THE RISE OF THE SIKH SOLDIER

About the Author

Gurinder Singh Mann
The author is an independent researcher in Sikh history and heritage. His work has appeared in print and on radio and television for two decades. He started researching in the late 1990s, which was formulated in his dissertation 'The Role of the Dasam Granth in Khalsa'. This was part of his MA in South Asian religions undertaken in 2001 at De Montfort University, Leicester, and was one of the first western works on Sikh martial scripture since Loehlin (1971). He is the author of three books: *Sri Dasam Granth Sahib: Questions and Answers* (Archimedes Press, 2011), *The Granth of Guru Gobind Singh: Essays, Lectures and Translations* (Oxford University Press, 2015) and *The British and the Sikhs: Discovery, Warfare and Friendship C1700–1900* (Helion & Co, 2020).

Mann also discovered a rare English translation by Dr John Leyden of *The Prem Sumarag Granth* in 2006. This was presented in a project titled the 'Anglo-Panjabi Literature and Publishing Initiative', which showcased the translations in 2011. As part of this project, he undertook the lecture 'The Lost British Account of Sikh Texts' in Leicester. Related to this, Mann has also presented on Anglo-Sikh relations at the Punjab Research Group (PRG) where he gave his paper 'The Impact and Legacy of Colonial Dominance in the Punjab' at the University of Wolverhampton in 2012, and published the small booklet, *Dr Leyden's Punjabi Translations* (Panjab Cultural Association). This highlighted the tensions between the East India Company and Christian missionaries in the Panjab.

At the Max Arthur Macauliffe Conference in 2014, at University College, Cork, Ireland, he also considered how Sikh scripture translation had changed over a century and delivered the paper 'Translating the Sikh: An Assessment of the Works of Leyden, Trumpp and Macauliffe'. At the International Sikh Research Conference 2014 at the University of Warwick, he provided vital information on Sikh artefacts in his paper 'The Importance of Sikh Relics and Manuscripts in the UK'. As a result, he has continued this research and lectured on this theme across the UK, as well as in Amritsar and Delhi, India.

Mann is also head of the Sikh Museum Initiative, the primary platform which works with existing organisations and private individuals to locate and uncover Sikh relics. The initiative undertakes research on documents and artefacts linking the British and the Sikhs as well as using new technologies to spearhead Sikh history. He has contributed towards several exhibitions from 2008 onwards, including curating the highly successful and influential exhibition 'Anglo–Sikh Wars: Battles, Treaties and Relics' (2017) at Newarke Houses Museum and Gardens, Leicester. As a result, he appeared on the acclaimed *Celebrity Antiques Road Trip* on BBC TV (2017). He has surveyed the battlefields of the First Anglo–Sikh War and has received an award from the village of Aliwal, Panjab, for his research in this area. Since 2018, he has managed and curated the Anglo Sikh Virtual Museum which allows users to interact with Sikh relics in 3D (www. anglosikhmuseum). This is the only truly 3D interactive Sikh resource in the world.

His work on relics has also allowed him to analyse materials at the Royal Collection Trust, and he delivered the lecture 'Sikh Arms and Armour in the Royal Collection' at New Walk Museum, Leicester, to supplement the exhibition 'Splendours of the Subcontinent: A Prince's Tour of India 1875–1876' (2017). He has written and partnered on Sikh collections for the Royal Armouries, Leeds (2019–22) where he is presently developing a Sikh digital resource. Mann has also been co-convener of the International Sikh Research Conference (ISRC) at the University of Warwick since 2014. He continues to work on discovering new perspectives on the Sikhs through relics, manuscripts and rare accounts and digital technologies.

The Rise of the Sikh Soldier

The Sikh Warrior through the ages, c.1700–1900

Gurinder Singh Mann

 Helion & Company

Helion & Company Limited
Unit 8 Amherst Business Centre
Budbrooke Road
Warwick
CV34 5WE
England
Tel. 01926 499 619
Email: info@helion.co.uk
Website: www.helion.co.uk
Twitter: @helionbooks
Visit our blog at blog.helion.co.uk

Published by Helion & Company 2022
Designed and typeset by Mach 3 Solutions Ltd (www.mach3solutions.co.uk)
Cover designed by Paul Hewitt, Battlefield Design (www.battlefield-design.co.uk)

Text © Gurinder Singh Mann 2022
Images © as individually credited
Maps drawn by George Anderson © Helion & Company 2022

Front cover: A sketch of three Akali Nihangs. Portraits of the Princes and People of India /
by Emily Eden, Drawn on stone by L. Dickinson. 1844.

ISBN 978-1-915070-52-4

British Library Cataloguing-in-Publication Data.
A catalogue record for this book is available from the British Library.

For details of other military history titles published by Helion & Company Limited contact
the above address or visit our website: http://www.helion.co.uk.

We always welcome receiving book proposals from prospective authors.

Contents

List of Illustrations and Maps

In text

In colour plate section

Acknowledgements

There have been many individuals and groups who have supported me in completing this project. This support spans many individuals from across the world. I would like to thank the staff at the British Library, the British Museum, the Victoria and Albert Museum, Maidstone Museum, RMN-Grand Palais (MNAAG, Paris) and the great team at The Royal Armouries.

Thanks to all the staff at Helion & Co Ltd, Duncan Rogers and the Series Editor, Dr Christopher Brice, for the great continued support they have provided me throughout the process of publishing this book. This is my second book published in their *From Musket to Maxim 1815–1914* series. Other mentions include Peter Bance, Sukhbinder Singh Paul, Neil Carleton (the Victoria and Albert Museum), Simon Dixon (University of Leicester), Rajwant Mann, Kartar Singh, Kumal Singh Haripuria, Dr Kamalroop Singh, Rav Singh (*A Little History of the Sikhs*), Harpreet Singh Bhatti, Jean Marie-Lafont, Natasha Bennett (The Royal Armouries), Dr Paramvir Singh (Punjabi University, Patiala), Dr Kashmir Singh (Punjabi University, Patiala), *Sarpanch* Pargat Singh (Aliwal), Punjab 2000, Dr Kristina Myrvold (Sweden), Anurag Singh (Ludhiana), Colonel Harinder Singh Attari, Michael Perry (Perry Miniatures), Bhayee Sikander Singh and Roopinder Singh, Bobby Singh Bansal, John Steedman, Bhajan Singh, Dalvir Singh Pannu, and Dr Opinderjit Takhar (University of Wolverhampton). To Tejpal Singh for providing useful suggestions on the final chapter. To the podcasters: Amar Singh (*Ramblings of a Sikh*), Sat Mann, and many others. To my brother Manjinder Singh Mann (aka Memphis), for the idea of the title and concepts contained within the book. Taranjit Singh (Taran3d) for applying his digital magic to the images. Jeevandeep Singh (Ludhiana), deserves major credit for always answering my queries in relation to Sikh coins. To my wife-Permjit Mann and children-Kimran Kaur and Amar Singh for bearing with me during the usual hibernation and battle mode status whilst preparing the book.

I would also lastly like to thank visitors to my website: www.sikhscholar.co.uk. Their comments and questions provide me with the daily motivation to write and ensure that projects like this have value. This project has also been endorsed by the Sikh Museum Initiative (SMI), www.sikhmuseum.org.uk, which is bringing out new research on Sikh artefacts and relics in the UK.

Introduction: Sikh Military History

The Sikh religion, while forged from the same environments of the Hindu and Islamic faiths, has stood apart from its counterparts in many ways. The Sikh Gurus or preceptors, numbering ten, embraced in their early incarnations a saintly persuasion, but they were definitely not passive. Guru Nanak (1469–1539), who was the first preceptor, created a community that not only looked inwardly in terms of venerating God but also had a worldly persuasion that would enable his followers to stand up to tyranny. He created verses that would later be incorporated into a living Guru or Guru Granth Sahib, the venerated scripture of the Sikhs. Many of these verses are a repository of faith in the almighty as well as a rebuttal to invaders who would sack the country and the rich inhabitants who would not stand up to these invaders. The Panjab has witnessed many invasions and the frontier has had to defend and repel various incursions, including the Mughals and Afghans, who set up their dynasties in India, firstly under Emperor Babur (1483–1530).

Guru Nanak rebuked Babur and composed verses to show his discontent.[1] Whilst the Guru is renowned for travelling to many corners of the world espousing his philosophy his householder philosophy has largely been neglected in favour of the ritualistic reciting of scriptures.[2] Yet his outlook was very much that of *miri piri*, the Sikh tradition which denotes the close relationship between the temporal and the spiritual aspects of human life. *Miri* denotes commander, governor, lord, prince, and so on, and signifies temporal power or civil authority. *Piri* means senior man, saint, holy man, spiritual guide, or head of a religious order and stands for spiritual authority. Guru Nanak was followed by Guru Angad (1539–52), Guru Amar Das (1552–74), and Guru Ram Das (1574–81), who built up his following and helped create an order of initiates across the Indian subcontinent. However, this following was being monitored by the authorities. The execution in 1606, of Guru Arjan (1581–1606), under the orders of Emperor Jahangir (1569–1627), marked the Mughal authority's response to

1 These verses are referred to as *Babur Vani*, the verses of Emperor Babur, contained in the Sikh scripture, the Guru Granth Sahib.
2 The householder lifestyle in this sense refers to one who has a family and actively engages in society. This is opposed to religious ascetics who lived in the forests and renounced the world. "Instead of wearing these beggar's robes, it is better to be a householder, and give to others," Guru Granth Sahib, p.587.

a growing religious order asserting the principles of freedom of conscience and human justice. The fifth Guru had essentially created a 'state within a state' and was mobilising his followers for the times ahead.

This is most prominently seen in the fact, generally overlooked, that it was under his direction that the Sikhs undertook their first protection of the faith from a military perspective. A flock of warriors came to the *Durbar* or court of Guru Arjun. The names of these warriors have come down to us as Bhai Kalyan Sood, Bhai Adit Soni, Bhai Pratap, Bhai Jaita, Bhai Piraga, Bhai Bhanu, Bhai Ganga Sehgal,[3] and Bhai Bidhi Chand.[4] However, before the ascension of Guru Arjun, his Sikhs were being prepared for the fight ahead. In the sixth incarnation, Guru Hargobind (1606–44) would come to embody the image of the saint-soldier, replacing the traditional *seli topi* with a turban and adopting two swords. The swords represented the swords of *miri* and *piri*. He was aided in this design by one pious Sikh named Baba Buddha who outlived six Gurus and became an elder statesman with a clear vision and purpose. He is credited with the evolution of *Shastravidia* or the knowledge of weapons, essentially the Sikh martial art. This, like any change in policy, would indeed be met with suspicion and there was a lack of will to embrace the warrior life. The Sikh theologian, Bhai Gurdas, refers to the Guru's martial qualities in his *vars* or odes, writing, 'This Guru, the vanquisher of armies, is very brave and benevolent.'[5] He states that the Sikh faith required protection which he describes as 'an orchard requiring the defence of thorny and hedgy Kikar trees.'[6] However, this change was also reflected in Sikh institutions, and the Throne of the Almighty or the Akal Takht was created under his supervision. This shrine was created to administer and dispense rulings on Sikh affairs. The Akal Takht would have a separate purpose to the Harimandir Sahib and hence Guru Hargobind commanded, 'For peace of mind go to the Harimandir Sahib and for *Rajoguni* [kingship] go to the Akal Takht Sahib.'[7]

His court mirrored that of any king except he imbibed the values of the spiritual together with the martial. The Guru sat under a canopy, and there was a *Nishan* or flag and he wore a *Kalgi* or plume on his turban. His followers brought him arms and horses. The poets and bards would infuse martial spirit into the populace by reciting poetry expressing *vir ras* or martial qualities with the *Shastras*, or weapons, while at the central Akal Takht. It was noted that the congregation 'were donating horses and clothes and came to do *Puja* [worship] of the weapons.'[8]

---

3   Ganga Sehgal was employed by the Mughal army but was asked by Guru Arjun to fight battles for the Sikhs and as a result 'he attained salvation'.
4   In the text translated as *The Rosary of the Sikhs and Bhagats* we see the names of these warriors. Trilochan Singh Bedi (ed.), *Sikhan di Bhagatmala* (Patiala: Punjabi University, 1994).
5   Bhai Gurdas, *Var* 1, *pauri* 48. *Var* is a reference to the ballad number and *pauri* the line number.
6   Bhai Gurdas, *Var* 26, *pauri* 25.
7   Sohan Singh, *Gurbilas Patishah Chhevin* (Amritsar: SGPC, 1988), p.216.
8   Michael Nijahawan, *Dhadi Darbar: Religion, Violence, and the Performance of Sikh History*, (New Delhi: Oxford University Press, 2006).

This was highly significant as the spiritual Sikhs were asked to become martial themselves and to worship weapons as 'delivers of justice' and 'emancipators of the downtrodden'. It was this concept that would guide the Sikhs in the future. This martial policy again was noticed by the authorities but Bhai Buddha's instructions in *Shastarvidia* proved most beneficial in the incursions against the Mughals. Guru Hargobind fought several battles against the Mughals where the imperial forces were defeated. It was seen that the Sikhs had embraced cavalry and the feats of dashing horsemanship were exhibited by warriors like Bidi Chand (1579–1638).[9]

Under the sixth preceptor Guru Har Rai (1630–61), and seventh Guru Harkrishan (1656–64), times were relatively peaceful. However, things came to a head during the ninth preceptor, Guru Tegh Bahadur (1621–75). The Mughal policy under Emperor Aurangzeb was becoming zealous and the notion of a *Dar-al-Islam* or Islamic state was initiated together with the introduction of the *Jizya* or taxation on non-Muslims. A congregation of Kashmiri pandits of the Hindu faith petitioned the Guru to protect their religious freedom. The Guru agreed to go to Delhi and further their case. Guru Tegh Bahadur was ordered to embrace Islam or meet the sword of Mughal rule. His refusal to convert led to him being executed at Chandni Chawk in Delhi. This act would later become a catalyst for better interfaith relations and humanity.

His son Gobind, then just a minor, consoled the Sikhs, at the Durbar at Anandpur, Panjab. He saw this as a natural progression of forging the religion into a military outfit aided by the design of God. Gobind had not only learnt several languages but was also taught *Shastarvidia* which he later imparted to his followers. He made Anandpur his abode and set about transforming his Sikhs. His court became the talk of India; poets fled from Emperor Aurangzeb's court and joined the prestigious group of poets and artisans at his Durbar. Many texts of heroism and valour were translated and hence his court also became an educational centre. He fought battles, kept a large war drum referred to as a *Ranjit Nagara* and became an envious figurehead. But the kings in the hills started causing strife with the Guru and soon his battle was with both the Hindus and the Muslims. The Guru had no option but to encourage the martial tradition in an organised way. He recited his own verses in *vir ras* or 'warrior spirit' which he incorporated into the secondary scripture or the Dasam Granth, 'Scripture of the Tenth King.' Compositions like *Jaap Sahib*, *Shastar Nam Mala* and others gave the Sikhs a scripture of valour to complement the spiritual Guru Granth Sahib. Next, the transformation of the faith incorporated a military strain formalising the Sikhs into the Khalsa or 'fraternity of the pure' through the *Khande ki Pahul*, or the 'initiation of the double-edged sword.' This initiation, which tradition asserts began in 1699, became unique in the Indian subcontinent, involving the consecration of water mixed with sugar and stirred with a sword or *Khanda*. The recitation of the prayers from the

---

9   Bidi Chand was Commander-in-Chief of the Sikh army and his feats of heroism are legendary. He also maintained the army during the tenure of the sixth preceptor, Guru Har Rai.

Guru Granth Sahib and the Dasam Granth gave the spiritual and martial blessing to the holy nectar. The initiates to the Khalsa would drink this water and commit to the 5 Ks: the keeping of the *Kesh* (uncut hair), *Kara* (a steel bracelet), *Kanga* (a wooden comb), *Kaccha* (underwear) and *Kirpan* (steel sword). The hair would be tied under the turban. In a sign of humility and comradeship, Guru Gobind undertook the initiation from the initiates. Tradition asserts that the male members took the appellation Singh and the female members Kaur. Hence the 10th preceptor was renamed Guru Gobind Singh. His *hukamnamas* directed the Sikh congregations to bring arms and armour to further the Khalsa movement.[10] He also created an ammunitions factory at Anandpur. All in all, his followers became militarised and the sword became a recourse of last resort.

This novel initiation of the Khalsa was noted by the authorities. The Guru fought many battles and his beloved Anandpur was sacked by the Mughals. The Guru introduced the military religious occasion of *Holla Mohalla*, a yearly event marked by mock battles demonstrating the martial prowess of the Sikhs, an occasion which is still marked to this day with tent pegging and feats of daredevilry by the Akali Nihangs. The concept of the Misl or 'confederacy' had been noted at the time of the Guru Gobind Singh and refers to an army unit or battalion. The court poet of the Khalsa, Sainapat, states:

Guru Gobind Singh marched to the battle-field.
Hearing the din of battle drums being beaten,
The battle standards were brandished in front.
Observing the deployments in four fold formations [Misl]
The Guru made his own deployments on several points.
Hearing the bugles heralding war on all the fronts
The enraged warriors responded and jumped into the field[11]

10   The sacred weapons of the Guru are viewed with major importance. Many of these exist today in many different collections. The historic *Khanda* used in the *Khande ki Pahul* ceremony is kept at Takht Keshgarh Sahib, Anandpur. A similar *Khanda* depicted within these pages from the seventeenth century can be described as follows, 'with the design taken from the 11th Century Chola swords, complete with an iron strap around the blade to the forte. A long intricately chiselled languet runs along the central portion of the blade and adding to the rigidity of the sword.' Thanks to Sukhbinder Singh Paul for the description. An interesting breastplate was worn by the Guru at the Battle of Bhangani in 1688. The plate is kept at the private collection of Captain Amarinder Singh in Patiala. This was recreated in 3D by the Sikh Museum Initiative. See <https://www.anglosikhmuseum.com/charaina/> (accessed 10 August 2021).

11   The text is believed to be written around 1711. Kulwant Singh (Trans), *Sri Gur Sobha Sainapati* (Chandigarh: Institute of Sikh Studies, 2014), p.21. There are also other references to Misls in the text. Sainapat (Mann) was part of the literary symposium created by Guru Gobind Singh where scholars, writers and scribes created a corpus of literature spanning different themes and traditions.

Left: Portrait of Guru Gobind Singh. (*The Sarvasiddhantattvacudamani* or 'Crest-jewel of the
Essence of all Systems of Astronomy.' British Library. Or. 5259.)
Right: Seventeenth Century Khanda. (Courtesy of Sukhbinder Singh Paul Family Collection)

The Khalsa in essence became *Chakravati* or 'always on the move.' After the death of Emperor Aurangzeb, his successor Bahadur Shah was deemed to be more favourable towards the Sikhs' cause.[12] The Guru encamped at Delhi and moved to Hazur Sahib, where he was stabbed and unable to recover from his wounds. He invested authority to the scripture, Guru Granth Sahib, which became known as a 'living Guru.' His own writings, the *Dasam Granth*, were held in equal esteem and became regular recitals in peace and war times. Various compositions from the text were recited when undertaking *Shastarvidia*. In essence, before and during battle, the inscriptions from the text would be a form of protection on the Guru's swords and armour. Verses from the text would contribute towards a military framework to this very day. He, however, instructed a relatively new member of the Khalsa, Banda Singh Bahadur (1670–1716), to take on the fight in the Panjab together with a war council of five. Banda would strike terror into the Mughal armies and some foundations of an early Sikh Empire was laid by him with the minting of coins, and the issuing of edicts.[13] However, this reign was short-lived and similar to the martyred Gurus, he was captured and executed at Delhi.

The Foundation of the Misls

The Sikhs then assembled under Akali Darbara Singh (1644–1734)[14] who vested authority into Kapur Singh (1697–1753). He had received the Khalsa initiation from Mani Singh, a pious and respected Sikh within the Khalsa. He earned the title Nawab in 1733, the honour given to him by the Muslims to confer rights and sovereignty. He was the head of the Sikh *Panth* or congregation and essentially the head of the Sikh armies, which he set about consolidating. His first role was to divide the Sikhs into smaller units or Misls. He set about creating a division comprising the veterans of the Khalsa, which was hence termed Buddha Dal. These were the warriors who most likely had a connection with Guru Gobind Singh and would have understood the concepts of early Sikh military tradition via *Shastarvidia* and other military skills. The next division was termed Taruna Dal, for the new younger Sikhs who wanted to be part of this new setup. The division was important as it introduced some stability and purpose within the *Dal Khalsa* or 'army of God.'

This initial division was into a group of five *Jathas* or battalions: 'The whole Khalsa *Panth* was organised into five contingents, with five distinctive emblems for their

---

12   Bahadur Shah was also known as Muhammad Mu'azzam, the eighth Mughal Emperor.
13   See my *The British and the Sikhs: Discovery, Warfare and Friendship* (c.1700–1900) (Warwick: Helion & Company, 2020). Here on *British and the Sikhs*.
14   Darbara Singh was from the family of Guru Hargobind and also served under Guru Gobind Singh.

identification. The five standards representing each contingent were planted within the precincts of the Akal Takht.'[15]

These markers were an initial sign of Sikh Sovereignty and the five groups were composed of the Shaheed contingent, Deep Singh and Karam Singh; Karam Singh and Dharam Singh of Amritsar; Sikhs from the Trehan-Bhalla clans; the Dashonda Singh contingent and the Bir Singh Ranghreta Contingent.[16]

It was during the lifetime of Kapur Singh that he handed over the leadership of the Sikh fraternity to Jassa Singh Ahluwalia (1718–83). He was considered to be the ablest, and due to his upbringing under the wing of Guru Gobind Singh's consort Mata Sundari, he ensured a continuation of military strategy.

Massacres and Battles

During the early period of the Sikh Misls, they faced tremendous odds fighting against the Mughal regime, both locally and nationally and against the Afghan invaders of Nadir Shah (1688 –1747) and Ahmed Shah Abdali (1722–72) of the Durrani Empire. Abdali was born in Multan, the Panjab or Herat and is considered the founder of the state of Afghanistan. At the height of his reign, his empire extended from the Amu Darya (ancient Oxus River) to the Indian Ocean and from Khorasan into Kashmir, the Panjab, and Sindh. He was a noble of the Abdali tribe whose rise occurred under the tenure of Nadir Shah where he led his cavalry forces and learnt the politics of the Indian subcontinent. Nadir Shah first rattled the Indian subcontinent with a ferocity not seen in many ages, and as a result, the Mughal regime was shaken.

The Panjab was subjected to constant invasions and persecution. The Governor of Lahore, Zakariya Khan (d.1745), followed the previous hard line of massacring Sikhs and asking the neighbouring warlords to bring Sikh heads for payment. He was also responsible for unleashing an untold horror on the Sikhs which was known as the *Choota Ghallughara* or 'smaller holocaust', in which over 10,000 Sikhs were killed over a period of two and half months.[17] The initial campaign in March 1746 centred on Yahiya Khan and Lakhpat Rai marching against the Khalsa and entrapping them within the hills of Kahnuwan, Gurdaspur. Many were killed and others were captured and taken as prisoners to Lahore and executed at the location later named *Shahid Ganj* or Martyrs' Square. A *Sarbat Khalsa* (conclave)[18] took place at Amritsar on 29 March 1748; during the auspicious occasion of Baisakhi, the entire force of the Khalsa was

15   Kulwant Singh (trans.), *Sri Gur Panth Prakash* (Rattan Singh Bhangoo), Volume II, (Episodes 82–169) (Chandigarh: Institute of Sikh Studies, 2008), p.91. Subsequent references will be *Sri Gur Panth Prakash*.
16   *Sri Gur Panth Prakash*, p.91.
17   Although other estimates consider this to be much higher over the course of this period.
18   This is a reference to the congregation of the Sikhs coming together to resolve any differences and agreeing to collective action.

divided into 11 Misls, each under its own chief or sardar. A list of these confederacies and their leaders were as follows, they developed over a number of years.

Buddha Dal
1. Ahluwalia Misl named after the village Ahlu and under Jassa Singh Ahluwalia.
2. Singhpuria (Faizullapuria) Misl under Nawab Kapur Singh, named after the area Singhpuria.
3. Karorasinghia Misl (Panjgarh) named due to their leader Karora Singh.
4. Nishanvalia Misl under Dasaundha Singh, named due to their role as *Nishan* or flag bearers of the Khalsa forces.
5. Shaheedi Misl under Baba Deep Singh, named due to their bravery and their commitment to *Shaheedi* or martyrdom.
6. Dalewalia Misl under Gulab Singh, named after Fort Dalla.

Taruna Dal
7. Sukerchakia Misl under Charhat Singh, named after the village Sukerchak.
8. Bhangi Misl under Hari Singh Dhillon, named due to him being fond of *Bhang* or cannabis plant.
9. Kanhaiya Misl under Jai Singh, possibly from the village Kanha.
10. Nakai Misl under Hira Singh, named after Nakka which was the territory in between the two rivers of Ravi and Sutlej.
11. Ramgarhia Misl under Jassa Singh Ramgarhia and named after the Fort Ram Rauni.

The Phulkian Misl was named after the original head of the family, Choudhary Phul Brar, and was composed of the leaders and territories of Patiala, Jind and Nabha. It would on occasion join with the Dal Khalsa but never took part in the decisions, even though Misl edicts were binding on them. This independence and neutrality served them well, much to the chagrin of many of the Misl leaders. There were also smaller rulers and even non-Sikh territories which helped and supported the Dal Khalsa in their battles and campaigns.

It is also important to stress the reason for the use of the word Misl. Whilst it has been outlined in a military sense, it is also plausible that it relates to a physical file or record. The Misl system involved a leader being chosen and his name and number of soldiers being recorded in a file known as a Misl, hence one possible reason for the origins of the name. This file would have been kept at the Akal Takht in Amritsar. However, with the number of attacks and desecrations by the Afghans and Muslims, this information has only come down to us second-hand with no surviving files. The number of heads of the Misls was whittled down to eleven so clear records could be kept of army numbers. In order to support the administration throughout the eighteenth century, the Misls built living quarters, education centres and forts. Around the Harimandir Sahib, these quarters were known as *Bungas* which continued to exist until the time of Maharajah Ranjit Singh. There were also *Katras* around Amritsar with living quarters and shops administered under Misl chiefs, the main ones being Katra Ahluwalia, Katra Bhagian (Kanhaiya Misl), and Katra Bhangian. The conquests and resources won by the Misls all resulted in helping to preserve the sanctity of Amritsar, providing *langar* (community kitchen) for the populace, and even depositing spoils of war within the city.[19] Supplementing this was protection around Amritsar which is relatively unknown. This was an underground network of tunnels for the Sikhs to hide in when the hordes of invaders attacked Amritsar. Recent research shows there is some merit to this idea, but it requires further research.

Military Methods and Strength

The Dal Khalsa, with its total estimated strength of over 70,000, consisted primarily of cavalry, with very little artillery or infantry. There have been widely varying estimates of the strength of Sikh forces. James Browne, in 1785, estimated it at 98,200.[20] Forster claimed that the Sikh military strength was a highly exaggerated 200,000;[21] similarly according to Francklin in 1793–4, 'The collected force of the Seiks[sic] is immense, they being able to bring into the field an army of 250,000 men.'[22] According to Alexander Dow, they could muster 60,000 horse in the field as noted below, and he also states the territorial aspects and levies introduced by the Khalsa as follows:

> The Seiks are, at present, divided into several states, which in their internal government are perfectly independent of one another, but they form a powerful alliance against their neighbors. When they are threatened with invasions, an assembly of the states is called, and a general chosen by them, to lead their respective quotas of militia into the field; but, as soon as peace is restored, the power of this kind of dictator ceases, and he returns, in a private capacity, to his own community. The Seiks are now in possession of the whole province of Punjab, the greatest part of Moultan and Sind, both the banks of the Indus from Cashmire to Tatta, and all the country towards Delhi, from Lahore to Sirhind. They have, of late years, been a great check upon the arms of Abdalla [Abdali]; and, though in the course of the last year they have been unsuccessful against

19   I have ascertained that there were several treasuries of the Sikhs during the time of Maharajah Ranjit Singh, some of which have origins in the Misl period. As Amritsar was prone to attack, it is uncertain where this treasury existed, but the underground chambers would be one answer. The other is the Buddha Dal as a moving army would carry the relics with them.
20   Bhagat Singh, *A History of the Sikh Misals* (Patiala: Punjabi University, 1993).
21   George Forster, *A Journey from Bengal to England: Through the Northern part of India, Kashmire, Afghanistan, and Persia, and into Russia by the Caspian Sea* (London: Printed for R. Faulder, 1798), Vol. 1, Letter XI, p.289. Forster's travels give some important observations of the Panjab and the Sikhs. His works were published posthumously in 1792.
22   This information was given to the author when he was in Panipat. Francklin, *History of Shah-Aulum*, p.75.

that prince in three actions, they are, by no means subdued, but continue a severe clog upon his ambitious views in India. The chief who leads at present the army of the Seiks, is Jessarit Singh [Jassa Singh]; there is also one Nitteh Singh, who is in great esteem among them.[23] They can, upon an emergency, muster 60000 good horse, though in India they are esteemed brave, they choose rather to carry on their wars by surprize and stratagem, than by regular operations in the field.[24]

James Browne states, '…in the districts not occasional incursions they levy a tribute which they call Raukey and which is about one-fifth (as the Maratha Chouth is one-fourth) of the annual rent; whenever a Zamindar has agreed to pay this tribute to any Sikh chief, that chief not only himself refrains from plundering him but will protect him from all others; and this protection is by general consent held so far sacred, that even if the grand army passed through a Zamindari where the safeguards of the lowest Sikh chiefs are stationed, it will not violate them.'[25]

In the above references, there is an observance of the term *Rakhi* which can be described as tribute or even protection money.[26] It comes from the word *Rakha*, the Panjabi word for protector. This was levied on areas the Khalsa had conquered or where landowners needed protection from other sardars or common criminals. This system also applied to external invaders and so paying around a fifth of their income to the Khalsa benefitted the landowners. This was also needed as the state had become weakened by invaders and so lawlessness was prevalent, with the populace not knowing whether they were dependent on the Afghans or the Mughals.[27]

The preferred method of warfare for the Sikhs was cavalry; although some Khalsa were proficient in the use of artillery, it appears it was seldom used. Many of the other powers, whether the Afghans, Mughals, or Marathas, started employing guns in their modes of warfare, together with employing European officers in some capacity to improve their methods of warfare. The traditional weapons of swords, guns and other weapons used in hand-to-hand combat were seen in action by the Sikhs in the eighteenth century, some of which had become outdated. Francklin states:

> The Seiks are armed with a spear, scymetar, and excellent match-lock. Their horses are strong, very patient under hardship, and undergo incredible fatigue. The men are accustomed to charge on full gallop, on a sudden they stop, discharge their pieces with a deliberate aim, when suddenly wheeling about,

23   The name of Nitteh Singh is not known amongst the Sikh names recorded in literature.
24   Alexander Dow, *History Of Hindostan: From the Earlies Account of Time to the Death of Akbar*, Vol. 2 (London: Printed for T. Becket and P.A, De Hondt), pp.82–83.
25   Major J. Browne, *India Tracts: Containing a description of the Jungle Terry districts, their revenues, trade, and government: with a plan for the improvement of them. Also an history of the origin and progress of the Sicks* (London: Logographic Press, 1788), p.viii.
26   Some commentators have also referred to it as blackmail.
27   Bhagat Singh, *Sikh Polity*, p.78.

after performing three or four turns, they renew the attack. The shock is impressive when offered only to infantry, but again artillery they cannot stand. It is a fact well known and established, that a few field pieces is sufficient to keep in check their most numerous bodies. Injured from their infancy to the hardships of a military life, the Seiks are addicted to predatory warfare, in a manner peculiar to themselves alone.[28]

Due to their low numbers and lack of artillery, the Khalsa adopted what can be described as guerrilla tactics, with an attack and retreat policy as described above. According to Rattan Singh Bhangu (d.1846), who was asked by the British to write a history of the Sikhs, 'The wise and the experienced were of the opinion that in battle there are two and a half movements. Rushing on the enemy and retreating make two and to strike is the half. The Guru [Gobind Singh] has taught us to run away and to come back again to fight. This is a great tactic. The Guru himself adopted these and in it there is no dishonour.'[29] The hit-and-run tactics were known as *Dhai Phat*, or 'two-and-a-half strikes' and were a distinguishing feature of the Sikhs. They were deployed mainly against the Afghans who commanded superior numbers in the field. These tactics became a staple method of warfare for the Sikhs and provided great dividends by picking off a small section of the enemy. It was this element of surprise after their withdrawal that meant the enemy expected that they were chasing a fleeing army, only for them to turn around and give them a surprise attack before melting away into the forests.[30]

The government of the Sikhs was considered to be of equitable benefit to both leaders and the common populace, following their own precepts of serving the poor and needy but using iron mettle when required. The Sikh chief, it was said,

...exerts an exclusive authority over his vassals, even to the power of life and death; and to increase the population of his districts, he proposes a ready and hospitable asylum to fugitives from all parts of India. Hence, in the Sikh territories, though the government be arbitrary, there exists much less cause for oppression than in many of the neighbouring states; and hence likewise, the cultivator of the soil being liable to frequent change of masters, by the numerous

28   Francklin, *History of Shah-Aulum*, p.76. He also states their 'fire arms superior to most parts of Hindostaun.'
29   Bhangu, *Sri Gur Panth Prakash*, pp.345–46. In response to a commentary written on the Sikhs commissioned by Colonel David Ochterlony (1758–1825), the account was deemed to be inaccurate; as a result, the *Panth Prakash* was written to give an authentic account of the Khalsa in the eighteenth century.
30   Arjan Das Malik, *The Sword of the Khalsa: The Sikh Peoples War 1699–1768* (New Delhi: Manohar, 1999), p.81.

resolutions that are perpetually occurring, may be considered as one of the causes of the fluctuation of the national force.[31]

The Sikh Art of War

It was the same Afghans under the Durrani Chief, Ahmed Shah Abdali, who created havoc in the Indian subcontinent. Their invasions led to a feeling of helplessness amongst the Indian populace and there was very little opposition to his campaigns. The Marathas had been decimated in 1761 in the battle of Panipat, but the Sikhs, who were constantly subjected to the Mughal and Afghan incursions, would strike back. On the seventh invasion of Abdali, the diarist named Qazi Nur Muhammed, not only participated in, but also vividly documented the battles with the Sikhs.[32] Using derogatory terms like 'dog' for the Sikhs, it was clear that the battle tactics of the Sikhs were having a great impact on the battlefield:

Do not call the dogs [the Sikhs] 'dogs' because they are lions, and are courageous like lions in the field of battle. How can a hero, who roars like a lion in the field of battle, be called a dog. If you wish to learn the art of war, come face to face with them in the field. They will demonstrate it to you in such a way that one and all will praise them for it. If you wish to learn the science of war, O swordsman, learn from them how to face an enemy like a hero and to get safely out of an action. Singh is a title [a form of address for them]. It is not justice to call them dogs. If you do not know the Hindustani language [I tell you that], the word Singh means a Lion. Truly they are like lions in battle, and at the time of peace they surpass Hatim.

When they take the Indian sword in their hands, they overrun the country from Hind [-ostan, meaning Northern India] to Sind. Nobody then stands in opposition to them, however much strong he may be. When they manipulate the spear they shatter the ranks of the enemy, and when they raise the heads of their spears into the sky, they would pierce even through the Caucasus. When they adjust the strings of their Chachi bows and place in them the enemy-killing arrows and pull the strings to their ears, the body of the enemy begins to shiver with fear. When their battle-axe falls upon the armour of their opponents, that armour becomes their coffin. The body of every one of them is like the piece of a rock, and, in physical grandeur, every one of them is more than fifty persons. It is said that Bahram-Gore killed wild asses and set the lions shrieking. But if

---

31 William Francklin, *Military Memoirs of Mr. George Thomas; Who, by Extraordinary Talents and Enterprise...* (London: reprinted for John Stockdale, Piccadilly, 1805), p.114.
32 He was a *Qazi* or judge in the service of Nasir Khan, the Chief of Kalat whose troops accompanied Abdali.

Bahram were to come face to face with them, even he would bow before them. During a battle when they take their guns in their hands, they come jumping into the field of action, roaring like lions. They tear the chests of many and shed the blood of several [of their enemy] in the dust. It is said that the musket is a weapon of the ancient days. It, however, appears to be the creation of these dogs rather than of the great Socrates. Although there are so many of the *tufangchis* [musketeers], but nobody can excel them in its use. To the right and to the left, and in front and towards the back, they go on firing regularly. If you do not believe in what I say, you may enquire of the brave swordsmen who would tell you more than myself and would praise them for their fighting. The fact that they grappled with thirty thousand heroes bears witness to my statement.[33]

This description gives us plenty to appreciate; namely their bravery equated with a lion, about their use of weaponry whether it be spears, bow and arrows, or battle axes together with the use of the musket. This serves as important testimony of the Misls, their method of warfare and their fearlessness on the battlefield.

Attire

There are varying descriptions of the Khalsa in terms of the dress or *Bana* (form). The majority of descriptions all point to the colour blue as the trademark colour of the Khalsa as prescribed by Guru Gobind Singh. In the codes of conduct referred to as the *Rahitnamas* namely the Bhai Daya Singh *Rahitnama*, the Khalsa colour is blue and it states that, 'An Akali is known by the blue garments he wears' as well as mentioning that the prohibition against wearing red is paramount.[34] According to the bard Bhai Gurdas II, the Khalsa was created by Guru Gobind Singh and 'thus were born the Bhujangi [young Sikhs] who wore the blue robes.'[35]

The Akali Nihangs to this day observe this tradition as the true warriors of the Guru. The blue colour was also described by many commentators in relation to the Misls. Francklin states:

---

33   Ganda Singh, *Qazi Nur Muhammad's Jang Namah Giving An Account Of The Seventh Invasion Of Ahmad Shah* Durrani [1764–1765] (Amritsar: The Sikh History Research Dept. Khalsa College, 1939), p.54.

34   See *Bhai Daya Singh Rahitnama*. The *Nashit-nama* (manual of instruction) attributed to Bhai Nand Lal, states, 'do not clothe yourself in red'. Similar sentiments are echoed in the *Prahalad Rahitnama*. This may have a played a part in the Tat Khalsa (Real Khalsa) and Bandeis (followers of Banda Singh Bahadur) divide where they wore red much to chagrin of the Sikhs of old.

35   *Bhujangi* known as 'sons of a snake', a reference to the Akali Nihangs. The quoted verses are credited to the poet Bhai Gurdas II, quite possibly a contemporary of Guru Gobind Singh. See Prithpal Singh Kapur and Dharam Singh, *The Khalsa* (Patiala: Punjabi University, 1999), p.143.

The Seiks, in their persons, are tall, and of a manly erect deportment; their aspect is ferocious, their eyes piercing and animated and in tracing their features a striking resemblance is observable to the Arabs who inhabit the banks of the Euphrates. The dress of the males consists of a coarse cloth of blue cotton, thrown loosely over the shoulders, and coming down between the legs, is confined round the waist by a belt of cotton. An ample turban of blue cloth covers the head, and over this is frequently wore a fafli [?] of silk and cotton mixed, resembling both in colour and pattern a Scotch Tartan.[36]

The Female Warriors and Administrators

The role of women has been largely side-lined. They have been ignored and remain faceless with depictions of them being non-existent. Commentators have been ignorant of female members of the Khalsa in the eighteenth century. In the Guru period, heroic names like Mai Bhago [Bhag Kaur] a contemporary of Guru Gobind Singh, are prevalent and generally known but not in much detail, even though a huge *Bunga* or watchtower was built in her memory during 1788, at the height of the Misl period. When we consider testimony from many sources we see that the female warrior was also considered with awe on the battlefield. As a result, in this text, we have considered the role of two Patiala Princesses, Rajinder Kaur and Sahib Kaur, to highlight this point. Indeed, British observers recognised their bravery and valour. Thomas observes, 'Instances, indeed have not unfrequently occurred, in which they [women] have actually taken up arms to defend their habitations from the desultory attacks of the enemy, and throughout the contest behaved themselves with an intrepidity of spirit highly praiseworthy.'[37] To quote Lepel Griffin, Sikh women 'have on occasions shown themselves the equals of men in wisdom and administrative ability.'[38]

Interestingly, the wives of some Misl leaders were seen as being equal to the men. The region of Patiala witnessed a number of important women in politics and warfare including Sahib Kaur (1771–1801), Rajinder Kaur and Aus Kaur. Some of these strong women also held onto territories even after their husbands' demise until Ranjit Singh subdued most of them. Sada Kaur (1762–1832) of the Kanhaiya Misl was prominent amongst the women during the late eighteenth century and aided Ranjit Singh in his quest to become Maharajah as well as wrestling Amritsar from another female leader, Sukhan Kaur (Bhangi Misl). The territories of the fearless warrior Baghel Singh (Karorasinghia Misl) were held by Rup Kaur, Ram Kaur and Rattan Kaur and that of the Nishanvalia Misl by Daya Kaur (d. 1823). During the Sikh Empire, Rani Chand Kaur (1802–42), wife of Kharak Singh also from the Kanhaiya Misl, was

---

36   Francklin, *History of Shah-Aulum*, p.76.
37   Francklin, *Military Memoirs of Mr. George Thomas*, p.133.
38   Lepel Griffin, *Ranjit Singh* (Oxford: Oxford University Press, 1905), pp.62–63.

the ruler of Panjab albeit briefly. The most famous female ruler in the form of regent was Maharani Jindan Kaur, wife of Ranjit Singh. She was exiled by the East India Company after the First Anglo-Sikh War due to her influence and power. We discuss the important role of several valiant Sikh women throughout the book.

Maharajah Ranjit Singh and the Sikh Empire

Towards the end of the eighteenth century, the Sikh Misls had either become too comfortable, or their leaders had become aged, thereby limiting their conquests. This left a void in leadership and the advancement of the Sikhs. It was the determination of a young Sikh boy aged twelve, named Ranjit Singh, the head of the Sukerchakia Misl, who would change the fortunes not only for himself but also for the Panjab. He was determined to pose a challenge to Zaman Shah Durrani (c.1770–1844), the grandson of Ahmed Shah Abdali, which he achieved successfully.[39] Ranjit Singh worked in unity with the other Misls who had formed a barrier around Panjab to thwart a Durrani attack between 1797 and 1798. However, this led to his determination to take on the ageing Misl leaders and he soon conquered Lahore in 1799. His crowning ceremony as Maharajah in 1801 and his taking of Amritsar in 1802 from the Bhangi Misl paved the way for almost complete dominance of the Panjab until his death in 1839.

Far from keeping in tune with the military tactics of old, the Maharajah set a course of introducing major reforms in his army. The employment of Europeans in the army would benefit the Sikhs by ensuring that they improved on their drills and methods of warfare. There were also a number of British personnel and other mercenaries from around the world who joined the Sikh army.[40] These western soldiers, known as *Ferengis* (foreigners), were given senior command in the Khalsa army including the Frenchmen Jean-Francois Allard (1785–1839) and Claude Auguste Court (1793–1880), and the Italians Paolo Di Avitabile (1791–1850) and Jean-Baptiste Ventura (1794–1858).[41] The *Fauj-i-Khas*, the elite wing of the army raised by Generals Ventura and Allard, was strictly trained under the French pattern and had a separate emblem and flag consisting of the words *Degh-Tegh-Fateh* written in Persian. The commands and language used were in French, which showed the faith the Maharajah had put in the foreign generals. The artillery was reorganised by General Court and Alexander

---

39 It was fate or perhaps irony that Zaman Shah would plead for Sikh support many years later when he was given sanctuary in the Panjab.
40 These included John Holmes (d. 1848), a trumpeter in the Bengal Horse Artillery; Dr Harvey, attached as a medical officer and a soldier named Ratray or Lesli who was part of the infantry battalion of the Sikh army. For a list of other British officers at the Lahore court, see Devinder Kumar Verma, *Foreigners at the Court of Maharaja Ranjit Singh* (Patiala: Arun Publications, 2006).
41 Verma, *Foreigners at the Court*.

Gardner (1785–1877),[42] but commanded by the Muslim Ilahi Bakhsh.[43] The artillery was mainly composed of Muslim recruits, and they served the Khalsa well. The army's weapons and equipment (including clothing) were of the best kind. The *Fauj-i-Khas* was supplied with the best available ammunition and were very loyal to Ranjit Singh, whom they usually escorted. The *Fauj-i-Ain* (regularly army) was a well-drilled force composed of infantry, cavalry, and artillery. The *Fauj-i-Be Qawaid* (*Jagirdari Fauj*), or irregular Army, were horsemen furnished by holders of large estates of the Misls. These were the feudal levies from the old Sikh landowners. The Akali Nihangs were part of the irregular Army, but the best of them were promoted to the *Ghorchurahs* or *Fauj-i-Sowari* who were the cavalry army and formed part of Ranjit Singh's personal elite bodyguard and troops.[44] The clothing differed from branch to branch with European innovations adopted together with the traditional attire.

The development of artillery and other important inventions in the Sikh Empire is credited to one Lehna Singh Majithia. His accomplishments surpass many of those in the Sikh Empire yet he remains relatively unknown, though his introduction of reforms in military methods helped the Sikh army immensely. This included the control of Sikh ordnance factories at Lahore and Amritsar and the re-creation of Sikh guns based on British designs. This was together with his understanding of many languages, mathematics, and a thorough understanding of astronomy. He was responsible for the development of a sundial at Amritsar. He was given the governorship of Amritsar and so introduced many infrastructure reforms including the development of buildings and gardens.

It was during the first Anglo-Sikh War (1845–1846) that we see the Khalsa go head to head with the East India Company. It was after the second Sikh War (1848-1849) which led to the defeat of the Sikhs and ultimately the annexation of the Panjab.

The Sikh military methods were praised by the British and were seen as being on par with them in many respects. However, their leadership failed to obtain the victory that they might have achieved. The delivery of Sikh arms to General Walter Raleigh Gilbert (1753–1853) was a humbling moment at Rawalpindi.[45] Yet from the remnants and the ashes of the Sikh Wars a way was made possible for the Sikhs to be employed en masse for the British Indian Army, leading to their many campaigns in Africa, Europe, and across the Indian subcontinent. The continued struggle in the North West Frontier (now known as Khyber Pakhtunkhwa) continued to be a major

---

42   Gardner's work was published posthumously by Major Hugh Pearse as *Soldier and Traveller; Memoirs of Alexander Gardner, Colonel of Artillery in the service of Maharaja Ranjit Singh* (London: William Blackwood and Sons, 1898). The accounts by Gardner are considered untrustworthy.

43   He effectively commanded the artillery in the Sikh Wars, but after the Battle of Chillianwallah, he went over the British side.

44   Sita Ram Kohli, *Catalogue Of Khalsa Darbar Records*, Volume 1 (Lahore: Printed by the Superintendent, Government Printing, 1919).

45   1st Baronet Sir Walter Gilbert, Colonel of the 1st Bengal European Fusiliers, fought in both Sikh Wars. A descendant of the famed Sir Walter Raleigh (d. 1618) of the Elizabethan era, he is buried at Kensal Green Cemetery, London.

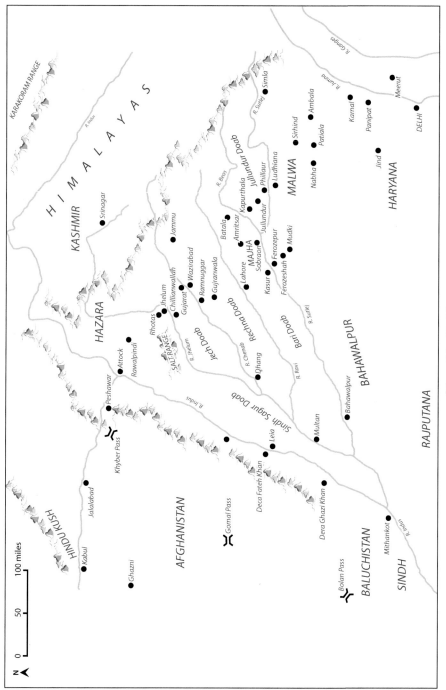

Map of the Panjab.

area of deployment for Sikhs. This was decades before the general view that Sikhs should be employed in mass numbers during the First World War and the Second World War. The story of the Sikh soldier is multi-faceted and demonstrates inevitable change. The common goals and themes of the soldier, however, remain: righteous, compassionate, adhering to codes of conduct and committed to uprooting tyranny. This was paramount and in line with the original role of the Khalsa as formulated by Guru Gobind Singh.

1

Jassa Singh Ahluwalia: Early Sikh Leadership

After the ascension of Guru Gobind Singh in 1708, the Khalsa was in dire straits, being hounded at every opportunity and with bounties placed on every Sikh head. It was either a case of bowing down to the constant threat from all fronts or taking the fight head-on with their opponents. Banda Singh Bahadur had taken the mantle from the Guru, uplifted the common person and not only struck fear into the Mughal regime but struck coins to denote sovereignty.[1] This strike was short-lived but the Khalsa would bounce back firstly under Darbara Singh, who as an elder statesman paved the way for Nawab Kapur Singh (1697–1753) to be the de facto leader of the Khalsa.

Kapur Singh would be the guiding light for the Sikhs in the early eighteenth century, creating a number of Sikh battalions or *Jathas* into an early Misl system. He had the idea of accepting a *Jagir* or land rights from a Mughal governor, Zakariya Khan, which was pivotal in keeping a small kind of peace in a forthcoming century of battles; it implied a vassal-chief relationship. This was a decision made in unison on the part of the Khalsa, hence the title of Nawab being attributed to him. This allowed for Sikhs to build up a small treasury and also allowed for the upkeep of an army at the time.[2] This deal was short-lived. It was during Kapur Singh's leadership that many Sikhs and later leaders all took the Khalsa initiation rites from him, which directly showed the importance of his position and authority. According to Latif, 'He converted a large number of people, carpenters, weavers, Jhiwars, Chhatris, and others to the persuasion of Govind, and the religious respect in which he was held was so great, that initiation into the *Pahul* of the Guru with his hands was considered a great distinction.'[3] This included many future Sikh leaders including Ala Singh of Patiala and others. Yet he was building the Khalsa Army from this small foundation

---

1   Read more about Banda Singh Bahadur in my, *The British and the Sikhs*.
2   *Sri Gur Panth Prakash*, p.87
3   Syad Muhammad Latif, *History Of The Panjab From the remotest Antiquity to the Present Time*, (Calcutta: Calcutta Central Press Company, 1891), p.322.

to rally around his successor, Jassa Singh Ahluwalia. His contribution was marked with a tomb or *Samadhi* situated near to the Gurdwara Baba Atal within the precinct of the Harimandir Sahib.[4]

Jassa Singh 'Kalal' (1718–83) from the community of distillers had a unique upbringing.[5] He was the son of a family headed by Sadhu Singh who had been serving the Sikh cause at the time of Guru Hargobind. He founded several villages around Lahore including the area of Ahlu in present-day Pakistan from where the name Ahluwalia derives.[6] Jassa Singh was considered to be born there to one Badar Singh (d.1723) whose brother Bagh Singh was already serving under Kapur Singh. After his father's passing, he was looked after by his mother, and on meeting the consort of Guru Gobind Singh, Mata Sundari, his mother offered her son to her for upbringing. This was a major blessing for the young Jassa Singh, who would be guided by Mata Sundari and tutored in various languages and arts and the recital of the Sikh scriptures. To be living in Delhi would have left a lasting imprint on his future ambitions which included one day conquering the Mughal regime, a prophecy which was envisaged not only by Kapur Singh but which was a continual recital within scripture, prayer and individual personal achievement.[7] He would see several Sikhs come to Delhi and visit Mata Sundari, and be witness to the edicts that were sent to the Panjab denoting the importance of a great female leader in a turbulent time. He would have also seen the dangers which were being faced under the Mughal Regime in the Panjab although there did not appear to be any threat to them at Delhi. He would also have come to an early understanding of the court politics of Delhi.

Many Sikhs took *Pahul* from the great leader including Amar Singh of Patiala, to whom he gave a special sword (see colour pages). When Jassa Singh came to the Panjab he was taken under the wing of Nawab Kapur Singh, from whom he learnt the art of war and eventually progressed to having a number of soldiers reporting directly to him. On Bhag Singh's death, he became head of the Ahluwalia Misl. His confederacy was based within Jalandhar and later, by 1767, covered the territory of Kapurthala where the dynasty still survives. His qualities and leadership paid off with Kapur Singh rewarding Jassa Singh with the mantle of the *Jathedar* or head of the Sikh Panth. This investiture was signified by the holy weapons of the Khalsa being handed down to Jassa Singh.[8] His first strategy was to re-organise the Sikh *Jathas* into a full-fledged Misl system. The system involved a leader being chosen and his name

---

4   The *Samadhi* is no longer there and it must have been destroyed, presumably as part of improvements at the Harimandir Sahib. Regrettably, much damage has been undertaken to the heritage of the Panjab in the name of progress.

5   *Sri Gur Panth Prakash*, p.93.

6   Griffin, *Chief and Families of Note in the Punjab*, Vol. 2, pp.495–496 .

7   'The Khalsa Panth which had made Kapur Singh a Nawab, would one day make the boy (Jassa Singh) a sovereign,' *Sri Gur Panth Prakash*, p.97.

8   These weapons belonged to Guru Gobind Singh and were given to Mata Sundri and then Nawab Kapur Singh.

and number of soldiers being recorded in a file known as a Misl, hence one possible reason for the origins of the name. This file would have been kept at the Akal Takht in Amritsar. However, with the number of attacks and desecrations by the Afghans and Muslims this information has only come down to us second-hand with no surviving files. The peasantry of Panjab and the landowners, who had seen their crops being ravaged by many rulers as well as witnessing famines, flocked under Banda Singh Bahadur. This continued through the years to the time of Jassa Singh Ahluwalia who went through villages ensuring their allegiances and support in return for protection. These villages would have also been a recruiting ground for soldiers who would be given a horse and arms to protect themselves but more importantly, they would be part of the Misl system.[9] The political situation was complicated by a Mughal regime that was beginning to crumble and there were many vying for position in northern India from the Marathas, Rohillas, other Muslim Nawabs from places such as Oude, and the East India Company whose rise should be a mandatory consideration in the discussion.

Jassa Singh's first strategic action was to reorganise the early groupings into two groups, namely the Buddha Dal and Taruna Dal. Whilst this task was undertaken by Kapur Singh, it would be under the leadership of Jassa Singh with both groups reporting to him. The historic occasion or a *Sarbat Khalsa* (conclave) is said to have taken place in 1748 at Amritsar. The Dals would still retain autonomy in decisions and excursions. They would meet on auspicious occasions like Diwali and Dussehra and whenever there was an imminent threat.[10] These were subject to *Gurmatas* (resolutions) taken at Amritsar, which were binding on all. The two-fold plan was first to face the local Mughal governors in Lahore and Sirhind and eventually remove them from office, and secondly to protect the Panjab from the incursion of the Afghans. These conquests, firstly under Nadir Shah, had created an industry of plunder for the invaders from central Iran. This group was eventually under the Durrani Chief, Ahmed Shah Abdali, who continued the massacres, abduction of women, and merciless killings in the name of loot and money. The Mughal regime was only too ready to either call for their help or stand by and watch the carnage being unleashed.

Jassa Singh's early conquests included attacking the baggage train of Nadir Shah in 1739 which was laden with treasures and booty. This led him to develop new areas and many forts including that of Dalewal.[11] Jassa Singh guided the Khalsa through the

---

9   M.L. Ahluwalia, *Life and Times of Jassa Singh Ahluwalia* (Patiala: Publication Bureau-Punjabi University, 1989), p.10

10   The occasion of Dussehra was a celebration that Sikhs considered sacred until the time of the Sikh reform movements. An Indic-themed story based on the defeat of Ravana of Lanka by Rama and narrated in the *Ramayan*. Guru Gobind Singh reinterpreted the passive nature of the story and instilled the military ethos of what the story was missing. See the composition *Ram Avatar, Dasam Granth*.

11   Jaspreet Kaur Sandhu, *Sikh Ethos-Eighteenth Century Perspective*, (Patiala: Vision and Venture), 2000, p.7

dangerous times in Sikh history that witnessed the large-scale massacres of the Sikhs named the *Choota Ghallughara* (smaller holocaust) and *Vadhha Ghallughara* (bigger holocaust). The former was a surprise attack on the Sikhs in 1746 where the Khalsa was encamped. The Mughal military commander Jaspat Rai was killed in action by Jassa Singh's unit and much of the treasure at Eminabad was taken as spoils in 1743.[12] Lakhpat Rai, who was a revenue minister at Lahore, and brother of Jaspat Rai, vowed his revenge. Together with the Lahore Governor, Yahiya Khan, they mobilised the Lahore troops, summoned reinforcements, and the local leaders were alerted for a large-scale genocide of the Sikhs. Many were rounded up and executed on 10 March 1746. Lakhpat Rai next set out for the forest of Kahnuvan near Gurdaspur where Sikhs were reported to have concentrated. Lakhpat had with him a large force of mostly cavalry, supported by cannon, with which he surrounded the forest and began a systematic search for the Sikhs. Initially, the Sikhs held out for some time and struck back whenever they could. Heavily outnumbered, Jassa Singh and Sukha Singh decided to escape to the foothills of the Himalayas to the north.[13] The Sikhs crossed the River Ravi and came in sight of the foothills, with the enemy in pursuit, only to find the armies of the hill Rajas waiting for them. Caught between these two armies, the Sikhs suffered heavy casualties. Battling their way through the forest, they recrossed the River Ravi in a desperate attempt to reach safety. However, there was further danger, and many injured Sikhs were swept away by the current. With Lakhpat Rai's forces still in hot pursuit, they crossed two more rivers, the Beas and the Sutlej, before finally arriving at the sanctuary of the Lakhi Jungle in Bhatinda. An estimation of the slaughter of the Sikhs was around 7,000 to 10,000 but the figure is considered to be much higher across the period.[14] The captives were marched back to Lahore, paraded in the streets, and publicly beheaded. Given the small numbers of the Sikhs in those days of persecution, the losses will have been a very substantial proportion of their population.

Not dismayed, Jassa Singh and the Khalsa continued the tactics of *Dhai Phat* or 'two-and-a-half strikes.' In 1756, one of the Durrani Chiefs, General Sabuland Khan, was defeated in Jalandhar. Adina Beg, the *Faujdar* of Jalandhar, was constantly accepting and rejecting Sikh authority and eventually asked for Maratha and Sikh help in turfing out the Afghans. In 1758 this pan-alliance of Sikhs/Marathas and Mughals defeated their enemy at Sirhind and Lahore. The Sikhs brought back captives and made them clean the Harimandir Sahib which had been destroyed by Ahmed

---

12   *Sri Gur Panth Prakash*, p.335

13   Sukha Singh of the Misl to be known as Karorasinghia was a daring Sikh who some years earlier with Mehtab Singh had killed Massa Ranghar who had desecrated the Harimandir Sahib.

14   'Some others reckoned the number of those killed at fifty thousand, Of whom forty thousand had been done to death. Still others put this figure much higher than fifty thousand, As no definite head count of those killed could be made.' *Sri Gur Panth Prakash*, p.377.

Shah Abdali months earlier. However, the Marathas did not view the Sikhs as a formidable body of soldiers, and they entrusted Lahore and other territories to Adina Beg. This was much to the annoyance of the Khalsa, who were 'the sons and daughters of Panjabi soil.' This left a deep distrust between the Sikhs and the Marathas, and as a result, no such alliance was ever undertaken again much to the detriment of the Hindustani nation-building and matrimony. The decimation of the Marathas at the battle of Panipat in 1761 by the Afghans may have seen a different result with the aid of the Sikhs.

In 1759, Jassa Singh Ahluwalia, after receiving a heavy tribute by Adina Beg, fought at Mahilpur, Hoshiarpur to keep the Afghans at bay.[15] This battle is seldomly cited and even inhabitants of the area are unaware of this important event. However, Jassa Singh kept his area of jurisdiction in Jalandhar right under the nose of Adina Beg, something which the Mughal administrator was hard-pressed to admit to. During this time, the Buddha Dal chief extended his territories across the Panjab. In 1761 Charhat Singh Sukerchakia was being besieged by the Governor of Lahore, Khajwah Abed Khan; the Dal Khalsa attacked Lahore and captured the fort briefly which brought great tribute and fame to Jassa Singh. There has also been a suggestion that the Misls minted their first coin to celebrate this occasion.[16] In the aforementioned Battle of Panipat, as the Afghans were traversing back to their territories, the Sikhs pounced on the baggage trains and rescued many female captives. The women were restored to their families, citing the Sikhs as protectors. The concept of *bandi chhoor* or liberators was paramount within descriptions of the Sikhs.[17]

In 1762, during the larger holocaust or *Vadhha Ghallughara* the Khalsa resolve was further tested. In another surprise attack, the forces of Ahmed Shah Abdali, aided by the local rulers of Zhain Khan of Sirhind and Bhikhan Khan of Marlekotla, fell upon the Sikhs on 5 February 1762. The Sikhs numbered about 30,000, but most of them were non-combatants. It was decided that the Sikh fighters would form a cordon around the slow-moving baggage train consisting of women, children, and old men. The strategy was to keep fighting while moving, so they kept the baggage

15 Jassa Singh was joined by venerable Wadhbhag Singh of Kartapur who had been left for dead by the Afghans and the Khalsa Chief Sham Singh of Panjgarh (whose soldiers would later form the Karorasinghia Misl). My family comes from this region of the Panjab and this battle seems to have been forgotten.

16 There has been much speculation regarding this coin. Some commentators have stated the inscription bearing Jassa Singh's name would not be possible as the spirit of Khalsa was in the name of the Gurus. However, others have contended a small number may have been circulated. To consider the various theories on the coin see Gupta, *History of the Sikhs*, Vol. 2, pp.174–178.

17 The concept was first used to describe Guru Hargobind's role in liberating captive princes at the Fort of Gwalior around the time of Diwali. However, in modern times the concept of *Bandi Choor Diwas* has been described as the liberation day itself, equating it with the festival of Diwali.

train marching, covering it as a hen covers its chicks under its wings.[18] Jassa Singh and Charhat Singh showed much courage and conviction and without their protection and resolve this attack would have seen the whole Sikh caravan massacred. More than once, the troops of the invaders broke the cordon and mercilessly butchered the women, children, and elderly inside, but each time the Sikh warriors regrouped and managed to push back the attackers. Jassa Singh suffered many wounds in the battle, but the Khalsa forces managed to make their way to a large pond. Both parties stopped their fighting for some respite and the Sikhs managed to head off to Barnala, with Ahmed Shah Abdali choosing not to continue his pursuit into the desert. The estimates of the Sikhs' loss of life vary from 20,000 up to 50,000 which essentially would have seen the end of the Sikhs. However, the self-belief of the Khalsa and their faith in themselves as handed down to them by Guru Gobind Singh saw them regroup. Within three months of the *Vadhha Ghallughara*, the Dal Khalsa rose to defeat Abdali's governor Zain Kan at Sirhind in April and May 1762. He saved himself by paying a large tribute. In October of the same year, Abdali was pushed out of Amritsar, which shows the tenacity of the Khalsa who were not willing to be subdued by the invader. In 1764, one of the most important conquests of Jassa Singh was leading 10,000 of his own Misl and seven other Misls to defeat Zain Khan, resulting in the portioning-out of Sirhind province. The Sikh sardars became holders of large estates overnight and this single conquest put them in an enviable position.[19] The Khalsa had now begun their path to complete dominance of the Panjab. However, it was also an issue that some Misls did not receive any share or were not part of this conquest, namely the major Bhangi sardars and the Sukerchakia Misl. They would receive their rewards with Jassa Singh directing them to push towards west Panjab.

Jassa Singh had realised that the rise of the Khalsa was not only for defence and he had to take the fight to the Mughal regime. Leading over 40,000 horsemen in February 1764, the first major conquest of the Ganga Doab took place. Many of the areas surrounding Delhi were attacked, including Shamli, Ambli, Miranpur, Deoband, Muzaffarnagar, Najibabad, Chandausi and Anupshahr, which was an outpost loyal to the East India Company.[20] They took tribute and booty all the way back to the Panjab. This would be the first incursion of the Khalsa's depredations and conquests around Delhi which lasted until 1803-4. However, there were still Afghan forces to contend with. In 1764, the seventh invasion of Ahmed Shah Abdali took place, where a contingent of thirty Sikhs headed by Gurbakhsh Singh (1688–1764) of the Shaheedi Misl were defending the Harimandir Sahib. They spilt their blood to the 30,000-strong Afghan force. During this invasion, the Durrani Chief's Chronicler, Nur Mohamed, wrote his description of the Sikhs and the events that unfolded. Whilst calling the Sikhs 'dogs', he recognised their prowess on the battlefield, writing, 'If you

18   *Sri Gur Panth Prakash*, p.509.
19   Gupta, *History of the Sikhs*, Vol. 3, p.37.
20   Gupta, *History of the Sikhs*, Vol. 3, p.47.

wish to learn the art of war, come face to face with them in the field.'[21] He described the martyrdom of the *Shahids* at Amritsar:

> When the Shah arrived at the Chak [Amritsar] there was not a single Kafir to be seen there. But a few of them had remained in an enclosure so that they might spill their own blood. And they sacrificed their lives for the Guru. When they saw the renowned King and the army of Islam, they came out of the enclosure. They were only thirty in number. But they had not a grain of fear about them. They had neither the fear of slaughter nor the dread of death. Thus they grappled with the Ghazis, and in this grappling they spilt their own blood. All the accursed Sikhs were killed and went to hell.[22]

The spoils and raids around Sirhind provided the Sikhs with much-needed money. This was used to rebuild Amritsar which again was desecrated by the Afghans. Repairs to the Harimandir Sahib together with other fortifications of the city were supervised by Jassa Singh. The area around Harimandir Sahib and the Akal Takht became the focal point for Sikh religion and its politics. All the leaders or sardars visited the shrine frequently and held meetings there. It was the duty of every sardar to ensure the proper management of the shrine. They were to guide and instruct the persons working there. Under the supervision of Jassa Singh, many of the sardars constructed their residential dwellings known as *Bungas* in the periphery of the Tank.[23] These initially served as defence locations for any impending attacks. Later, the complex had watchtowers. The largest *Bunga* was constructed under Jassa Singh Ramgharia where his soldiers rested and were housed. These *Bungas* also served as educational institutions. In essence, they were named after their respective confederacies, individuals of importance, communities of importance and religious orders like the *Udasis*, *Nirmalas*, *Sewapanthis* and Akalis.[24] These places were used as rest houses for accommodating pilgrims during festive occasions by various Misls. The main *Bunga*, known as the *Akal Bunga*, was also a record office of the Sikh bands and fighters. This file we understand was known as a Misl, so in essence, it was a record of the number of warriors and the name of the sardar who commanded them. This file would have also held details on territorial acquisitions, the idea being to prevent boundary disputes.[25] This came about due to some sardars deciding to take each other's territories; Jassa Singh acted on numerous occasions to get these territories back for them.[26]

---

21 Singh, *Jang Namah*, p.54.
22 Singh, *Jang Namah*, pp.34–35.
23 The lake surrounding the Harimandir Sahib.
24 Madanjit Kaur, *The Golden Temple Past and Present* (Amritsar: Guru Nanak Dev University Press,1983), p.180
25 Kaur, *The Golden Temple Past and Present*, p.169
26 This was never completely acted on but during his tenure, the Misl was the actual record of possessions.

The Ahluwalia Katra, Amritsar. (By Felice Beato. Courtesy of Getty's Open Content Program. Negative 1858–1859, print 1862)

Jassa Singh also allocated land for the formation of *Katras* (residential quarters) around Amritsar with shops administered under Misl chiefs. His was named Katra Ahluwalia, whilst other prominent ones included Katra Bhagian (Kanhaiya Misl), and Katra Bhangian (Bhangi Misl).

The final time that the Durranis pulled down the Harimandir Sahib was in 1764, but the Khalsa made sure it was the last. It was also in this year that Jassa Singh began the main repairs to the sacred shrine; however, they could not complete it due to an impending invasion. In 1765 the work was assigned to Des Raj, who collected funds for the job.[27] With the construction of some *Bungas* and *Katras*, this began to

27   Kaur, *The Golden Temple Past and Present*, p.16. The construction of the other areas of the complex was undertaken incrementally throughout the eighteenth century.

draw very large numbers of devotees who, along with their sardars, contributed liber-ally to the treasury for running the *langar* and undertaking the construction work of the sacred shrine at Amritsar. Jassa Singh Ahluwalia's name is inscribed at the Harimandir Sahib for his services at the shrine.[28]

The Afghan army met the Sikhs in their first direct battle in 1765. Jassa Singh distinguished himself in the campaign and is described as leading the other Misl chiefs:

> From the other side, the dogs were also coming forward with their well-arrayed army, with Jassa [Singh] Kalal like a mountain in the middle. He was accompa-nied by another Jassa [Singh] Thoka who was a lion in fury and strength among these dogs. He had also kept several other dogs experienced in war along with him there. The right was led by Charht [Singh], Jhanda [Singh] and Jai Singh while the left was under the command of Hari Singh, the lame, Ram Das, Gulab [Singh] and Gujjar [Singh].[29]

This description shows the Khalsa as being formidable and noticeably showing their might and prowess. The description of a dog for the Khalsa was a blunt reminder of how much of a thorn they were in the side of the Afghans. The names of the other Misl chiefs were: Jassa Singh, described as 'Thoka' of the Ramgharia Misl; Charhat Singh Sukerchakia (whom we discuss later); Jai Singh of the Kanhaiya Misl; and Hari Singh, Ram Das, Gulab Singh and Gujar Singh, all of the Bhangi Misl. After seven days of battle, the Afghans were driven out of the Panjab. Many of them perished crossing the River Beas, the number of dead equalling those who died in the current campaign. This paved the way for further success for the Khalsa forces who took over Lahore in 1765 and established their authority, and this was marked by the minting of coins by the Misls.[30] The apportioning of territories established the Misl leaders in various territories. Jassa Singh possessed some areas in the Bari Doab and Bist Jullundur Doab, and in 1769 Jassa Singh captured Jalandhar together with the Singhpuria Misl Chief, Khushal Singh. In 1771 he started making plans for the territory of Kapurthala. Initially, he just sought tribute but he captured the area after the ruler Rai Ibrahim was dealing with his subjects with cruelty. Jassa Singh lived at Kapurthala until his death.[31] The Misls unfortunately did not have

---

28 This is on the northern side of the complex, towards the *Ghantaghar* (clock tower). It records that Jassa Singh undertook *Sewa* (selfless service) of the shrine together with the names of Maharajah Kharak Singh and Prince Nau Nihal Singh.

29 Singh, *Jang Namah*, p.49.

30 Whilst this is understood to be a collective Dal Khalsa coin, the Bhangi Misl deserves major credit for the victory at Lahore and as a result, the coin is sometimes solely attributed to them. See next chapter.

31 Several of the historic buildings remain but require restoration including the Haveli of Jassa Singh and the place of Nihal Singh.

Historic buildings at Kapurthala, c.1900. (Courtesy of Peter Bance)

the unity required to keep hold of their own territories and respect the territories of others. There occurred an unfortunate incident where Mali Singh (brother of Jassa Singh Ramgharia) came to blows with the Buddha Dal Chief. Jassa Singh was held captive and eventually released. As a result, Jassa Singh Ramgharia and his Misl, upon hearing of these unfortunate events, tried to placate Jassa Singh. However, this was seen as a matter of national disrespect, and several Misls combined and ejected the Ramgarhia Misl out of their territories.

One of Jassa Singh's biggest achievements was leading the Khalsa forces against Shah Alum II and taking over Delhi in 1783 together with Baghel Singh of the Karorasinghia Misl and other prominent sardars. With a force of 30,000 Sikhs, they poured into the Ganga Doab and took their depredations again all the way to British territories. After some hard-fought battles with the Delhi armies of Emperor Shah Alum, they were defeated. On 11 March 1783, the Buddha Dal made for the Red Fort, where the royal palace was located, entering virtually without a fight and hoisting the Khalsa battle standards.[32] This is recognised as a great victory in Sikh history, together with turning the tide against the Mughals and sending the forces of the Afghan King Ahmed Shah Abdali back across to Afghanistan.[33] Whilst one of these events would be seen as remarkable, to dent two power bases was due to the character of Jassa Singh Ahluwalia. With the Sikh forces congregated at the court of Delhi, Jassa Singh took the important step of sitting on the same throne as the Mughal Emperors. Jassa Singh hence was given the name of *Padshah* (king).[34] The concept of 'Raj Kharega Khalsa' or 'the Khalsa will rule' was materialised. Baghel Singh, the ablest Misl leader around the Ganga Doab, cemented the victory by negotiating the terms with the Shah Alum and signifying Sikh authority with the building of seven Sikh shrines around Delhi. The takeover was not deemed appropriate for a long-term presence and Baghel Singh, as commander of the Sikh armies in the region, raised revenue by receiving octroi duties or taxation on a regular basis.[35] This occasion also sent a strong message to the various players around Delhi including the Marathas and Rohillas. The role of other Misls should not be discounted including the heavy tribute procured by Jassa Singh Ramgharia. This included the so called platform on which the Mughals once sat on.

These players also included the East India Company, and several of the Sikh chiefs started writing to the British to seek out their intentions. A demarcation of territories had been intended ever since the British took over Diwani rights from the Mughals in

---

32   Mann, *The British and the Sikhs*, pp.38–39.
33   In 2020, in response to changes in farm laws, a year-long protest took place in Delhi. The imagery of the Khalsa conquest of 1783 became a rallying point for the predominantly Sikh protestors.
34   However, it is also claimed that Jassa Singh Ramgharia objected to Jassa Singh Ahluwalia taking the throne. As a result, Jassa Singh Ahluwalia withdrew from the throne, so as not to mar the important victory.
35   Mann, *The British and the Sikhs*, pp.34–46.

1765 and their power base was increasing. Jassa Singh moved quickly to open a channel with the envoy of the Governor-General, Major James Browne, who proceeded to Delhi on learning that the Sikhs had made their conquest of Delhi.[36] Fourteen documents show the language and diplomacy shown by the Khalsa in dealing with the British.[37] Jassa Singh, Lehna Singh Bhangi, Amar Singh of Patiala, and Baghel Singh deferred negotiations and suggested communications should be made to Jassa Singh as the 'highest and greatest and in that country called Badshah Singh.'[38] There were also hints of a possible treaty that would keep the Sikhs from gaining more territories and threatening British interests. The diplomacy and the idea of curtailing the activities of the Sikhs failed and the Sikhs continued their warlike depredations on the borders of British territories until General Gerard Lake (1744–1808) took over Delhi in 1803-4.[39] However, Jassa Singh was not able to witness the success of his conquests to their logical fruition as he passed away in the same year. He was succeeded by his cousin Bhag Singh Ahluwalia (d.1801). The Kapurthala Royal Family would carve out their principality during the Sikh Empire and after the annexation of the Panjab. Fateh Singh Ahluwalia (1784–1837) was very prominent during this time and one of Ranjit Singh's first steps was to form an alliance with him. As a plenipotentiary of the Maharajah, he signed the First Anglo-Sikh treaty known as the Treaty of Amritsar in 1806 with General Lake. The Ahluwalia dynasty would support the British during the so-called Indian Rebellion of 1858. The descendants continue to reside at Kapurthala.[40]

The Dal Khalsa established its authority over most of the Panjab region in a short time. As early as 1749, the Mughal governor of Panjab solicited its help in the suppression of a rebellion in Multan. In early 1758, the Dal Khalsa, in collaboration with the Marathas, occupied Sirhind and Lahore. Jassa Singh, due to his position as the Buddha Dal chief, had the privilege of his *Samadhi* being positioned within the

36   'But the real cause of Major Brown's arrival was in consequence of orders he had received from his government, not to decline any overture that might be made for affording a military aid to the royal cause. The Seiks had for several years back, by their predatory incursions into Doo Ab and Rohilcund, excited alarm in the government of Majud Al Dowla: and Mr. Hastings, the British governor, with his usual discernment, deemed the exertions of the court of Delhi might, at the present juncture of affairs, prove a beneficial counterpoise to the rising power of the Seiks.' Francklin, *The History of the Reign of Shah-Aulum*, pp.115–16.
37   For the letter and reply by Jassa Singh Ahluwalia see my book *The British and the Sikhs*, pp.136–137.
38   Krishna Dyal Bhargava (ed.), *Browne Correspondence* (Delhi: Pub. for the National Archives of India by the Manager of Publications, Government of India, 1960), pp.74–82. Browne states: 'From all these letters the Readiness of these Sirdars to enter into a friendly communication with the English Nation, is sufficiently evident, at the Same Time they are in some Degree alarmed at the apparent Union between Us and the Shah's Servants, which they are apprehensive may lead to some attempts on their Possessions.'
39   Gerard Lake, 1st Viscount Lake. Also known as Lord Lake who was Commander in Chief of the British forces.
40   The present head of the family is H.H. Brigadier Sukhjit Singh.

precincts of the Harimandir complex in Amritsar.[41] He had the unique position of being called *Sultan-ul-Quam* and *Badshah* (king). However, he did not live to see the entire fruits of his selfless actions, with the other Misls building on his strategy. He guided the Sikh forces for nearly 40 years and was witness to the two largest massacres of the Sikhs. However, under his authority, the Khalsa fought back against the Afghans and took the fight to Mughal Delhi. He also foresaw the rise in British power. The Marathas had lost their friendship with the Sikhs back in 1758 and this never healed; otherwise, the history of Hindustan may have been a different affair. His leadership would be the forerunner for Maharajah Ranjit Singh some years later. His achievements can be summed up by Sinha as the following:

> For the successful termination of Sikh war of independence, we should give the credit to the entire nation, not to any individual.....But an exception must be made in favour of Jassa Singh Ahluwalia. To a large extent, he was the soul of many of these apparently isolated undertakings that ultimately brought the war of liberation to a successful termination. The Sarbat Khalsa would invariably nominate him as the commander in all its combined undertakings. But his ascendancy was precisely that which superior minds acquire in times of difficulty. ...The Sikh horseman recognised his general in the most handsome, tall, figure and by the fact he surpassed every one of his men in temperance as well as in toil; in valour as also in conduct. [42]

Whilst according to modern Buddha Dal tradition the Sikhs would be guided by the Nihang leader Naina Singh of the Shaheedi Misl, it appears the Misl system continued with each leader independent as before.[43]

---

41 This is near the shrine of Baba Atal and next to Jassa Singh's mentor Nawab Kapur Singh. These are rarely recognised by the congregation as with many other important aspects of the Harimandir complex.

42 N. K. Sinha, *Rise of the Sikh Power*, pp.90–92.

43 There are limited sources on this transition but the Nihang tradition is steadfast on this point of history. It appears that Naina Singh's successor Akali Phula Singh definitely held the glory of the Khalsa.

2

Charhat Singh: Building the Sukerchakia Dynasty

The Sukerchakia Misl was one of the prominent Misls of the eighteenth century and the depth of its strategic leadership would lead to the creation of the Sikh Empire. It was this Misl which, under Maharajah Ranjit Singh in the nineteenth century, would carve out a nation from the warlike Sikh people. To understand their origins we need to discuss the history and importance of Charhat Singh (1733–70) who played a pivotal role against the Afghans and the Mughals. He was always on the frontline in the battles that he fought, as a result of which he was recognised as a fearless warrior. The origins of this Misl, however, started under one Budh Singh (d.1715) who fought under Guru Gobind Singh and Banda Singh Bahadur.[1] After his death, his two sons settled in different regions. Nodh Singh (d. 1752) was based in Sukerchak (Amritsar district) from where the Misl received its name and Chanda Singh settled in Sandhanwalia in Sialkot district. These two branches played an important part in Sikh history and politics throughout the eighteenth and nineteenth centuries. Nodh Singh also served under Nawab Kapur Singh. As his confidence increased, he gathered a small number of soldiers to form his own unit and in 1758 the national Sikh assembly sanctioned him to form his own Misl. He died in 1763 whilst in battle. He was superseded by Charhat Singh who also served under Kapur Singh. However, this dashing Misl leader started carving out territories of his own and through marriage resulted in his possessing areas of Gujranwala where he established himself and his Misl.[2]

His early campaigns including working in unison with Jai Singh Kanhaiya of the Kanhaiya Misl. In 1754 they together plundered the area around Lahore. He was adept in various weapons including the musket and the *Khanda* or double-edged sword. His bravery was noted when an Afghan warrior covered with armour challenged the

---

1   The probable date of death is given as 1715 at Gurdas Nangal. Gupta, *History of the Sikhs*, Vol. IV, p.294.

2   He married Desan Kaur, the daughter of a leading sardar, Amir Singh, of the Singhpuria Misl. *History of the Sikhs*, Vol. 4, pp. 294–295. 'He occupied the region reputed for breeding quality horses. Establishing a police post in the city of Gujranwala, He decided to loot and plunder the rest of the region', See Bhangu, *Sri Gur Panth Prakash*, p.591.

Sikhs in a one-to-one encounter. Charhat Singh stepped up but was stopped from fighting as Sukha Singh realised the danger he would face, but he was not afraid of a challenge.[3] In 1758 a fort was built at Gujranwala from where the Misl leader would be best placed to lead his forces. He was part of the pan-alliance comprising of Marathas, Sikhs and Mughals. They fought the Afghans in the Panjab who found themselves being hounded by the Dal Khalsa, instrumental of whom was Charhat Singh Sukerchakia and his Misl. By using his forces to attack at odd times of the day and night, picking off the Afghan army, he caused much annoyance to the Durrani troops.[4] However, the Durrani forces under Prince Taimur and Jahan Khan escaped across the river, but the entire treasury which was still east of the river was captured by the victors.[5] This was not about spoils alone and the Durrani prisoners were captured and made to clean the Harimandir complex: 'Some regiments of the Singhs under the command of S. Charat Singh gave a hot chase to the Afghans, and brought about 200 Afghans prisoners to Amritsar. These persons were made to cleanse the holy tank in Sri Darbar Sahib, which had been filled by Jahan Khan.'[6]

It was 1761 which brought much glory and prestige to Charhat Singh. It was after the third battle of Panipat where Ahmed Shah Abdali had decimated the Marathas that he also despatched General Nur-ud-din Bamezat with a 12,000 strong contingent to chastise the Sikhs. Charhat Singh checked his advance and they were made to advance to Sialkot, where the Durranis surrendered after being besieged, Nur-ud-din reportedly managed to escape disguised as a beggar.[7] In response to this humiliating defeat, Khwaja Ubaid Khan, the Afghan governor of Lahore, marched upon Gujranwala. The town was surrounded but Charhat Singh fought with courage and surprised the besiegers by his night sallies. In the meantime, other Sikh sardars, under the leadership of Jassa Singh Ahluwalia, came to the aid of Charhat Singh. Ubaid Khan was attacked by the Dal Khalsa and was defeated with the governor fleeing to Lahore leaving behind siege guns, ammunition and stores.[8] Around November 1761 they fell upon Lahore, killing him.

3   Bhangu, *Sri Gur Panth Prakash*, pp.185–191. In this encounter, Sukha Singh was giving words of advice about choosing your battles carefully and knowing your adversary's strengths.

4   Composed of Jassa Singh Ahluwalia, Tara Singh Ghaiba, Jassa Singh Ramgarhia, Hari Singh, Jhanda Singh, Ganda Singh of the Bhangi Misl and others. Also see Ganda Singh, *Ahmad Shah Durrani (Father of modern Afghanistan)* (New York: Asia Publishing House, 1959), pp.205–206.

5   P. Setu Madhave Rao, *Thamas Nama: The Autobiography of a Slave* (Bombay, Popular Prakashan, 1967), p.70, 'In the afternoon (19th April 1758) Taimur Shah crossed the river [Ravi]. The Vazir followed him. A general movement of the army began.' Based on the testimony of Tahmas Khan better known under the pen name Miskin. Bhangu, *Sri Gur Panth Prakash*, Vol. 2, pp.441–443.

6   *Tareekh-e-Gujjran- wala, Haqiqat-e-Firkai Sikhan*, quoted in Ganda Singh, *Sardar Jassa Singh Ahluwalia*, p.92.

7   Gupta, *History of the Sikhs*, Vol. 2, p.171.

8   Rao, *Tahmas Nama*, p.104.

The fact that Charhat Singh had taken the fight to the Afghans and Mughals greatly enhanced his prestige and made him stand out amongst the Sikh Misls. These events led to the aforementioned *Vadhha Ghallughara* where Abdali made his pronouncement to kill every Sikh – lock, stock and barrel. It was during this battle that once again Charhat Singh demonstrated much courage and valour similar to Jassa Singh Ahluwalia (whose role we discussed), his bold military tactics preventing a complete annihilation of the Sikh army and non-combatants. To get a military understanding of this battle and the part played by the Sukerchakia Chief, the actual events need to be explored in detail. In February 1762, the Sikhs were attacked by the Afghan and Mughal forces. As a result, the strategy was to ensure that the *Vahir* or baggage train or caravan was protected. This train was composed of women and children and the Dal Khalsa had to make an immediate decision as to whether to fight or retreat.

Initially, Jassa Singh and Sham Singh's contingent went to protect the caravan with the rest of the Dal Khalsa fighting directly with the enemy.[9] Charhat Singh wanted to divide the Khalsa forces into smaller divisions but there was little time to make these plans in the immediate theatre of war. Whilst a number of Sikhs protected the main caravan, another contingent would push forward and attack and then retreat.[10] After four miles Abdali, with his four brigades of troops, spilt the main Sikh forces from the baggage trains. Another attack however resulted in the caravan being split into two. The Afghan king was getting frustrated with his general, Zhain Khan, who had been unable to encircle the Sikhs. A further attack was made to finish off the Khalsa army, during which time Charhat Singh directed and protected the caravan.[11] During a fit of rage, the Misl leader proclaimed that he would seek out Abdali and fight him on the spot. He left the caravan to seek the Durrani chief whom he was unable to locate, cutting through the enemy forces, 'Like a fast running water spider did horses run back and forth, Like a flash of lightning would Charhat Singh enter the Pathan forces.'[12] At one point in the battle he picked up a spear to use in his fighting; this broke into pieces and he then proceeded to use a small firearm. He also had access to several horses which he changed during the course of the battle. Charhat Singh received many wounds and despite this he kept fighting: 'Though many a wound did S. Charat Singh receive on his body, He kept on fighting without feeling frustrated by so many wounds.'[13] The caravan eventually reached Gahal village and Ahmed Shah Abdali's forces stopped their pursuit due to lack of water and food. This gave a respite to the Khalsa. The eloquent description of the battle tactics cannot be better described then as follows: 'As a mother hen protects her newly hatched chicks, She spreads both her wings to keep her brood protected. So did Khalsa Panth Singhs provide protection

---

9   Karam Singh and Karora Singh are singled out.
10   Bhangu, *Sri Gur Panth Prakash*, Vol. 2, p.493.
11   Bhangu, *Sri Gur Panth Prakash*, Vol. 2, p.499.
12   Bhangu, *Sri Gur Panth Prakash*, Vol. 2, p.505.
13   Bhangu, *Sri Gur Panth Prakash*, Vol. 2, p.505.

to the caravan.'[14] When the caravan was moving through the villages, he had to fight those loyal to the enemy. After a number of miles, they reached a location where there was drinking water and again both forces stopped to quench their thirst. Eventually, the Sikhs moved a further ten miles to safety.

Charhat Singh is singled out by the chronicler, Rattan Singh Bhangu. He states the Misl leader who, despite being subjected to numerable attacks and wounded, made the crucial difference in the battle:

> Uncountable was the number of wounds which S. Charhat Singh received, Innumerable were the arrows, lances and swords which hit his body. Whosoever did S. Charhat Singh hit like the mighty Bhim Sain, His every blow resulted in wounding his adversary in fight.
>
> From the concluding day of this massacre of the Sikhs, Did S. Charhat Singh's stock sore high among the Singhs. Many a life of Sikhs in the caravan had he saved, Putting his own life at a great risk determinedly.
>
> Praise be to S. Charhat Singh said each member of the caravan, They owed their life to S. Charhat Singh's valorous deeds. Whosoever survived, survived because of S. Charhat Singh's efforts, Thus did they praise S. Charhat Singh all in one voice.
>
> Thus did they bless him gathering in a congregational prayer, Undoubtedly would he be a chief among the Singhs. May he become a chief among the Khalsa Panth, Unitedly did they shower their blessings on this great Singh…
>
> In whatever direction did S. Charhat Singh move, Thither would the whole caravan follow in his footsteps.
>
> In great reverence did the Khalsa Panth hold him, **Attributing the whole victory to S. Charhat Singh's brave deeds** [author emphasis].
>
> Such great gratitude did he earn from the Khalsa Panth, That he would be the star attraction in every Sikh congregation. For each expedition would he be consulted in advance, Offerings in plenty would he be offered for his sacrifices.[15]

This bravery shown by Charhat Singh catapulted him into becoming one of the strongest and best-recognised Misl leaders. It was due to this important victory that he was consulted with the other chiefs, and this is demonstrated when the Hari Singh Bhangi in 1763 wanted to attack the area of Kasur due to reports of a Brahmin woman being abducted. There was, however, a numerical disadvantage, with the Kasur forces numbering 14,000 yet it was Charhat Singh who impressed on the Bhangi chief that an attack was warranted and helped towards boosting the morale of the combined forces.[16] Their eventual attack resulted in the capture of Kasur and the plundering of

---

14   Bhangu, *Sri Gur Panth Prakash*, Vol. 2, p.509.
15   Bhangu, *Sri Gur Panth Prakash*, Vol. 2, pp.515–516.
16   Bhangu, *Sri Gur Panth Prakash*, Vol. 2, p.557.

Rohtas Fort depicted late in the late nineteenth century. James Grant, Recent British Battles on Land and Sea (1884).

the whole town, and the return of the lady to the Brahmin.[17] The friendship between the Sukerchakia and the Bhangi Misl, however, did not continue as they were both jostling positions for grounds nearby; as a result, they were eventually on top of each other territorially.

In November 1763, Charhat Singh, whilst at Sialkot, engaged Abdali's Commander-in-Chief, Jahan Khan, who had been sent to punish the Sikhs, and whom he inflicted upon a severe defeat. The Afghan king, who came out himself, was forced to return home harassed by the pursuing Sikh bands. This allowed Charhat Singh to sweep across Rachna and Chaj Doabs and reached Rohtas.[18] The Afghan commander of the fort, Sarfaraz Khan, offered stiff resistance but was overcome near Attock.

---

17   Bhangu, *Sri Gur Panth Prakash*, Vol. 2, p.565.
18   Rohtas Fort was built in the 16th century under the regime of Sher Shah Suri, founder of the Suri Empire.

The Zamzama Gun: The Battle for Possession

This famous gun has been given several different designations in history being known as the Lion's Roar as well as the *Bhangian-di-Topp*, the 'Gun of the Bhangis' or later in history as Kim's Gun.[19] It was cast at Lahore, with another of the same size, in 1757 by Shah Nazir, under the directions of Shah Wali Khan, prime minister of Ahmed Shah Abdali. It was used in the third battle of Panipat of 1761 which helped the Durranis in their conquest of India and subjugation of the Marathas. In 1765, when the Bhangi sardars captured Lahore, they obtained possession of it. Charhat Singh came to welcome them and showered praise on the Bhangis, and he expected some share of the spoil. Indeed at this time, the partitioning of key areas took place with the Sukerchakia gaining possession of Gujranwala, Sheikhupura, Jhelum, and the salt mines of Khewra and Pind Dadan Khan after receiving sanction from the Bhangis; essentially, some regions of the Rachna and Chaj Doabs. Meanwhile, the Bhangis took Sialkot, Gujarat, Rawalpindi, and Attock, and the hilly tracts around Kashmir were assigned to Gujar Singh Bhangi amongst other important territories.[20] This contributed towards a small peace between the two Misls and the Zamzama Gun was indeed offered by the Bhangis, suggesting that the Sukerchakia Chief could not muster the strength to carry it to Gujranwala. Charhat Singh, seeing he could get nothing more, called his men together and, with great labour, carried it off to his camp, and then to his fort at Gujranwala.[21] The Misl was always in a constant fight with the group known as the Chattas. The gun was captured by Ahmad Khan Chhatha, who took it to his fort of Ahmadnagar, Chiniot. However, this started a war over the gun with his brother, Pir Muhammad, who called in Gujar Singh Bhangi to his assistance. He entrapped Ahmad Khan, and kept him captive unless he relinquished it. Gujar Singh, however, cheating his ally, carried it to Gujarat and kept it himself. Two years later, the Bhangis took it with them on an expedition against Charhat Singh. The Bhangis were beaten, and the gun, too heavy to remove quickly, fell again into the hands of the Sukerchakia chief. In 1772 the Chattas recovered the gun, placed it in the fort of Manchar, and a short time afterward removed it to Rasulnagar (Ramnuggar).[22] The following year it was captured by Jhanda Singh Bhangi on his return from Multan. It was sent to Amritsar, where it remained in the *Bhangian da Killa* (fort of the Bhangis)

---

19   Named so after Rudyard Kipling (1865–1936) who describes the gun in his novel *Kim* set amidst the backdrop of the 'Great Game', the political conflict between Britain and Russia in Central Asia.

20   Gupta, *History of the Sikhs*, Vol. 4, p.297. The emphasis is on the comparison between the Sukerchakia and Bhangi, but other Misls possessed areas should not be down played. The Bhangis also had the Bari Doab with Amritsar being an important part of their possessions.

21   Griffin, *Chiefs And Families Of Note In The Punjab*, Vol. 1, p.458.

22   Griffin, *Chiefs And Families Of Note In The Punjab*, Vol. 1, p.458. This is the location of one of the battles of the Second Sikh War that took place in 1849.

The Zamzama Gun. (Courtesy of Gurinder Mann)

until 1802.[23] The history of the gun would have been known to the Sukerchakia Chief and so Ranjit Singh desired to repossess the gun back to his Misl. He used it as a pretext to drive the Bhangis out of Amritsar and seized it with the assistance of Sada Kaur of the Kanhaiya Misl (whom we discuss in the next chapter).[24]

Jhelum fell into the power of Ahmed Shah Abdali, and as a result, he made his uncle Sarbuland Khan the *Faujdar* of Rohtas. The Rohtas Fort was of strategic importance and so in 1767, Charhat Singh, together with 500 of his sowars and Gujar Singh Bhangi's 400 sowars, 2,000 infantry, several pieces of artillery, and the common populace laid siege to it.[25] Sarbuland Khan was taken prisoner and eventually let go and a new Afghan governor was installed. Charhat Singh took Jhelum at the same time as Rohtas. Interestingly, the location was cited as where Guru Nanak had stayed and as a result a commemorative structure was built by Charhat Singh, who installed a *Sarovar or* pool, and an area for the recitation of the Guru Granth Sahib.[26] He

23   Now known as Gobindgarh Fort after Ranjit Singh took possession of it. Named after Guru Gobind Singh, it would become a treasury and haven for some relics during the Sikh Empire.

24   *Griffin, Chiefs And Families Of Note In The Punjab*, Vol. 1, p.458.

25   Shahamat Ali, *The Sikhs and Afghans, in connexion with the India and Persia, immediately before and after the death of Ranjeet Singh: from the journal of an expedition to Kabul through the Panjab and the Khaibar Pass* (London: John Murray, Albemarle Street, 1847).

26   A larger Gurdwara dates from 1834 and was commissioned by Maharajah Ranjit Singh.

followed these victories with the occupation of a large portion of the areas of Dhanni and Pothohar. He then took Pind Dadan Khan, and built a fort there. The salt ranges of Kheora and Miani were the next to fall to him. The rapid success, especially in the salt ranges, aroused the animosity of the Bhangi sardars who had started seeing these locations within their sphere of influence.[27] This was played out in the open when Charhat Singh and the Bhangis took sides in the family dispute at Jammu. The ruler, at the time Ranjit Deo, wanted to pass on the succession to his younger son but was opposed in this attempt by Brij Raj Deo, the elder son, who managed to secure the active support of Charhat Singh and Jai Singh of the Kanhaiya Misl. Ranjit Deo enlisted the support of Jhanda and Ghanda Singh Bhangi. The rival armies marched into Jammu in 1770. Charhat Singh was fatally wounded when his gun was accidentally discharged, and he died at age of 45.[28] The mighty warrior's empire-building came to an end. However, there were several reasons as to why the Sukerchakia Misl was able to build and continue to rise. The real success of Charhat Singh was his ability to employ loyal *Kardars* or governors or revenue officers in the areas where he conquered and occupied. This was not an easy task as most of these regions were Muslim areas and he required the support of both the general populace and the strategic people in charge there. This is why the Sukerchakia Misl managed to have greater success than the Bhangis. After Charhat Singh's death, his wife, Desan Kaur (1740–94) was able to convince the *Kardars* to continue their allegiance to the Misl. She was a very able administrator, and she undertook many allegiances whilst her son Mahan Singh (1756–92) was a minor. She also undertook the rebuilding of the fort at Gujranwala and named it *Mahan Singh ki Garhi* or Fort of Mahan Singh. Building on the success of Charhat Singh, Mahan Singh would further strengthen the Misl. This foundation led to his son Ranjit Singh becoming the empire-builder of the future. Mahan Singh was aided by the Kanhaiyas and this partnership continued during his tenure, to which he added Sialkot (Kotli Ahangaran, a place well-known for the manufacture of guns), Ramnuggar and Akalgarh (Alipur), as well as humbling the powerful Chatta Chief, Pir Mohd Khan. Another important alliance was with the Mann sardars of Mughalchak, Gujranwala, who eventually settled at Mannawala in the Sheikhupura district. Mahan Singh married the daughter of the chief of the Mann family, Jai Singh Mann (d. 1812). From the time of Charhat Singh, the Mann sardars provided continuous support to the Sukerchakia Misl. This can be seen by the alliance taking full advantage of the Jammu succession dispute and looting the wealth

27   Bhangu, *Sri Gur Panth Prakash*, Vol. 2, p.591.
28   Jai Singh Kanhaiya, in retaliation, arranged for the killing of Jhanda Singh. Also see Gupta, *History of the Sikhs*, Vol. 4, p.305. His *Samadhi* was built at Gujranwala, 'Pass through the Mandi, or market-place and town to the left, when an open space will be reached, and on the right is the small *Samadhi* of Charat Singh.' John Murray, *Handbook of the Panjab* (London: Thacker, Spink, and Co., 1883), p.227.

of the area to their satisfaction.[29] This led to the defeat of Brij Raj Deo in 1780. Mahan Singh would also add substantially to the prestige of the family by the acquisition of many heirlooms belonging to the Islamic faith after this conquest. These important relics were kept with the Sukerchakia Misl throughout the Sikh Empire.[30]

The Misl also supported campaigns of the Dal Khalsa into the areas around Delhi. With all these developments, the Bhangi sardars were unable to hold onto their military forts due to their leaders either dying early or not adding to their overall conquests and bad leadership. All this left Ranjit Singh as the Sukerchakia Chief, the strongest of all the Misls especially in the regions of the Rachna and Chaj Doabs.

29 This alliance with the Mann sardars continued into the reign of Maharajah Ranjit Singh. 'At one point there were no fewer than twenty-two members of it holding key military appointments of great trust and honour.' Griffin, *Chiefs And Families Of Note In The Punjab*, Vol. 1, p.157.

30 The relics pertain to the Prophet Mohammed and his immediate successors. The relics were shifted from place to place, and Ranjit Singh showed them to the visitors. He was offered huge sums of money for them but he refused to part with them. Dr Ganda Singh, 'Muslim Relics with the Sikh Rulers of Lahore', *Proceedings of Indian History Congress*, (1943), pp.284–289.

3

Sahib Kaur: Protector of the Patiala State

The history of the Patiala state is heaped with tales of self-preservation, which is a kind statement considering how many have felt about the chiefs of that location playing the political game throughout the ages. The patronage, however, seems to have been given by Guru Gobind Singh to Chaudhari Phul and his sons Ram Singh and Tilok Singh. It is from there that descended the houses of Patiala, Jind and Nabha, also collectively known as the Phulkian Misl. The son of Ram Singh was Ala Singh (1691–1765), a Misl chief who founded and developed the state of Patiala after the capture of Sirhind in 1764. Taking the rites of Khalsa initiation from Nawab Kapur Singh, they captured the towns of Barnala and defeated Rai Kalha of Raikot, and the Bhatti Chiefs, and so set about making Malwa a strong territory. However, his reign was not of parity with the Khalsa and he was seen as being a sympathiser to the Durrani conquerors who gave him patronage and support. The title of *Raja-e-Rajgan Bahadur* was bestowed on the chief.[1] This was not to the liking of the Dal Khalsa although Jassa Singh Ahluwalia maintained the peace between the Sikh forces and Ala Singh. The Phulkian states including Patiala which played in favour of their self-interest against the Afghans and Mughals. Ala Singh was succeeded by Amar Singh (1748–82) who took initiation rites from Jassa Singh Ahluwalia, who intervened in a war of struggle for chiefdom with his half-brother Himmat Singh. Amar Singh added to the glory of the Patiala state by siding with Ahmed Shah Abdali as well as occupying Bathinda and occupying lands south of Patiala. The Mughal conquests of the Cis-Sutlej areas in 1771 were thwarted by the Patiala chief with the help of the Buddha Dal and Taruna Dal. As a result, he expanded the territories between the Yamuna and Sutlej territories.

He was succeeded by his son Sahib Singh (1773–1813) who consolidated his position within the Misls by marrying Rattan Kaur, the daughter of deceased Ganda Singh of the Bhangi Misl. His second marriage was to Aus Kaur, daughter of Gurdas

---

1   Although given by the Afghans, the title made no difference to the views held by the Dal Khalsa. If anything, it infuriated many of the Misl leaders.

Singh Chattha. His ascension to the Patiala State was guided by an inner circle that included Diwan Nanu Mal, who was a shrewd politician. He was the most trusted advisor during the reign of Amar Singh's period. Unfortunately, after the master's death, this trust in Diwan quickly evaporated and he became selfish. He aligned with the Marathas and initiated efforts for the destruction of the Patiala rule, starting from its roots. Diwan's attitude also influenced the other servants of the empire. They too initiated pursuits for their own selfish gains.[2] As a result, corruption, looting, and injustice reigned supreme in the Patiala state. His subjugation of Khalsa territories was not going to be taken lightly, especially after recovering lands that belonged to the Singhpuria Misl under Khushal Singh. Nanu Mal also smoked the *Hukka* (pipe) in the Durbar which was openly objected to by the Sikhs.[3] The state was in immediate danger now. On one hand, the inner situation was fast deteriorating while on the other hand, external enemies were also eager for its destruction. The child, Maharaja Sahib Singh, was terrified of the emerging situation.

However, the Patiala state had been guided through the ages by the strength of their womenfolk who were very politically astute and at times, were more in tune with efforts to maintain the state from foreign invasions and Misl attacks. Sahib Singh was initially guided by his grandmother, Mata Hukman, together with his aunt, Rajinder Kaur (1739–91) and his elder sister Sahib Kaur (1771–1801). Lepel Griffin notes the importance and statesmanship role played by the women of Patiala and his indictment of the male rulers of Phulkian states:

> Rani Rajindar was one of the most remarkable women of her age. She possessed all the virtues which men pretend are their own—courage, perseverance, and sagacity without any mixture of the weakness which men attribute to women; and, remembering her history and that of Ranis Sahib Kour and Aus Kour, who, some years later, conducted, with so much ability, the affairs of the Pattiala State, it would almost appear that the Phulkian Chiefs excluded, by direct enactment, all women from any share of power, from the suspicion that they were able to use it far more wisely than themselves.[4]

Rajinder Kaur (1739–91), the Patiala princess was known for her valorous qualities, was the granddaughter of Baba Ala Singh.[5] Her husband died at a young age which left her in charge of the family estate, consisting of over two hundred villages. When

---

2   Lepel Griffin, *The Rajas of the Punjab Being the History of the Principal States in the Punjab and their Political Relations with the British Government*, 2nd Ed. (London: Trubner & Co., 1873), pp.56–58.
3   The smoking of tobacco is considered forbidden within the Sikh faith.
4   Griffin, *The Rajas of the Punjab*, p.67.
5   The only child of her father, Bhumla Singh, who died when she was barely four, she was brought up by her grandfather, and, in 1751, married to Chaudhari Tilok Chand, of Phagwara.

Fresco of Panjabi women leading a hunting expedition. (Bhuman Shah Durbar, Dipalpur.
Courtesy of Dalvir Singh Pannu)

Ala Singh was arrested in 1765 by Ahmad Shah Durrani for having fallen into arrears
in paying tribute, he was taken to Lahore. Rajindar Kaur went to her grandfather and
offered to pay the money to secure his release. But he declined.[6] In 1778, Amar Singh
of Patiala, who was Rajindar Kaur's cousin, was defeated by Hari Singh of Sialba.[7]
Rajindar Kaur came to his rescue with three thousand soldiers marching through the
territories of the chiefs who had fought on the side of Hari Singh. During the reign of
the minor Sahib Singh, Rajindar Kaur was again in Patiala to defend the town against
Maratha onslaughts. At the head of a strong force, she marched as far as Mathura
where peace parleys were opened with the Marathas. The princess died in 1791 at
Patiala after a short illness.

Diwan Nanu Mal died not soon after in 1792 and, due to the mounting dissensions
within his state, Sahib Singh recalled his sister, Sahib Kaur, to Patiala and offered her
the role of prime minister, which she accepted. It was unusual at that time for a woman
to leave her husband to aid another person or territory even if they were family. Sahib
Kaur was a warrior and leader of men who played a prominent part in the history
of the Patiala and her story is seldom taught or discussed. She was extraordinarily
intelligent and brilliant, not only mastering languages but learning horse riding and
the use of arms. Sahib Kaur married at an early age to another powerful Misl leader,
namely Jaimal Singh (1712–93) of the Kanhaiya clan, who resided at Fatehgarh and
was master of a greater part of the Bari Doab in the present-day Gurdaspur district

6   There is a tradition within the Sikh community that a father does not accept money from
     a daughter of the family.
7   He was from one branch of the Dalewalia Misl who held the territories of Ropar, Sialba,
     Avankot, Sisvan and Kurah.

of the Panjab.[8] Her first show of strength was witnessed not soon after that, when she came to the rescue of her husband, Jaimal Singh, who had been captured by Fateh Singh, arriving at the head of a large Patiala army to rescue him. It was in 1794 that she came face to face with the Marathas who had attacked Jind and Kaithal.[9] Bhag Singh, ruler of Jind state, had asked the other Sikh rulers and chiefs for help. Sahib Singh was non-committal, but Sahib Kaur, 'a woman of masculine and brave spirit', put pressure on Sahib Singh.[10] He flatly refused and forbade her to help. She replied that if Jind was captured, nobody could save Patiala for long. She collected her troops and left Patiala without the approval of her brother.

She was aided by the Misl chiefs Jodh Singh (Kalsia) and Bhanga Singh (Thanesar), both of the Karorasinghia Misl, whilst Tara Singh Ghaiba (Dalewalia Misl) sent a detachment of troops. During the night, she ordered the sounding of the battle drums, *Nagara*, while preparing to face the invading forces. The joint force, numbering about 7,000 men, met the Marathas led by Anta Rao and Lachhman Rao at Mardanpur near Ambala. A tough exchange took place; when they faced each other, it became evident that not only the Maratha force was large in numbers, but they had heavy artillery and cannons. In comparison, the Sikhs were few in numbers and did not possess any artillery. The Marathas sent envoys asking Sahib Kaur to surrender, which she considered deeply before sending back messages stating that she would kill every Maratha to the last man. Sahib Kaur, who was said to have dressed in male attire and ride on horseback, directed her soldiers. Some Sikhs fled the battlefield. She left her chariot, unsheathed her sword, sat on the back of a horse, and gave an enthusiastic lead to the army. [11] As Griffin writes:

> Retreat would have soon turned to flight had not Bibi Sahib Kour... stepped down from her chariot (*Rath*), and, drawing her sword, declared that the Sikhs would be ever disgraced if they allowed her, a woman and the sister of their Chief, to be slain, for she was determined never to retreat. This gallantry so shamed and encouraged the soldiers, that they returned with renewed fury to the fight, which they maintained, though with considerable loss, till nightfall, neither side being able to claim the victory.[12]

8   Jaimal Singh or Jai Singh, whose Kanhaiya Misl dominated the area referred to as Fatehgarh Churian. He was another high-ranking Sikh who received the Khalsa initiation rites from Nawab Kapur Singh. The festivities of the marriage in 1780 lasted ten days and consisted of visitors numbering 10,000. The prime minister of the Mughal Empire, Najaf Khan, sent a *Khila'at* to Sahib Kaur. Gupta, *History of the Sikhs*, Vol. 4, p.165.
9   Some of the smaller Sikh chiefs had started paying their submission to the Marathas.
10 A modern poem highlighting the exploits of Sahib Kaur can be seen in *Rani Sahib Kaur – Kasumbhrha*, Prof. Mohan Singh (Lahore: Lahore Book Shop), p.53.
11 Kahn Singh Nabha, *Mahan Khosh*, Vol. 3, p.1876.
12 Griffin, *The Rajas of the Punjab*, pp.71–72.

Hand-to-hand combat took between the two forces before they retired for the night. The Khalsa forces had to consider their position, with some Sikhs stating that the situation was dire and that tomorrow they would be killed. Sahib Kaur was not despondent and rallied her forces who were equally sharp in battle strategy. The following morning, her contingent made a surprise attack on the Marathas, and even before the enemy became aware of what happened their soldiers were killed by Sikh swords. In minutes the field was filled with dead bodies. The suddenness of the attack as well as the darkness made it difficult to distinguish between their own and Sikh soldiers. As a result, many enemy soldiers died fighting among themselves. Sahib Kaur moved around, encouraging her soldiers with *Jaikaras* (utterances of victory). Her sword, too, killed many enemy soldiers. This surprise attack by the Sikhs completely changed the status of the battle. With additional Khalsa reinforcements nearing the battlefield, Anta Rao and Lachhman Rao found escape to be the best way out. They quickly collected their remaining companions and ran towards Hisar.[13] The true status of the battle became evident with sunrise. Uncountable enemy soldiers lay dead, and enemy cannons, ammunition, ration, and treasury were all left behind. Sahib Kaur was awarded all this wealth and she distributed it among the Sikh soldiers. She captured the cannons and the ammunition and took them to Patiala. Upon reaching Patiala, she was welcomed with huge celebrations.

Bedi Sahib Singh (1756–1834) of Una, a man of repute and a descendant of Guru Nanak, charged the Pathan chief of Marlekotla with cow-killing and attacked him.[14] He was saved by the timely succour given him by Sahib Kaur acting in response to the request of the Raja of Nahan, who had friendly relations with the Patiala state and who often sought their intervention when faced with internal disturbances. Sahib Singh was more than happy to respond to this request and in 1796, Sahib Kaur, with a force of one thousand, rushed to Nahan, and restored peace and settled the affairs of the state and reduced the insurgents to obedience. The ruler of Nahan presented her with a tall and strong elephant that she kept for her own use.[15] In the same year, at the time of the famous *Kumbh Mela* at Hardwar, a famous pilgrim station, a dispute arose between two groups of saints – the Gosains and the Udasis. Sahib Singh, who with his followers was camping nearby, took the side of the Udasis. Sahib Kaur was away in the state. She came to know of it, rushed in with reinforcements, and saved the situation.

During 1796-7 the Panjab was waiting for the impending attack of Zaman Shah Durrani (1770–1844).[16] All the various Misls combined for this invasion. Sahib Kaur was at Shakgarh near Sialkot and monitoring the situation. The Patiala policy was

---

13   Griffin, *The Rajas of the Punjab*, p.72.
14   Sahib Singh Bedi was recognised by many; he coronated Ranjit Singh on his investiture as Maharajah as well as provided military assistance in his campaigns.
15   Griffin, *The Rajas of the Punjab*, p.73. Gupta, *History of the Sikhs,* Vol. 4, p.176.
16   During the time of the Sikh Empire, he took refuge in the Panjab after a war of succession in Afghanistan. He later lived as a pensioner in Ludhiana under British jurisdiction.

always of appeasement with the Durannis. When the *Vakils* of Zaman Shah had reached Patiala, Sahib Singh promised his support to them. However, Sahib Kaur informed her brother that he should unite his forces with Lal Singh of Kaithal. His choices were to submit or fight the Durannis. Sahib Singh, in this instance, geared his troops with Kaithal and got ready for a war footing. The other Misls had moved their families out of harm's way. Sahib Kaur was to make the final decision on the course of events and was preparing to send her force to Patiala. The Durrani Chief on this occasion did not go any further and left for Kabul. The following year, Zaman Shah again threatened the Panjab and whilst fear was induced across the land, he again failed to make any headway.[17]

Portrait of George Thomas (William Francklin, *Military Memoirs of Mr. George Thomas; Who, by Extraordinary Talents and Enterprise...* (Piccadilly, London: reprinted for John Stockdale, 1805)

A number of fascinating encounters took place between Sahib Kaur and an Irish adventurer known as George Thomas (c.1756–1802), who had become a powerful ruler in the neighbourhood of Hansi and Hisar.[18] He had sought fortune for many years and came under the wing of a formidable female ruler of Sardhana, Begum Samru (c.1753–1836). He later joined the ranks of the Marathas, instructing them in European methods of drill. The district of Jhajjar was renamed 'Georgegarh', corrupted to become known as Jahazgarh, where he raised a fort. He commanded eight regiments of foot, a thousand horsemen and around fifty guns. He states that he:

> ...established a mint, and coined my own rupees, which I made current in my army and country...I now judged that nothing but force of arms could maintain me in authority I therefore increased their numbers, cast my own artillery, commenced making musquets, matchlocks and powder.[19]

---

17   Gupta, *History of the Sikhs*, Vol. 4, pp.176-180.
18   Thomas was born in Tipperary, Ireland, and came to India in 1781.
19   Francklin, *Military Memoirs of Mr. George Thomas*, p.133.

He asked the Sikhs for an alliance but they refused, so with the Dal Khalsa combining their forces for the onslaught of the invasion of Zaman Shah, he saw this as an opportune time to take Sikh territories. In 1799, his rise under the Marathas and his thirst for power went to his head and he thought he could take on the might of the Sikhs all the way to Amritsar and Lahore, something which the East India Company not only scoffed at but would not be a party to. This wishful thinking was recorded in his biography as follows: 'At length, having gained a capital and country bordering on the Seik territories, I wished to put myself in a capacity, when a favourable opportunity should offer of attempting the conquest of the Punjab, and aspired to the honour of planting the British Standard on the banks of the Attock.'[20]

George Thomas attacked Jind bordering Patiala. The Phulkian Chiefs, who were at the time busy preparing for the Durrani attack, came back to their territories. Sahib Kaur led out a strong contingent to relieve the besieged town and, assisted by the troops of other Sikh chiefs, she forced George Thomas to withdraw. Sahib Kaur managed to get the veteran Sikh leader Baghel Singh (in one of his final battles) and various Karorasinghia Misl leaders, including Gurdit Singh, Bhanga Singh, and Mahtab Singh, to assist her. This also included Tara Singh Dalewalia and Nabha Chief Jaswant Singh. This showed the respect that Sahib Kaur had from her male counterparts. More importantly, they wanted George Thomas out of their territories. Francklin states:

> The sister of Sahib Sing, of Puttialah, a woman of a masculine and intrepid spirit, attended by a large force, arrived to succour the place: with her also came Bugheel Sing, and other chiefs of the Seiks.[21]

Thomas opposed them with heavy artillery fire and the Sikhs had to retreat. At the beginning of 1799, Sahib Kaur collected nine thousand Sikh troops under her command and attacked Thomas's strongholds. She cut his supply lines and many of his best men were cut to pieces. Her bravery inspired others and the number of her forces increased. After a blockade of one hundred days, Thomas retired from Jind and hurried back to his camp. The Sikh forces pursued him but had to retreat when Thomas attacked them while they were sleeping. When they returned to Jind, they were scolded and taunted by Sahib Kaur for their cowardice, '...who had said that the Nabha soldiers, in comparison those of Pattiala, were no better than sweepers (*Chumars*).'[22] She said that she would take to the field personally to show them how to fight.

---

20 Francklin, *Military Memoirs of Mr George Thomas*, p.133. Griffin asserts that the reason for the attack was that the Sikhs were not prepared in joining Thomas in his selfish acts of making his own principality. Griffin, *The Rajas of the Punjab*, p.76
21 Francklin, *Military Memoirs of Mr George Thomas*, p.190.
22 It was suggested that the soldiers of Nabha were in collusion with George Thomas and hence why it led to these remarks.

The warrior princess, who, as we have seen before, had on several occasions exhibited a spirit superior to what could have been expected from her sex, and far more decisive than her brother, now offered to take to the field in person.[23]

They felt humiliated and resolved to conquer or to perish. The Sikhs then regrouped and again attacked Thomas, who now offered peace terms. This amounted to each party keeping possession of its territories held before the siege of Jind.[24] Every Sikh chief except Sahib Singh was in favour of accepting the terms. Like a wise politician, Sahib Kaur tried her best to persuade her brother to agree to the peace terms, but he, being a stubborn man, did not agree. Sahib Kaur signed the treaty on behalf of the Patiala state in March 1799. It was noted, 'He alone refused to sign the treaty, although, in spite of his remonstrances, it was done by his more spirited sister.'[25] This enraged Sahib Singh, who arrested Sahib Kaur and imprisoned her at Patiala.[26] She appealed for help from the Irishman, Thomas, who marched to Patiala. He had to fight the Patiala forces on his way and the forces of Tara Singh Ghaiba, and consequently, both sides suffered heavily. When he reached near Patiala, the weak-minded Sahib Singh yielded, accepted the peace terms, and released his sister. Sahib Singh was extremely vindictive and possessed a cruel nature. He again imprisoned Sahib Kaur in the fort of Patiala. Owing to differences with her brother, Sahib Kaur escaped to take up residence in Bherlan, Sangrur, which fell within her *Jagir* (where she had built a fort) changing the name of the village to Ubheval.[27]

She was yet again caught and imprisoned. This was the tragic end of the 'Joan-of-Arc' of the Patiala state. In character, bravery, and in statesmanship, she occupies first place in Sikh history. Thomas called her a man and not a woman. Kahn Singh Nabha, the celebrated author of *Mahan Khosh* or Sikh Encyclopaedia writes, 'if Sahib Kaur had not protected the state, undoubtedly many disasters would have befallen it.'[28] Mohamad Latif writes that the Marathas' defeat was due to the fact that Sahib Kaur herself took part in the battlefield and thus exhorted her army. There is no doubt that Sahib Singh would not have survived as the ruler of Patiala but for the help of his brave and self-sacrificing sister. She was cremated in the royal cemetery of Patiala known as Shahi Samadhan.[29]

23   Francklin, *Military Memoirs of Mr George Thomas*, p.192.
24   Griffin, *The Rajas of the Punjab*, p.78.
25   Francklin, *Military Memoirs of Mr George Thomas*, p.193.
26   Apparently on the instigation of his wife, Aus Kaur, who may have had designs for their son Karam Singh to be a rightful heir.
27   These acts were also used by the forces opposed to her, stating that she was taking independent decisions which she had no right to impose.
28   *Mahan Khosh*, Vol. 3, p.1876.
29   A college in Patiala is also named after Sahib Kaur.

Shahi Samadhan or Royal Tombs of the Patiala dynasty. (Courtesy of John Steedman)

4

Sada Kaur: The Kanhaiya Queen

The Sikh Empire was built on the tenacity and foresight of Maharajah Ranjit Singh; however, the foundations and the events leading up to his success are overlooked. The lynchpin of his success was partly due to the influence of Rani Sada Kaur (c. 1762–1832). According to Latif, 'Sada Kour, one of the most artful and ambitious of her sex that ever figured in the Sikh history, conduced materially to the success of Ranjit Singh in his early exploits, and it is truly said of her that she was the ladder by which Ranjit Singh reached the summit of his power.'[1] This female leader had great vision and influence but her story has been side-lined in mainstream Sikh history, partly due to the relationship with the Maharajah fracturing in the later years. However, her leadership skills brought great fruits for the conquest of Panjab by Ranjit Singh.

Sada Kaur was from the Misl known as the Kanhaiya, a confederacy whose origins lie in the area of Kanha, a village 15km from Lahore. The village name has the same origins as the Misl name.[2] The leader of the Misl was one Jai Singh Kanhaiya (1712–93) who, together with other early Misl leaders, received the Khalsa rites of initiation from Nawab Kapur Singh. Originally joining the band of warriors under Amar Singh Kirigra, he eventually branched into creating his own Misl. He seized a part of Riarki, comprising of the district of Gurdaspur and the upper portions of Amritsar together with Sohiari, where he made his headquarters. He later shifted to Batala and thence to Mukerian. His territories lay on both sides of the Beas River and Ravi River. The Kanhaiyas played an important role in the major conquests of the Misl as previously outlined, including receiving a share in the spoils during the conquest of Lahore in 1765, and the retrieval of the Zamzama Gun with the Sukerchakias.

Jai Singh's son, Gurbakhsh Singh, was instrumental in the rise of the Misl. He married Sada Kaur. Gurbakhsh Singh was unfortunate enough to get involved in the fratricidal Misl-against-Misl warfare which continued to the detriment of the

---

1   Latif, Syad Muhammad, *History Of The Panjab*, p.346.
2   Another theory suggests that the name is associated with the handsome appearance of Jai Singh Kanhaiya.

Kanhaiyas when Mahan Singh Sukerchakia, together with Raja Sansar Chand, offered to give back to Jassa Singh Ramgharia his possessions and estates.[3] The condition was that he needed to provide assistance against Jai Singh Kanhaiya, which he readily agreed to. Gurbakhsh Singh advanced with 8,000 men but was defeated and killed by this confederacy and Jai Singh was compelled to return the estates and forts to Jassa Singh and Sansar Chand. The effects of the death of Sada Kaur's husband would continue to play out with the Kanhaiya and Ramgharia Misls continuing their feud.

Sada Kaur became the leader of the Misl after her father-in-law Jai Singh passed away, and in 1789 she seized the territories of Naushera and Haytnagar Kalan from another part of the Kanhaiya confederacy. A few years earlier in 1786, with the blessing of the Kanhaiya chief, Jai Singh, she had her daughter Mehtab Kaur married to Mahan Singh's son, the young Ranjit Singh. This matrimonial alliance would keep her in good stead leading to dominance due to the combining of the resources of both Misls. After the death of Mahan Singh, Ranjit Singh was made the chief of the Sukerchakia Misl and Sada Kaur would become his regent. Sada Kaur wielded much influence over Ranjit Singh and some other advisors were dispensed with, leading to greater participation in his affairs.[4]

The Kanhaiyas, like many of the other Misls, held a *Katra* within Amritsar. It was managed by the Chaudry Chajju Mal who had been a confidant of Jai Singh Kanhaiya. He fought alongside him at the battle of Achal in 1783. He was also present when Sada Kaur's husband Gurbakhsh Singh was killed in 1785. The protection of Sada Kaur's territories was of paramount importance and they may have been seen as an easy target (due to her being a women) by other Misls within Amritsar. She managed to hold on to her base due to Chajju Mal's support even though he was attacked by Jassa Singh Ramgharia on occasions. He would also be very useful to Sada Kaur when Ranjit Singh attacked the Bhangis later on.[5] It was important to note that many people supported her even it was a detriment to themselves; for instance, Ruldu Ram, who was in charge of the estates of Mukerian, developed the area and was the tutor of Rani Mehtab Kaur's son Sher Singh, the future ruler of Panjab.[6]

3   The estates of Jassa Singh Ramgharia was taken under the instructions of Jassa Singh Ahluwalia after he was kidnapped by his brother Mali Singh. A confederacy of the Ahluwalia, Bhangi, Karorasinghia and the Kanhaiya drove the Ramgharia chief into the districts of Hansi and Hisar.

4   There have been suggestions that Ranjit Singh and Dal Singh were involved in the poisoning of his mother. This seems a stretch of the facts. Henry Thoby Prinsep, *Origin of the Sikh Power in the Punjab and political life of Maharaja Ranjit Singh; with an account of the Religion, Laws, and Customs of Sikhs* (Calcutta: G.H. Huttmann, Military Orphan Press, 1834), p.49.

5   Griffin, *Chief and Families*, Vol. 2, p.43. Chajju Mal was later employed in Ranjit Singh's service and became a customs collector for him in 1813. He was also sent to the Kangra Hills by the Maharajah from 1815 to 1816.

6   Ruldu Ram was however admonished by Ranjit Singh when he was out of favour with Sada Kaur and his estates removed but were later returned to him. Griffin, *Chief and*

Portrait of Sada Kaur by Kehar Singh. Central Sikh Museum, Amritsar.

In 1796, Sada Kaur besieged Jassa Singh Ramgharia in his stranglehold of Miani, a fort in the Hoshiarpur district near the River Beas. She was supported by her son-in-law, Ranjit Singh, and his Sukerchakia Misl and the forces of Bhag Singh of the Ahluwalia Misl. It was these three Misls which essentially enabled Ranjit Singh to eventually become the head of the Sikh Empire. Jassa Singh held out for some time but his provisions ran very low, and he despatched messages to Sahib Singh Bedi of Amritsar asking him to intervene. They were advised by the veteran holy sage to raise the siege. For Sada Kaur this was not an option as revenge for her husband's death was in her mind. However, it seems that good fortune saved the Ramgharia Chief when the River Beas came down in a flood and swept away a large portion of the Kanhaiya camp, taking men and horses and camels. Sada Kaur and Ranjit Singh escaped with difficulty and retired to Gujranwala.[7] Sada Kaur had also been encouraging Ranjit Singh in his endeavour to fight back against the invasions of Shah Zaman which took place between 1793 to 1799. Her military forces were used in the successive invasions and helped rid the provinces of Panjab of the Afghan chief. In his last invasion, Sada Kaur's army had defended Amritsar.[8] This support together with that of the other Misls helped achieve victory for Ranjit Singh. This important fact has been lost in history and is the last time when the ageing leaders of the Misls like Baghel Singh, Jassa Singh Ramgharia, Tara Singh Ghaiba and others took part together in closing the borders to the invader.

Ranjit Singh was now in a good place to conquer Lahore and by taking Sada Kaur's advice he proceeded to besiege the town. The Bhangi Misl, as noted earlier, held sway in neighbouring areas of the Sukerchakia Misl but their rule in Lahore had become unpopular. The triumvirate Sikh Chiefs – Sahib Singh, Chait Singh and Mohar Singh – ruled parts of the city with the latter two chiefs fighting amongst themselves, leading to their unpopularity.[9]

Together with Zaman Shah endorsing the operation, the conditions were now ripe. The townsfolk of the city had also written to the Kanhaiya chief asking for assistance in removing the Bhangis from the city.[10] The attack by Ranjit Singh and Sada Kaur, whose troops numbered 5,000, took place with the help of the local populace. It was instigated that the gates be open whilst the city was attacked from different vantage points. Chait Singh Bhangi and Mohar Singh Bhangi escaped but were captured. Chait Singh negotiated terms with Sada Kaur. They were given *Jagirs* and removed from Lahore. Sada Kaur has been credited with her careful advice both politically and military in procuring the city.[11] However, this victory was going to be short-lived as a powerful coalition was formed in 1800 between Jassa Singh, Ramgarhia, Gulab Singh Bhangi, Sahib Singh Bhangi, Jodh Singh of Wazirabad and Nizam-ud-din Khan of Kasur. The confederate forces, several thousand strong, left Amritsar for Lahore under the command of their respective chiefs.[12] Sada Kaur's forces, together with the Ranjit Singh's, took part in skirmishes which lasted for two months, until Gulab Singh Bhangi succumbed to the vices of alcohol and died on the expedition. As a result, the confederacy was disbanded.[13]

---

7   Sahib Singh predicated that only God could intervene and the floods were seen as this intervention. Griffin, *Chief and Families of Note in the Punjab*, Vol. 1, p.480.
8   Gupta, *History of the Sikhs*, Vol. V, p.16
9   Gupta, *History of the Sikhs*, Vol. V, p.26.
10   Latif, *History Of The Panjab*, p.349.
11   Prinsep, *Origin of the Sikh Power*, p.52.
12   Jassa Singh conducted the plan from further afield and did not take part in the action.
13   Prinsep, *Origin of the Sikh Power*, p.53.

Hazuri Bagh and Lahore Fort, 1866. (Samuel Bourne. Courtesy of Getty's
Open Content Program)

In 1801, the Akalis were monitoring the situation and if Ranjit Singh was staking his claim to the Panjab, they would ensure that it was undertaken without bloodshed within Amritsar. The head of the Buddha Dal and Nihang leader, Akali Phula Singh had started to lay claim to the Gurdwaras around the city. This was to play out when Ranjit Singh and Sada Kaur took hold of the Bhangi estates within the city. As Gulab Singh Bhangi had died during the confederate attack on Lahore, Amritsar was ruled by his widow, Rani Sukhan, in the name of her minor son, Gurdit Singh. Ranjit Singh and Sada Kaur, aided by Fateh Singh Ahluwalia, approached Amritsar with the pretence of acquiring the Zamzama Gun for a campaign. They attacked the *Bhangian da Qila* after which time the Bhangis fled to *Lohgarh Qila*, and this too was captured.[14] The Bhangis were given *Jagirs* and their domination of Amritsar and Lahore ended. The ascendency of the Sikh Empire under Ranjit Singh was underway and Sada Kaur was pivotal to his success. In 1802, Sahib Singh Bhangi attacked Gujranwala and again both Misl forces repelled the attack. Sada Kaur provided her forces for the campaigns of Chiniot, Kasur and Kangra as well as for the expeditions

14   Prinsep, *Origin of the Sikh Power*, p.54. There has been some suggestion that the many forts and *Katras* were linked by underground tunnels most likely built during the Misl period. Hence why the Bhangis were able to escape from fort to fort. See 'Discovering Amritsar's Secret Tunnels' at Living History India website, <https://www.livehistoryindia.com/snapshort-histories/2020/07/08/secret-tunnels-amritsar> (accessed 31 January 2021.)

against the turbulent Pathans of Hazara and Attock. In January 1820, the people of Hazara had rebelled against the Lahore Durbar and so Prince Sher Singh and Sada Kaur were dispatched to quell the disturbances. They were successful in defeating the *Ghazis* and the sounds of Sat Sri Akal were heard across the area. Sada Kaur made a declaration to the people informing them of their duties and the consequences if they did not follow the rules:

> Rani Sada Kaur held a darbar and announced that whosoever would raise the banner of revolt would be severely dealt with. Complete peace should prevail and nobody should create trouble. Land revenue should be paid regularly in future and previous dues cleared. War indemnity was imposed on the Ghazis which they promised to pay, putting their hand on the Quran.[15]

Ranjit Singh's conquest also included additional matrimonial alliances and this was not to the liking of Sada Kaur. This began the gradual decline in relations between the two parties. If Mehtab Kaur was the only wife of Ranjit Singh then that would have been an ideal situation for Sada Kaur. Her interest was for the future prospects of her children and the continuation of the Kanhaiyas but Ranjit Singh had other motives. He strengthened his union with various Misls by having many marriage partners. He was betrothed to Datar Kaur (d.1838) better known as Mai Nakkain of the Nakai Misl in 1798, who bore him a son, Kharak Singh. She played a major part in Maharajah's life including taking part in the Battle of Multan (1818). He was also carrying on parlays with Moran Sarkar, much to the chagrin of all around. This all led to further estrangements with Sada Kaur and his wife, Mehtab Kaur. However, change was afoot when in 1804 Mehtab Kaur gave birth to a son, Ishar Singh, although he, unfortunately, passed away aged one and a half. In 1807, twin sons were born to Mehtab Kaur who was now living with Sada Kaur in Mukerian. They were named Sher Singh (later Prince) and Tara Singh. The Maharajah's mind was poisoned by rumour-mongers that they were not his children. Sada Kaur was extremely upset when the Maharajah refused to acknowledge them as his own sons. Relations became even more tense when in the same year, Ranjit Singh sent Diwan Mohkam Chand to extract tributes from various chiefs around the Kangra Hills, which were under the protectorate of the Kanhaiyas. These events began the continual decline of Sada Kaur's fortunes.[16]

Sada Kaur always had to fight for her cause and she was a capable administrator as well as a warrior. In 1808 the area of Wadni was given to Sada Kaur; this was originally the territory of Tara Singh Ghaiba. However, after the Treaty of Amritsar in 1809, she petitioned the British for her territory. It was granted by Colonel Ochterlony,

---

15   Johar, *Sikh Warrior: Hari Singh Nalwa*, p.38.
16   Prinsep, *Origin of the Sikh Power*, p.61. Diwan Mokham Chand between 1814-25 was virtually the commander in chief of the armies that conquered Multan and Kashmir.

agent to the Governor General at the Ludhiana Political Agency. However, she still had to expel Amar Singh, whose family were administering the area. In 1813, her daughter Mehtab Kaur died.[17] The Maharajah absented himself from the cremation and other ceremonies. Finally, he was persuaded by Diwan Mohkam Chand to go to Sada Kaur's place and participate in the ceremonies for his deceased wife. It is claimed that during this time Sada Kaur's estrangement led to her entering into correspondence with the British. According to Cunningham, 'Sada Kaur perceived that she could obtain no power in the names of the children, and the disappointed woman addressed the English authorities in 1810 and denounced her son-in-law as having usurped her rights, and as resolved on war with his new allies. Her communications received some attention, but she was unable to organize an insurrection, and she became in a manner reconciled to her position.'[18] The time came when Sada Kaur arranged the marriage of her grandson, Sher Singh, and adopted a conciliatory attitude towards Ranjit Singh. Sher Singh's marriage took place in December that year, but without the kind of pomp and ceremony which was witnessed at the time of the marriage of another child of the Maharajah, Prince Kharak Singh.[19] After this reconciliation, the armies of Sada Kaur, Sher Singh and Tara Singh were included in military campaigns. In 1814, Sada Kaur heard the news that Ranjit Singh had told her grandsons, Sher Singh and Tara Singh, they would soon get *Jagirs*. However, this was not to be and, in 1820 Ranjit Singh sent a *Farman* to Sada Kaur asking her to set apart half of her estate for maintenance of her own grandsons; this was indirectly asking her to surrender her territory to him. With very few options she had no alternative but to sign the deed. Not soon after this, she escaped from the camp in a covered palanquin. She was captured and committed to close confinement. The arrest would now lead to Ranjit Singh seizing all the possessions of the Kanhaiya leader. All her wealth and territory were taken at Batala, after a small resistance at the Kanhaiya Fort at Atalgarh by one of her female attendants.[20] Interestingly, one of the areas taken by Ranjit Singh was Wadni which Sada Kaur had fought so hard to hold onto. The British, on hearing this news, restored the estate to Sada Kaur. Ranjit Singh avoided the political and military pressure needed to reclaim the area despite Akali Phula Singh offering to reclaim the territory.[21] However, he was

---

17   Gupta, *History of the Sikhs*, Vol. V, p.51.
18   Cunningham, *History of the Sikhs*, p.175. Gupta goes further and states that Mehtab Kaur and Sada Kaur were in touch with Captain A. Mathews and were plotting Ranjit Singh's downfall. Gupta, *History of the Sikhs*, Vol. V, pp.223–227. Any overtures from the Sikhs were seen as a weakness of Ranjit Singh, and Charles Metcalfe also saw this in 1809 and realised that he would be able to successfully negotiate the Treaty of Amritsar successfully.
19   Prince Kharak Singh's wedding took place to Chand Kaur, the daughter of Jaimal Kanhaiya. There may have been a sense of resentment in Sada Kaur upon seeing another member of the Kanhaiya Misl being taken into confidence within the Sikh Empire.
20   Prinsep, *Origin of the Sikh Power*, p.128. A Gurdwara is now situated at this location.
21   According to Cunningham, Akali Phula Singh offered to take back the territory single-handed with 1,000 of his troops. This would have started an escalation of British-Sikh

able to negotiate this back from the British, causing much resentment for Sada Kaur after her imprisonment.

Thus fell the spirited figure of Sada Kaur, who figured prominently in Panjab politics for about thirty years. She was one of the most remarkable women in the history of the Panjab. She had been the mainstay of Ranjit Singh's power, the ladder whereby that monarch had been enabled to reach the summit of his greatness. She was the companion of his toils, and to her energy, intrigues and influence he chiefly owed his success in his early exploits. She maintained an unbending disposition to the last, and her ruin was bought about by the course of events, not less than by the high tone she was in the habit of assuming and the independence of character she asserted, both of which the Sikh monarch had become incapable of tolerating by the growth of his power. She bore the calamity of her confinement with great restlessness and impatience, upbraiding and execrating her ungrateful son-in-law, beating her breast with vehemence, and renewing her curses and lamentations every day.[22]

Sada Kaur died in 1832 while still closely confined by Ranjit Singh, who had risen to a pinnacle on her shoulders. She was just as ambitious and climbed up her own ladder, bearing in mind she was a widow who controlled the resources and army of a powerful Misl. She was to come into conflict with her domineering son-in-law, who did not discriminate when it came to a chief either male or female; both had the same treatment meted out to them. After Sada Kaur's death, he granted the title of Prince to Sher Singh whilst Tara Singh was neglected.

relations and the British were already looking to eliminate the hardened Akali leader. Cunningham, *History of the Sikhs*, p.145.

22   Latif, *History Of The Panjab*, p.424. Prinsep, *Origin of the Sikh Power*, p.128.

5

The Military System under Maharajah Ranjit Singh

The Sikh Misls had provided a grounding from which a consolidated Panjab could prosper and from which an offensive position could be taken rather than a defensive one. Ranjit Singh of the Sukerchakia Misl had conquered Lahore in 1799 and taken Amritsar in 1801. However, the youthful king needed support; not from the Misls of old, but a new strategy to build and strengthen a Sikh Empire if it was to last. This would be undertaken through numerous ways, including the subjugation of the Sikh Misls through force, dynastic alliances and most importantly through the reorganisation of the Sikh military. It is the latter statement that we are mainly concerned within this chapter.

In 1801, there was a recognition of Ranjit Singh as ruler of Lahore and Amritsar and with the attendance of chiefs, nobles and prominent citizens it was clear that this was the start of something formal and structured. Ranjit Singh was anointed as Raja of the Panjab by Sahib Singh Bedi, a man of repute and a descendant of Guru Nanak. What is clear is that the investiture and the names given, whether that was 'Maharajah' or otherwise, was not something he seemed to be overly concerned with and this was reflected in the minting of his coins and his servitude to the Gurus. The Nanakshahi Coins bore the traditional signatures of victory and reverence to Guru Nanak and Guru Gobind Singh, the couplet from the time of Banda Singh Bahadur and the Sikh Misls.[1] His ambitious strategy of creating a system of governance was created with the help of the populace and his government would be *Sarkar I Khalsa;* an all-encompassing populist rule which gave power and rank not just to the Sikhs but to the existing Hindu and Muslim citizens. This also extended to the influx of European mercenaries.

---

1   The development of coins took a new turn under his regime and various mints were created across Panjab. About 12 different mints operated examples included the following: Lahore, Amritsar, Multan, Peshawar, Kashmir, Derajat, Dera Ghazi Khan, Mankera and so on. Thanks to Jeevandeep Singh for his help in deciphering Sikh coinage.

With his power base on the increase there was another rising power which Ranjit Singh was aware of: that of the East India Company, and whilst there was no direct threat, there was a matter which would bring together the British and the Sikhs in a more diplomatic arena. The so-called Cis-Sutlej states, which were several Sikh small states, some of which were bordering the River Jamuna, had become all too powerful. They were, however, stopped by the British from receiving their traditional tribute, *Rakhi*. This also led to a stop to their depredations into the areas around Delhi where they had become masters after subduing the Marathas and Mughals. Jaswant Rao Holkar (1776-1811) of the Marathas was being hunted by General Lake into Panjab. The question was posed to the Sikh Court as to whether to give sanctuary to the Maratha Chief or to undertake a policy of appeasement. The latter route was chosen. Ranjit Singh could ill afford to embroil his newly-created leadership in a war with the British. The Maharajah was young in age and his courtiers, like Sada Kaur and others, advised him to keep the peace with the British. The First Anglo-Sikh Treaty was enacted in 1806 with Fateh Singh Ahluwalia being a cosignatory of the alliance. This effectively saved Jaswant Holkar and consequently his territories were restored to him. (See appendices).

The Cis-Sutlej states found themselves being squeezed between the might of two emerging superpowers, that of the Sikh Empire and the East India Company. These states viewed the British as being a more favourable option; they had already accepted British suzerainty from 1803. However, a new petition was to be created by territories of Kaithal (Lal Singh), Jind (Bhag Singh), Patiala, Nabha and Kalsia for formal recognition by the EIC in 1808. The protracted negotiations continued, with Ranjit Singh's encroachments causing discomfort to the Cis-Sutlej states. Forced by the approaching British army, he signed the second Anglo-Sikh treaty with the EIC on 25 April 1809.[2] This, however, was subject to scrutiny and whilst paying attention to Lahore and Amritsar he failed to consider the lands near the Jamuna. As a comparison with the territories possessed by the Sikh Misl versus the Sikh Empire, there was a big concession in terms of the lands lost.[3]

This treaty, whilst handicapping the Sikh Empire from making territorial gains below the Sutlej River, allowed expansion south-west towards Multan and Derat, north-west into territories beyond the River Indus including Peshawar, to the northern areas of Jammu and Kashmir and the south-eastern territories of Kangra and the Shivalik Hills.[4] These areas would be subdued in due course and completely close the

---

2   See Appendices for the Treaty of 1806. Other treaties can be viewed in *The British and the Sikhs* or by visiting 'The Anglo-Sikh Treaties: 1806–1846' at <https://www.sikhmuseum.org.uk/portfolio/the-anglo-sikh-treaties-1806-1846/> (accessed 14 February 2021).

3   For a discussion on this, See *The British and the Sikhs*. A simple solution would have been to send a Sikh army to be stationed at the Jamuna River with help of the Cis-Sutlej States.

4   The treaty requires further qualification; essentially any territory which was administered by Ranjit Singh or paid tribute to the Sikh Empire was allowed to continue this relationship.

borders to conquest from any region. Ranjit Singh had knowledge of these lands due to the Sukerchakia Misl already having conquered these territories.

Sikh Military System

The Dhai Phat system employing cavalry yielded great results during the eighteenth century. Yet an evolution of the Sikh Military system was warranted. A mixture of the old and the new was something Ranjit Singh would eventually adopt. A state army would ensure the stability of the Sikh Empire and the move to the employing artillery, infantry, engineers, to fight conventional warfare.

The Maharajah had seen the armies of General Lake and was aware of the strength of the Pathans and Muslim rulers. A popular anecdote that is cited is when General Charles Metcalfe (1785–1846) and his escort visited Amritsar, they were attacked by the Akali Nihangs, which they repelled in a disciplined way. This discipline he felt was missing from the Sikh army, and the Nihangs would still play a part but in a different way. The development of infantry and artillery would be the key components of these changes, adding to the cavalry and guerrilla attacks mentioned previously. This was together with a standing army replacing many of the old feudal levies raised by the Sikh chiefs and Misls.[5] The classification of the Khalsa army can best be depicted by the following table. It was essentially composed of the state army and the *Jagirdari* or feudatory army:

The classification of the Sikh army.

Khalsa Army							
State Army					Jagirdari Fauj		
Irregular Army		Regular Army (Fauj-i-Ain)			Artillery	Cavalry	Infantry
Fauj-i-Sawari	Fauj-i-Kilajat	Artillery	Cavalry	Infantry			

It should be noted that whilst the notion of the European innovations was applauded, some changes in Sikh army formations are evident from an earlier period when we inspect the Khalsa Durbar Records (KDR). Intricate records were kept of soldiers, rates of pay, promotions and replacement of commanders, as well as the number of troops allocated to a regiment. Fines and injunctions are also clear to see. This challenges the accepted idea of records not being available; if anything they have not been scrutinised enough.[6] There is also detailed information on the practice of branding horses and camels as soon as a trooper was enlisted in the army.

5   Sita Ram Kohli, 'The Reorganisation of the Khalsa Army', in Teja Singh and Ganda Singh (eds.), *Maharajah Ranjit Singh* (New Delhi: Nirmal Publishers, 1986), p.66.
6   The KDR furnishes us with much information on the army of Ranjit Singh. It is surprising the text has not been quoted more in Sikh history. The main challenge has been the original records were in Persian, a language that many Sikhs are no longer versed in.

Belt Buckle depicting the three branches of the Military: Artillery, Infantry and Cavalry.
(Lahore, circa 1830. Courtesy of Sukhbinder Singh Paul Family Collection.[7])

Infantry

Infantry, whilst seen as an inferior branch of the military by the Sikhs, was modified
so that it became attractive, leading to important battalions being formed. The Sikhs
described the drills introduced as *Ruqs-i-luluan* or the 'fool's ballet.' Initially, *Purbias*,
a small number of deserters from the EIC, as well as Sikhs formed this branch.
Examining the payrolls of the KDR from 1813 the bulk of the infantry consisted of
Hindustanis, Gurkhas and Afghans. This changed by the year 1818 when the Sikh

Sita Ram Kohli has made a great start in this area and requires additional work for this
information to be translated. The records are kept at Anarkali, Lahore.
7   A 80.5 mm x W 95mm, cast bronze Khalsa Force's belt buckle which was worn at the
central chest juncture of the soldier's chest straps. A similar one was sold in a Bonhams
auction in June 2020.

SING   SEPAHEE.   MOOSELMAN SEPAHEE   GORKHEE   SEPAHEE

Sikh Empire Infantry. (John Martin Honigberger, *Thirty-Five Years in the East* (London, 1852))

recruitment expanded amongst this branch and became predominant.[8] The Maharajah took to attending military parades and extending favours to infantry personnel. The showering of monetary gifts and clothing were all key in the name of raising the profile of this branch and encouraging enlistment. The exact date of when Ranjit Singh raised his first battalion of regular infantry is hard to ascertain. However an examination of the payrolls in 1807, shows he had three such battalions. With Charles Metcalfe later seeing five such battalions.[9]

In 1838, the year before the death of Ranjit Singh, the infantry increased to over 26,000 men with a monthly salary of Rs2,27,600. One of the main innovations in the Sikh army was the introduction of European instructors whose changes paid huge dividends to the Sikh Empire. This was inevitable in this branch which required a major upgrade. Battalions that numbered in the region of 800 men and were commanded by a Commandant or *Kumedan*, assisted by an adjutant and a major

8   Sita Ram Kohli, *Catalogue of Khalsa Darbar Records:* Vol.1 (Lahore: Printed by the Superintendent, Government Printing, 1919), p.2. From here referred to *Khalsa Darbar Records* or KDR.
9   *Khalsa Durbar Records*, p.2.

in his duties. There was also a *Subedar, Havaldar, Naik, Quarter Havaldar, Nishanchi* (banner bearer) and privateers.[10]

Various posts were attached to the battalion, and this included a clerk or *Munshi* to check the payrolls, plus an accountant or *Mutasaddi*. The unit also had a reciter of the Sikh scriptures or *Granthi* who was fundamental to warfare in all branches. There were also other non-combatants of the camp which can be described as follows: *Saqqa* (water carrier), *Sarban* (camel-driver), *Gharyali* (gongsman), *Jhanda bardar* (flag bearer),[11] *Belder* (spadesman), *Mistri* (blacksmith), *Najjar* (mason) and the all-important *Langri* or cook.[12] Light tents and animals were attached to each battalion in a fixed proportion.

The following table shows the expansion of Ranjit Singh's Infantry.

Table 1. Strength and pay rates of the infantry

Year	Strength	Monthly Salary (Rs.)
1819	7,748	60,172
1823	11,681	84,162
1828	15, 825	1,16,284
1833	20,577	1,167,962
1838	26,617	2,27,660
1843	37,791	4,83,056
1845	53,962	5,70,205

The subsequent increase in numbers and rates of pay within seven years after the Maharajah's death (1839) had a negative effect on the army in terms of organisation and unruly behaviour which was one reason for the downfall of the Sikh Empire.

Artillery

The artillery or *Topkhana*[13] was another branch that during the Misl period witnessed short bursts of enthusiasm. However, it was limited, partly due to their infrastructure at the time. The possession of the Zamzama Gun from the Durranis and the use of swivel guns or *Zamburaks* (guns mounted on camels) was in vogue but only in a limited way. The influx of European mercenaries and the EIC whose predominant introduction of artillery helped various groups, had been evident in the development and success of the Mughals, Rohillas and Marathas in their campaigns. The

10   Kohli, 'The Reorganisation of the Khalsa Army', p.70.
11   As noted earlier in the preceding century a whole Misl was named the Nishanvalia Misl and these standard-bearers were a fighting unit in themselves.
12   Kohli, 'The Reorganisation of the Khalsa Army', p.70.
13   The KDR records this term through the papers.

Afghans had this capability and were successful in the subjugation of Northern India by employing this method of warfare in the eighteenth century.

This branch was also reorganised like the infantry and developed into a regular ordnance department. Initially, the main recruits were *Purbias* but the Sikhs took to artillery relatively easily and the introduction of matchlocks proved popular. The Europeans were at the helm of these innovations but the Sikh Army held their own with improvements made to existing Indian and European mechanisms. Two *Ferengis* who are singled out in this area were Claude Augustus Court (1793–1861) and Colonel Gardner. The later entering the Panjab stated, 'At the time of my arrival at Lahore the Maharajah was in want of an instructor of artillery, M. Court being employed principally as superintendent of the gun-factory. He was a very amiable and accomplished man.'[14] The recruitment and training of gunners became a highly organised and efficient arm of the army and was predominantly composed of Muslim recruits with high-ranking officers. Mian Ghaus Khan (d.1814) who in 1812 was in command of the *Topkhana* he was superseded by his son Mohammad Khan. Other important officers included Mian Qadir Baksh, Mahsar Ali Beg in charge of horse battery as well as the celebrated Ilahi Bakhsh.[15] Their expertise and enthusiasm were borne out in Ranjit Singh's campaigns and the later discussed Anglo-Sikh Wars.

The *Topkhana* was split into:

1) *Topkhana Jinsi* – mixed batteries of *Gavi*, driven by bullocks, *Aspi*, driven by mules and horses and *Hoboth* or the howitzer.
2) *Topkhana Aspi* – purely horse batteries.
3) *Zamburaks* and *Ghurbaras* – mortar sections.[16]

The organisation and structure of the artillery unit resembled that of the infantry in terms of ranks. The number of guns in a *Jinsi* battery varied from ten to in excess of twenty-five guns, whilst the horse batteries averaged eight pieces. Each gun in a battery had eight to ten men attached to it, under the charge of a *Jamadar* assisted by a *Havaldar* and a *Naik*.[17] The following table shows the expansion of the artillery during Ranjit Singh's reign. Interestingly, whilst aspersions have been cast on lack of artillery in the early period, before 1809, he still possessed 40 guns and maintained two *Topkhanas*.

14   Pearse, *Soldier and Traveller*, p.180.
15   G.L. Chopra, *The Punjab as A Sovereign State* (Lahore: Uttar Chand Kapur and Sons, Lahore, 1928), p.97.
16   Kohli, 'The Reorganisation of the Khalsa Army', p.73.
17   Kohli, 'The Reorganisation of the Khalsa Army', p.73.

Table 2: Strength, number of guns and swivels, and pay rates of the artillery.[18]

Year	Strength	Guns	Swivels	Salary (Rs. monthly)
1818–1819	834	22	190	5,840
1828–1829	3,778	130	280	28,390
1838–1839	4,535	188	280	32,906
1843–1844	8,280	282	300	82,893
1845–1846	10,524	376	300	89,251

Again, the increase in the size of the artillery branch was assisted in the early period by the introduction of European recruits, General Court joined the ranks in 1827. The EIC had also given the Sikh Empire several guns as gifts. The Sikhs used this opportunity to improve on their patterns. One could question this motivation but it was definitely to the detriment of the British as witnessed in the Anglo-Sikh Wars, particularly the first one. William Bentinck had presented to Ranjit Singh two six-pounders at the splendorous meeting at Ropar in 1831. Another important person in the Sikh Empire, considered in a later chapter, was Lehna Singh Majithia, considered to be instrumental not only as an inventor but as a key asset in improving and developing the ordnance factories. His guns were used in the battles of Ferozeshah and at Aliwal. Also at the latter battle, two six-pounder guns manufactured by Rai Singh measuring 4 feet and 10 inches, and 4 feet and 11 inches respectively were evident. Only fragments of information exist about where these factories were but with some certainty we can say the casting of guns took place at Lahore, Amritsar, Kotli Lohran and Nakodar (*Top Nikodarwali*)[19] amongst others.[20]

There were several foundries in Lahore for the casting of guns and the manufacture of shells. They were all under the control of Ranjit Singh and supervised by the following men. One was under Mian Qadir Bakhsh, an engineer of repute, who received much training in artillery and also wrote a book on the subject. He was aided by Anup Singh. The foundry at Shahdara was under Sarup Singh and Jawahar Mal and the Mazung foundry was under Sobha Singh. Finally, there was a foundry under Nahar Singh.[21] William Barr writes about the foundry within the Lahore Fort, saying, 'Amongst other pieces of ordnance, we were shown two very respectable-looking brass 4-pounder howitzers, lately cast from the models of those presented to Runjeet Singh by Lord William Bentinck; and the superintendent told us there were ready for service, in and about the immediate neighbourhood of Lahore, 700 guns, of various calibres.'[22] Osbourne also notes the strength of the guns in 1838:

---

18 Kohli, 'The Reorganisation of the Khalsa Army', p.74.
19 Names of those in charge include Khalifa Nir-ud-Din and Qade Khan.
20 Alexander Burnes, whilst inspecting the guns in 1831, states: 'The guns, however, were well cast, and the carriages in good repair: they had been made at Lahore, and had cost him 1,000 rupees.' Burnes, *Travels in Bokhara*, Vol. 3, p.165.
21 Verma, *Foreigners at the Court*, p.44.
22 He was accompanying Colonel Wade and his army in 1839 and made many important observations of the Sikhs. Lieut. William Barr, *Journal of a March from Delhi to Peshawur*,

9-pounder howitzer inscribed with the *Kaukab-i-Iqbal-i-Punjab*. (Acc. No:XIX.247.
@Royal Armouries)

There were thirteen brass nine-pounders on the ground, protected by two squad-
rons of his regular cavalry, under the command of Rajah Dheean Sing. After
manoeuvring for about an hour, and executing several of the more simple movements with considerable precision and steadiness, and at a tolerable pace, they
commenced practising with grape at a curtain, at two hundred yards' distance;
the practice would have been creditable to any artillery in the world. At the first
round of grape, the curtain was cut clean away, and their shells at eight and
twelve hundred yards were thrown with a precision that is extraordinary, when
the short period of time since they have known of even the existence of such a
thing is taken into consideration. I rode up to the curtains with Dheean Sing at
the conclusion of the practice and found them almost cut to pieces.[23]

and from thence to Cabul, with the mission of Lieut.-Colonel Sir c. M. Wade, kt. C.b. Including
travels in the Punjab, a visit to the city of Lahore, and a narrative of operations in the Khyber
Pass, undertaken in 1839 (London: James Madden & Co., 1844). pp.102–103.
23   Osbourne, *The Court and Camp of Runjeet Singh*, pp.163–164.

A 9-pounder howitzer was presented to Maharajah Ranjit Singh by Governor-General Auckland in Ferozepore. These guns were studied by the Sikhs and the design improved upon, one example of which is a 'hardwood carriage' design with ornate designs added to it.[24] The *Zamburak* were swivel guns that were mounted on and fired from camels. These were smaller and easier to use and could be carried through mountainous terrains. They were limited in range but proved important when moving to different arenas of a battle. Examples of these were used in the Sikh Wars. (See colour pages).

The cannons were given elaborate names and provided a source of amusement. Inscriptions on the guns include that of *Ram-ban*, *Fateh Jang* (victorious in war), *Jang-i-Bijli* (destroys like lightning) etc. This development also continued under Maharajah Sher Singh; examples include a pair of two Bronze Mountain howitzers, one of which was named *Shirin* (sweet), cast by Fazl Ali Khan and Colonel Gardener. The other, presented by Nihal Singh Ahluwalia, bore the inscription 'Sher Singh Bahadur, may his good fortune and majesty endure, was presented by the famous sardar of high dignity Nihal Singh Bahadur Ahluvalia.'[25]

This all pointed to the Sikh Empire being independent in regard to raw materials, design, production, construction, and maintenance. The fusion of European innovations with the existing methods proved to be beneficial for the Sikh Army.

Cavalry

The Khalsa army, from its inception, was primarily cavalry and they were astute horse riders during the Misl period whilst fighting the Mughal, Afghan and other armies. The main body or *Ghorchurah Fauj* was kept under Ranjit Singh's command and served as an independent branch of the army. Then there was also the cavalry which was raised on western lines. These two systems of cavalry worked well for Ranjit Singh and allowed for the sardars and chiefs to contribute a large body of men. Added to this were the regular troops known as the *Fauj-i-Ain*. The breakdown of the cavalry is as follows: the Regular Cavalry, *Fauj-i-Ain;* and the Irregular Cavalry which consisted of *Jagirdari Fauj* and *Ghorchurah Fauj*.

Regular Cavalry: Fauj-i-Ain
There were only a handful of men recorded in the year 1819; just 837 in three regiments with a fourth added in 1821. This branch was trained in due course by General

---

24   The hardwood carriage is of a block trail type based on General Sir William Congreve's 1792 design for British service.

25   These can be seen at Fort Nelson, The Royal Armouries. *Shirin*, Acc.No XIX.108 has inscriptions praising Fazl Ali Khan and 'General Gornar Sahib Bahadur' who is considered to be General Gardener. The Bronze Howitzer, Object Number XIX.109 by Nihal Singh Ahluwalia (1817–52), Raja of Kapurthala.

Allard who in 1822 had entered the service of the Maharajah. He was commissioned to raise a corps of dragoons, disciplined and armed in a similar fashion as that of the Europeans. These Sikh soldiers were put through a different set of paces than they were previously used to and it would have seemed strange to them at first. This body of troops was fine not only in appearance but equally in drill; however, they were only a small part of the overall cavalry.

As the table below shows, there was no major increase in the numbers in this area after 1828 until the figure rises marginally in 1845.

Table 3: Showing the year, strength and salary of the regular cavalry

Year	Strength	Salary (Rs)
1819	750	11,723
1823	1,656	41,609
1828	4,345	1,03,970
1833	3,915	86,544
1838	4,090	90,375
1843	5,381	1,61,660
1845	6,235	1,95,925

Jagirdari Fauj

This cavalry, which was raised on a feudal system, had to furnish a number of soldiers and horses based on the amount of *Jagir* they received. An estate was held by a superior on condition of military service. The *Jagirdar* and his forces were required to present themselves for review at the state parade which was normally at the time of certain festivals like Dussehra. Punishments and fines were also introduced to ensure that the troops were in order. Later, the *Jagirs* were revised so that rolls describing the number of soldiers in a contingent were deposited in the state's administrative offices, as well as horses being branded. Any discrepancies were again met with punishment or fines.[26] Their services were constantly requisitioned throughout the year, either to chastise a recalcitrant chief or to realise revenues from defaulting Zamindars. There does not appear to be any accurate records of this branch of the army.[27]

Ghorchurah Fauj

In the KDR the irregular cavalry was defined as the *Ghorchurah Fauj, Sowari Fauj,* and *Fauj be-qawaid*. The latter means 'ones that follow no prescribed rules'; since this branch of the army did not accept the introduction of European methods of military drill and discipline, which were enforced by the Maharajah with full vigour in his

---

26   Even the high-ranking Khalsa, Hari Singh Nalwa, was fined for not maintaining the stipulated number of men.
27   Sita Ram Kohli states that he was unable to compile this information due to the records not being complete.

regular army, the *Ghorchurahs* were known as the *Fauj be-qawaid*. This salaried branch of the army was partly inherited and absorbed from the families of the Sikh Misls. There was indeed a period of appeasement, with tests of loyalty and the dispersion of favours. Originally the divisions created were a *Ghorchurah Sowar*, but later another regiment was raised known as the *Khass* orderlies.[28] The force was divided into *Derahs*, each of which formed a complete unit. Each *Derah* was formed of several subordinate groups called Misls (taking their name from Sikh Confederacies). Two large divisions, that of the Ramgharia Misl and the troops of Milkha Singh Thepuria, formed the *Derah* Ramgharia and *Derah* Pindiwala respectively.[29] This was after Ranjit Singh's deposition of the Ramgharia Misl, firstly by befriending Jodh Singh Ramgharia and then on his death in 1816 by completely stripping their territories. It was originally commanded by Diwan Mokham Chand and then by Lehna Singh Majithia in 1824. The *Derah* Pindiwala was composed of soldiers whom in 1804 were under the command of Jiwan Singh. After his death in 1815, Ranjit Singh absorbed his troops and took direct control over Rawalpindi. The contingent was commanded by Diwan Radha Kishan and Lala Das Mal.[30] Prince Kharak Singh took over the troops of the Nakai Misl and Prince Sher Singh, the Kanhaiya Misl. Other troops were absorbed into divisions known as Derah Naulakha commanded by Suchet Singh, the name being derived from the troopers cantoned in the vicinity of Naulakha. *Derah* Ardalyan was another contingent that was composed of different regiments after 1818, originally commanded by Mehtab Singh and then his son Bhima Singh.

The tactics and methods of warfare followed the style of old; hit and run tactics and bold assaults on the enemy. Ranjit Singh felt that modernisation would not work within the predisposition of these particular soldiers. However, there was no fixed uniform or strength in these units. In 1822, the smaller groups were grouped into larger divisions under the command of a high ranking officer. This included Diwan Mokham Chand, Jamadar Khushal Singh (1790–1844), Suchet Singh, Lehna Singh Majithia, and the Attariwala and Sandhanwalia sardars.[31] On the death of the subordinate members of the divisions, there was a tendency for them to be replaced from within their own families. The irregulars were paid originally by the *Jagirs* and interestingly they were the best paid within the whole Khalsa army; however, this was not sustainable in the long run.[32] This would eventually be replaced with a system of regular pay. In keeping with the Misl system, military service required the soldier to possess their own horse

28   *Khalsa Durbar Records*, Vol. 1, p.104.
29   Milkha Singh Thepuria was a great sardar who faced the Afghans head-on and
       commanded great respect in the Misl period. He possessed the area around Rawalpindi.
30   *Khalsa Durbar Records*, Vol. 1, p.115.
31   Ali, *An Historical Account of the Sikhs and Afghans*, p.24. *Khalsa Durbar Records*, Vol. 1,
       p.106. Jamadar Khushal Singh rose up from the ranks firstly as the personal attendant
       of the Maharajah and then the high office of chamberlain to the Durbar. He served in
       several military campaigns.
32   *Khalsa Durbar Records*, Vol. 1, p.106.

and a sword but even this was eventually relaxed and the state would begin to let the entrant in without the necessary requirements, allowing them to pay any monies in instalments.[33] Many of the recruits were also aligned with this branch as it was seen as being prestigious and an honour to fight for the Maharajah and the Empire. At times, when the regular army failed, the bold and fearless *Ghorchurahs* saved the day. Hugel, commenting on their dress, states that he never '...ever beheld a finer nor a more remarkably striking body of men. Each one was dressed differently, and yet so much in the same fashion that they all looked in perfect keeping.'[34] The massive swelling in numbers as previously mentioned can be seen again in the figures after 1838.

Table 4: Showing the year, strength and annual salary of the Irregular Army.

Year	Strength	Annual Salary (Rs)
1813	374	1,65,117
1817	2,464	2,78,318
1819	3,577	11,13,782
1823	7,300	22,45,000
1828	7,200	21,94,000
1838	10,795	31,68,714
1843	14,383	44,18,840
1845	19,100	58,27,597

Akali Nihangs

It should also be mentioned that the remnants of the Buddha Dal order were still intact and composed of the weapon-clad Akalis. Whilst they were anti-British and opposed Ranjit Singh's friendship towards them, they supported the Sikh Empire more impressively than any other group. They also formed part of the Irregular Army and were called into action as necessary. They went into battle based on their own convictions, without authority from the Sikh Empire, and many of them were given roles as part of the aforementioned *Ghorchurah Fauj*. We discuss the qualities of the Akali Nihangs in chapter nine, regarding Akali Phula Singh.

Fauj-i-Khas

The *Fauj-i-Khas* refers to the elite or royal army which was essentially a 'French' Legion within the regular army. The arrival of Generals Allard and Ventura in 1822 brought about many changes to the regular army, mainly from the French system in which they were trained.[35] This included development and organisation, drills, flags and even commands given in the French language. Allard raised two cavalry

33   It was Rs100 for a horse, Rs16–Rs20 for a matchlock, Rs10 for a sword.
34   Baron Charles Hugel, *Travels In Kashmir And The Panjab* (London: John Petheram, 1845), p.331. See Appendix for the full description.
35   Initially, Ranjit Singh was suspicious of their motives. They had written letters in Persian; he gave them a few hurdles to cross, requesting that they write in the French language.

regiments, whilst the artillery was raised by Ilahi Bakhsh, comprising of 15 to 20 guns, and General Ventura totally reorganised the infantry. In total, four infantry battalions, two cavalry regiments and artillery were the hallmarks of the *Fauj-i-Khas*.[36] The number of soldiers which comprised the regular army was around 5,500. The British were certain to take notice of this well-drilled part of the army. This legion fought in many of the main battles including at Naushera (1823), Dera Ismail Khan, Multan and Peshawar (1837–39) and the conquest of Kalu and Mandi (1841). After Allard's death in 1839, command was given to General Ventura and after he left for France in 1843, the command was given to Diwan Ajudhia Prashad. He steadied the ship during the turbulent years of Sikh anarchy in the Sikh Empire and commanded the legion in the First Sikh War.[37] The role of this elite part of the army also acted as a border force of the River Sutlej. They ensured that the British did not encroach on Sikh territories as well as trying to prevent the Akalis crossing the border.

Weapons of Warfare

The different types of weapons would obviously change over time. Although the Sikhs still retained their staple arms from the Misl period, with developments in technology and the introduction of European arms, the makeup was changed. There was also a fusion of arms manufacture which combined the patterns of the Europeans with Indian ideas and modified them for use in the Sikh Empire. Using the three types of classification by Bajwa (1964) we can determine what key arms and armour were used.

1. With regards to defensive arms we can start with helmets (*Khods*), usually made of gold; these close-fitting steel caps were modified for the Sikhs to ensure that they held the long unshorn hair in a topknot. Hence, these were sometimes referred to as Turban Helmets. They were surrounded by a curtain of small chainmail. Some had a nose guard and others had small shafts to support feathers, usually of heron. Many of the *Jagirdars* and royalty adopted these helmets to great effect.[38] The breastplate or *Charaina* alluded to earlier was worn by many of the officers in the Sikh army. These four plates of armour, usually of gold, was damascened with

The English translation can be seen in the Appendices. Prinsep, *Origin of the Sikh Power*, pp.131–133.

36 Ian Heath, *The Sikh Army 1799–1849* (Oxford: Osprey Publishing, 2005), p.12.

37 General Venture praised the work of Ajudhia Prashad. 'I have never had a cause to repent appointing him my deputy, for on my return from France I have found the troops in as a good a condition as I had been present myself.' See Griffin, *Chief and Families of Note in the Punjab*, Vol. 1, p.273.

38 Many of these types of helmets can be seen in UK collections particularly at The Royal Armouries. One has been recreated in 3D by the Sikh Museum Initiative. See helmet, XXVIA.35a, <https://www.anglosikhmuseum.com/sikh-helmet/> (accessed 5 November 2021).

Koftgari. This was worn together with chain armour known as *Zira* (mail), whilst a complete suit was known as *Kurta Zira.*[39] The inclusion of the cuirass from France also added to the depth and type of armour used within the Sikh Empire. With this classification we can also add arm guards or *Dastana*, generally consisting of two plates hinged together on one edge and fastened by straps and buckles on the other. These would provide protection on the lower arm. An example of a Turban Helmet, *Chariana* and *Dastana* can be seen in the colour pages.[40]

2. The short arms used by the Khalsa were originally bows and arrows, battle-axes, and maces. These would still be used by the Akali Nihangs. These were being phased out within the main branches of the army, and the short arms here were composed of swords, daggers and spears or lances. Swords of various types had been used by the Sikhs in the eighteenth century, and in the Sikh Empire the most popular was the *Talwar* (curved sword) and the *Kirch* (straight sword).[41] The nobility opted for more lavish swords with hilts, blades, guards encrusted with jewels and gold. There were also different types of daggers. This included the *Kartar* (punch dagger) which was composed usually of a triangular-shaped blade, with an inset allowing the hand to grip in such a way that resulted in the blade sitting above the user's knuckles. The *Peshkabz* essentially was a curved blade with a handle usually made of hardened animal bones or tusks. The *Bichua* a dagger with a waved (curved) blade and usually with a handle of iron-gilt. The *Chhura* a long knife of Afghan origin. The blades of these daggers were elaborate swords inlaid with gold. Spears and lances were from the fighting methods of the past but still in vogue, particularly amongst the cavalry. These long shafts of steel or bamboo were fitted with sharp-pointed blades on the tip.[42] The *Chakram* or *Chakkar* was a quoit that was wielded by rotating it around a finger and then deployed over large distances with deadly effect. Some were decorated and inscribed with verses from the Sikh scriptures. Quoits are discussed in detail in the section on Akali Phula Singh.

3. Small firearms. There was a variety of these arms used and deployed with great effect against the enemy. This included the matchlock, flintlock, carbine, percussion cap, and other pistols. The matchlock was a firearm which was ignited by a lighted slow-match held in a device called the serpentine. The trigger on the gun brought the match in touch with the powder held in the pan. The Indian variety referred to as *Torador* and various other types had been introduced through the Mughals. This was the staple firearm of the Sikhs and appeared to be of a superior

39 Bajwa, *Military System of the Sikhs*, pp.231–232.
40 This set of military attire is considered to have a connection with Maharajah Ranjit Singh or his Durbar. This has been ascertained after a comparison with the *Toshkhana* records. Acc.No: XXVIA.36, The Royal Armouries.
41 Bajwa, *Military System of the Sikhs*, pp.232–234.
42 For a finely decorated lance depicting hunting scenes possibly belonging to Jowala Singh. See The Royal Armouries, Acc.No: XXVII.221.

design. The flintlock was a European gun introduced into India by the French and the British, and one style, popularly known as the 'Brown Bess', was used primarily by the Sikh infantry. This was long-barrelled gun, firing with flint and pan.[43] Many of these had a bayonet attached like their European equivalents. Another type of firearm, referred to as a *Bharmar*, was designed by Mirza Bharmar from Lahore. It had a dual design with both flint and a slow match serving as a backup. This was used by the Gurkha Battalions in the Sikh Empire. There was also a type of carbine, a gun of the flintlock variety but with a trumpet-styled shorter muzzle, popularly known as a blunderbuss. Having a shorter barrel allowed the horseman to shoot and ride with ease. These were also imported from France. Others included the percussion cap gun, *Sherbacha* (mountain gun), the double-barrelled gun and the pistol. The latter was known as *Tamancha* and varieties were again imported from France and interestingly some were bought from the EIC.[44]

Attire and Clothing

The clothing of the Sikh army poses challenges. Whilst there was some consistency within the branches, the *Jagirdars* and the royalty dressed with laxity and without any fixed prescriptions. However, we can ascertain that European innovations influenced some of the branches and it would be inevitable that it would lead to confusion between friend and foe during the Anglo-Sikh Wars. The Sikh infantry wore scarlet jackets which were looser and longer than the British coatee and blue linen trousers. These scarlet jackets were worn together with black cross belts, again also popular with the EIC. The regular cavalry wore scarlet tunics and turbans with blue trousers. The artillery was distinguished by their black coats, white trousers, and black turbans. The irregular cavalry, the *Ghorchurahs* and *Jagirdari Fauj*, wore what they wanted. The senior officials wore more elaborate shawls, helmets, and round shields.[45] Turbans were of different colours whilst blue was still favoured amongst the soldiery, particularly the Akali Nihangs.

Rewards, Titles, and Medals

Several titles and rewards were introduced to further boost morale and reward service for the soldiers within the Khalsa Army. These came in many forms and included

---

43   Indian names include Banduk Pathar Kala and Banduk Chaqmaq.
44   Bajwa, *Military System of the Sikhs*, pp.234–237. Also see, B.H. Baden Powell, *Handbook Of The Manufactures And Arts Of The Punjab*, Vol. 2 (Lahore: Punjab Printing Company,1872), pp.291–292.
45   Cook, *The Sikh Wars*, p.38.

Sikh arms and armour. (G.W. Osbourne, *The Court and Camp of Runjeet Singh* (London: Henry Colburn, Publisher, 1840))

the awarding of a grant or *Khila'at*. This was not new within the Indian subcontinent and was probably expected. There were several ornaments contained within it, usually eleven for first-class officers. The *Khila'at* could include a shawl, turban, long coat, waistband, bracelets, bangles, aigrette, and other weapons, some made of gold. There were also rewards of elephants and kettle drums.[46]

The Maharajah also introduced several titles that were conferred on the best of the rank and file. This included *Zafar-Jang* (victorious in war), *Shujah-ul-daulah* (valour of the state), and *Hizbar-Jang* (the lion in fight). One interesting innovation was the institution of the Order of Merit in 1837, presumably at the time of the marriage of his grandson, Prince Nau-Nihal. Indeed, the tradition was borrowed from his western counterparts, in particular from the French *Légion d'Honneur* as created by Napoleon Bonaparte in 1832. The title was referred to as *Kaukab-i-Iqbal-i-Punjab* (Star of the Prosperity of the Panjab). The European practice of awarding service medals was also discussed at length with the British local representative, Captain Wade, in April 1838. This seems to have led indirectly to an order that henceforth the uniforms of all of his platoons should have their own identifying mark. The medals were in the shape of a star with ten rays radiating from the centre, bearing an effigy of the Maharajah and his name on the obverse. It appeared to have three classes:

1. First class: ornamented with a diamond and reserved for family members of the Maharajah and high-ranking officials.
2. Second class: containing a diamond and emerald, reserved for courtiers, nobles, government officials.
3. Third class: containing a single emerald, which was reserved for military officials of the rank of colonel, major or captain who had displayed feats of bravery, as well as state officials and any individual showing a display of prowess within the state.

All these orders were rewarded together with the aforementioned *Khila'at*. Medals were given out to a range of royals and other individuals including Faqir Aziz ud-Din, Hira Singh (1816-44) and Lehna Singh Majithia. This was together with the *Ferengis* being generously rewarded, Generals Allard, Avitabile, and Court amongst others. The tradition continued after the Maharajah's death. See the colour pages for example which belonged to Maharajah Duleep Singh. This Order of Merit was also inscribed on Sikh cannons and depicted earlier in the chapter.

The Amazons

Other notable military factors include the inclusion of women at the Durbars, who were attired in military uniform but were *Nautch* girls known as the 'Amazons.' There

---

46   Kaur, *The Golden Temple Past and Present*, p.77.

has been much speculation regarding their role and whether it was just functionary or whether they took part in battle. The overwhelming evidence points to their role as being dressed up in military outfits and bearing arms whilst undertaking their dance routines. This is confirmed by Sohan Lal Suri in his chronicles:

> ...special floorings were spread out very artistically and dancing girls, putting on suits of various colours like those of gold and gold-threaded, came forward in a very wonderful style – dressed in manly garments, some of them holding swords, bows, guns, and spears in their hands like the soldiers, and some had tied up their hair or had let them loose in a dishevelled manner, decorated with gold ornaments and articles of jewellery, and presented themselves to the Maharaja with their crests working as spears of beauty against the buds of men's hearts.[47]

Osbourne notes there were corps developed for entertainment who were 'magnificently dressed, armed with bows and arrows, and used frequently to appear on horseback, mounted en cavalier, for the amusement of the Maharaja.'[48] They were also reportedly seen as being Ranjit Singh's bodyguards, albeit this was misguided: 'At the great festivals here are hundreds of them at Lahore and Amritsar, whom he makes dress up in the most ridiculous way, ride on horses and follow him; on such occasions they form his bodyguard.'[49] Amongst the weapons wielded by the 'regiment of amazons' were spears, several of which were brought to the UK after annexation of the Panjab.[50]

Diplomatic Ties

The idea of the Sikh Empire having a global reputation is borne out the fact that Ranjit Singh had correspondence with many governments across the world. Whilst it has been noted the Sikhs had been in correspondence with the EIC since the late eighteenth century, it was more profound during this period. This is also borne out by

47   Sohan Lal Suri, (trans, V.S.Suri), *An Outstanding Original Source Of Panjab History Umdat-Ut-Tawarikh*, Vol. 3 (Delhi: S. Chand & Co., 1961), p.83. Henceforth *Umdat-Ut-Twarikh*.

48   See W.G. Osbourne, *The Court and Camp of Runjeet Singh* (London: Henry Colburn, 1840), pp.95. A dancing girl named Lotus is identified as one member of the 'Amazons' and he notes that there were originally about one hundred and fifty of these fair warriors, who were selected from the prettiest girls from Kashmir, Persia, and the Panjab.

49   H.L.O. Garrett (trans. and ed.), *The Punjab A Hundred Years Ago: As Described by V. Jacquemont* (1831) & *A. Soltykoff* (1842) (Delhi: Nirmal Publishers, 1986).

50   In the original list of relics listed by Lord Dalhousie, they are described as 'spears used by Mah Ranjit Singh's Corps of drilled women.' Sotheby's, *Sotheby's Colstoun Auction Catalogue*, May 21–22; 1990, pp.24–25.

letters and gifts from the King and later the Queen of England.[51] Additionally, there was much correspondence with the King of France, Louis Philippe I (1773-1850), in main due to the French soldiery connection. Interestingly, we also see correspondence between the authorities in Cairo and the Sikh Empire. This is together with ties to the other nations in the Indian subcontinent including the Marathas, Afghans, Mughals and others. The idea of a nondescript place called the Panjab having only a local or national presence is not true, and the splendour of Sikhs and the Panjab reached an international zenith during Ranjit Singh's reign.

Flags

The so-called national flag of the Khalsa has baffled many and still poses issues as to the origin, style, motifs and colour. In the modern-day, the *Khanda* motif (a double-edged sword) is associated with the Khalsa, and is seen on Sikh flags of a more recent origin.[52] We need to distinguish between a *Nishan Sahib*, which was hoisted in buildings and Gurdwaras, and those military banners carried in battle. The depictions on the eighteenth-century Khalsa flag have been considered to show possibly three weapons: the *Kartar* (punch-dagger), *Dhal* (shield) and *Tegh* (sword).[53] An early depiction of this flag dated c.1770–80 shows Guru Gobind Singh with five followers on his journey to the Decan. This flag is carried by an Akali which is painted in yellow. In terms of the Akalis or Nihangs, whilst we have alluded to the colour blue, however, we also find from certain accounts that the Akali flag was black in colour. This is borne out by the British accounts, as well as a black banner being captured at the battle of Ferozeshah and kept at Lichfield Cathedral. This idea is compounded by examining the most numerous types of a flag that were taken to the UK by Governor-General Dalhousie after the annexation of the Panjab and found on the battlefields of the Anglo-Sikh Wars. The flag is composed of a triangular form with three seams, one side with a central gilt solar motif on a floral ground, the other with a depiction of three deities; the Goddess Durga on her tiger flanked by Hanuman and Kartikeya set on a ground of floral sprays. The green silk borders have a gilt scrolling floral vine, and the wooden pole is in three sections with a steel spearhead terminal and steel handle

51   The meeting of Captain Burnes and the presentation of horses to the Maharajah from King William IV (1765 – 1837) of England is one example. Suri, *Umdat-ut-Twarikh*, Vol. 3, p.63. See appendices for the letter.
52   There is no conclusive data or accounts as to when the modern Khalsa insignia was given credence. There is a strong possibility that it was based on military regiment insignias in the latter part of the nineteenth century or early twentieth century.
53   There is a possibility that the round circle is that of a pot and as a result the flag depicts the concept of *Degh-Tegh-Fateh*. See mine and Kamalroop Singh's book, *The Granth of Guru Gobind Singh: Essays, Lectures and Translations* (New Delhi: Oxford University Press, 2015), pp.215–216.

ਨਕਸ਼ਾ ਦਰਬਾਰ ਸਾਹਿਬ ਜੀਅ।

The Harimandir Sahib. (Coloured transfer lithograph. Wellcome Collection, with permission)

with two fluted bosses with brass fittings (see colour pages).[54] Whilst traditionally the colour of the Khalsa attire and flags have been known to be blue, at least in the eighteenth century, there does appear to have been certain changes during the Sikh Empire which many Sikhs may find difficult to accept. This is due to the Hindu motifs employed on the Khalsa flags, the argument being that these would not have been used by Sikhs. The fluidity of the motifs should be seen in the light of a Khalsa common-wealth representing different denominations as opposed to a strict Sikh sentiment. The facts show this was the most common flag of the Sikh Empire that we know about; indeed other information may come to light that could challenge this assumption or show an array of different flags.[55] Red flags are mentioned in Panjab *Akhbars* or newsletters which records in September 1839, that 'at the request of Raja Heera Singh, flags of gold and silver cloth and Kinschah (Kimkhab, brocaded silk) were promised to the troops at the time of Dusshera.'[56] *Kimkhab* is generally of red colour.

54　These standards were also referenced within *The Illustrated London News* of 19 December 1846 which confirms at least two of these flags were found at Ferozeshah and Sobraon. Indeed two flags could be seen at Lichfield Cathedral (now taken off display), as well as the two at Maidstone Museum, Kent together with many kept in private collections.

55　Another erroneous argument made is these flags belonged to Dogra Regiments; again there was no such thing as a Dogra regiment.

56　Newsletter dated 28 September 1839, quoted in Ganda Singh, *The Panjab In 1839–40 Selections from the Punjab Akhbars, Punjab Intelligence, etc preserved in the National Archives of India* (Amritsar: Sikh History Society, 1952), pp.132–133. There was a great demand for

Baron Hugel states that he saw *Nishan Sahibs* of red colour at the Darshan Deori of the Harimandir Sahib: 'Before the entrance to the bridge are two large banners of red; on one is written, "Wah! Guruji-ke fatih!" in white letters; and on the other, the name of Ram Das [Guru]. These banners are from thirty to forty ells long, and are stretched on masts and confined with iron chains.'[57] There are several portraits depicting these *Nishan Sahibs* in different colours inscribed with the *Kartar*, *Dhal* and *Talwar*.[58]

However, these *Nishan Sahibs* should not be equated with the military banners as described above. The *Umdat-ut-Twarikh* gives us information on the royal standards of the Sikh Empire. We learn that before the Maharajah visited places and locations, the standards would be sent in advance signifying his imminent arrival. This is noted on his visit to the Harimandir Sahib and the Rambagh. It appears that the standards were of major importance. Suri writes, 'Maharaja ordered the departure of his heaven-kissing standards from Lahore, reached the garden of Shalabagh with an incessant march and afterwards went to the fort of Gobindgarh.'[59] We also note the standards of the Sikh Empire, apart from military expeditions, were also taken on hunts.[60] The author does not mention the colours of these standards. There was also a French variety of standards introduced which we discuss in the next chapter.

fabrics of all varieties at the Sikh Court, where artisan flourished. Powell, *Handbook Of The Manufactures And Arts Of The Punjab*, p.156.

57 Hugel, *Travels In Kashmir And The Panjab*, p.394.
58 Hand-coloured print c.1890. Museum number 1994,1216,0.1.IND, The British Museum. Also see the print depicting Amritsar, Acc.No: IM.148-1914, Victoria and Albert Museum.
59 11 April 1832. Suri, *Umdat-ut-Twarikh*, Vol. 3, p.137.
60 On 11 February 1832, the 'departure of the royal standards took place from Lahore to the other side of the river for hunting. The village was Thukriala.' Suri, *Umdat-ut-Twarikh*, Vol. 3, p.124.

6

The *Ferengis* of the Sikh Empire

It is important to add a discussion on the so-called *Ferengis* or foreigners within the Sikh Empire. As noticed earlier, the Indian subcontinent was home to many mercenaries hoping for employment within the various armies of the Mughals, Marathas, and even the Sikhs. Whilst the EIC had come prepared with their own army, the French continued to furnish armies through the late eighteenth and early nineteenth'centuries. Early innovators included Joseph François Dupleix (1697–1763), Governor-General of French India (Pondicherry) and a rival to Robert Clive, who introduced French officers to fighting with the local troops. Most notable were De Boigne and Perron of the Maratha army, whom who we touched upon in relation to George Thomas. There were also a number of French officers who worked under Begum Samru.

However, it was not only the French who sought employment in the Sikh Empire. It also became a haven for many nationalities, mostly of European descent who frequented, traded with and ultimately became a pivotal part of the Sikh army. The rise of the Sikh soldier would not be complete without paying some attention as to what the Europeans brought to the Sikh Empire and what role they played. There have been many lists documenting the different denominations of the foreign fighters in the Sikh court. It is out of our scope to consider all the other soldiers in the employ of the Sikh Empire. It has been noted there were over 62 foreigners working or passing through the Sikh Empire.[1] Nationalities varied from across the globe including British, Austrian, Prussian, Portuguese, Spanish, Greek, Russian, and American. Examples include Alexander Gardner of the artillery; Josiah Harlan, an American general and later governor of Gujarat; General Henry Charles van Cortlandt, Governor of Dera Ismail Khan; and Dr Johann Martino Honigberger, physician to the Maharajah. There were several deserters from the East India Company as well.

The Maharajah was suspicious at first and would test these foreigners before they were employed in various duties. Several of them were promoted to high ranks but

---

1   Verma, *Foreigners at the Court*, p.vii. We can say with certainty and add many more names to the list by Verma's number of 62.

their movements were still controlled, and they were only allowed a fixed amount of personnel under their command. Other injunctions included keeping a beard, refraining from eating beef, and not smoking. In the event of a clash with a European power, they would stay loyal to the Empire and if unmarried they would be advised to seek marriage and raise their families in the Panjab. Holidays and returning to their native lands were only to be granted by permission of the Maharajah. If anything, some of these rules, being of a military nature, were a normality if not a formality. The Maharajah looked upon his European officers as men who held universal traits, and it was his regular habit to compel them to undertake other duties in addition to those for which they were specially employed. These included administrative functions and roles as governors.

As stated in the previous chapter, Ranjit Singh's aim was to primarily strengthen the army and make improvements to the artillery and infantry. Furthermore, he was to make general improvements to ordnance and other medical and technical innovations which could improve the Sikh army in the long run. Ranjit, as noted, did not completely change the military system; he retained many of the old ways of warfare, ensuring both served their purposes. It was for this reason he acquired an advantage over the other armies whether it was the Afghans or the EIC. Indeed, the *Ferengi* would have had full knowledge of the battle tactics of the British as many had fought against them in the Napoleonic wars or were themselves from Britain or America. The plethora of information that comes down to us alerts us to the fact that many powers were fully aware of each other, with ministers and dignitaries having both casual and formal conversations regarding their armies.

Military Manuals of Maharajah Ranjit Singh

Before considering the history of several pivotal *Ferengis* we need to better understand how their fighting methods were instilled into the Sikh Empire. We learn that several manuals were translated and then used within the Sikh army. This tremendous feat deserves merit on its own. The texts, known as the Military Manuals of Maharajah Ranjit Singh, were essentially a translation of military methods from French into Persian. There were three texts in total:

1. Infantry (Translated by Allard and Ventura). c. 1822–30.
2. Cavalry (Translated by Allard and Ventura).
3. Artillery (Translated by Court). c. 1830.[2]

---

2   Jean-Marie Lafont, *Maharajah Ranjit Singh Lord of the Five Rivers* (New Delhi: Oxford University Press, 2002), p.146.

The latter two, the Cavalry and Artillery manuals, are no longer traceable. The extant Infantry manual furnishes us with great details of French military tactics. Attributed to Imam Bakhsh Lahori, it contains a number of illustrative portraits including Maharajah Ranjit Singh with Dhian Singh (1796-1843) meeting Generals Ventura and Allard. Standing next to the *Ferengis* is Hira Singh, and at the bottom are officers from the *Fauj-i-Khas*. (See colour pages).[3] This sets the scene for the rest of the text which was also known as the *Zafarnama*.[4] The text is composed of three military systems and a synopsis is given below.

1.   Drill: military movements composed of falling in, drill without arms and drill with arms.
2 and 3. Weapons training/Evolutions: composed of twelve stages of loading arms, two quick methods of loading, firing in two stages, range practice, four methods of marching, alignment, tactical training in columns and lines, four methods of the formation of squares.

Each command for these drills was undertaken in French like the lifting of arms ('*Levez Arms*'). Each soldier moved onto the next area after mastering the first. The sheer determination by the French generals to introduce these methods is an eye-opener considering the populace was not familiar with the French language and the practice of drill was alien. The military manual also contains portraits of the manoeuvres outlined. (See colour pages). Apart from the methods of drills, another important set of manoeuvres was the formation of squares. This is where parts of the infantry would form a square to face the opposition. This would become a vital part of the drills. The Battle of Aliwal is renowned for this formation which was adopted by the Sikhs.

The manual also gives training in bayonet exercises which were also useful for changing tactics mid-battle. The text is now kept at the Ranjit Singh Museum, Rambagh, Amritsar. It is a text which should be studied more widely as the rich battle drills described within it are a great asset to students of military history. Moreover, the addition of these drills to the strength of the previous tactics carried from the Misl period would benefit the Sikh army immensely. Indeed, it is a testimony of the innovations introduced by Generals Allard, Ventura, Court, and Avitabile, and therefore we will take a few moments to look at their careers.

---

3   Shaikh Basawan visited Allard and Ventura every evening to learn the commands in French and understand their meanings. Lafont, *Maharajah Ranjit Singh*, pp.146–147.
4   In the text by Fauja Singh Bajwa is an English translation of the key parts of the military manual. Bajwa, *Military System of the Sikhs*, pp.243–260.

Portraits of Generals Allard, Court, Avitabile and Ventura. (Painted by and courtesy of Harwinder Kaur)

Jean-Francois Allard

Jean-Francois Allard (1785–1839) was born at Saint-Tropez, France and joined the 23rd Dragoons in Napoleon's army. As a cavalryman, he rose up in the ranks between 1803 and 1814 and served in Italy and Spain. It was at the latter where he was wounded serving with the Imperial Guard. Napoleon promoted him to captain and he was made aide-de-camp to Guillaume Marie-Anne Brune (1764–1815). The defeat of the French at Waterloo left Allard without a military post and he was watched by the authorities in France as he was considered dangerous by some loyalists. His role in the new order, known as the Bourbon Restoration, was not required.[5] Leaving for the middle east in 1815, he was to join the army of Shah Abbas, where he met the Italian, Ventura, and seeking alternative opportunities they headed to the Panjab and the Kingdom of the Sikhs.

At Lahore in 1822, he settled into family life and married Pan Dei, with whom he had six children, one dying in infancy.[6] He was given a house in front of the Anarkali Tomb which was built incorporating Persian and European designs. After undergoing the tests of loyalty and his credentials being confirmed, his initial role was to raise a corps of dragoons which bore the hallmarks of the Europeans. Given a liberal salary of Rs2,500 a month, he set to work together with General Ventura. As seen in the previous chapter there was expansion in the cavalry to nearly four times that at the time of his arrival. Ranjit Singh would make it a habit to see the army drills. Suri writes: 'Allard Sahib presented five gold ducats [coins] to the Maharajah, who ordered him to set up his camp in the estate of Parmanand on the bank of the river in an extensive land, and to watch the drill of the regular troops every day.'[7]

Together with Ventura, he took command of Shaikh Basawan's Paltan Khas and later Paltan Deva Singh (1822), and the Gurkha Paltan (1823). Shaikh Basawan would learn much from the generals, leading to his formidable presence in the hoisting of the Khalsa flag in Afghanistan in 1839. These Paltans formed the infantry of the *Fauj-I-Khas*. The cavalry (*Fransisi Sowar*) was composed of two regiments (*Rajman*) raised by Allard on 16 July 1822. The *Rajman Khas Lansia* (Lancers), composed of mainly Pathans and *Rajman Daragun* (Dragoons) composed mainly of Sikhs.[8] Allard raised another regiment of dragoons in 1823. By 1825, the *Fauj-i-Khas* (infantry, cavalry and artillery) had reached the standard number of around 5,000-6,000 strong. He also took part in the major campaigns of the Sikh Empire and became a trusted confidant that Ranjit Singh could rely on. He took command of the military forces in operation in 1825 in Peshawar and Derajat for pacifying the Muslim tribes along the

---

5   The period from 1814–30 when Napoleon abdicated and Louis XVIII became king until the 100 days' campaign by Napoleon leading to the second restoration.
6   Pan Dei was the daughter of the Raja Menga Ram of Chamba. Their first daughter, Marie Charlotte, only lived a few months and a tomb was built in her memory at Lahore.
7   22nd May 1831, Suri, *Umdat-Ut-Tawarikh*, Vol. 3, p.36.
8   Ian Heath, *The Sikh Army 1799–1849* (Oxford: Osprey Publishing Ltd., 2005), p.15

Indus in 1827. At the North West Frontier, together with Hari Singh Nalwa in 1830, they quelled the *jihad* of Sayyid Ahmad Barelvi. In 1837, in the attack on Jamrud after the death of Hari Singh Nalwa, his troops played an important role in securing the surrounding territories. From 1824 onwards, Allard was also responsible for the Anglo-Sikh border along the Sutlej, and his *Fauj-i-Khas* undertook patrols from the Himalayas down to Hari ka Pattan. This was an important job ensuring border security, not only from infringement by the Sikhs (mainly the Akalis) but also from the threat of the British.

One of the innovations which can be attributed to General Allard is his troops or cuirassiers adopting the metal helmets and the wearing of the cuirass (body armour). The body armour or *Charaina*, whilst not a new innovation, as we know was also worn by Guru Gobind Singh in the late seventeenth century and some Misl soldiers also wore them in the eighteenth century. However, it appears that Allard had brought over arms and armour from France, these being gifts from King Louis Philippe I.[9] This was noted by Governor-General Lord Auckland, who wrote, 'You will have seen in the papers the arrival of General Allard in a French frigate. He brings a present of 500 cuirasses and 2,000 stands of arms from the French king to Ranjit Singh, and is accredited French Charge d' Affaires at Lahore.'[10]

An example of a cuirass can be seen in the writings of the Hungarian doctor, John Martin Honigberger (1795–1869), depicting a cavalry officer wearing an Indo-Persian style helmet and body plate armour. It does appear to be one piece as opposed to the traditional four-piece *Charainas*.[11] General Allard also acted as host to European visitors to the Maharajah's court. On ceremonial occasions, he was chosen for special duties. He, for instance, escorted Maharajah Ranjit Singh at the time of his visit to Ropar in October 1831 for a meeting with the Governor-General. He was also proud of his troops and when asked about a war with the British and the success of an operation, he replied, '...that first of all it was impossible for anyone to dare or venture war against the Maharaja on account of the awe and prestige exercised by the enemy-trampling glory of the Maharaja and that, if any one thought of waging war under the misfortune ordained for him by his star, he (Allard) would first put forward his four companies as checkmate and after that he would make advance and go ahead so far in the field of battle that the whole world would talk of it.'[12] It was this confidence that

9   On Allard's visit to France he presented a letter from Lahore: 'The King and his associates examined it and asked why the seal was so small and he replied that the eye is the smallest of all the limbs and yet sees the whole of the world, nay the whole world can be surveyed by it.' This response greatly pleased Ranjit Singh. Suri, *Umdat-ut-Twarikh*, Vol. 3, p.291.

10 Letter dated 3 December 1836 from Lord Auckland to Sir Charles Metcalfe. Jean-Marie Lafont, *Fauj-i-Khas, Maharaja Ranjit Singh and his French Officers* (Amritsar: Guru Nanak Dev University, 2002), p.101

11 Another example includes Lal Singh depicted during the Anglo-Sikh Wars. See James Duffield Harding, *Recollections of India Part 1. British India and the Punjab* (London: Thomas M'lean, 1847).

12 Suri, *Umdat-Ut-Tawarikh*, Vol. 3, p.385.

Lahore Fort Armoury: arms and armour including the cuirass and carbines.
(Courtesy of Peter Bance)

A Charaina Sowar
(Cuirassier).
(John Martin
Honigberger, *Thirty-
Five Years in the East*
(London, 1852))

Allard and his *Fauj-i-Khas* had been instilled with, along with a level of training, that had made the Sikhs into an improved fighting unit. This order was demonstrated in the Sikh Wars.

Allard was also sent on many administrative duties. In 1838, he went to Peshawar to help General Avitabile in the running of the administration of the city. However, Allard passed away in 1839, some months before Ranjit Singh who was now also experiencing failing health. It was a dark day for the Sikh Empire as testified by Lieutenant William Barr: 'On the occasion six regiments of the Maharajah's were paraded for the purpose of paying respect to the memory of the deceased, who was beloved both by natives and Europeans, and whose death has cast a gloom over the city.'[13] During his lifetime the general had been given several honours such as the *Légion d'Honneur* by Napoleon Bonaparte, and the *Bright Star of the Punjab* by Maharajah Ranjit Singh. He also contributed to the study of coins and was fluent in several languages. His legacy still continues in France.[14]

Jean-Baptiste Ventura

Jean-Baptiste Ventura (1794–1858) was from Modena, Italy and he was a soldier who was equally as important as General Allard for improvements within Sikh warfare in the Panjab. He joined Napoleon's infantry in 1810 and rose to the rank of captain. He served in many of the French campaigns including the Battle of Wagram, the Moscow campaign of 1812 and finally at the Battle of Waterloo in 1815.[15] His infantry was disbanded, and not long after this he followed the same route into the Panjab as General Allard.

It was within the infantry that the Maharajah required major changes, due to the unpopularity with which it was held by his Sikh soldiers, and Ventura was well placed to undertake this job. Ventura also lived within the precincts of Lahore at the Anarkali Tomb; he created a garden that added to the splendour of his residence. (See colour pages).[16] It was also here that European visitors stayed and were entertained.[17] He was given land and *Jagirs* including the area of Sanhewal (to his daughter) and land at Talwandi Rajputana to supplement his income of Rs2500.[18] He married an Armenian

13   Barr, *Journal of a March from Delhi*, p.73.
14   In 2016 Maharajah Ranjit Singh's *Fauj-i-Khas* received renewed recognition in the fashionable resort of St Tropez on the French Riviera. A bust of Maharajah Ranjit Singh, General Allard, and his wife Pan Dei was unveiled. This was undertaken by the great-grandson of Allard, Henri Prevost-Allard, the Mayor of the City.
15   Verma, *Foreigners at the Court*, p.1.
16   Anarkali was built by Emperor Jahangir for his favourite dancing girl Anarkali in the early 1600's.
17   On Captain Burnes's visit to the Panjab, the garden was cleared and much expense was given to make it a befitting venue. Suri, *Umdat-ut-Twarikh*, Vol. 3, p.120.
18   The *Jagir* of Sanhewal is noted in Suri, *Umdat-ut-Twarikh*, Vol. 3, p.381.

Christian in 1825 with whom he had one child named Victoria. The Maharaja and other dignitaries attended the wedding and he was given lavish presents by the sardars of the court. However, his nuptials were short-lived when his wife left him and retired to live in Ludhiana.

He received the command of the elite brigade or *Fauj-i-Khas*. The idea was to bring improvements in the infantry branch of the army. Together with Allard, the innovations as noted earlier were set in motion. Indeed, this was a product of many years of working within the Sikh Empire to bring about these changes. He proceeded to keep four infantry battalions. This was reduced from five and deemed to be a manageable number together with two regiments of cavalry. The improvements would raise the army to equal of that of the British. This was indeed a bold claim but one that was borne out in the Anglo-Sikh Wars. According to Osbourne, 'His [Ranjit Singh's] regular infantry have been all raised and drilled by General Ventura, an Italian officer in his service, and to whom this present soldier like appearance and state of discipline are entirely due.'[19] Gardener, who served with Ventura, states, 'The four infantry battalions of this brigade were the models on which the remainder of the army was formed, and it was by the conversion of his main strength from indifferent irregular cavalry to infantry of a very high class that Ranjit Singh effected the marvellous results which establish his claim to be considered a great military organiser.'[20] Captain Wade, with whom Ranjit Singh had much communication, had given him a book on drills and regulations in English. It was left for Ventura to find a suitable translator who could impart this information to him.[21] When the *Vakils* of the Raja of Nepal were shown Ventura's troops drilling, they were also impressed by their discipline.[22]

Ventura also saw and participated in several battles for the Sikh Empire, including at Naushera (1823) which was the epic last battle of Akali Phula Singh. In Ventura's first battle, within a year of coming to the Panjab, his troops caused a division in the ranks of the Afghans which contributed towards the success of the battle. He was also at Bethier (Kangra) in 1828. In 1831 he was given senior command at Dera Ghazi Khan and controlled vast areas of lands. He raised new garrisons at forts and appointed *Kardars* for the collection of taxes.[23] This led to peace in the area which had been fraught with incursions from the Mazari tribes. The Maharaja's fondness of horses also led Prince Sher Singh and Ventura to start a campaign against Sultan Yar Mohammed Khan who possessed the 'famous mare Lalli, known for its beauty

19   Osbourne, W.G., *The Court and Camp of Runjeet Singh* (London: Henry Colburn Publishers, 1840), p.161.
20   Pearse, *Soldier and Traveller*, p.305.
21   'The Captain Sahib (C. M. Wade) sent a book in English pertaining to the regulations of the troops of the platoons and the horsemen.' Suri, *Umdat-ut-Twarikh*, Vol. 3, p.254. Ventura after considering various suggestions opted for the chronicler, Sohan Lal Suri, to translate it. The title of the book is not known or whether it was translated.
22   Suri, *Umdat-ut-Twarikh*, Vol. 3, p.370.
23   4 May 1831. Suri, *Umdat-ut-Twarikh*, Vol. 3, p.26.

in Afghanistan and Panjab.'[24] They were given instructions to possess the horse by any means necessary. After some initial enquiries which failed, Ventura arrested the Sultan and procured the mare by paying Rs60,000; an extravagant amount. In 1834, together with Ranjit Singh and Hari Singh Nalwa, he launched an attack on Peshawar. Ventura's troops dealt with the army of Azim Khan which fled to Kabul; this contributed to the prestige of the Sikh Empire.[25] In 1837, Hari Singh Nalwa was besieged by the forces of Dost Mohammed Khan and in the same battle, the Sikh general lost his life. Kanwar Nau Nihal Singh (1821-40) and Ventura managed to save the Jamrud fort and Peshawar from falling into Afghan hands. This was an important juncture and was a measure of some success amidst the ferocious battle Hari Singh Nalwa fought.

Ventura had taken an interest in the manufacture of guns and in 1840 he presented to Maharaja Kharak Singh and Nau Nihal Singh three newly built cannons, which they were excited and ecstatic to see. This led to him preparing five more cannons in the same style and fashion.[26] Ventura was briefly given the governorship at Derajat together with Kashmir and Multan. These were all important areas in the Sikh Empire, thus demonstrating Ranjit Singh's faith in him. At all these locations, his administrative and military interventions raised his prosperity and increased his command. Another innovation, which many are not aware of, was the development of a paddleboat and steamboat for the Maharaja. Together with General Gardener, he constructed a double-roofed boat that was fitted with two guns. It was a crude attempt to please the Maharaja but if innovations in this field had been continued and resources had been put into this area, this could have also been a great source of power in the rivers of the Panjab.[27] The general was also given various titles including *Matih-ul-Hukam Wafadar Haq Guzar Khidmat Guzar* (faithful and devoted).

Suri writes, 'On the 9th [21 December, 1836] letters were issued to the officers and the Mutsadis of the platoons, Ahlkars and Daftaris and others informing them that, on account of his well-wishing, faithfulness, service, devotion, sacrifice in rendering meritorious services to the Maharaja, General Chevalier Ventura Sahib was granted the title of "Faithful and Devoted" out of great kindness of the Maharaja and ordered them to proclaim this order all over his dominions.'[28]

Ventura had also trained the able Ajudhia Parshad in officiating as commander of the *Fauj-i-Khas* when he was on leave. After Ranjit Singh's death, the European position had become precarious, and with this battle over power in the Durbar, his main ally was Nau Nihal Singh. However, after his death he promised Maharajah Sher

---

24 Verma, *Foreigners at the Court*, p.6. Pearse, *Soldier and Traveller*, p.309.
25 Pearse, *Soldier and Traveller*, p.307.
26 Suri, *Umdat-ut-Twarikh*, Vol. 4, p.101.
27 Gardener states, 'This was the first and only steamer built for the Sikh monarchy.' Pearse, *Soldier and Traveller*, pp.202–203.
28 Suri, *Umdat-ut-Twarikh*, Vol. 3, p.318.

Singh of his loyalty. On seeing the court descend into chaos and the insubordination of the army and his own troops, he tried to resign but was given only leave. After Maharajah Sher Singh's death, seeing the writing on the wall, he made for Shimla then left India in 1844. Sohan Lal Suri states, 'Ventura Sahib, who was a brave and capable man, gifted with foresight, remarked that at that time the ill-going sky had taken a different revolution and the book of control and administration of Khalsa Ji had become absolutely scattered and that the changes of the sky did not seem to preserve the old style of the deceased Noble Sarkar.'[29] Ventura died in Toulouse, in the south of France on 3 April 1858.

Claude Auguste Court

Claude Auguste Court (1793–1880) was born in 1793 in Grasse, France and in 1812 he entered the *École Militaire Polytechnique*. A year later he joined the 68th Infantry Regiment of Napoleon's army as a commissioned officer. He was part of his French campaigns in the years between 1813 and 1815, and also at the Battle of Waterloo. With the swift changes permeating the country, he resigned in 1818. Looking abroad, he joined the service of Mohhamed Ali Mirza, the Shah of Persia and was to meet a certain Avitabile who was in service there. The fame and fortune of Allard and Ventura had spread across the world, and it was the latter who informed Court of the possibility of finding a role at Lahore. Similarly, like their counterparts, Court and Avitabile arrived in Panjab in 1827.

Ranjit Singh had already started his reforms and was now in need of additional artillery improvements. Colonel Gardener, on arriving in the Panjab, also commented on the course of army improvements, writing, 'At the time of my arrival at Lahore the Maharaja was in want of an instructor of artillery, M. Court being employed principally as superintendent of the gun-factory. He was a very amiable and accomplished man, as was General Ventura.'[30] He set about his task by consolidating the changes made by Allard and Ventura and proved himself to be an efficient artillery commander and ordnance officer. His pay was increased until it reached Rs2,500. In 1829, he married a Muslim woman, but she died in 1837 whereafter he constructed a mosque at his residence. He was later to marry a Kashmiri woman who converted to Christianity in due course. As a man fluent in various languages and historical research, he devoted much time to additional pursuits as well as his paid roles. This included research into antiquities and numismatics. He was particularly interested in the ruins between the Jhelum and Indus rivers. He produced the first archaeological surveys and maps of the Panjab and adjoining areas north-west as far as Kabul and was also one of the first to excavate and record the Buddhist sites and to collect coins

29   Suri, *Umdat-ut-Twarikh*, Vol. 4, p.268.
30   Pearse, *Soldier and Traveller*, p.180.

of the region.[31] His literary pursuits included writing for the *Journal of the Royal Asiatic Society* as well as two books, *Journey from Persia to Kabul* in French and then later translated into English and *A Brief Narrative of the Anarchy in the Punjab, 1839–45*.

As stated in the previous chapter, the *Topkhana* was organised into modern or European lines. Gardener states Court was placed in 'full command of a camp of eight horse-artillery guns. Two mortars and two howitzers. I was likewise deputed to teach most of the principal officers attached to the artillery, at the head of whom was General Sultan Mohamad Khan and several colonels.'[32] Court had moulded his troops into an effective fighting machine:

> ...their movements being executed with a celerity and precision that would have done honour to any army. The orders were given in French, and the system of gunnery used by that nation has also been adopted. At the conclusion of the exercise, we walked down the line and inspected the ordnance. The two guns on the right of the battery were six-pounders, and were the same that Lord William Bentinck had presented to Runjeet Singh at Roopur. The rest were cast by himself from their model, and appear almost equally good.[33]

For many observers, the work undertaken by General Court was breath-taking. Barr writes, 'When it is considered that all we saw was the work of the general's own knowledge, and we reflect on the difficulties he has had to surmount, it is a matter almost of wonder to behold the perfection to which he has brought his artillery.'[34] He worked with Lehna Singh Majithia and this fusion of Indian and European artillery methods would have been the catalyst for some of the improvements, including the casting of shells.[35] Indeed, his initial development of shells which was showcased at Ropar was worth Rs300,00 to Court.[36]

Court, whilst based at Lahore, also participated in some campaigns, including taking control over Nauner (Dera Baba Nanak) in 1833, a task he undertook with ease. He was also with the other *Ferengis* in the battle against Dost Mohammed Khan in 1835 and the occupation of Peshawar. Court was with Misr Sukh Raj (d.1842) stationed two *kos* (around 4 miles) from the Afghan forces. After experiencing victory there, in 1837 he was sent to quell the disturbances of the Afghans where he managed

---

31 It was assumed that his coin collection was lost until 1994 the sale of three small albums entitled *La Collection Numismatique du General Court* (book of rubbings) helped identify coins that were already at The British Museum. They were part of the coins purchased by Alexander Cunningham in 1880 and bequeathed to the museum between 1888–94.
32 Pearse, *Soldier and Traveller*, p.182.
33 Barr, *Journal of a March from Delhi*, p.259.
34 Barr, *Journal of a March from Delhi*, p.260.
35 Shells were manufactured by Raja Kalan, Lehna Singh, and Court in 1838. Suri, *Umdat-ut-Twarikh*, Vol. 3, p.475.
36 Hugel, *Travels In Kashmir And The Punjab*, p.329.

to push their forces back past Ali Majid. Interestingly, he also provided support to the EIC in their campaign to reinstate Shah Shuja on the throne of Kabul, proving successful at the operation of Garhi Dilsa Khan in May 1840. He was recommended for a dress of honour.

His brigade was equally dressed to impress. Barr writes, 'The men dressed something like our own horse [English] artillery, except that, instead of helmets, they wear red turbans (the Jamadars; or officers being of silk), which hang down as to cover the back part of the neck: white trousers, with long boots, black waist and cross belts and black leather scabbard with brass ornaments.'[37] The Maharajah would also inspect the foundries himself and even visited the cantonment of General Court. Suri states, '... the Maharaja went to the cantonment of Court Sahib and inspected the factory where the cannons were prepared and saw the iron-smiths, the carpenters, and the melted materials of the cannons.'[38]After the death of Ranjit Singh, his own troops decided to take action against him including attacking his house during the reign of Kharak Singh. He had served Nau Nihal Singh faithfully and was also liked by Maharajah Sher Singh, for whom he helped secure the Lahore Fort. The continued turbulence, which led to his master being killed, led him to cross the Sutlej and into British Ferozepur. He relinquished his post and after securing some recompense he returned to France with his wife, and he died in his native Grasse in 1861.

Paolo Di Avitabile

General Paolo Crescenzo Martino Avitabile, known as Paolo Di Avitabile, was from Naples, Italy. The corrupted name of *Abu Tabela* was frequently used. At the age of 16 he joined the Militia of Naples and at the time of Napoleon's occupation of the city, the army merged, allowing him to serve in his Royal Corps of Artillery. He rose to the rank of captain. However, in 1815 Naples became an independent state under the Bourbons, at which point he shifted allegiances to the new dynasty which he served until 1817. He was unable to be selected for promotion due to his serving under Napoleon, so he looked for other opportunities, arriving at the court of Mohammed Ali Mirza, Shah of Iran. He served there for six years between 1820–1826. He received information from General Ventura of the glory of the Panjab and together with his colleague Court he joined the Lahore Durbar in 1826. Avitabile served in the infantry on his arrival, where he was unable to make any major progression or impression on Ranjit Singh. He took part in the campaigns of Jasrota to confiscate some estates[39] and he also took part in the previously discussed campaign against Dost Mohammed Kahn in 1835. All was not lost, and on the recommendation of General

37   Barr, *Journal of a March from Delhi*, p.260.
38   15 August 1837. Suri, *Umdat-ut-Twarikh*, Vol. 3, p.372.
39   Suri, *Umdat-ut-Twarikh*, Vol. 3, pp.193–196.

Ventura, he was given administrative and civil duties and appointed as the Governor of Wazirabad and nearby territories.[40]

Lieutenant Barr observed the opulence of the *Ferengi*. The Europeans dressed lavishly and they also wore weapons of value:

> 'He wore an open horse-artillery full-dress jacket, displaying beneath it a red waist-coat, equally profusely ornamented with lace…sabres attached to embroidered belts, the plate of Avitabile's being of gold studded with valuable jewels, as was also his scabbard, a very small portion of green velvet being visible in the centre of it. The blade of his scimitar, which belonged to Akhbar, is a very superb one, and cost the governor 2,000 rupees, which, added to 1,000 more for the setting, may be considered a tolerably large sum for a weapon.'[41]

It was within the administrative functions that he shone and brought governance in the districts he managed, particularly at Peshawar which was given to him in 1835. Captain Henry Havelock observed at Peshawar, 'His reputation as an excellent governor had been fully established in the Punjab, and had even reached India, whilst he was in charge of the town and the surrounding country of Wuzeerabad.'[42] It was at this location that some members of the EIC were given passage on their campaign in Afghanistan and they had also stayed within his fortress at place of Bala Hisar. This was a well-built building made of sun-dried mud, able to withstand siege and attack. All commentators refer to his improvements at Peshawar which made it a prosperous location for trade. He also ensured that there was protection from the Afridis who attacked travellers; 'Between the Khyber Pass and Peshawer, the Afreedees were in the constant habit of rushing down from their hills, and plundering and wounding the Sikh villagers, till Avitabile erected a line of towers and guard-houses, which have had a good effect in controlling the depredations of the mountaineers in that quarter.'[43] Indeed General Avitabile issued a proclamation to the effect that any traveller from Kabul who visited any inhabitants in Peshawar, needed permission from him. Failure to do so would lead to severe punishment.[44]

40   On Ranjit Singh's visit to Wazirabad, Avitabile had prepared a map of the city which would help in the future. Suri, *Umdat-ut-Twarikh*, Vol. 3, p.168.

41   Barr, *Journal of a March from Delhi*, p.232.

42   Captain Havelock, 13th Regiment Light Infantry, later Major-General. He took part in the First Anglo-Afghan War of 1839. He fought in the First Anglo-Sikh War and the Indian Rebellion of 1857. The road named after him in Southall, London was renamed Guru Nanak Road in 2021. Many people were oblivious to the fact that Havelock had many Sikh serving under him. Captain Henry Havelock, *Narrative of the War in Afghanistan in 1838-39*, Vol. II (London: Henry Colburn, 1840), p.195.

43   James Atkinson, *The Expedition into Afghanistan; notes and sketches descriptive of the country, contained in a personal narrative during the campaign of 1839 and 1840. Up to the surrender of Dost Mahomed Khan* (London: W.H. Allen & co., 1842), pp.386–387

44   Ali, *The Sikhs and Afghans*, p.182.

Due to the various atrocities committed by the local populace, Avitabile ruled the city with an iron hand. This was not lost on his visitors and the inhabitants who were terrified to cause offence on the pain of death.[45] Indeed, he had big shoes to fill as the previous governor, Hari Singh Nalwa, ensured that he too had an imposing grip on the city. The Christian Missionary Joseph Wolff (1795–1862) refers to him as adding much to the town of Wazirabad and having a major presence in the area:[46]

> I arrived at the hospitable dwelling of Signor Avitabile, Governor-General of Vizir Abad [Wazirabad], in the service of Runjeet Singh. This ingenuous man has made this the finest town in the Punjaub, and added to it a new town with a gate, to which he has given the name of 'Ram Katera,' the quarter of God. He has established gallows, which he calls the ornament of civilization; for he has the power of life and death; but he is devoted to his Royal Master, and to the welfare of the country…He has made Vizirabad the asylum of the oppressed Cashmeerians, and his name is far known.[47]

However, these reports of capital punishment, justified or not, came to the notice of Maharajah Ranjit Singh who would intervene to ensure that sentencing was more humane. This led to Avitabile sending reports to Lahore advising of his decisions and land revenue collected.[48] He also advised on possible conquests including the country of the Isafzais, which could yield Rs500,000 per year.[49] He was also rewarded for his services and given various gifts during his time at Lahore.[50] It was Allard who suggested that Avitabile should be rewarded with a *Khila'at* for his services.[51] It was also in 1838 that he was given additional robes of honour and a medal. When Colonel Wade went to see the *Topkhana* of General Court, he had visited '…the camp of Avitabile and had observed the whole of Topkhana, well-equipped and well set, and he was himself making every effort to bring to a successful end every one of the affairs.'[52] He took an leave of absence in 1836 due to ill health but continued as governor from 1838 to 1842.

---

45   'We counted thirteen bodies, in all, on the gibbets around Peshawur, when we first arrived, and seven delinquents were executed during our stay.' Havelock, *Narrative of the War in Afghanistan*, p.200.

46   A Jewish Rabbi from Germany who converted to Christianity and became a zealous missionary.

47   Joseph Wolff, *Researches and Missionary Labours among the Jews, Mohammedans, and other sects by the Rev. Joseph Wolff During his travels between the years 1831 and 1834* (Philadelphia: Orrin Rogers, 1837), p.181.

48   Suri, *Umdat-ut-Twarikh*, Vol. 3, p.263.

49   Suri, *Umdat-ut-Twarikh*, Vol. 3, p.271.

50   Suri, *Umdat-ut-Twarikh*, Vol. 3, p.335, p.648.

51   'Allard Sahib said that, on account of good services rendered by Avitabile, he must be granted a special robe of honour.' Suri, *Umdat-ut-Twarikh*, Vol. 3, p.385.

52   Suri, *Umdat-ut-Twarikh*, Vol. 3, p.644.

On the retirement of General Allard, the additional responsibility fell on Ventura and Avitabile. The Maharajah wanted it to be known that it was business as usual;

> a letter was issued to Avitabile and Court Sahibs that they must maintain the convention of the troops according to the old custom and should not display any kind of slackness in any way and added that shortly after that troops would be appointed by the Noble Sarkar in their place. Letters were issued to the officers of the platoons, regiments and the Topkhana that they must always be obedient and loyal to Avitabile and that they must not go against him in any way.'[53]

The British were fond of the general as he had been hospitable to them and afforded them much support on their campaigns in Afghanistan. This was not pleasing to many in his division and they did not want to support the British, nor see Lahore supporting them. In 1841, he was attacked by his own troops due to delays in pay and them not being afforded the same privileges as some of their counterparts in Lahore. However, despite this, he continued to serve the Sikh Empire for several more years but eventually his governorship was removed. Staying aloof of the intrigues at Lahore, he left for Shimla in 1843, then reaching Calcutta (modern name Kolkata; hereafter simply Calcutta) and eventually returning to his native Naples. He died on 28 March 1850, after apparently being poisoned.

The French Flag

Interestingly, one flag which deserves consideration is the so-called French flag, generally considered to be that of tricolour and having inscriptions including the words *Degh-Tegh-Fateh*. Hugel states that he presented to the Maharajah Ranjit Singh a portrait of a 'Sikh, who holds the flag of the French legion, tri-colored, with Govind Singh on horseback.'[54]

Murray refers to the *Fauj-i-Khas* having their 'own emblems, the Eagle and tricolour flag with an inscription of the martial Guru Gobind Singh embroidered in it.'[55] Other commentators have also stated that they witnessed seeing a French flag carried by Sikh troops. It is interesting that whilst we see many of the red coloured standards captured during the Anglo-Sikh Wars there was very little evidence to support the idea of the French flags. However, some years ago I came to learn of a possible flag at Maidstone Museum which I was able to inspect.[56] The museum notes it as follows:

53   Suri, *Umdat-ut-Twarikh*, Vol. 3, p.621.
54   Hugel, *Travels In Kashmir And The Punjab*, p.336.
55   Letter from Dr. Murray to Colonel Wade quoted in Chopra, *The Punjab as A Sovereign State*, p.91.
56   I visited the museum in 2019 and inspected the French Flag and others in their possession.

Ranjit Singh Durbar with his courtiers and *Ferengis*. (G.W. Osbourne, *The Court and Camp of Runjeet Singh* (London: Henry Colburn, Publisher, 1840))

One of Three Sikh Colours. Sikh colour tri-colour pattern, rectangular. Five panels, blue, red white, blue, white with overlapping stripes, panels of 50cm circa. A unique flag from the Sikh Wars made for troops commanded by French. Historically mounted in oak diamond shaped case…Frame incorporated standards of the colours; silver tablet at bottom; badge missing from top; 149cm width, 177cm circa long. Main panels circa 50cm wide, first blue panel 20cm wide.[57]

This is the only known flag of the *Fauj-i-Khas* surviving today. A portrait of the flag and the red flags are shown in a portrait noting that they were captured by the 50th Queen's Own Regiment during the Anglo-Sikh Wars. Comparing the flag at Maidstone and the portrait, we can confirm that this is the French Flag used by the Sikhs. (See colour pages).

In conclusion, we can say that the European soldiers or *Ferengi* contributed immensely to the development of not just the military but also in administrative and political areas in the Empire. Their service was absorbed into the burgeoning Sikh Empire and, if anything, the innovations of military expertise were synthesised with the traditional Sikh soldiery from the Misl period. This is why the old methods of warfare were not dispensed with completely and instead the European units were added on. There is, however, one point of note and that is whilst they played a great

57   As per Maidstone Museum's records and details sent to me by staff members.

role during the time of the Maharajah, they were unable to completely follow-through during the Sikh Wars and this would have been an interesting arena to see their innovations in action against the British. They did, however, leave their tactics and drills in place, so in essence, their mark was still felt in the Sikh Wars. It would seem that the Sikhs were underestimated by the EIC. But the work of these *Ferengi* was done and left to the commanders to follow up. Within forty years, the Maharajah had created an elite body of soldiers which surpassed many of those which had been seen before:

> ...if you could but have seen the splendour of the sight we saw this morning, you would simply have died of it. As it is, you will only turn sleepy over the description. But I think that the entrance to the camp this morning was the finest thing I ever saw anywhere. There were altogether four miles of Runjeet's soldiers drawn up in lines. We passed through a mile-and-a-half of them – his bodyguard. A great number of these are uniformly dressed in bright orange turbans, tunics and trousers, the others provide their own dresses for which they have an enormous allowance. They are all of the same form, made of 'kincob' – gold and silver . . . cloth of every possible shade of colour. They have long black or white beards half down to their waists and a large expenditure of shawls and scarves disposed in drapery about them. Their matchlocks are inlaid with gold or steel or silver, and some of them with bows and arrows, some with long spears, and all the chief ones with . . . black heron's plumes. Everything about them is showy and glittering – their horses with their gold or silver hangings, their powder flasks embroidered with gold.[58]

---

58   Emily Eden describing her arrival at Amritsar on the 12th December, 1837 with her brother Governor-General Auckland. Janet Dunbar (ed.), *Tigers Durbars And Kings Fanny Eden's Indian Journals* (London: John Murray, 1988), p.180.

7

Lehna Singh Majithia: Inventor and Technologist

Lehna Singh Majithia was one of the leading administrators and military leaders in Maharajah Ranjit Singh's court.[1] However, unlike his contemporaries, he was able to surpass their accomplishments with his own abilities in astronomy, architecture, mathematics, and literature and military inventions; hence he was a polymath. Similar to many of the other individuals we have recounted here, his work has seldom been discussed and hence it is befitting to analyse his role during the Sikh Empire. Lehna Singh was the son of Desa Singh, belonging to the well-known and illustrious family of the village Majithia. Desa Singh was a capable administrator who held senior command within the Sikh Empire. He governed Amritsar and upon his death in 1832, Lehna Singh took over the territories and his duties. The Majithia soldiers served under Ranjit Singh with at least ten of them being counted during the Durbar, the three main ones being Surat Singh, Amar Singh and Lehna Singh.

A robe of honour, consisting of eleven pieces of valuable cloth, *Jigha* (an ornament of gold worn on the turban) and a *Turra*, or tassel, and gold earrings, was sent by the Maharajah for Lehna Singh. He was appointed governor of the hill territory between the Ravi and the Sutlej, the appointment which he held until the beginning of 1844. The sardar, however, did not reside in the hills, but at Amritsar, or at Majithia, and made periodical tours in the states under his charge to examine accounts and make any necessary fiscal and administration arrangements. He was in charge of the Harimandir Sahib, an office of great honour, which his father had held before him.[2] He was to become the governor of Kangra. Yet during his life, he pursued a life of intellectual pursuits unmatched by anyone within the court. He was given the prestigious title of *Hussam-ud Daula* (the sword of the state).[3] Lehna Singh had served the Sikh Empire with great distinction and one of his first campaigns was at the battle

---

1   Lehna Singh is sometimes confused with Lehna Singh of the Bhangi Misl and Lehna Singh of the Sandhanwalia clan.
2   Latif, *History Of The Panjab*, p.458.
3   Griffin, *Chiefs And Families Of Note*, p.420.

of Multan in 1818. He was also sent to seize the possessions and territories of Sada Kaur, who had once guided Ranjit Singh. She was taken prisoner and that was the end of the Kanhaya Misl, as no one came to her aid. In 1825, on the death of Diwan Mokham Chand, part of the irregular company or *Ghorchurahs* was placed under the command of Lehna Singh.[4]

Lehna Singh exhibited excellent diplomacy skills and was sent on occasion to negotiate treaties. On the ascension of the reign of Kharak Singh in 1839, he was sent to Shimla to continue dialogue with the British over territories.[5] Similarly, in 1842 he was deputed by the Lahore Court to wait upon Governor-General Ellenborough (1790–1871) at Ferozepore.[6] He held a superior command and was also responsible for deputing many other sardars in his care including the Ramgharia sardars, the most famous of which was Mangal Singh Ramgharia (1800–79), who later became custodian of the Harimandir Sahib.[7] The Majithia sardars also had many feudal retainers. In the internecine war between the Sikhs, Lehna Singh sided with Prince Sher Singh, providing his army to help in removing Rani Chand Kaur. He also was also called upon to settle disputes amongst families and the dividing of *Jagirs*.

When the Christian Missionary Lowrie met the sardar, whilst trying to seek out his religious convictions and thoughts on Christianity, he was drawn to the instruments in his care, and '...seeing a thermometer and compass lying on the table, he soon showed that he perfectly understood the uses of each, and wished to know why the magnet always pointed to the North.'[8] He was aware of the healing properties of metal; he was inquisitive about magnetic properties and he possessed instruments of whose use and purpose he was examining. Lowrie was impressed with his scientific questions and knowledge. The aforementioned Alexander Burnes had not seen much invention on his travels, but upon meeting Lehna Singh he was surprised by '...his knowledge of mathematics, of the movement of the stars and his insatiable curiosity about the working of scientific instruments. He presented the sardar with a thermometer.'[9]

4   *Khalsa Durbar Records, Vol. 1,* p.109.
5   Griffin, *Chiefs and Families of Note,* Vol.1, p.297.
6   Edward Law, 1st Earl of Ellenborough, a British Tory politician, who was four times President of the Board of Control of the EIC and also served as Governor-General of India between 1842–1844. Griffin, *Chiefs and Families of Note*, Vol. 1, p.299.
7   Mangal Singh was the nephew of Jassa Singh Ramgharia. Under the British, he was the custodian of the Harimandir Sahib from 1862 till his death in 1879. In 1876, the Prince of Wales conferred upon him the honour of CSI or Companionship of the Order of Star of India.
8   *The Foreign Missionary Chronicle*, Volumes 3–4 (Pittsburgh: M. Maclean Printer, 1835), p.185.
9   Madan Gopal, *Dyal Singh Majithia* (New Delhi: Publication Division, Ministry of Information and Broadcasting, Govt. of India, 1994).

Architecture

Lehna Singh left his mark on the city of Amritsar through various engineering and architectural pursuits, and a gold plate at the entrance to the sanctum sanctorum records the name of Maharajah Ranjit Singh. It reads: 'The Guru was kind enough to allow the privilege of service to the temple to his humble servant Sri Maharaja Singh Sahib Ranjit Singh.' It was due to the devotion of the Maharajah that the Harmandir Sahib was covered with gold-plated copper sheets. However, the name of sardar Lehna Singh Majithia, written at the marbled *Dalhij* (steps) of the entrance to the sanctum sanctorum is now barely visible.[10] The *Pradaksina* or circumambulatory path around the Harimandir Sahib was also the work of the great sardar. He arranged for the flooring to be covered in marble. He sent Ahmed Yar, brother of Muhammad Yar Mistri, to Makrana quarry in Rajasthan. Ahmed Yar despatched marble for nine months from Makrana and the work of covering the floor was completed in 1834.[11] This great Sikh intellect, with his remarkable engineering skills, made an invaluable contribution to the expansion of the Harmandir Sahib. In fact, the stone inlay and the murals by painters from the famous Kangra School of Art were executed under his supervision. Lehna Singh also designed the Ram Bagh gardens in Amritsar, filling it with rare specimens of trees and fountains. Other improvements made at the Harimandir Sahib included the repairing of the *Nishan Sahibs*. The first wooden flag post was erected by Udasi Pritam Das and it broke in 1823. This was replaced with an iron stand with gold plates on it by Desa Singh but it eventually fell down in 1841. Lehna Singh improved on the design and raised another gold standard in its place. Sher Singh, on his enthronement as Maharajah in 1841, placed another flag by its side, with more costly gold plating.[12]

One of his most interesting inventions was that of a *Dhupghari* or sundial, which shows the time, date and lunar changes. Located at the bridge which connects the *Darshan Deori* (gateway) to the Harimandir Sahib is something quite unusual. On either side of the bridge are fixed ten marble lamp posts with gold lanterns on them. A fine marble railing runs throughout the length between the lamp posts. However, on the left side, a lamp post bears a sundial instead of a lantern. This is actually fixed on a pillar between the fifth and sixth lamp post. This is usually completely missed by worshippers to their visit at the holiest shrine of the Sikhs. This instrument can be described as follows: 'There seem to be two scales in the rectangular border; the outer one of modern hours, with sub-divisions marked for 30 minutes and 10 minutes,

---

10   Sundar Singh Ramgharia, *Guide to the Darbar Sahib or Golden Temple of Amritsar* (Lahore: Mufid-i-Am Press, 1903), p.25. It reads that the pavement around the Harimandir Sahib was constructed by sardar Lehna Singh Majithia through Gurmukh Singh Gyani.

11   P.S.Arshi, *The Golden Temple – History Art And Architecture* (New Delhi, Harman Publishing House, 1989), p.61

12   Arshi, *The Golden Temple*, p.67.

Sundial at the Harimandir Sahib.

and the inner one of the traditional *ghatis* (of 24 minutes), subdivided in ½ ghaṭis.'[13] (A *ghati* is an Indian unit of time.) Sundar Singh Ramgharia in 1903 records the Gurmukhi engraving as follows: 'The Sun-dial was devised and made by sardar Lahna Singh of Majthia in 1909 [1852]. In 1951 [1894] the pillar and sundial were renewed in marble under the superintendence of Bhai Gurbaksh Singh, Gyani.'[14]Another astronomical instrument or weapon created by Lehna Singh was a 'singular iron sun-dial; called a Pratoda or Pratola, (serving also for an hour-glass a gun and a spear)

13   S. R. Sarma, *A Descriptive Catalogue of Indian Astronomical Instruments* (Germany: author, 2021), p.3646.
14   Ramgharia, *Guide to the Darbar Sahib*, p.23

believed to have been made by him for Lord Hardinge.'[15] This was notably made after the Anglo-Sikh Wars.

As well as these innovations he assisted in the development of a Sanskrit astrological chart called the *Sarvasiddhantattvacudamani* or 'The Crest-Jewel of the Essence of all Systems of Astronomy.' It was written by Durgashankar Pathak from Benares (modern name Varanasi). This was a centre of learning for many Indian scholars. The text contains a comparison in Sanskrit of the astronomical systems of Europe, Islam, and India.[16] The text is now understood to have been commissioned after 1845 by Lehna Singh Majithia and provides us with a better understanding of his genius.[17] The text contains allusions to Hindu deities as would be expected as per the author's roots in the Brahminical tradition. The text then goes on to provide horoscopes of Guru Nanak, Guru Gobind Singh, Ranjit Singh and Lehna Singh. The text is furnished with elaborate depictions of each of them except surprisingly Ranjit Singh. The horoscope has only been properly translated recently and can be read as follows:

The lotus named Laihna Singh excels, which grew in the lake of nectar (Amritsar), which is filled with the pollens of fame of, and made to bloom by, the Sun, [that is] Ranjit Singh.

May this glorious Laihna Singh flourish! He is endowed with radiance; he vanquished the Muslim rulers with his valour and other virtues; expert in the observance of the daily rituals and conduct; brave, devotee of Guru [Nanak], one who has a detailed knowledge of military formations and hunting, one who collects tributes from [other] chiefs, the foremost of the valiant, the crest-jewel of the chiefs, the producer of victory.[18]

This new revelation emphasises the importance that Lehna Singh held as well as his focus on astronomy. There are well-illustrated portraits of him within the text. One shows him using the telescope and sitting with his alleged mentor in technical matters, Sivalala Pathaka. The other shows him sitting with Durgashankar Pathak, the writer of the text, together with his own son, Dyal Singh, who would later become famous

15   Journal of the Asiatic Society of Bengal. v.29, 1860.
16   The manuscript is held at the British Library: MS or.5259. It has been erroneously been given attribution to Prince Kharak Singh as well as being said to containing Nau-Nihal Singh's horoscope. However, based on recent research, it actually contains the horoscope of Lehna Singh and other details which confirm the importance of this manuscript. See C.A. Bayly, *Empire and Information: Intelligence Gathering and Social Communication in India, 1780–1870* (Cambridge: Cambridge University Press, 1999), p.254.
17   S. R. Sarma, 'Who is the Native of the Sarvasiddhantatattvacudamani?', *History of Science in South Asia*, 9, (2021), 167–208. https://doi.org/10.18732/hssa57. I have removed the diacritics for clarity.
18   S. Sarma, 'Who is the Native', p.176

in his own right in the nineteenth century.[19] The portrait also shows a number of astronomical instruments including an armillary sphere, two globes, a sine quadrant, and a Jacob's staff. This is together with a telescope, a universal equatorial sundial. Both Lehna Singh and Durgashankar have their pocket watches in front of them. (See colour pages). Another text with which he was involved was Euclid's *Elements* (Euclid was a 3rd–4th century BCE Greek mathematician, known as the 'Father of Geometry') which he translated from Arabic into Panjabi.

Diplomatic missions

Ranjit Singh was greatly impressed by Lehna Singh's diplomatic finesse and, therefore, sent him on several diplomatic missions to negotiate with the British on important political matters. In this role, he met Lord William Bentinck and escorted Lord Auckland. Lord Ellenborough, in the letter addressed by the Maharajah to his officers, refers to Lehna Singh as 'the great and the wise', whom he met as part of his diplomatic mission to escort Alexander Burnes to Lahore in 1831.[20] Together with Prince Sher Singh in 1837, he escorted General Henry Fane (1778–1840), Commander-in-Chief of the EIC forces, for the nuptials of Prince Nau Nihal Singh. According to the fictional account of Colonel Bellasis in *Adventures Of An Officer In The Punjab*, it is stated, 'My new ally will be mentioned more at large hereafter; suffice it now to say that he was a mechanic and an astronomer, as well as a good soldier and a virtuous man. He was by far the best specimen of the Sikh Surdars.'[21] When trying to attain favour with the polymath, he wrote, 'The fame of Lena Singh has burst the bounds of the Punjab, it has swept to the furthest comers of Hindustan, and has reached the western countries, where the wise men pant to become acquainted with the Plato of the age, the Aristotle of the East.'[22] Whilst the description maybe farfetched, it was still an indictment of the talents of Lehna Singh.

19   Dyal Singh was chairman of the Punjab National Bank, but widely known for establishing *The Tribune* newspaper in Lahore in 1881,
20   Burnes, *Travels in Bokhara*, Vol. 3, p.103.
21   The account, whilst fictional, was written by Major Lawrence (1806–1857) who spent much time in the Panjab and had direct contact with many of the key players there. He is best known as being in the group of administrators known as the Lawrence brothers in the Panjab after the Anglo-Sikh Wars; he died at the Siege of Lucknow during the Indian Mutiny. Major H. M. L. Lawrence, *Adventures Of An Officer In The Punjab (Vol. 1)* (New Delhi: Punjab National Press, 1970), pp.76–77.
22   Lawrence, *Adventures Of An Officer In The Punjab*, pp.160–161.

Military Inventions

The most important of Lehna Singh's innovations was that he excelled in manufacturing 'ultra-modern' weapons, including cannons and pistols, some of them even superior to those used by the British forces. These accelerated the development of artillery to such an extent that by the late 1830s, the Sikh artillery rivalled that of the East India Company in both quantity and quality. All this shows the technical and artistic expertise of those working in the Sikh foundries and workshops. There is a barrel, produced in Lahore in 1838, which is based on the British Light 6-pounder, while the carriage takes its idea from the Bengal artillery pattern introduced in 1823. He was also involved in the development of shrapnel shells (1831) and other ammunition types. When the sardar took over command of the *Topkhana* of Mohammed Khan in 1838 he was instructed '...to look to various repairs that were needed and submit to the Maharaja the estimate of money required to set them right so that the same be awarded to him and he be enabled to put the gunners to drill everyday.'[23] This was a role in which he was comfortable in undertaking.

Baron Hugel, upon being escorted by Lehna Singh, noted a cannon manufactured by him and interestingly a British-manufactured gun was offered to him:

> Lena Singh, accompanied me on his elephant a good way out of the city, attended by a servant carrying a double-barrelled gun, and to my surprise on taking it in my hand, I found a new and beautiful Joe Manton, which he, according to custom, offered to me, and which I, of course, refused. Before the gate lay an immense gun formed of metal cast from iron bars. I asked how old it was, and how it came there, and was told by the Thanadar [Lehna Singh] that he had only recently manufactured it, and expected to receive the carriage for it from Lahor.[24]

Osbourne notes that Ranjit Singh:

> ...introduced one of his Sirdars to us, Llana Sing [Lehna Singh], who is a clever mechanic, and in great favour with Runjeet from his success in casting shrapnell shells, an instrument of war he has been very anxious to possess ever since his interview with Lord William Bentinck at Roper [October 1831] where he first saw them used. They are of pewter, and answer the purpose very well.'[25]

---

23   Suri, *Umdat-ut-Twarikh*, Vol. 3, p.397.
24   Hugel, *Travels In Kashmir And The Punjab*, p.396. Joseph Manton (1766–1835) was a gunsmith who innovated the sport of shooting, improved weapon quality, and paved the way for the modern artillery shell. He however was at odds with the British army and this led to court cases over payments due to him. This led him to become bankrupt. One of his workers was James Purdey would later go on to form James Purdey & Sons, a manufacturer of specialist high-end bespoke sporting shotguns and rifles.
25   Osbourne, *The Court and Camp of Runjeet Singh*, p.80.

Colonel Baird Smith of the Asiatic Society remarked on the quality of his workman-ship, including the previously described Pratoda sundial as well as the manufacture of cannons:

> Lena Singh Majeteeah, the constructor of the Pratoda Dial, was the representa-tive of a well-known distinguished Sikh family. He did not take any very promi-nent part in the Sikh campaign [First Sikh War], but his brother Runjoor Singh commanded the Khalsa army at the battle of Aliwal where, as all know, he was signally overthrown by the force under Sir Harry Smith. On that occasion an exquisitely beautiful battery of six field guns, the property of Lena Singh, and the produce, probably, of the same workshops which produced the Pratoda Dial, was captured. Nothing could surpass the whole design and details of these guns, and while they were ornamented with great taste, they were at the same time good working guns, and had been vigorously used during the day. Lena Singh had very considerable mechanical capacity. He enjoyed greatly hearing of all forms of mechanical invention. The long range and explosion shells for guns were favourite subjects of experiment and discussion with him, and he was altogether a notable man among his race, and in his position as a Sikh Chieftain of large possessions, having strong intellectual tendencies in spite of the semi-barbarism amid which he lived.[26]

This gives us important information about his factories, which would have been manufacturing many types of devices and mechanisms. More importantly, we can now also link the cannons that were manufactured by him and used within the Sikh wars. This would also infer that his guns might have been provided to his half-brother Ranjodh Singh at Buddowal and Aliwal.[27] His designs were possibly superior to the European types, even though after the wars some thought they were odd and would not have worked:

> A fancy existed to obtain the use of a mortar from an howitzer, by fitting its carriage with a sliding transom, on withdrawing which, the howitzer could be elevated to 45 degrees, its cascable resting on an additional transom fixed underneath. Major Green constructed a carriage of this kind in 1796, which was experimented on at Dum-Dum, and spoken favourably of, but eventually not found to answer, and therefore discarded.
>
> Whether the result of imitation, or of half-informed mechanical taste, we find Lena Sing Majeetiah, commandant of the Punjab artillery, indulging in a

26 'For November, 1860', *Journal of the Asiatic Society of Bengal*, Vol. 29 (Calcutta: Printed by C.B Lewis, Baptist Mission Press, 1860), pp.424–427.
27 Ranjodh Singh would be joined by Ajit Singh of Ladwa (Karorasinghia Misl). They failed however to take the advantage of the situation and would be defeated at the battle of Aliwal a few days later.

similar fantasy: a carriage adapted for the double purpose. It is scarcely possible that such a one could be useful; the shock acting vertically on the axle, would be too severe for any moderate dimensions to bear; this was found in Major Green's carriage, and the proposed remedy was shortening the axle, which would, while strengthening, have rendered it very likely to overturn.[28]

However, it was this type of technology that was perfected by Lehna Singh, an example of which exists today at Quila Mubarak, Patiala. This type of ordnance allowed the Khalsa to punch well above their weight and was underestimated by the British.[29] Kashmiri artisans and trained craftsmen were under the supervision of officers like Lehna including Faqir Nur-ud-Din, Doctor Honigberger and other Europeans who carried on the work of casting, boring, polishing and decorating guns and pistol barrels. His units were always considered to be fit for purpose, and in regular parades, Lehna Singh's artillery on review was always up to the mark. [30]

Proposals for Prime Minister

During Rani Chand Kaur's brief regime, it was proposed to appoint Lehna Singh as the prime minister, but he was considered too mild a person for such a challenging task which needed ruthlessness and the twisting of politics. During the impending Anglo-Sikh Wars, Lehna Singh's skills would have been much needed but he decided to vacate the Sikh Empire which was combusting in all directions. In March 1844, Lahina Singh fell afoul of Pandit Jalla's (d. 1844) regime and, feeling insecure at Lahore, he left the Panjab for Haridwar. This was noted by the Panjabi poet Shah Mohammed, in his monumental epic *Jangnamah*, who wrote about his leaving at this critical time.[31] He left the management of his estates to his half-brother Ranjodh Singh Majithia. His *Jagirs* were promptly confiscated and usurped by Hira Singh. Lehna Singh settled in Banaras, where he could pursue his astronomical studies. He declined to return to the Panjab after various letters and solicitations were sent by the Lahore Durbar.

28   E. Buckle, *Memoir of the services of the Bengal artillery from the formation of the corps to the present time with some account of its internal organization*, ed. J. W. Kaye, (London: W.H. Allen and Co., 1852), pp.180–181.
29   Thanks to Neil Carleton for supplying me with this information.
30   Nau-Nihal Singh had 'reviewed Sirdar Luhna Singh's Artillery and given a horse with a golden saddle, a gun and five hundred rupees to the Surdar as well as two hundred rupees to his Golundazes,' newsletter dated 10 June 1839 quoted in Singh, *The Panjab in 1839–40*, pp.42–43.
31   He describes Lehna Singh as the 'epitome of wisdom' and as someone who did not want to get involved in the intrigues and political machinations taking place. P.K. Nijhawan, *The First Punjab War Shah Mohammed's Jangnamah*, (Amritsar: Singh Brothers, 2001), p.115. Henceforth *Jangnamah*.

He was once again offered the office of Wazir, this time by Maharani Jind Kaur during her regency, but he refused this offer. Due to Ranjodh Singh's fight with the British at Buddowal and Aliwal, Lehna Singh was also implicated; 'The Governor-General has determined that the property of Leina Sing Mujithea in our provinces shall be held responsible for the damage which has been, or may be done to the station of Loodhiana by the instrumentality of that sardar's representative and manager.'[32] As a result, his movements were restricted and he was kept under surveillance and any contact with the Panjab was prevented. On his arrest, he protested, as was described by Captain M. F. Gordon to the Governor-General:

> He said that to escape from the disturbances in the Panjab he had left it, more than two years ago, against the wishes of Hira Singh and others, who had since then frequently solicited him to return, but he was tired of their intrigues and dissensions and had disregarded their invitations . . . he ought not, he maintained, to be held responsible for the acts of his brother, which he had not prompted, nor could he control them; and he dwelt particularly on the indignity which, he said, had been put upon him, by surrounding his house with sepoys, seizing the arms of his followers and making himself a prisoner.[33]

He felt he was been victimised for no other reason than being Ranjodh Singh's brother; on the contrary, he provided letters showing the Lahore Durbar begging him to return. His counsel would have been welcome in the affairs of the Panjab as well as the innovations for which he had become famous. During March 1846, news arrived from the Panjab that hostilities between the Sikhs and the British Government had ceased and that 'friendship' had been re-established between the two powers. On 6 March, 1846, it was stated that:

> The President in Council is of opinion that in consideration of the late progress of events in the war with the Seikhs, Sirdar Lehna Sing may be properly relieved from the condition of surveillance in which, on requisition from the Governor-General, he has for some time been held, and His Honour in Council, therefore, desires that the guard now stationed at the Sirdar's residence may be withdrawn.'[34]

In 1846, Henry Lawrence, who was now the British Resident, also suggested his nomination as Wazir in place of Lal Singh, but Governor-General Hardinge did not accept the proposal. Lehna Singh returned to the Panjab in 1851, but two years later went back to Banaras where he died in 1854.

---

32 Ganda Singh, 'The Arrest and Release of Sardar Lahna Singh Majithia', *Proceedings of Indian Historical Congress* (Allahabad: General Secretary, Indian History Congress, 1940), pp.392–399.
33 Singh, 'The Arrest and Release of Sardar Lahna Singh', pp.392–399.
34 The Officiating Secretary to the Government of India, Foreign Department.

The contribution of Lehna Singh to science, astronomy and artillery in the Panjab has yet to be fully recognised and his work deserves greater recognition for his achievements. The Panjab looked to him for leadership, but it was apparent that his strengths lay in the pursuits of the mind, which could contribute to the great heritage of the Panjab. His contribution to the cannons was a pivotal one, adding to the strength of the Khalsa army. His legacy can be seen throughout Amritsar and within the precincts of the Harimandir Sahib.

8

Hari Singh Nalwa: Conqueror and Commander-in-Chief

The houses of the Sukerchakia and Uppal clans, from which Hari Singh descended, are linked, going back to the eighteenth century. During the testing time of the *Vadhha Ghallughara*, Hari Singh's grandfather Hardas Singh lost his life fighting against Ahmed Shah Abdali. Hari Singh (1791–1837) was born in Gujranwala to the family of Gurdas Singh Uppal and Dharam Kaur. Gurdas Singh had joined the Sukerchakia Misl and was a great warrior, firstly under Charhat Singh and then Mahan Singh. The Uppal family had conquered the territory of Balloki, in the region of Kasur. When he died in 1798, Hari Singh was around seven years old and was then brought up by his mother. He undertook the Khalsa rites of initiation shortly afterwards at the age of ten. He started learning horse riding and archery skills at this early age. He also learnt languages including Persian which would keep him in good stead in the future. Tradition notes that in 1804 during a hunting expedition, a tiger attacked Hari Singh and killed his horse. In a moment of courage, he single-handedly held open the tiger's mouth and ripped it apart, hence he was given the appellation of *Nalwa*.[1] This term has generally been referred to as tiger claws or tiger killer.[2] At the age of 13, this was indeed a brave feat which was noted by all who witnessed it. Baron Hugel, the German traveller, on meeting Hari Singh surprised him by being aware of this heroic feat:

> Hari Singh's manner and conversation are very frank and affable; and having acquainted myself beforehand with the history of this most distinguished

---

1   However it is noteworthy that he did not use the appellation himself. It was popularised later in the nineteenth century. Vanit Nalwa, *Hari Singh Nalwa Champion of the Khalsaji*, 1791–1837 (New Delhi: Manohar, 2009), p.324.

2   An alternative suggestion based on family tradition recounts the story of Raja Nal from the epic *Mahabharata*. The Raja kills a tiger in the story. So the suggestion is that Ranjit Singh was present when Hari Singh killed the tiger and exclaimed 'Wah Mere Raja Nal, Wah' – Well done my Raja Nal Wa, which was then abbreviated into Nalwa. Nalwa, *Hari Singh Nalwa*, pp.24–25.

member of Ranjit's court, I surprised him by my knowledge whence he had gained the appellation of Nalwa, and of his having cloven the head of a tiger who had already seized him as its prey. He told the Diwan to bring some drawings, and gave me his portrait, in the act of killing the beast.[3]

Prinsep also notes the sardar's killing of the tiger: 'Huree Singh Nalooa, a Sikh Jageerdar, who had killed a tiger single- handed on horse-back, with the sacrifice, however, of his horse.'[4] When Hari Singh was 14, he joined the service of Maharajah Ranjit Singh where he showed letters detailing his lineage and family association with the Sukerchakia Misl. This was timely as Ranjit Singh started recruiting the sons of sardars at an early age for warfare. Impressed with Hari Singh Nalwa's commitment and family associations, he sent him for training amongst the 'boys' regiment' within the Sikh army.[5]

Hari Singh accompanied Ranjit Singh in his early campaigns and showed all the signs of becoming a great warrior. He was made a sardar and given command of the Sher Dil Regiment consisting of 800 horsemen and infantry, which was more than some of his experienced counterparts.[6] Nalwa as a commander of the Khalsa forces was either in charge of or directly participated in 20 major battles. These were pivotal to the advancement of the Sikh Empire and include Kasur (1807), Sialkot (1807), Attock (1813), Kashmir (1814), Multan (1818), Peshawar (1818 – becomes tributary), Shopian (1819), Mangal (1821), Mankara (1821), Naushera (1823), Sirikot (1824), Saidu (1827), Peshawar (1834 – annexed) and Jamrud (1836). By examining the KDR, we have knowledge of the expenditure incurred by the Khalsa general for his uniforms, saddles, matchlock, tents, banners, camels, cooking, utensils, and musical instruments which came in at a cost of Rs16, 526. The pay of Hari Singh's men was Rs42,791 for combatants and Rs264 for combatants within his establishment.[7]

Yet Nalwa's life in the Sikh Empire was synonymous with his governorships of troublesome areas, namely Kashmir (1820–21), Greater Hazara (1822–37), and Peshawar (1834–36). Hari Singh was responsible for expanding the frontier of the Sikh Empire beyond the Indus River right up to the mouth of the Khyber Pass. This is why Hari Singh was considered the most feared and able amongst the ranks of the Khalsa.[8] He

---

3   Hugel, *Travels In Kashmir And The Punjab*, p.254. This informs us that Hari Singh would have had portraits commissioned of this heroic act.

4   Prinsep, *Origin of the Sikh Power*, p.23.

5   Surinder Singh Johar, *Sikh Warrior: Hari Singh Nalwa* (Delhi: National Book Shop, 2012), p.14.

6   Desa Singh Majithia (400 horsemen), Hukum Singh Chimmi (200 horsemen and infantry), Nihal Singh Attariwala (500 horsemen and infantry). Singh, *Sikh Warrior: Hari Singh Nalwa*, p.15.

7   Kohli, 'The organisation of the Khalsa Army', p.70.

8   Interestingly, in 2014 according to a poll by Australia Millionaires, Nalwa was considered No. 1 in their 'Top Ten World Conquerors.'

did not shirk from his duties and was seen as the mighty vanquisher of the regions from which the Sikhs had faced hordes of Afghan invaders for centuries.

The Early Battles

Kasur, in 1801, was one of the first targets for Ranjit Singh after his investiture as Maharajah. It was ruled by the Pathan chief, Nizam-ud-Din. This would lead to a protracted affair for several years. Early expeditions to take the territory proved ineffective and support was given to the Nizam-ud-din by Sahib Singh Bhangi. The Pathan chief eventually paid *Nazrana* and lent some of his men to Ranjit Singh. Trouble brewed a year later, and the Lahore Durbar subdued the fort and received tribute. After Nizam-ud-din's death, Nawab Qutab-ud-din took over and the area again gave trouble, but after a siege last several months, the Nawab surrendered. It was in February 1807 that the Nawab once again challenged the authority of Ranjit Singh, this time under Jodh Singh Ramgharia; Kasur was attacked. Hari Singh Nalwa accompanied the commander and was in charge of one division of the army. After communication lines had been cut, food supplies ran short within the fort and artillery was used to level the city walls. After a month, Qutub-ud-din surrendered and the Sikhs plundered the city and treasury, gaining jewels, shawls, and animals.[9] Hari Singh showed his military prowess in the battle and was showered with praise and was given a *Jagir*. It was the first feather in the turban for the young Hari Singh.[10]

Multan

Multan was a rich fertile area in the southern part of Panjab, and it held a strategic position as a centre of trade with countries across the Bolan Pass; there was also a direct route to Kandahar. It was close to Lahore and so posed a threat to Ranjit Singh. Initial attempts to conquer the area in 1802 resulted in the defenders under Nawab Muzaffar Khan having limited strength in comparison to the Khalsa forces, and so he offered *Nazrana* and paid tribute to the Maharajah. In 1806, and again in 1807, *Nazrana* was given, but the latter attempt at a conquest still did not result in the capture of the fort. In 1810, the fort was again attacked and the neighbouring Muslim chiefs all paid a tribute, fearing their territories would also be subdued. Nawab Muzaffar Khan remained steadfast in his opposition, however. Ranjit Singh himself commanded the operation, with big guns installed outside Hathi and Khizri gates. After heavy bombardment there was still a stalemate, so it was decided to lay mines under the walls of the fort. This operation was hazardous, with death almost

9   Latif, *History Of The Panjab*, p.367.
10 Singh, *Sikh Warrior: Hari Singh Nalwa*, pp.18–20.

a certainty, at least from the Pathans firing from the walls. The Maharajah asked for the bravest men to volunteer for the mission. Hari Singh Nalwa was the first to stand up followed by Nihal Singh Attariwala (father of Sham Singh) and Attar Singh Dhari. Numbering seventy-five in total, they proceeded towards the fort. After indiscriminate firing by the Nawab's soldiers, many of the Sikhs were killed and Attar Singh Dhari and his battery were blown up. Even deploying the Zamzama Gun had no effect on the besieged. During this time, Diwan Mokham Chand, commander of the overall forces fell ill, and Nihal Singh and Hari Singh were injured. Whilst, not a success, this gave the Maharajah thoughtful insights into the early phase of siege mechanics, an area that required additional science and strategy. Ranjit Singh, however, received a tribute and service from the Nawab's soldiers. The Khalsa soldiers who placed the mines were rewarded with *Jagirs*, with Hari Singh Nalwa receiving Rs20,000.[11] More importantly, this raised the profile of Hari Singh amongst the army and his peers.

In 1816, again Multan was attacked, *Nazrana* was obtained, and Sikh forces moved to Mankara where the fort was bombarded with heavy artillery. Hari Singh was instrumental in the capture of this territory. He was rewarded with a *Jagir* at the famous location of Gujranwala, which was the envy of all, even Ranjit Singh's son, Prince Kharak Singh. The services rendered by Hari Singh were amply rewarded and he set about developing the area, including repairing the old fort, adding a bungalow and encouraging people to move into the area. In 1818, the Lahore forces again attacked Multan with Hari Singh as a commanding general. The final battle of the fort took place with better use of artillery under Ilahi Bakhsh and Jamadar Khushal Singh. After the Akalis has breached the fort wall, it was all over. Nawab Muzzafar Khan and his sons all died in the encounter. Ranjit Singh finally secured the victory which alluded him for many years, the area was plundered and this brought great wealth to the treasury of Lahore as well great riches of the city. Hari Singh Nalwa was pivotal in the victory and his *Jagir* was doubled as a result of the conquest.

Ranjit Singh bestowed all the regions of the Tiwana chiefs in *Jagir* to Hari Singh in 1819. This was a result of the battle at Mitha Tiwana where Diwan Mokham Chand and Hari Singh crossed the River Chenab to set up a Sikh camp in Pindi Bhattian near Chiniot. Hari Singh captured the area, again using artillery. This area became a breeding ground for camels.[12] The area of Nupur was also given as *Jagir* and these two areas formed the areas of the prestigious salt mines. Shortly afterwards, he subdued the Sayyids people, who were constantly harassing the mainly Hindu populace who they viewed as second-class citizens. The Pirs of the region Uch were attacked and they surrendered, after paying a tribute of Rs25,000. Hari Singh was again duly rewarded with the *Jagir* of the area.

11   Johar, *Sikh Warrior: Hari Singh Nalwa*, p.27.
12   Nalwa, *Hari Singh Nalwa*, p.101.

In 1813, Ranjit Singh had secured the fort of Attock, which was the route by which Asian invaders had to come through to plunder.[13] He was in control of this passageway and would block any further incursions. Kashmir was being occupied by Fateh Khan with the help of Ranjit Singh's army but when the share of plunder was not received, he prepared his forces for battle. The governor of Attock, Jahandad Khan, was afraid of the Lahore Durbar and after receiving payments he relinquished control of the fort and his soldiers. Dia Singh's contingent took charge of the fort. Fateh Kahn was furious at learning that his fort was taken so easily and sent a force of 15,000 soldiers. The Lahore Durbar sent a detachment of forces. On July 1813, when the forces of the Khan had depleted their reserves, Diwan Mokham Chand separated the Sikh cavalry forces into four divisions, one being led by Hari Singh. The Sikh infantry was under Ghaus Khan. Other notable Sikh figures included Jodh Singh Kalsia from the Cis-Sutlej State and Nihal Singh Attari. The Ghazi forces, now under Dost Mohammed (brother of Fateh Khan), led their charge which was repulsed but they gained ground and managed to capture some of the Sikh guns. The balance, however, now swayed into the Sikh hands and the constant harassing of their forces by Mokham Chand led to a Sikh victory. Fateh Khan and his forces were driven out of Khairabad across the Indus River. Ranjit Singh was overjoyed that a complete victory over the Afghans had taken place, and salutes were fired at Amritsar and Lahore.

Kashmir was also on Ranjit Singh's list of conquests. It was a territory famed for its trade route, the growth of different types of fruit, and its great beauty spots. Trade between Kashmir and Tibet had flourished for many years. In the area's capital, Srinagar, shawls were made which were famous around the world. In 1814, Ranjit Singh's attack on the area was a failure and he could not capture the area. It would take another five years until he was more fully prepared to go all out to capture the territory. In April of 1819, with a 30,000 strong force, he prepared for his attack. Hari Singh commanded one of the divisions. On route, they captured Bhimber and Saidabad, and on reaching Rajouri, Hari Singh gave the locals a crushing defeat. The Ghazi leader, Agar Kahn, was defeated and was allowed to keep Rajouri in payment for helping in the attack of Kashmir. The Bheram Pass was captured next, followed by Poonch and Basana. This essentially secured the route to the Pir Panjal Pass. Diwan Mokham Chand separated the forces into three divisions. They attacked Kashmir from different directions in June 1819. The soldiers were now on a war footing: 'The Bugles sounded and the sky was rent with cries of Sat Sri Akal.'[14] After a fiercely fought battle, Kashmir was captured and Jabhar Khan was driven out; he escaped to Peshawar. On capturing the city, law and order were maintained and no plunder was undertaken. Hari Singh was again instrumental in the battle. On his return to Lahore, he was showered with praise from the public and the Durbar.

13   The campaign has been known by various names including the battle of Haidru/Chuch/ Attock.
14   Johar, *Sikh Warrior: Hari Singh Nalwa*, p.41.

The Governorship of Kashmir was taken up by Diwan Moti Ram (1770–1837).[15] His taxation policies crippled the economy and signs of rebellion were on the cards. In the following year, Hari Singh Nalwa was sent to turn things around and ensure the assistance of the populace but to keep a tight grip on law and order. He was a formidable general, but it was now time to test his administrative abilities. On his investiture, he noticed that tax receipts were lax and army pay was in arrears. Within a short time, he received the cooperation of the people. As a result, he also had coins struck in the area to show the strength of the Lahore Durbar in the area. He undertook land reforms and ensured a fair system of taxation was operated. He banned bonded labour, which was effectively the carrying of officer's articles and luggage. He introduced grants for papier-mâché industries and improvements in shawl manufacture.[16] He undertook the construction of forts at Uri and Muzaffarabad, and the gurudwaras at Matan and Baramula (after taking the territory) were constructed. This was together with work that was started on laying out a spacious garden on the banks of the River Jhelum. Ranjit Singh was pleased with his work and rewarded the sardar with gifts. His work was now done and he was recalled by the Maharajah after two successful years. On his departure, the locals lined the route with hails of 'Long Live Hari Singh Nalwa.'

Hari Singh minted many coins and the ones issued at the Kashmir mint included a silver rupee with a standard '*Degh Tegh Fateh Nusrat Bedarang, yaft az Nanak Guru Gobind Singh*' couplet. Additionally, the coin also contained the word '*Har*' in Gurmukhi script. The reverse shows the mint name of Khitta Kashmir and it is dated VS1878/79 (1821/22). These coins were reported to the Maharajah at Lahore and it was alleged that Hari Singh Nalwa had commissioned them in his name. However, this was not possible and the word 'Har' was most likely used in the context of God; the usage of Gurmukhi on the rupees, the standard currency, signifies the takeover of Kashmir from foreign Islamic forces into Sikh hands.[17]

In November 1821, he took the area of Mangli (Hazara) after a hotly-contested battle leaving 2,000 Ghazis dead with losses to the Khalsa army of 180 and 350 injured. One of his commanders, Megh Singh Russa, was killed. Hari Singh managed to obtain tribute and plunder of weapons and animals. He raised a memorial for his fallen soldiers. The area of Mungher was now presenting a problem for the Lahore Durbar and a strong force was sent to depose Hafiz Ahmad Khan whose forces numbered 25,000. Hari Singh captured seven forts on route to the area to give him the protection needed. He captured the area after several days of hostilities and desertions from Khan's camp. The Nawab was given honourable terms by Ranjit Singh and another victory was secured by Hari Singh.

---

15   The son of Diwan Mokham Chand, he officiated as the governor of the Jalandhar Doab during the absence of his father on military expeditions. He was also part of diplomatic missions with the British. He died in Benares in 1837.

16   Johar, *Sikh Warrior: Hari Singh Nalwa*, p.50.

17   Thanks to Jeevandeep Singh for the interpretation of the coin.

Hari Singh Coin, Mint Kashmir 1821/1822. (Courtesy of Jeevandeep Singh)

The main area of Hazara was taken with tribute given to the Lahore Durbar; however, in 1819 they rebelled, with Makhan Singh being slain. Hukma Singh Chimni launched an attack from Attock which failed. Prince Sher Singh and Sada Kaur, as recounted earlier, went to quell the disturbances in 1820. This was undertaken relatively easily but the governor, Diwan Ram Dayal, was killed by a loyal subject of the Durbar. Another governor, Amar Singh Kalan, was killed in 1822.[18] The Maharajah had no choice but to send a man of expertise to the area. Hari Singh became governor of Hazara in the same year and he attacked Hasham Khan Karal who had killed Amar Singh. He relented and surrendered to the Sikh general. Forts were constructed at Narra (Abbottabad) and most importantly at Harikishangarh which was named after the eighth Guru, Har Krishan.[19] The nearby town of Haripur was constructed with a strong wall was to fortify the area. It was described as a popular town and 'it has a large and densely-crowded population, and a respectable bazar, and was the largest town I had seen in Ranjit Singh's territories in this direction. The streets were full of life, and the shops glittered with everything to delight an Indian's taste.'[20] A water tank was built, and a shrine named *Shahid Ganj* (Martyr's Abode) was built in commemoration of the martyrs who died in the battle. In the same year of 1822, Mankara, a tributary of the Sikh Empire, was slow in sending their money until a show of force was sent. The Nawabs of the Saddozai clan were now going to be subdued. In November 1822, Hari Singh's forces established their batteries within reach of the fort. Trenches

18   Amar Singh Majithia, but called Kalan (senior) to distinguish him from another Amar Singh, the junior (Kalan). These soldiers both hailed from the village of Majithia.
19   Received as a *Jagir* from Ranjit Singh, Hugel, *Travels In Kashmir And The Punjab*, p.206. Hugel recounts meeting Hari Singh's son Chattar Singh who was riding a fine horse with trappings of gold and enamel and Kashmiri shawls.
20   Hugel, *Travels In Kashmir And The Punjab*, p.207.

were dug and the siege lasted 25 days, after which the Nawab accepted defeat and the last Saddozai stranglehold fell to the Sikhs.[21]

Seeing the Afghan grip disappearing and the loss of Kashmir, the forces of Mohammed Azim Barakzai marched from Kabul towards Peshawar in 1823. They had also made overtures to the EIC requesting an alliance against the Sikhs. This was refused. Governor Yar Mohammed Khan had been giving tribute to Ranjit Singh but fled upon seeing his half-brother's forces approaching. Prince Sher Singh and Hari Singh were despatched to meet the invaders; they crossed the Attock and reached the fort of Jahangira. A small skirmish took place with the Afghans and now both sides mobilised their forces. Ranjit Singh learnt that Sher Singh was surrounded and, with no time to waste, led the charge at the Attock River and vanquished the besiegers of the fort. The Afghans were stationed at Naushera, the area between Attock and Peshawar. They encamped at Pir Sabd hillock with around 40,000 troops. Akali Phula Singh, who we discuss later, fell in the attack against the Ghazis after being struck by a musket ball. The Nihangs did not waver and were hell-bent on avenging the Khalsa general. Ranjit Singh, on hearing the news, gave a great fight in the battle but 2,000 Sikhs had laid down their lives. The Ghazis fled to the hills. Hari Singh Nalwa halted the Azim Khan's forces and showered artillery fire on the soldiers. The Sikhs undertook their *Dhai Phat* methods of old and though two Sikh guns were captured, the Khalsa cavalry rode through the Ghazis with Hari Singh Nalwa leading the attack. This was now the end of the Ghazis. The Afghans were finished off, and Hari Singh Nalwa was showered with blessings upon entering Peshawar. Yar Mohammed and Dost Mohammed repented for their actions in the battle and were exonerated after their forgiveness was granted by the Maharajah.

The peace was not going to last long and the tribes of Tarin and Torkheli around Hazara were looking at settling scores and undertaking plunder. As a result, Hari Singh attacked Sirikot in 1824; he was faced with 15,000 tribesmen and his routes were blocked. On entering the village of Narra, the ammunition dump blew up and Hari Singh was nowhere to be seen. It was presumed that the Khalsa general had fallen, and news of his death spread like wildfire. The Sikhs under Maha Singh Miripuria and Tek Singh sent out search parties to locate Hari Singh. He was found injured under a tree and was carried into the Sikh camp, bandaged up and then taken to Haripur to recover. A few days later, the Sikhs attacked Narra and plundered the village. Sirikot was strengthened and the Ghazi leader Mohammed Khan Tarin was taken captive. Ranjit Singh rushed to Hazara to find out the reasons for Hari Singh's injuries and was happy to learn of his recovery. This showed the deep respect the Maharajah had for the Khalsa general. Additional defences were prepared in the area. A year later a small rebellion took place, and this was also squashed.

21   Nalwa, *Hari Singh Nalwa*, pp.105–106.

Hari Singh Nalwa dressed in military attire. (Watercolour by a Company artist, Punjab, 1865. Courtesy of the Council of the National Army Museum, London.)

In 1827, there was further troubling brewing when Sayyid Ahmad 'Barelvi' raised a *jihad* of revolt against the Sikhs. He became the champion of the Yusufzai tribe. He was from the Malwa region and was a Hindu convert to Islam. He stood for a return to the purity of the Islamic religion and was a promoter of social reform under the banner of Wahhabism.[22] After meeting Amir Dost Mohammed of Afghanistan, the Sayyid promised to turf out the Sikhs. He got the attention of Sultan Mohammed Khan and Yar Mohammed Khan who then joined him. Thousands of Pathans joined the Sayyid on his conquest to expel the Sikhs. Budh Singh Sandhanwalia, accompanied by 4,000 horsemen, was sent towards Attock to assist in suppressing the Yusufzai. The Sayyid marched from Peshawar in the direction of Naushera. Sardar Budh Singh wrote to the Sayyid seeking clarification of his intentions. The Sayyid replied that he wished to first take the fort of Attock and then engage Budh Singh in battle. Hari Singh Nalwa was stationed at the fort waiting for reinforcements, but the rebellion was now underway. The battle of Saidu took place on 23 February 1827 and the Sikhs over-powered the enemy with a cannonade which lasted two hours. The Sikhs charged at their opponents, routed them, and continued a victorious pursuit for six miles, taking all their guns, swivels, and camp equipment. The Sayyid retreated into the hills.[23] The Sikhs outnumbered them and gave a big defeat to the fanatical leader.[24]

In 1828, the Sayyid tried again with fewer numbers but was again repulsed. In 1830, another attack took place but Hari Singh and Colonel Ventura routed them. Hari Singh arrived and attacked the Pathans and a heavy engagement took place, but rain then separated the forces and they both retired. The following day, with 6,000 troops and marched onto Village Tulundi; the Sayyid fled to the Panjtar Hills. After some fierce fighting, the Ghazis fled and Nalwa and his troops won the day. They then captured Panjtar and collected ammunition and fortified the area before returning to Hazara. Ranjit Singh sent a *Khila'at* as a reward to the Khalsa general. Later in the year, the Sayyid captured Peshawar. This was, however, going to be short-lived.

In May 1831 the threat of the Sayyid was still evident. He had been hiding in the hills since the first incursion. He reached the area of Kagan and took a few villages. Hari Singh had been recalled in order to head a delegation to meet Governor-General William Bentinck. The response, therefore, would be under Prince Sher Singh and Hari Singh's deputy Mahan Singh Mirpuri with 1,000 troops being sent. The Ghazis attacked Balakote and face-to-face encounters took place; Prince Sher Singh decapitated Sayyid Ahmad Shah's head. Colonel Gardener describes the scene:

Syad Ahmad and the *maulvi*, surrounded by his surviving Indian followers, were fighting desperately hand-to-hand with the equally fanatical Akalis of the Sikh

22 Reform movement by Muhammad Abd al-Wahhab in the eighteenth century and adopted by the Saudi families where it is still prevalent today.
23 Nalwa, *Hari Singh Nalwa*, p.119.
24 Ranjit Singh was ill during this time but hearing of the victory he recuperated very quickly.

army. They had been taken by surprise and isolated from the main body of the Syad's forces, which fought very badly without their leader. Even as I caught sight of the Syad and *maulvi* they fell pierced by a hundred weapons. Those around them were slain to a man, and the main body dispersed in every direction.[25]

The Ghazis were defeated with 3,000 dead, the Khalsa army losing 800 and one prominent commander Pratap Singh Attariwala losing his life. This was a prominent victory of the Sikh army over the troublesome tribesman and sent a strong message. Hari Singh's troops held their own against the preacher. He regretted the fact that he was not present at the battle, having pursued the Sayyid for many years.[26] Hari Singh was to remark, 'that a wolf had been shot in the hunting ground; but the game became spoilt.'[27] Much of the booty of the Sayyid was presented to the Lahore Durbar.[28]

In 1833, Hari Singh turned his attention on the Ghakar people, who had provided support to the Sayyid in the battle of Balakote. They had lapsed in their payments to the Lahore Durbar, and Hari Singh took Khanpur with ease, built a fort and stationed parts of his army there. Hazara was now completely in the hands of the great general. The Sayyid in his rebellion against the Lahore Durbar had also captured Peshawar temporarily. Whilst it was still a Lahore tributary, Dost Mohammed Khan decided to annexe the territory of Peshawar completely. He made the proclamation that the area should be handed to him. Most of the tribes refused to join in and instead favoured the Sikhs. Letters were sent asking for Sikh involvement and the dissolution of Khan's power not just from the Muslim tribes but also the Hindu Diwans.[29] It was also an opportune moment as the struggle between Shah Shuja and Dost Mohammed Khan was intensifying, so allowing Ranjit Singh to make his move. The North West Frontier had many defences, but Peshawar was a strategic post within the region. In 1834, Hari Singh, Prince Nau-Nihal, Mohan Lal and General Court were sent to take the city. Charles Masson who witnessed the action saw:

> ...the young shahzada [Nau Nihal Singh] on an elephant, with Hari Singh and a variety of Sikh chiefs, attended by a host of cavalry. Behind them followed the battalions of M. Court, advancing in columns at a brisk pace. On reaching the gardens attached to the house we were in the first shots were fired, some Afghans

25   Pearse, *Soldier and Traveller*, pp.171–172.
26   Nalwa, *Hari Singh Nalwa*, p.127.
27   Suri, *Umdat-ut-Twarikh*, Vol. 3, p.271.
28   'Sardar Sham Singh Attariwala along with Jai Singh and Pratap Singh presented himself to the Maharajah in union with Kanwar Sher Singh. He presented 15 gold ducats, nine Persian guns, axes, pistols, three flags and one elephant, which the wicked Khalifa (Syed Ahmed) used to ride.' Suri, *Umdat-ut-Twarikh*, Vol. 3, p.48.
29   Charles Masson, *Narrative Of Various Journeys In Balochistan Afghanistan The Panjab And Kalat* Vol. III (London: Richard Bentley, New Burlington Street, 1844), p.226

being concealed among the trees. They were soon cleared out, and the march of the force was not affected by the desultory opposition.[30]

Indeed the opposition was weakened by a lack of tribal support and Hari Singh's forces of around 9,000 soldiers easily subdued the territory which was now completely in the hands of the Sikh Empire.[31]

After surrounding the area, the fort of Bala Hisar was taken. The fort was garrisoned and further reinforcements were sent by the Lahore Durbar. Ranjit Singh visited and supervised the activities. It was a tremendous victory by the Sikh Empire and took their kingdom to the very doorsteps of Afghanistan. Hari Singh was made the governor of the province and honours were conferred to the *Vakils* who broke the news.

The rule of Hari Singh Nalwa has been described as being ruthless and heavy-handed but this opinion comes as a product of defiance and rebellion by the tribesman. His reputation was such that people used the name of *Nalwa* as a scare tactic to obtain obedience from man and child. In essence, he was held in awe and his visitations were used by mothers as a term of affright to hush their unruly children. It is said this story, is still used to this day in some areas of Pakistan. The post at Peshawar was held till his death in 1837. Further defences included the improvements at Bala Hisar (Sumergarh) and the deployment of strong contingents at Attock, and Jahangira. Coins synonymous with Nau Nihal and Hari Singh were also struck.

Battle of Jamrud

The final battles of Hari Singh took place within the region of Jamrud. This was another region that was strategically rebuilt to ensure the defences of Durbar territories. The foundation stone was laid on October 1836, and on its completion, there was great fanfare and the recitation of Guru Granth Sahib took place. The fort had 800 infantry, 200 horsemen, and over 22 guns in different sizes.[32] Mahan Singh was put in charge of the fort.[33] He created a well for the provision of the garrison. Nearby he had constructed a fort named Burj Hari Singh as well as Barra Fort under the charge of Jhanda Singh Butalia.[34] Michni Fort was constructed on the banks of the Kabul River and put under the command of Nichatar Singh (son of Dhanna Singh Malawi (1775-1843) and Shankergarh was looked after by Lehna Singh Sandhanwalia.

---

30   Masson, *Narrative Of Various Journeys*, Vol III, p.227.
31   Masson, *Narrative Of Various* Journeys, Vol III, p.229.
32   Johar, *Sikh Warrior: Hari Singh Nalwa*, p.94.
33   Raja Mahan Singh Mirpuri Bal was bestowed the title of sardar by Ranjit Singh. The town of Mansehra derives its name from him. His name has also been spelled Mehan or Mihan.
34   Another resourceful commander of the Sikhs, he fought at the battle of Ferozeshah. In the Second Sikh War, he supported the British against Chattar Singh's revolt at Hazara.

THE SIKH INSCRIPTION

THE INSCRIPTION ON THE ARCH GATE PERTAINS TO THE SIKH
DYNASTY. THE SIKHS INVADED PESHAWAR, REBUILT THE FORT AND
NAMED IT SAMEER GARH. THE INSCRIPTION READS AS FOLLOWS:-

پورکھ ـــــ ج

بفضل سری اکال

سرکارفیض آثار جارہ رجیت سنگھ بہادرپشاور درجہت یک ہزار دشت صدونود ویک راجہ بکرماجیت ... تعمیر کردایں سمیر گڑھ نامود

VICTORY TO PORAKH.THROUGH THE GRACE OF SRI AKAL UNDER THE
LIBERAL GOVERNMENT OF MAHARAJA RANJEET SINGH BAHADUR OVER
THE REGION OF PESHAWAR, IN THE YEAR 1891(VIKRAM SAMRAT)
(A.D 1834) THIS   WAS   BUILT   BY   RAJA   BIKRAMAJIT   AND
WAS NAMED SAMEER GARH".

Hari Singh Nalwa residence at Bala Hisar. (Courtesy of Bobby Singh Bansal)

These innovations and walls of defence deeply disturbed the Afghans. They viewed this as an afront for further aggression in Afghanistan, therefore Amir Dost Mohammed Khan started making preparations against the Sikhs. He was aware of Hari Singh Nalwa's military successes and did not want to meet him head-on in the battlefield. So he first created a *jihad* and roused the passions of the Afghans and gave his five sons to his generals to take into battle. This had a stirring effect on the populace and he received many recruits for his crusade. Nalwa had prepared his defences from region to region. The army of Hari Singh Nalwa was the talk of every town. For the marriage of Prince Nau Nihal, to the daughter of Sham Singh Attariwala, his troops were sent from Peshawar and shown off to the British as a show of strength and force. Henry Fane, commander of the British forces, commented:

> The larger proportion of them were dressed in yellow silk, armed with match-locks or spears, and tolerably mounted; and if they did not do much else they made a very splendid show. Some few were beautifully dressed in chain armour, and looked so like the pictures one sees of warriors in the time of Richard Coeur de Lion, that one might almost fancy one's self transported back to the time of the Crusaders; for which all these gentlemen in yellow and all the colours of the rainbow, would make a good appearance as the soldiers of Saladin.[35]

The recalling of forces from Peshawar was indeed a risk and the Afghans may have known about the garrison having limited forces. Nalwa, sensing an attack, sent a despatch for more forces and this was received by Dhian Singh on 26 April 1837. Hari Singh received a reply three days later. In the meantime, the Afghans had started marching with a 10,000 strong army swelling to 20,000 which were commanded by Prince Akbar Khan and Sami Khan. The Jamrud Fort was attacked on 27 April with Mahan Singh keeping the Afghan forces at bay. Despite a day of fighting the Sikhs still held the fort:

> The evil-minded [ghazis] had carried on an incessant shower of cannon balls upon the walls of the fort all day long, and had thereby demolished utterly one side of the wall of the fort, and that Mehan Singh had lost no time in throwing balls from inside, and that 500 Afghans and some sardars had rolled upon the bed of death.[36]

They were well aware that Hari Singh was at Peshawar and the onslaught intensified on the fort with a cannonade. There were heavy losses on both sides during the next day. There was no sign of reinforcements. The situation was getting worse, and the Sikhs had to get a message to Hari Singh. Several officers stood up to leave the fort but Mahan Singh had found a volunteer in a woman named Harsharan Kaur. She stated that the menfolk should repair the fort and she would ride out, knowing full well the risk of capture. She disguised herself as an Afridi woman, and a letter was written to

35   Henry Edward Fane, *Five years in India; comprising a narrative of travels in the presidency of Bengal, a Visit to the Court of Runjeet Sing, a residence in the Himalayah mountains, an account of the late expedition to Cabul and Affghanistan, voyage down the Indus, and Journey overland to England*, Vol. 1 (London: Henry Colburn, 1842). pp.156–157. Richard Coeur de Lion or Richard the Lionheart a reference to King Richard I (1157–1199). Salah ad-Din Yusuf (1137–1193) or Saladin is a reference to the Sultan of Egypt and Syria and the victor against the Christian Crusaders at the decisive Battle of Hattin in 1187.
36   Suri, *Umdat-ut-Twarikh*, Vol. 3, p.353.

Hari Singh Nalwa requesting help. She also stated that she would acknowledge her safety at Peshawar with the sound of cannon fire. After several hours, of traversing a difficult terrain through the Pathan battalions she reached Peshawar around 2:00 a.m.

She saw Hari Singh on his bed suffering from sickness. This illness did not deter him, and he managed to collect his troops of 6,000 foot soldiers, 1,000 regular cavalry and 3,000 irregular cavalry. Suri writes:

> …with folded hands himself got up and said to the Panth of the Singhs that that was the time of fighting and bloodshed and they must not show the least delay or postponement, adding that though the Maharaja had made a Sankalp [order] to him in order to save his troops from war, yet at that time in agreement with one another they must kindle up the fires of war. The Panth of *Khalsaji* rejoined that they were ready to sacrifice their lives.[37]

At the same time, he despatched another letter to Ranjit Singh requesting reinforcements urgently. Another letter was sent to Lehna Singh Sandhanwalia but the passage to Hashat Nagar was being blocked. Ranjit Singh received the letter but this delay allowed the Afghans to take the advantage. The Lahore Durbar despatched Tej Singh, Gullu Khan of artillery, Sham Singh Attariwala, and others but their arrival would take time. On 30 April 1837 the scene was set for the final battle of Hari Singh. Cannons were fired at Peshawar so alerting Mahan Singh that his letter via Harsharan Kaur had been received. This improved morale at Jamrud Fort.

On arriving at the Burj, Hari Singh divided his forces under his own command, another under Nidhan Singh 'Panjhatta', and the third under Amar Singh Majithia. Whilst he positioned himself in the middle, the other columns went right and left and managed to disperse the Afghan troops, but was routed by Shamsuddin Khan who struck two bullets at the general who fell down. Seeing Hari Singh wounded, the Sikhs retreated into the fort.[38] Reinforcements were needed as provisions were nearly depleted. The force under Prince Nau Nihal now made its way to Peshawar and cleared the enemy; there were great numbers on both sides:

> On arriving at Peshawar we found Amir Dost Muhammad with 40,000 or 50,000 of his own troops, and about 60,000 to 80,000 Ghazis, encamped at and about the mouth of the Khaibar Pass. The 'Francese Compo,' or French division of the Sikh army, then personally commanded by the four French and Italian generals – Messieurs Allard, Ventura, Avitabile, and Court – and having a strength of 20,000 to 22,000 men, marched towards Hashtnagar, and thence slowly and cautiously made its way westward and south-westward with the object of turning the left flank of the Dost's army; while the remainder of the

---

37   Suri, *Umdat-ut-Twarikh*, Vol. 3, p.353.
38   Shamsuddin Khan, nephew of Dost Mohammed Khan.

Sikh army, commanded by Ranjit Singh himself, and 60,000 to 80,000 strong, horse and foot, threatened Dost Muhammad's centre and right flank.[39]

There was continued skirmishing lasting a month. At this point, the Afghans retreated. The position at Jamrud was being attacked and the injured Hari Singh continued his onslaught on the Afghans. Mohammed Khan, who directly fought with Hari Singh Nalwa, was injured as was Nawab Jabbar Khan. Hari Singh made an attack on the forces of Zarin Khan, during which Mangal Singh Ramgharia's bravery was evident in the clash. The Afghans were losing the battle and were fleeing in all directions. Nalwa's forces saw the son of the Amir on the battlefield and gave chase to him and captured 14 guns of his division. They continued their pursuit and maybe they went too far as they were checked by a large body of horse led by Shamsuddin Khan. Hari Singh had been using Parmar rifles (manufactured at the ordnance factory at Lahore) and these proved very effective. The Khalsa general did not want to pursue the fleeing Afghans on the Khyber Pass but in a fit of enthusiasm, Nidhan Singh rallied the troops to give chase. As the command to chase was not given, Shamsuddin appeared with his troops. Hari Singh Nalwa was at Surkamar and pursuing the Afghans in the caves when his bodyguard Ajaib Singh Randhawa was killed. Hari Singh went towards the cave and was also shot, in the chest and stomach. The battle was now coming to a head. Hari Singh made it to Jamrud Fort and his army tried in vain to save him after bandaging him up. He thanked his forces for their service and he would now meet his maker. These were the final moments of the battle-hardy Commander-in-Chief.

The Maharajah had learnt of the last stand of the great general in May 1837, but there had been an idea to not let the word out in fear of additional reprisals by the Afghans. Ranjit Singh was tearful of hearing of the loss of such a great personality in the annals of Sikh history. Sohan Lal records the statement of the Maharajah on hearing the news of Nalwa's death:

> As it was ordained by the Immortal God, a bullet from the Persian gun struck the said sardar (Hari Singh) and put an end to his life, and an ignominious defeat befell the army. The said sardar (Hari Singh) came over to Jamrod and Mehan Singh engaged himself in concealing the news of his death with the result that the news of his death was not known to anybody in the camps of the Sikhs and the Afghans. The Maharaja felt very grieved on hearing this dreadful news and his eyes became wet with tears while he talked about the fidelity and sacrifices of the said sardar (Hari Singh) from the beginning to the end of his career.[40]

---

39   Pearse, *Soldier and Traveller*, p.185.
40   Suri, *Umdat-ut-Twarikh*, Vol. 3, p.354. General Allard also confirmed had it not been for Hari Singh's intervention, the forts would have been taken by the Afghans, Suri, *Umdat-ut-Twarikh*, Vol. 3, p.369.

Sword of Jassa Singh Ahluwalia given to Amar Singh of Patiala. © Roopinder Singh.
Courtesy of Bhayee Sikandar Singh & Roopinder Singh, *Sikh Heritage Ethos and Relics.*

i

Portrait of Maharajah Ranjit Singh by Imam Bakhsh. © RMN-Grand Palais.
(MNAAG, Paris) / Thierry Ollivier.

The French *Fauj-i-Khas* Flag. © Maidstone Museums. Photographed by Gurinder Singh Mann.

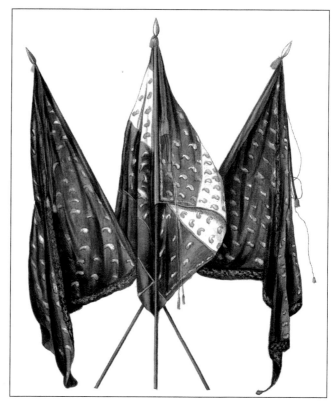

Sikh Colours captured by the 50th Queen's Own Regiment in the campaign on the banks of the Sutlej 1845–1846. Ackermann &Co. © Maidstone Museums.

Fresco of Akali Phula Singh in battle. From the Palace of Suchet Singh. Courtesy of Nick Fleming.

Military drill from *The Military Manual of Maharajah Ranjit Singh*. (1822-30). Maharajah Ranjit Singh Museum, Amritsar: Acc.No:1035. Photo courtesy of Jean Marie Lafont.

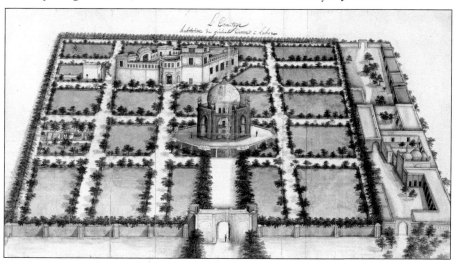

Residence of General Court, Anarkali, Lahore. *Memoirs of General Court*. (12-544165). (C) RMN-Grand Palais (MNAAG, Paris) / Thierry Ollivier.

Left: Order of Merit with a portrait
of Maharajah Ranjit Singh. ca 1837–1839.
Acc.No:IS.92-1981. © Victoria and Albert
Museum, London.
Above: Lieutenant Herbert Edwardes Anglo
Sikh War medal. Courtesy of Peter Bance.
Below: Sham Singh Attariwala and Chattar
Singh Attariwala. C.1860. Add Or.
1403.© British Library Board.

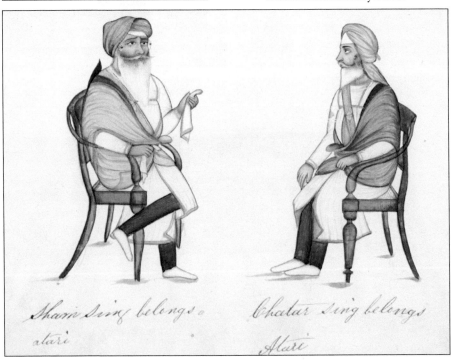

Sham Sing belongs
atari

Chatar Sing belongs
Atari

Right: Bodyguard of Ranjit Singh. Two horsemen on richly caparisoned mounts.# Inscribed in Persian characters: 'Sawardan I khass' or Lahore Life Guards, 1838. Add.Or.1385. © British Library Board.
Below: Portrait of a bodyguard of Ranjit Singh with a matchlock, and bow and arrows, mounted on a richly caparisoned horse. Skinner Album/Add Or.1248. © British Library Board.

General Allard's Sikh Lancer. 1838. Add.Or.1382. © British Library Board

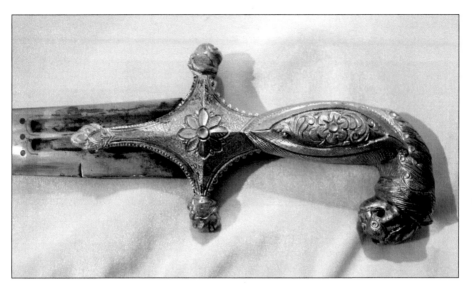

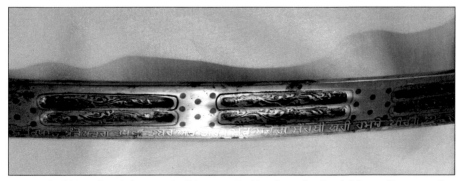

Sword of Sham Singh Attariwala. Photographed by Gurinder Singh Mann. Courtesy of Colonel Harinder Singh Attari.

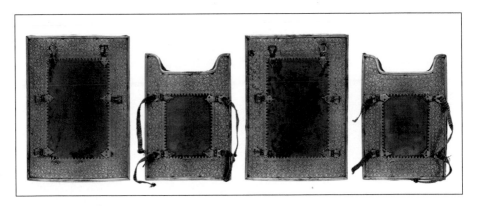

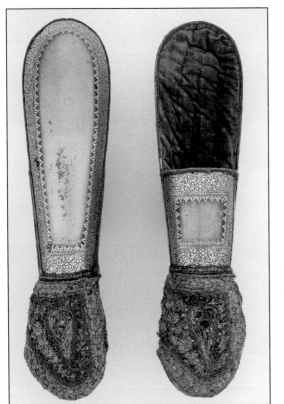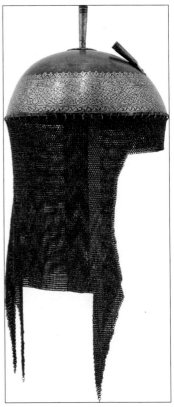

Helmet, Charaina and Dastana. Arms and Armour traditionally attributed to Maharajah Ranjit Singh. Acc.No:XXVIA.36. @Royal Armouries.

Sikh Mortar shell used during the siege of Multan,1849. Acc.No:1973-04-16. Courtesy of the Council of the National Army Museum, London. Photographed by Gurinder Singh Mann

Lehna Singh Majithia, Durgasankara Pathaka, and Dyal Singh. *Sarvasiddhantattvacadamani* or 'Crest-jewel of the Essence of all Systems of Astronomy.' Or.5259. © The British Library Board

Generals Allard and Ventura meeting Maharajah Ranjit Singh. *The Military Manual of Maharajah Ranjit Singh* (1822–30). Maharajah Ranjit Singh Museum, Amritsar: Acc. No:1035. Photo courtesy of Jean Marie Lafont.

Mounted Sikh Noblemen. Painting by L.H de Rudder based on Prince Alexis Soltykoff. *Indian Scenes and Characters: sketched from life. 1859.* Courtesy of Gurinder Singh Mann.

Maharajah Sher Singh and his troops, Lahore. Painting by L.H de Rudder based on Prince Alexis Soltykoff. *Indian Scenes and Characters: sketched from life. 1859.* Courtesy of Gurinder Singh Mann.

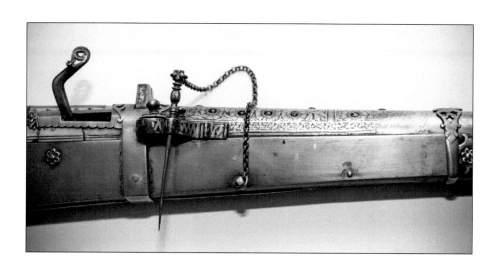

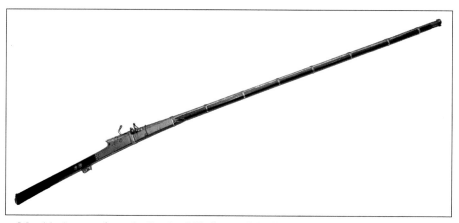

Matchlocks guns from the Battle of Chillianwallah. Courtesy of Sukhbinder Singh Paul Family Collection.

Watercolour of the Battle of Chillianwallah, 1849. 61st South Gloucestershire Regiment. Painted by A.C. Lovett after J. Marshman. c. 1895. © Soldiers of the Gloucestershire Museum.

Five Light guns with small jockey wheels, and one swivel Zamburak, Lahore Fort, late nine-teenth century. Courtesy of Peter Bance.

Sutlej Gun-6-Pounder, Field Gun, Limber and Carriage. Acc.No:XIX.329. @Royal Armouries.

Portrait of the Sikh Square of the Avitabile regiment facing the Bengal Horse Artillery. © Michael Perry/ perry-miniatures.com

Sikh Flags at Lichfield Cathedral. Photo courtesy of Amarpal Singh Sidhu.

Peshawar Fort and surroundings. 1878, John Burke.

Above: 15th Ludhiana Sikhs. 1900. K. E., Rose.
Right: Subadar-Major Jinwad Sing Bahadur,
45th (Rattray's Sikhs). 1903. Charles, Lyall.
Prints, Drawings and Watercolors from the
Anne S.K. Brown Military Collection.

Fort Attock with bridge of boats & Khairabad, from below the old serai on left bank of Indus. 1878, John Burke.

Indeed the idea was to keep the death a secret so as not to alert other warlords nearby and set the stage for any insurrections. Mahan Singh, one of Hari Singh's commanders, was rewarded for his valour in the battle with Jagirs. The Afghans did not capture Jamrud or Peshawar and they fled across the Khyber Pass. The Sikhs lost their most influential commander in the highly contested battle. He was cremated in Jamrud fort, a *Samadhi* being built for him later.[41] Another *Samadhi* was constructed at the general's homeland at Gujranwala, by his son.[42] There are various assessments of this battle concerning the withdrawal of troops of the battle for Nau Nihal's marriage, letters not acted upon at the Lahore Durbar and the pursuit by Nidhan Singh. Cunningham states:

> It seems that the Afghans were at first routed or repulsed with the loss of some guns, but that the opportune arrival of Shams-ud-din Khan, a relation of the Amir, with a considerable detachment, turned the battle in their favour. It is nevertheless believed that had not Hari Singh been killed, the Sikhs would have retrieved the day. The troops in the Peshawar valley had been considerably reduced by the withdrawal of large parties to Lahore, to make a display on the occasion of Nau Nihal Singh's marriage, and of the expected visit of the English Governor-General and Commander-in-Chief.[43]

Ranjit Singh now wanted to take revenge on the Afghans who had amassed a large army at Peshawar but the British thwarted this move as they had set their sights on Kabul. Dost Mohammed Khan sent letters to the British with the effect of checking Sikh designs.[44] He also tried to appease Ranjit Singh by coaxing him with flattery and presents of horses.

With the help and agreement of Ranjit Singh, who joined the Tripartite Treaty in 1838 with British viceroy Lord Auckland, Shah Shuja was restored to the Afghan throne in Kabul in August 1839.[45] Ranjit Singh died in June 1839, yet Sher Singh and Nau Nihal Singh still supported the British through this turbulent time. The British invasion led to the disastrous Anglo-Afghan War (1839–42), with the Sikhs providing nominal support. The interesting point to note is that whilst the Sikhs never conquered Afghanistan, they did subdue the Afghan nation. However, the banner of the Sikh

---

41   The brother of Mahan Singh was also killed and cremated at the same time. Gupta, *History of the Sikhs*, Vol. 5, p.181. The tomb of Hari Singh bears a plaque in three languages, erected by one Babu Gajjumal Kapur of Peshawar in 1892: 'Tomb of the Late Hari Singh Nalwa, Cremated 30th April 1837.'

42   The ashes of Hari Singh Nalwa were later taken for immersion in the River Ganges.

43   Cunningham, *History of the Sikhs*, p.191.

44   Mohan Lal, *Life of the Amir Dost Mohammed Khan of Kabul..... including the victory and disasters of the British army in Afghanistan* (London: Longman, Brown, Green and Longmans, 1846), pp.248–252.

45   Treaty between the British Government, Ranjit Singh, and Shah Shuja-ul-Mulk, concluded at Lahore on 26 June 1838.

Samadhi of Hari Singh Nalwa, Jamrud Fort. (Courtesy of Bobby Singh Bansal)

Empire supported the EIC in taking Kabul. This was under the leadership of Colonel Sheikh Bussowan, aided by Captain Auguste De la Lafont.[46] Mohammed Dost Khan was exiled to Mussoorie in November 1839 but was restored to his former position

46   It is worth digressing to labour the point about how the Sikhs supported the British in taking Kabul and restoring Shah Shuja to the throne. Ranjit Singh did not want the major EIC force passing through his territory. It was suggested that a large number of British forces should be collected at Firozpur, and proceed in company with Shah Shuja. They marched upon Kabul, passing through Sindh, the Bolan Pass, Qandahar, and Ghazni. The Shahzadah Taimur, with the Sikh contingent, would shape his course within the Panjab, so as to divert the attention of the Kabul chief from the Khyber side. Colonel Wade's Sikh escort was furnished with artillery as well as *Ghorchurah* and troops of the Najib battalion. The EIC, supported by the Sikh Empire, crossed the Khyber and defeated Afghan forces at the fort at Ali Masjid and then entered Jalalabad. When Shah Shuja and the supporting armies entered Kabul unopposed in August 1839 they decided to do a victory march where the Sikhs were present. The Afghans were much very surprised at the discipline of the Khalsa army which was trained by the French Generals. Shah Shuja gave medals only to British forces for the action at Ghazni. Sikh forces were given Rs5,000 to be distributed to their soldiers for action at Ali Masjid. Sikhs undertook law and order duties and dealt with the thieves who were robbing the cantonment at night. The Sikh commander Colonel Shaikh Basawan, after undertaking his duties, went back to Jalalabad and General Wade took his troops and Sikhs back to Peshawar. This ended the Sikh engagement in the First Anglo-Afghan War. See Ali, *The Sikhs and Afghans*, pp. 490–493. Lord Auckland expressed 'high satisfaction' with the conduct of Colonel Shaikh Basawan, to whom he sent a sword 'in testimony of his gallantry and determination.'

after the murder of Shah Shuja in April 1842. He thereafter maintained cordial relations with the Lahore Darbar with a regular exchange of embassies between the two governments. A representative of the Sikh kingdom was sent to Kabul, while an agent of the Emir was always present at Lahore. Khan also helped the Khalsa army in the Second Anglo-Sikh War.

Diplomatic Mission

In 1831, Nalwa also led the diplomatic mission to meet with Governor-General Bentinck, which culminated in the Treaty at Ropar between the British and the Sikhs. Something that was not lost on Hugel was the intelligence and knowledge of worldly matters by the general:

> Hari Singh Nalwa was the person sent by Ranjit Singh to invite Lord William Bentink to confer with the Maharaja at Shimla; and as I happened to know most of the persons he had met there, our conversation was very different from the majority of such interviews in India; and really consisted of a due exchange of ideas, and of references to events which had actually taken place. His questions proved him to have thought and reasoned justly: he is well informed on the statistics of many of the European States, and on the policy of the East India Company, and what is very rare among the Sikhs; he can both read and write the Persian language.[47]

Indeed, the idea was for Ranjit Singh to discuss the issue of Sind and hence this explains Hari Singh's presence but Governor-General Bentinck evaded the issue. On meeting the Governor-General he was presented with weaponry: 'After that the Military Lord [C.-in-C.] made them depart with a show of great respect to the Sikh representatives, giving one English gun and sword to the sardar [Hari Singh Nalwa].'[48] Also in the same year, the general met with Colonel Wade who was interested in his conquests of Kashmir, Multan, Peshawar and other places.[49] He also conversed with Colonel Burnes on his visit to the Attock Fort. These victories of the Sikh Empire were not lost on the British.

In 1832, Hari Singh also was visited by the missionary Joseph Wolff who was ordered to give him protection around Peshawar by Ranjit Singh. This included providing safe passage and money for his work. He met the Sikh general at Jahangira, which furnishes us with information on his court: 'We arrived at Jehaangeer. Serdar Hurry Singh, in a tent, sitting upon a chair, surrounded by about 80 Officers, and

47   Hugel, *Travels In Kashmir And The Punjab*, pp.254–255.
48   Suri, *Umdat-ut-Twarikh, Vol. 3*, p.28.
49   Suri, *Umdat-ut-Twarikh, Vol. 3*, p.22.

Nobles, and soldiers, rose and put his hands in mine, and welcomed me in the name of the Maharajah.'[50]

During his stay, he was given information on the Sikh religion by the *Vakil* Munshi Mool Singh who was versed in Sanskrit and other languages. Interestingly, the conversation of religion would come to a head with Wolff having a curious conversation on the Christian religion.[51]

Construction Projects

More than fifty-five buildings are attributed to Nalwa, including forts, ramparts, towers, Gurdwaras, water tanks, *Samadhis*, temples, mosques, towns, *Havelis*, *Sarais* and gardens. Some of these we have alluded to earlier. The territory of Guseroli, which once belonged to Charhat Singh Sukerchakia, was also in Hari Singh's possession, and according to Hugel, this '...consisted of a beautiful garden which was the most beautiful and best kept I had seen in India.'[52] Nalwa built all the main Sikh forts in the trans-Indus region of North West Frontier: Jahangira Fort and Naushera Fort on the left and right banks of the Kabul River, respectively. He also built Sumergarh Fort in Peshawar, Fatehgarh Fort in Jamrud, and Uri Fort in Kashmir, and reinforced Akbar's Attock Fort on the left bank of the Indus River. Nalwa never neglected his religious duties and he ensured that Sikh buildings and remembrance sites were built around his jurisdiction. This included Gurdwara Panja Sahib in Hassan Abdal which commemorated Guru Nanak's visit there. Here he constructed a tank and the steps were made from marble brought in from Rajputana. He attached a large *Jagir* for the maintenance and recitation of the Sikh scriptures there.[53] At Gujranwala he had constructed the *Samadhi* of Maha Singh Sukerchakia and his wife Raj Kaur,

50   Wolff, *Researches and Missionary Labours*, p.176.
51   Wolff, *Researches and Missionary Labours*, pp.177–178. He would later hear readings of the Guru Granth Sahib at Hassan Abdal and meet Ranjit Singh who once again held a discourse on God with him.
52   Hugel, *Travels In Kashmir And The Punjab*, p.253. Hugel also describes meeting Hari Singh at the palace which consisted of the finest carpets from Kashmir and Kabul.
53   Panja Sahib, named after the historic event in which Guru Nanak stopped a large stone from killing him. Tradition narrates that he left his handprint of *panja*, five fingers on the large stone. 'When I came to the marble steps leading to his Durbar, which was held before the celebrated stone, and saw him there seated on carpets, I took off my shoes, a courtesy which gained for me the loud praises of all present. The Guru [reciter of the scripture] received me with every mark of dignity, and accepted a present, which was certainly well bestowed, if only for the sight of the stone, on which the above-named marvel still remains imprinted.' Hugel, *Travels In Kashmir And The Punjab*, p.226. Ali, *An Historical Account of the Sikhs*, pp.158–60, records the Akalis being the recipients of offerings at the shrine.

the memorials of Ranjit Singh's father and mother respectively, which pleased the Maharajah immensely.[54]

In conclusion, we can say that there are numerous names that uphold the Khalsa spirit and the way of the sword, but Hari Singh Nalwa stands head and shoulders above others. The persecution faced by the Sikhs under the Afghans during the Misl period and then the uprisings during the Sikh Empire was met head-on. The name of Hari Singh still strikes fear into people across Afghanistan and Pakistan; he was a general whose achievements have never been repeated with a horse, musket, or sword. A French description sums up his accomplishments:

> The best of Ranjit Singh's Generals and the most feared by the Afghans. Every year, Hari Singh followed by his invincible Akalis [the Immortals] was going to raise taxes from Yousoufzais, stalking them down in the mountains and in their dens. A long time after his death, the mothers kept telling their crying child: 'Keep silent or Hari Singh will come'; and even to this day, old people still show the place where 'the tiger' chased them like a herd of sheep.[55]

Hari Singh was deeply religious and was versed in the Sikh scriptures and ensured that Gurdwaras were built to provide the Sikh congregations with spiritual nutrition. His success on the battlefield consisted of over 20 battles in which he participated or led. This is a testimony to the greatest of saint soldiers. The Afghan Empire, in a series of battles with the Sikhs, had been steadily losing their territories. Thus Panjab, Multan, Kashmir, Derajat, Hazara and Peshawar, which were once part of the kingdom of Kabul, were lost to the Sikhs. The loss of Peshawar was particularly galling as the inhabitants were fellow Pashtuns and the town was the summer capital of the Afghan Emirs.

---

54 Suri, *Umdat-ut-Twarikh*, Vol. 3, p.273.
55 Par James Darmesteter, *Chants Popularies des Afghans* (Paris: Imprimerie Nationale, 1889), p.260. Thanks to Amar Singh Mann for translating the text.

9

Akali Phula Singh and the 'Body of Immortals'

The Akalis were a strong contingent that idealised the saint-soldier ideal devised during the times of Guru Gobind Singh. They played an important part during the struggles against the Afghans and Mughals in the eighteenth century. Whilst traditionally the Buddha Dal and Taruna Dal were all seen as Akalis, wearing the blue clothes and armed to the teeth, during the late eighteenth century some of these innovations were dropped as wealth and modernity started influencing the faith. At the turn of the nineteenth century, only the Shaheedi Misl remained as the armed guardians of the faith spiritually and military, and they retained the martial elements of Guru Gobind Singh. We have considered the changes in methods of Sikh warfare during the time of Ranjit Singh. During this time, there was a continuation of the shock and awe skills of the Nihangs which denoted their bravery and determination. The weaponry of the Akalis did not differ much from the eighteenth century, with hand-to-hand combat and a one-man walking army being the operational strategy of these body of warriors. Weapons were worn as part of their attire; the swords, *Kartars* (punch daggers), *Bagh Nakkha* (clawed weapon) and the whirling *Chakkars* or quoits on the necks and around their turbans. These would be supplemented with pistols and other small arms. The *Charaina* was also favoured by them. The Akalis played an important part during the Sikh Empire and this was under the notorious Khalsa warrior, Akali Phula Singh. He was not only a general in battles, leading his troops, but also in his saintly role as protector and preserver of Khalsa institutions. As a result, he was the custodian of the Akal Takht where initiation into the Khalsa fraternity took place. In fact, at Amritsar you could only get initiated into the faith from the Akalis during his leadership.[1] According to John Malcolm, the Khalsa initiation ceremony took place as follows:

---

1   'A Sikh wishing to become a Singh finds no difficulty in accomplishing his proselytism. He goes to the Akalees, or priest of the sect, at Amritsur...after the performance of certain ceremonies he is given to drink a sherbet made of sugar and water, from the hand of an Akalee.' See *Tour to Lahore, The Asiatic Annual Register, vol. XI —for the Year 1809* (London: printed for T Cadelland W Davies, etc., 1811), pp.421–440.

He is then presented with the five weapons: a sword, a firelock, a bow and arrow, and a pike. One of those who initiate him says, 'The Guru is thy holy teacher, and thou art his Sikh or disciple.' Some sugar and water is put into a cup, and stirred round with a steel knife, or dagger and some of the first chapters of the Adi-Granth, and the first chapters of the Dasama Padshah ka Granth [Dasam Granth] , are read; and those who perform the initiation ceremony exclaim, Wa! Guruji ka Khalsa! Wa! Guruji ki Fateh! After this exclamation has been repeated five times, they say, 'This sherbet is nectar. It is the water of life; drink it.' The disciple obeys; and some sherbet, prepared in similar manner, is sprinkled over his head and beard...He is instructed to believe, that it is the duty of all those who belong to the Khalsa, or commonwealth of the Sikhs, neither to lament the sacrifice of property, nor life, in support of each other, and he is directed to read the Adi Granth and Dasama Padshah ka Granth every morning and every evening.[2]

Whilst the scriptures were fundamental to the initiation process, the eighteenth century notion of the *Gurumatta*, or binding resolutions of the Khalsa in the name of the Guru, was still evident in the early years of the Sikh Empire. The Akalis also maintained the tradition of the scriptures of the Guru Granth Sahib and Dasam Granth being ceremonially enthroned together. This was under the orders of Akali Phula Singh at the Akal Takht. All important decisions were made with both scriptures present, Malcolm again comments on the importance:

When Gurmata or great national council is called, (as it always is, or ought to be, when any imminent danger threatens the country, or any large expedition is to be undertaken) all the Sikh chiefs assemble at Amritsar. The assembly, which is called the Gurumata, is convened by the Acalis; and when the chiefs meet upon this solemn occasion, it is concluded that all private animosities cease, and that every man sacrifices his personal feelings at the shrine of the general good; and, actuated by principles of pure patriotism, thinks of nothing but the interests of the religion, and commonwealth, to which he belongs.

   When the chiefs and principal leaders are seated, the Adi-Granth and Dasama Padshah ka Granth are placed before them. They all bend their heads before these scriptures, and exclaim, Wa! Guruji ka Khalsa! Wa! Guruji ki Fateh! A great quantity of cakes, made of wheat, butter, and sugar, are then placed before the volumes of their sacred writings, and covered with a cloth. These holy cakes, which are in commemoration of the injunction of Nanac, to eat and to give to others to eat, next receive the salutation of the assembly, who then rise, and the Acalis pray aloud, while the musicians play. The Acalis, when the prayers are finished, desire the council to be seated. They sit down, and the cakes being

2   Malcolm, *Sketch of the Sikhs*, pp.182–185.

uncovered, are eaten of by all classes of Sikhs: those distinctions of original tribes, which are, on occasions, kept up, being on this occasion laid aside, in token of their general and complete union in one cause. The Acalis then exclaim: 'Sirdars! (Chiefs) this is Guru-mata!' on which prayers are again said aloud. The chiefs, after this sit closer, and say to each other: 'The sacred Granth is betwixt us, let us swear by our scripture to forget all internal disputes, and to be united.' This moment of religious fervour and ardent patriotism, is taken to reconcile all animosities. They then proceed to consider the danger with which they are threatened, to settle the best plans for averting it, and to choose the generals who are to lead their armies against the common enemy. The first Guru-mata was assembled by Guru Govind; and the latest was called in 1805, when the British army pursued Holkar into the Penjab.[3]

These important resolutions were pivotal for Sikh harmony amongst the Misls, but as Maharajah Ranjit Singh climbed his ladder as the ultimate leader of the Sikhs, many institutions were dispensed with. The importance of the Dasam Granth, however, was maintained. Maharajah Ranjit Singh had many copies of the Dasam Granth produced as well as ensuring that both Granths were carried in procession when his armies went to battle.[4]

Phula Singh was born to Ishar Singh as a member of the Nishanvalia Misl. After his father's passing, he was entrusted to the notable Akali Chief Narain Singh, better known as Naina Singh. It was at the holy precincts within Anandpur where he was trained in the warrior arts.[5] According to Buddha Dal tradition, after Jassa Singh Ahluwalia it was Naina Singh who was head of the warriors as well as the Sikh institutions. After his passing, the mantle was given to Phula Singh, who would be the chief architect of ensuring that the Khalsa traditions were maintained. The Akali was anti-foreign and hence his immortal army would come into regular confrontation with the *Ferengi*. Whilst serving Maharajah Ranjit Singh, Phula Singh would admonish his activities and practices. The law of the Nihangs was all-pervading and binding on the poor and the rich, with the Maharajah subservient to their practices and religious mantras.

3   Malcolm, *Sketch of the Sikhs*, pp.120–123.
4   'He was always attended on his tours by a priest with a volume of each of the two chief scriptures [Guru Granth Sahib and Dasam Granth]. They were wrapped up in rich pieces of silk, placed in a cotunder a big canopy, and thus borne from one place to another. A special military escort was provided; each member of which carried a Sikh banner. The procession was often followed by a number of priests on elephants. Besides this, every regiment had its own volumes of the Granths and religious insignia. Even the ministers of state carried separate copies of the Granths on their journeys', Mufti Ali ud-Din, *Ibratnama*, Quoted in Chopra, *The Punjab as a Sovereign* State, p.204.
5   Prof. Rajinder Singh, 'Akali Phoola Singh – The Great Warrior', *Sikh Review*, (India, Calcutta, March 1981), pp.42–45.

Fresco of Akali Naina Singh (right), Baba Atal, Amritsar. (Photo: Gurinder Singh Mann)

At the time of Ranjit Singh's takeover of Amritsar, it was Akali Phula Singh who stepped in ensuring that the holy city did not witness a bloodbath, with the Bhangi family being relieved and given a *Jagir*. At this juncture, the Akalis of Anandpur took over the Akal Takht and the rest of the army were situated in what would become known as Akali Phula Singh Burj.[6] Akali Phula Singh was an instigator of building projects, and he also repaired many Gurdwaras in Amritsar including Gurdwara Ramsar and so on. In 1808, the EIC sent General Charles Metcalfe to the court of Maharajah to develop friendly relationships between the two. Metcalfe's mission was attacked by the Akalis attached to Phula Singh; the intrepid warrior had no fear of man but only God who he worshipped in the form of all steel.[7] Metcalfe described the Akalis:

> [They are]…a military brotherhood who are considered as the peculiar defenders of the Temple and the Faith. Any person is admitted into this Brotherhood, who

6   Most likely built after his martyrdom. There now stands two Gurdwaras which are under the head of the Buddha Dal Nihang Singhs.
7   This is an allusion to the concept of God being equated with being all-steel by Guru Gobind Singh. This concept appears within verses within the Dasam Granth compositions namely *Jaap Sahib, Akal Ustat, Bachitra Natak*.

feels an inclination to join it. No qualification is necessary, but a sanguinary disposition, and any reinforcement to the body, from any religion, or any caste, is equally acceptable. Under the sanction of the supposed holy office, they commit every enormity. They seem to be the terror of the people of the country, in the town of Amritsar particularly and to be free from the control of the Government. Some of them are distinguished by the appellation of *Nungee Tulwar Akallee* [author emphasis] from their always carrying naked swords. Ranjit Singh tells me that he has confiscated the lands of the Akalis, concerned in the late disturbance. He informs me that, although he did not think it prudent, whilst the ferment lasted to make any severe example, he is determined henceforth to destroy by degrees, the power and influence of this ungovernable set of Ruffians.[8]

During the early 1800s the EIC would come in contact with the Akalis across Hindustan and many descriptions perfectly capture their practices and innovations. No other group would be understood more by the British than the Akalis, the biggest thorn to their later domination in the Panjab.

Whilst the Metcalfe incident would set the scene for the future, Phula Singh policed parts of the Panjab and would not tolerate western involvement in Panjab affairs. This standoff would continue with Ranjit Singh having issues with his policy of appeasement with the British. The signing of the Treaty of Amritsar in April 1809 may have also triggered the following events. These concern Captain White of the EIC who was surveying the boundary lines in the Nabha region. Since the British came to the shores of Hindustan they had brought many cartographers who essentially mapped city after city. This led to a better understanding of the country, not just for the present EIC but for future generations of soldiers and administrators. This would also prove to be fruitful in future conquests. Akali Phula Singh, on learning of the British intentions, led a pre-emptive attack. Captain F.S. White states, 'I was informed about 250 people had collected there with the design of attacking me. I immediately turned off into Jungle relinquishing all thoughts of proceeding to Mansah and taking the direct road to Ludhiaaah.'[9] On 18 December 1809, Akali Phula Singh and 80 of his men attacked the captain at the village of Chowki and many villagers also joined the attack until the numbers swelled. White took off in flight and in the retreat all the tents and baggage were lost; the little British force only found safety by storming the village of Patoki. They held up there until the arrival of Ram Singh, nephew of Raja Jaswant Singh of Nabha. In the skirmish, several of Captain White's party were killed and nineteen wounded.[10] White writes:

8   Metcalfe papers No.72, 7 March 1809. Quoted in Victor G. Kiernan, *Metcalfe's Mission to Lahore (1808–1809)* (Jullundur: Languages Department, Punjab, 1971), pp.100–101.
9   From Lieutenant F.S. White, Surveyor, to A. Seton, Resident at Delhi, 24 December 1809. Anon, *Records Of The Ludhiana Agency* (Lahore, Punjab Government Press, 1911), p.148.
10   Lepel Griffin, *The Rajas of the Punjab*, p.124.

By the time I had gone one *Kos* the enemy had augmented to about 500 men by small parties of horse and foot from different villages and began to press on me so close as to force me to commence firing; but, although the enemy were individually brave, particularly the foot, who frequently came so near as to spear the *Sipahees*…I was forced to sacrifice the baggage (a string of sixteen camels, several of which were severely wounded).

On our arrival, however, at this village [Patoki], which may be deemed a large one, as most of them are in this part of the country, we were greatly disappointed to find the inhabitants join the enemy, and with this addition to their force I do not hesitate to say that in my opinion we had to oppose one thousand men…

The only chance of saving the party was that of storming the village and procuring shelter amongst the houses; this plan was accordingly adopted, and possession of a part of the village taken with but little loss…

Early the next morning Run [Ram] Sing, the nephew of Jiswunt Sing, arrived from Phool, a small town sixteen Kos from Pukoke [Patoki], to my relief. Tranquillity was immediately restored in the village – the enemy having returned to their respective villages during the night.

The loss on our side is 3 *sipahees* killed, 11 wounded, 3 servants killed, 8 servants wounded, belonging to Captain Skinner's Irregular Corps; wounded 2 horses, Lieutenant White's killed, 4 horses belonging to Captain Skinner wounded, 2 of which were left at Pukoke as unfit for further service. The whole baggage excepting the ammunition and the Soobidar's property lost.[11]

Representations were made by the Raja of Patiala, Sahib Singh, stating that the issue was started by members of White's party. The captain had to write several letters to Delhi explaining the nature of events. The complaint of Sahib Singh was rejected by the Resident at Delhi, A. Seaton:

It would appear that the head of the gang of robbers, who attacked and plundered Lieutenant White, was Phola Sing, an Akaulee, is a subject of Runjeet Sing and joined the troops of that Chief near Kot Kapoorah when he found that the arrival of Run Sing prevented him from accomplishing his purpose, which seems to have been not merely to plunder but to destroy the party with Lieutenant White.[12]

11   From Lieutenant F.S.White, Surveyor, to A. Seton, Resident at Delhi, 24 December 1809. *Records Of The Ludhiana Agency*, pp.148–153. White also states that he lost his books, papers, and maps which he had collected during his four years' survey. He states that surveying this region was no longer advisable.

12   From A. Seaton to C. Lushington, Acting Secretary to Government in the Political Department, Fort William, 28 December 1809. *Records Of The Ludhiana Agency*, pp.157–158.

The Rajas of Nabha, Jind and Patiala were instructed to take measures against Akali Phula Singh. This was going to be a difficult if not an impossible task. Colonel Ochterlony, based at Ludhiana, was instructed to apprehend the Akali Chief as the attack of the British was considered a national insult. The British were aware that Akali Phula Singh was at Damdama with between '300 to 500' Akalis. The political machinations continued until May 1809, when Phula Singh, recognising that the British would come for him, rode out from Damdama to Amritsar. A party of Sikhs from the Cis-Sutlej Chiefs went to Damdama to seek him out; 'The place was taken, but the murderer, being a priest, was suffered to escape.'[13] Damdama had been an Akali stranglehold for many years and a special place of reverence. The Shaheedi Misl leader Deep Singh had his headquarters there after Guru Gobind Singh established a centre of education. The British were now looking to Ranjit Singh to apprehend the Akali and bring him to justice as it was posing difficult for them to apprehend him. It was enough for now that Phula Singh was ejected from the British protectorate territory but the Akalis would now be a marked group of soldiers by the British:

> That which further remains to be done can be accomplished at a future period when the conjuncture may be more favourable. Phola Sing is certainly deserving of the severest of punishments. Not content with being both the instigator and the leader of the murderous attack made upon the British mission when encamped at Amritser, in the month of February in 1809, his late attempt to cut off Lieutenant White's party seems to evince that his sanguinary malignity is as rooted and inveterate as it is ferocious. It is to be hoped that the time is not far distant when circumstances will no longer admit of so atrocious and blood-thirsty a criminal eluding the pursuit of justice.[14]

Whilst the EIC thought this would send a message to the Akalis, if anything it made Akali Phula Singh a notorious defender of the Khalsa way of life, subject to no laws of mankind. An application asking Ranjit Singh to eject him from Amritsar was made but this came to nothing. Whilst some representation would have been made, it would have been a simple order as opposed to sending any major personnel to remove him. According to Colonel Ochterlony:

> Runjeet Sing had sent most particular orders for the expulsion of Phola Sing, the Ukaulee. These reports have been confirmed by other letters, and that the delay which has occurred in their execution has been owing to the reluctance of his people at Umritser to carry them into effect...he has insisted on their immediate obedience, and has even threatened to order a Mussalman to enforce his orders,

---

13   A. Seaton to C. Lushington, 7 May 1810. *Records Of The Ludhiana Agency*, pp.211–212.
14   A. Seaton to C. Lushington, 7 May 1810. *Records Of The Ludhiana Agency*, pp.213–214.

and that the Ukaulees themselves and other priests of the temple have insisted on Phola Sing quitting the place.[15]

Akali Phula Singh had dared Ranjit Singh and Fateh Singh Ahluwalia to take action. If he was provoked, it would lead to bloodshed and from his standpoint would be a fight to the death.

> Phola Sing sent a harsh and indignant reply, declaring that Umritser had been the place of residence of Gooroo Baba Nanak; that he, Phola Sing, was one of that Gooroo's priests and would not leave the place, adding that, in the event of an attempt being made to expel him by force, he and forty or fifty Ukaulees who were devoted to him would resist to the last, being determined rather to perish than to yield.[16]

Ranjit Singh's forefathers' relationship with the Buddha Dal and the Akalis meant he would face a major backlash in the Panjab and create a major disorder, the likes of which even he could not prevent. This was indeed a test for the Maharajah, one which he could not concede to the British and in all probability he would not have wanted to. Ranjit Singh would make use of Phula Singh's talents and, as noted earlier, would turn the Akalis into a major force in his Irregular Army. Lepel Griffin describes the situation with regards to Phula Singh and his persona and reverence amongst the Sikhs. No one would dare try to attack the Buddha Dal leader, because:

> The garrison was accordingly marched against him, but when they approached, Phula Singh sent to ask them if they would kill their Guru (spiritual teacher). The Sikhs would not molest him; and the whole force was kept out some two months to prevent his plundering, marching where he marched, more like a guard of honour than anything else. Numberless stories of the same kind can be told of Phula Singh, who was a very remarkable man. He was a robber and an outlaw, but he was nevertheless a splendid soldier, and a brave, enthusiastic man.[17]

Indeed the prowess of the Akalis was a staple in stories of valour. Amongst the *Ferengi*, his 'Immortals' were well known:

---

15   Colonel Ochterlony to C. Lushington, 8 May 1810. *Records Of The Ludhiana Agency*, pp.214–215. The idea the Akalis wanted to expel Akali Phula Singh does not sound true but they may have advised him to seek alternative areas of protection.
16   A. Seaton to C. Lushington, 11 May 1810. *Records Of The Ludhiana Agency*, pp.215–216. The description that Guru Nanak had resided in Amritsar is erroneous. See Appendices for the full letter.
17   Griffin, *The Rajahs of Punjab*, p.350.

These men, whose designation signifies 'Immortal' were in the habit of rushing forward furiously upon the enemy in the beginning of a battle and throwing him into confusion, thereby often doing good service to their chief, who knew their value, and gave them every encouragement. They were led by one Phoola Sing, a desperado of a most fierce and sanguinary character and who figures prominently in the history of Runjeet's early career.[18]

Prominent Battles

Akali Phula Singh with his Nihang warriors were a force to be reckoned with even before the incidents with the British. The Akalis were in action at the Battle of Kasur. The Maharajah called upon the forces of the Akalis and employed them in laying siege to Kasur; this was on 10 February 1807. Two pitched battles were fought outside the city. Sikhs emerged victorious in both battles. Kutab-ud-din Khan went into the fort with his remaining army. The Sikh army laid a siege around the fort. Fire was exchanged by both sides for many days. One night, the wall of the fort was mined and brought down. The Khalsa army entered the fort and engaged the enemy in hand-to-hand combat. Soon, they overpowered their enemy. Kutab-ud-din was captured. The Akali was granted a *Jagir* on the bank of the River Sutlej. As a result, the territorial gains enhanced the ambitions of the Maharajah.

In October 1813, Maharajah Ranjit Singh ordered Diwan Ram Dayal, sardar Dal Singh, Phula Singh and Hari Singh Nalwa to capture all areas within Pir Panjal and annex them to the Khalsa Raj. Akali Phula Singh and the Akalis took a prominent part in this campaign and Rajouri Fort was captured by the Khalsa forces. In 1816, Ranjit Singh learnt the news that Mir Hafiz Khan had evicted Nawab Muhammad Khan. A small army was immediately sent on a campaign for punishing the miscreants under Akali Phula Singh and Fateh Singh Ahluwalia. Phula Singh attacked the fort of Ahmad Kot. The battle raged for three days. On 12 April 1816, the fort was blasted by a mine. The Nihangs of Phula Singh entered the fort and occupied it. The Mir was also captured.

One of the most prominent victories that the Nihangs won for the Maharajah was at the battle of Multan in 1818. After the Sikh army was unable to secure the fort, the Akalis were sent for. They reached there on 18 June. Phula Singh received a briefing from Prince Kharak Singh. The Zamzama Gun was deployed in front of Khizri Darwaza and firing commenced. It was about this time that an inspiring account was made by Ghulam Jilani, in his *Jang-i-Multan*. As the attack was commencing on the fort walls, one of the Sikh guns lost one of its wheels. It was decided that the Akalis

18   G. Carmichael Smyth, *A History of the Reigning Family of Lahore, with some account of the Jummoo Rajahs, the Seik soldiers and their Sirdars; with notes on Malcolm, Prinsep, Lawrence, Steinbach, McGregor, and the Calcutta Review* (Calcutta: W. Thacker and Co., 1847), p.21.

would hold up the gun on their shoulders. The Khalsa in the purest form was seen when there was no deliberating and all the Akalis rushed to be the first to lay down their lives. It was not until at least 11 Akalis had sacrificed themselves that a breach was made in the walls.[19]

The attack was led by Akali Sadhu Singh who broke the door into two. Akali soldiers entered the fort with the slogans or *Jaikaras* of 'Akal Akal.' Hand-to-hand fighting took place. The Ghazis fought with determination and did not yield an inch. The brave assault by Akali Sadhu Singh Nihang has been noted by many European, Muslim, and Sikh writers. Muzzafar Khan came face to face with Akali Phula Singh and was killed. His elder son Shah Nawaz attacked Phula Singh who then suffered a big wound. In the meantime, sardar Dhanna Singh Malwai and Sham Singh Attariwala reached Shah Nawaz and killed him there and then. The condition of the Ghazis became untenable. Reports say that more than 12,000 men including Nawab Muzzafar Khan and his five sons were killed in this battle. When Prince Kharak Singh, Akali Phula Singh and the other sardars reached Amritsar, the court was unanimous in their understanding of who was the hero of the campaign. Maharajah Ranjit Singh honoured Phula Singh with the title Protector of Khalsa Raj. The honour of the Multan victory rested on the head of Akali Phula Singh.

Akali-British Encounters

It is also worth recounting other practices of the Akalis which were described by the British. One description is of the Sikhs at the location of Nanden, in the Decan where Guru Gobind Singh ascended to the heavens. The author describes how a 'detach-ment of Europeans of the Madras Establishment, under the command of Lieutenant-Colonel Murray, was ordered by Sir Thomas Hislop, whilst at Hyderabad, to join his personal escort.[20] On their route the men experienced very great hardships from the badness of the roads, owing to the severe rains; and were also exposed to a most

---

19 Khushwant Singh, *Ranjit Singh: Maharaja of Punjab* (New Delhi: Penguin Books, 2009), p.33.

20 The anonymous author of this account in the *Summary of the Mahratta and Pindarree Campaign: During 1817, 1818, and 1819, Under Direction of the Marquis of Hastings: Chiefly Embracing the Operations of the Army of the Deckan, Under the Command of His Excellency Lieut. Gen. Sir T. Hislop, Bart. G.C.B.: With Some Particulars and Remarks* (London: E Williams, 1820), probably wrote his book under the pen name 'Carnaticus' because of his unsparing criticism of his superior officers and their conduct of the campaigns. He was actually an Irish officer in the Madras Army named Marshal Clarke. He was born in 1789, and he died at the early age of 44 in Peronne, northern France on his way home from India. His book, accompanied by beautifully engraved maps was first published in 1820 and gives a clear and lengthy account of the operations in 1817, 1818, and 1819 of the armies of the East India Company. This was particularly of the Army of the Deccan under the orders of the Marquis of Hastings and the direct command of Lt. Gen. Sir T. Hislop.

inclement monsoon.' The detachment reached the River Godavari where they came across the Sikhs of Nanden. A brief description is given of the Akalis at the Throne of Hazur Sahib. This early account enriches our idea not only of the Throne but also of the guardians – the Akali Nihangs,

> At this village [Nandere], we were much gratified by a visit to the Seik College, where there are upwards of 300 of that class instructed in matters of their religion, and the whole establishment is seemingly conducted with great regularity and application. The sages who preside there deliver out their lectures from their respective stalls, occupying at a convenient distance from each other, two sides of the hall of audience. These instructors appeared venerable, pious and respectable old men, seated upon carpels and having large and richly embroidered pillows before them, whence from their books they delivered out their discourses to their bearers. The Seik student always appears in public well dressed; and in stature, deportment, and habit, strikes the visitor at once with a prepossession in his favour. They are generally tall, of elegant symmetry, and in their countenance alone carry an expression of superiority and manliness, far above any other tribe in India. They generally dress in dark clothes with lofty blue turbans, and are on all occasions armed with a sword and shield, and many of them with an instrument of war which they wield with great dexterity and effect. This weapon resembles a common quoit, with this difference, that the plate of the former is perfectly flat on both sides, and not above the eighth of an inch in thickness. These are commonly carried in a dozen or two on the upper ball or crest of the turban, where they sit close together, and quite at hand for service. In using these missile weapons the fore-finger of the right hand is introduced into its cavity in the centre, and the inner edge brought to rest firmly on the ball of the same finger; the thumb is applied outside and over the edge (which is as sharp as a common knife) merely to direct the aim. The right leg is then drawn back, and the Seik, raising his arm above his head, and inclining his body downwards, discharges it in an horizontal direction, just as a boy skims a sheet of water with a slate. These weapons fly through the air faster than the eye can follow them; and the Seik makes as sure of hitting an object the size of a man at seventy or eighty yards as the best marksman could with a rifle. These weapons are used with best effect against bodies of cavalry, where, even at the distance of two hundred yards, one of them coming in contact with the horse's leg or body, will be sure to break the former, or plunge right into the latter. The Seiks use also bows and arrows with great skill, and are elegant horsemen, on these occasions using the spear and matchlock, and on all public ceremonies displaying their beautifully embroidered black banners, with curious devices upon them. This class of people bear the most deadly antipathy to the Mahomedans.[21]

21   Anon., *Summary of the Mahratta and Pindarree Campaign*, pp.85–88.

It is interesting to note that the Akalis at Nanden are described in the same manner as the Akalis at the Akal Takht and other places in India. This confirms the notion that the Buddha Dal continued its sway across all Gurdwaras and the Thrones of Polity from the eighteenth century to the start of the nineteenth century. The descriptions of the Sikh Scriptures, the *Dastar Boongas* and the wielding of the *Chakkar* are all traits that the British witnessed in the Panjab, which were also seen with the Akalis at this location. It was Charles Wilkins in 1781 who described the *Throne at Patna* as a college and again this inference is made based on the discourses made by the Gianis (reciters of the scriptures) at Hazur Sahib.[22] The Throne was not just a place of worship but also an educational establishment. Sikhs could get initiation in the Khalsa precepts and in the ways of wielding the sword or *Shastarvidia* at these thrones. The description also shows how the *Chakkar* was held in great esteem. It appears, however, on this occasion the British passing through the Sikh domain was a peaceful excursion.

The Growing Evil: The Babel Trees of Hazur Sahib

Some years later, the British would again come into contact with the Akalis at Hazur Sahib. The Throne was surrounded by a number of trees and hedges. This was a sort of protection from the outside world. In some ways, their way of life could be protected as the sacred ground of the Tenth Guru was indeed sacred. The babel trees, it is understood, were actually planted by Guru Gobind Singh during his sojourn; so not only did the Guru foresee his last breathing ground but gave the area lasting protection. The Akalis at Hazur Sahib, however, also had other reasons for growing the trees:

> The small Seikh colony at Nundour, in the Deccan, when asked why they hem in their settlement with a Babul hedge, reply, that the plantation is intended to supply tent-pins for the Seikh (Panjab) Army; implying, of course, that the Khalsa will so far extend their conquests.[23]

Gestures like these were treated with amusement by some British officers who underestimated the strength and the power invested by the Tenth Guru in the Sikhs. This particular notion of sovereignty was alien to the British, as to them, one Sikh represented one Sikh. The Sikh in their own psyche represented *Sawa Lakh* or were equal to 125,000. The concept of *Raj Kharega Khalsa* or the 'Khalsa will rule' continues to be a rallying cry for the Sikhs.[24] The supplying of tent pegs to the Panjab shows the relationship between the Sikhs of Nanded and Panjab. This respect was reciprocated by

---

22 See 'Charles Wilkins and the Throne at Patna', in my book *The British and the Sikhs*, pp.28–33.

23 *Calcutta Review*, Volumes 1–2, 1844.

24 This is not better represented than in the daily recitation of the Sikhs called the petition or the *Ardas* which resounds with the theme of Sikh sovereignty.

Maharajah Ranjit Singh when sending materials to Nanded. The British understood the military advantage the hedges gave the Sikhs; it was an enclosed centre of operations, so they cleverly disposed of these so they could see the activities of the Khalsa.

The Final Battle: Naushera

Akali Phula Singh would continue to serve the Khalsa with authority and sincerity and there was no campaign where he would not be seen leading at the front. This bold strategy would also cost him his life. The early morning congregation took place on 14 March 1823.[25] The entire Sikh army and the generals attended the assembly. The Afghan forces headed by Azim Khan from Afghanistan were buoyant and wanted to reclaim their lost territories. Maharajah Ranjit Singh and the generals had already discussed the impending battle. The view of the Darbar was that if they delayed the attack any longer, it would enable the enemy to muster their army in large numbers. So it was decided to launch an attack immediately. The Akalis were in favour of this move. Thirty thousand Ghazis, blinded by the enthusiasm of *jihad*, let loose a volley of fire on the Khalsa army. The Akalis kept advancing and wanted to take on the enemy in sword and lance battle. They were adept in their use and preferred it over the guns. Seeing the Akalis advancing fearlessly in the rain of bullets, Maharajah Ranjit Singh could not keep himself aloof from the scene of action. He ordered his army to march with the help of Akali brethren. He marched with his army and attacked the Ghazis who were trying to encircle the army of the Nihangs and were looking at that time to be succeeding. According to Smyth, his martyrdom was an epic encounter with the Afghans that defined not only Akali Phula Singh but his band of Akalis. His narration deserves to be recounted in full:

> Just at this critical juncture, however, he saw, to his great joy and equally great surprise, the black banner of Phoola Sing and his Akalees moving along the foot and then up the side of the disputed hill. The Akalee chief at the head of his five hundred desperadoes was advancing against the enemy. Runjeet had himself seen Phoola Sing, in the heat of the engagement, struck from his horse by a musket ball which shattered the cap of his knee. He had seen him borne to the rear to all appearance utterly disabled. But there was Phoola Sing seated on an elephant actually leading his little band to the assault. On went the Akalees after their leader who from his elephant shouted an invitation to the whole army to follow them. The army did not respond to his call, but up the hill and towards the foe went Phoola Sing and his men, determined to decide the fate of the day by a desperate assault. The Afghans waited not for their attack, but rushed down the hill to become

---

25   The description has been taken from Gurinder Singh Mann and Kamalroop Singh, *Akali Phula Singh and his Turban*, unpublished manuscript.

the assailants. At this moment, Phoola Sing ordered his men to dismount and let their horses go. This was done, and at the same instant the Akalees shouted their war-cry of Wah Gooroojee! of which the Afghans as loudly answered with their Allah! Allah! The horses set at liberty, either from habit or alarmed by the tumult, rushed wildly forward and into the ranks of the enemy. This strange and unexpected attack caused some confusion in the Afghan host, observing which the Akalees, throwing down their matchlocks, rushed forward sword in hand with impetuosity as to drive back the enemy, and to secure themselves a footing on the hill. The main body of the Seiks witnessing this success of the Akalees, now took heart, and with a loud cheer rushed forward en masse to take advantage of it. By this movement, a body of twelve or fifteen hundred Afghans placed betwixt the Akalee band and the advancing Seik army. Finding themselves thus exposed on both sides, they took to flight, endeavouring to elude the Akalees who were above them, and to make their way towards the summit, where their main body, some eight or ten thousand men, was strongly posted. But Phoola Sing was not the man to permit them to escape so easily; he turned and attacked them with such vigour that they were speedily brought to a stand, and in the attempt to check his advance, lost above six hundred men. The Akalee force, however, was by this time reduced to little more than one hundred and fifty. Yet this exploit of theirs, had so inspired the main body of the army with courage and spirits that hastening to the support of the little band of heroes, they completely routed the Afghan detachment, and followed up their advantage by a desperate effort to dislodge the more powerful body of the enemy from its position on the summit of the hill. Phoola Sing mounted on his elephant led the advance undeterred by the receipt of another musket ball in his body. The Akalees rushed on, in front of the attacking army, eager to close with the enemy. As they approached the position of the Afghans, they were met by a most destructive fire of matchlocks and musketry, which greatly thinned the small party of Akalees who now remained. At this moment the mahout who conducted the elephant on which Phoola Sing was seated, having already received three balls in his body, and being terrified at the close and destructive fire, hesitated to advance. In vain the chief urged him to proceed directly towards the enemy, the man was panic-struck and seemed rather to meditate a retreat. On this Phoola Sing drew a pistol from his belt and shot him through the head. He then with the point of his sword urged the elephant forward towards the enemy. He had not, however, advanced much further when a bullet from an Afghan matchlock entered his fore-head, and he fell back in his howdah a corpse. The death of their leader so infuriated the Akalees, that though their first charge was repulsed, they again and again returned to the assault with more desperate resolution, and in the end made a way for the Seik army into the midst of the enemy's position, and dislodged him from the height with great slaughter. Runjeet, now rejoined by many of his troops who had fled at the first reverse, followed up his advantage, and falling on the Afghans who had again formed at the foot of the hill, put them to flight in the greatest tumult and confusion, numbers of them hiding themselves in the long grass of a neighbouring swamp where they were cut to pieces or shot down by the victorious Seiks. The loss on the side of the Seiks was upwards of five thousand men, and it was thought that the Afghans lost nearly double that number.[26]

Thus Akal Phula Singh, the Jathedar of the Akal Takht and the Akali Nihangs, became a famous *Shahid* in 1823, which followed in the long line of the Khalsa martyrs. The battle was won for Ranjit Singh, after all hope of victory had fled, by the bravery of Phula Singh, so gallantly supported by his troop of his Akalis. The heroism of the chief won the applause of both Sikhs and Muslims. There were 3,000 losses and Sikhs lost 2,000 men in the encounter whilst the Afghans fled back to Kabul leaving their baggage, tents and guns.[27] A tomb was erected over his remains, on the spot where he fell, and although watched and attended by a party of Akalis, it also became a place of pilgrimage for Hindus and Muslims. At the location of his cremation, the Maharajah attached a big *Jagir* for its maintenance. The *Samadhi* stands at Pir Sabak, and can still be found four miles east of the Naushera side of the Kabul River.[28] Ballads and tales were recounted regarding the cult of Akali Phula Singh and this extended far beyond Sikh folklore with poems of valour written by the British as well.[29] The writer Ganesh Das paid his tribute as follows:

Phoola Singh fell a martyr
He fought a great battle, against the Turks
Along with many Sikhs, he waged a relentless fight,
He won salvation
He gave his life for the honour of the Panth,
He won against the Duranis
and won acclamation
He had a longing to fight the Ferengis too
Seldom will a lion of his sort be born again.[30]

---

26   Smyth, *A History of the Reigning Family of Lahore*, pp.189–191.
27   Another notable death was that of General Balbhadra Singh (1789–1823) Gurkha. A commander who was also known for his defence of Nepal during the Anglo-Nepalese War (1814–1816). Azim Khan died some time afterward dejected and heartbroken. Gupta, *History of the Sikhs* Vol. V, pp.150–151.
28   The tomb of Akali Phula Singh is in a dilapidated state and is difficult to get to as there is much growth of trees surrounding the area. Many Sikh shrines related to the Gurus and other historical places in Pakistan have been in neglect since partition. For a good understanding of Sikh shrines in Pakistan, see Dalvir Pannu, *The Sikh Heritage: Beyond Borders* (USA: Pannu Dental Group, 2019).
29   Henry F. Brookes in *The Victories Of The Sutlej, A Prize Poem: Together With The Sailor's Christmas Eve, And Other Pieces* (1848), pp. 100–102, wrote a poem describing the heroism of Akali Phula Singh. R. W. Bingham's book, *General Gilbert's Raid To The Khyber* (1850), pp. 98–102 is a testament to the heroic encounter at Naushera.
30   Singh, 'Akali Phoola Singh – The Great Warrior', pp.42–45.

Akali Phula Singh Burj, Amritsar. (Photo: Gurinder Singh Mann)

Another memorial, known as Burj Akali Phula Singh, was later erected in Amritsar. This land was given to the Akalis by Ranjit Singh, where Phula Singh had spent most of his time when free from military campaigns. The Burj at Amritsar had developed as a headquarters for the Nihangs and is known as the location where Guru Hargobind undertook *Shastarvidia*.

Phula Singh would be succeeded by Akali Hanuman Singh who led the Akali forces in the Anglo-Sikh Wars; he met his death partly on the treachery of the Patiala forces whose cannonade killed many of his followers. The Akalis were the national Sikh army and one which the whole Khalsa commonwealth recognised. Thus, the Sikhs had lost their great general, a true Sikh. He was a fearless and skilled commander. He maintained the *sant sipahi* tradition of the Khalsa. Akali Phula Singh remains a role model for all Sikhs to this day.

10

First Anglo-Sikh War

The Intrigues at the Lahore Durbar

The reign of Maharajah Ranjit Singh came to an end in 1839 and unleashed a series of events that the Panjab was not ready for. Succession within empires is always an important juncture that can maintain the hegemony or can collapse a state, and when chaos can run riot. It was the latter which was witnessed partly during 1839 up to the advent of the First Anglo-Sikh War of 1845. Some of these events need to be recounted to ensure the reader is aware of the conditions that the Sikh Army was in before the war with the EIC began.

The bid for succession was between the Princes Sher Singh, popular with the army, and Kharak Singh, the elder son of Ranjit Singh, with the latter ultimately taking the mantle. The investiture of Kharak Singh as Maharajah took place on 1 September 1839, two months after the death of Ranjit Singh. There has also been a suggestion that his son Nau Nihal Singh, popular with Ranjit Singh, would have been a better choice at this time. The coronation took place whilst Nau Nihal Singh was on his way to Delhi and was not informed of Ranjit Singh's death, hence leading to this view.[1] Dhian Singh, one of the Dogra Brothers, and the Prime Minister instigated the first shot and started the spiral into the depths of intrigue. He arranged for the confidant of the Maharajah, Chet Singh, to be killed. This essentially resulted in Kharak Singh being Maharajah in name only and his son, Nau Nihal, taking the official reins of government. This arrangement continued until a year later when Kharak Singh died after failing health in November 1840. It was during the funeral that matters took another twist. Nau Nihal Singh was riding through an archway of the Hazuri Bagh, Lahore, when he was crushed to death under the brickwork with his colleagues. This would lead to further speculation as to whether this was premeditated. The information was kept quiet until Prince Sher Singh was informed and a declaration was made on 7 December 1840.

---

1   He was also supported by Durbar courtiers.

Naul Nihal Singh and Kharak Singh. (John Martin Honigberger,
Thirty-Five Years in the East (London, 1852))

Chand Kaur (1802–1842), the widow of Maharajah Kharak Singh and mother of
Nau Nihal Singh, now petitioned for the position of Regent of the Panjab. This was
an interesting prospect especially as the claim was based on her daughter in law, Sahib
Kaur's, unborn baby who could be heir to the Sikh state. This was accepted by the
courtiers of the Durbar but she would only be in power for less than two months.
The child was stillborn and this ended the brief rule of the only female ruler of the
Sikh Empire. Dhian Singh and Maharajah Sher Singh looked to take power with the
support of the army and Lahore was attacked with a skirmish taking place between
the forces. The Maharani, now deposed, was allowed to retire peacefully and given a
pension. However, in 1842, she was considered to have been murdered by her attendants in her chambers.

Maharajah Sher Singh attained the reign of the Sikh Empire on 27 January 1842.
Once in power, he set about trying to stamp his authority on the Durbar but he was
also at the mercy of the power brokers-the Sikh army. They demanded an increase in
pay and other gifts. At this time, the treasury was in a depleted state, with revenues
not in the same condition as several years ago and the governors were taking advantage of the prevailing situation and not sending their receipts to Lahore. The troops
were now getting into an unruly disposition and the city of Lahore became a scene
of debauchery for six to eight weeks; this was a low ebb for the Panjab and a slap
in the face for the Empire that was built upon not only their hard work but by the
mighty sword of Ranjit Singh. Many governors and army personnel faced the wrath of
this new army of the Khalsa. Governor of Kashmir, Colonel Mian Singh, was at the

`wrong end of his troops who hacked him to pieces and other *Ferengi* officers were also subject to mistreatment and the sword.² Colonel Foulkes, who was present in Mandi and Kulu was killed, and Major Ford in Hazara met the same fate. The Amritsar Garrison commander was also deposed of. Colonel Avitabile and Diwan Mulraj of Multan played the ruse of increasing the armies' wages with a view of buying time to save themselves. This all led to the army developing into their own institution known as a *Panchayats*. They regarded themselves as the representative body of the Khalsa and so above the Durbar's rules. This left Sher Singh in a weakened position. A settlement was made between the Maharajah and the Sandhanwalia sardars in 1842 which was supposed to settle the differences within the court. However, this was an opportunity to get rid of Sher Singh and the minister Dhian Singh, which happened on 15 September 1843. The Sandhanwalia faction arranged an inspection of the troops and Sher Singh, without suspicion, undertook the duty. On the pretence of showing off a new gun, Ajit Singh shot the prince and then as he fell on the ground, decapitated him. The son of Sher Singh, Prince Pratap Singh, was killed by Lehna Singh Sandhanwalia. On the same day, Dhian Singh, who had managed to be a key player in Lahore Durbar affairs was also killed. The spiral of murders and death continued and within two days the Sandhanwalias now faced retribution from the son of Dhian Singh, Hira Singh. With the support of the *Fauj-i-Khas* and the troops of Colonel Avitabile and Court, they laid siege to the fort with cannons resulting in 1,000 dead, among them Lahina Singh and Ajit Singh Sandhanwalia. This period in September essentially saw over 1,000 deaths including the Maharajah, his son, the prime minister, the Sandhanwalia sardars and other dignitaries killed in succession.³

There was no shortage of successors of Ranjit Singh but there was no one adequate to manage the affairs and bring about a peaceful transition. Hira Singh, now Wazir or Prime Minister now required the Maharajah to serve his purposes. The period of military dominance was however in the hand of the *Panchayats*. For a few short months, Hira Singh tried to install stability into the lands and was successful in reinstating receipts from the provinces. Hira Singh may have thought his plan of a Dogra rule had succeeded and in part, this was true. However, he had put his own cronies into power including Pandit Jalla.⁴

The Regent or Queen Mother of the Sikh Empire and the younger wife of Ranjit Singh, Jindan Kaur had also to come to the fore during this time. Her son Duleep Singh, still an infant, was pronounced Maharajah. An incident took place where Pandit Jalla used foul language against her when she was giving out alms to the poor.

2   An unfortunate end to a colonel who had been Governor of Kashmir between 1834-1841 and was responsible for major improvements in the area and the minting of coins. Many of which can be seen at the British Museum, London.
3   Kohli, *Sunset of the Sikh Empire*, p.73.
4   The Pandit was the tutor of Hira Singh and remained his lifelong companion and became his adviser and deputy as he assumed the office of the prime minister of the Sikh kingdom.

Maharani Jindan Kaur and Maharajah Duleep Singh. (John Martin Honigberger, *Thirty-Five Years in the East* (London, 1852))

She appealed to the *Panchayats* for support and his arrest. Whilst this was pending, Hira Singh and Pandit Jalla, sensing their days were numbered, fled Lahore with jewellery and cash when they were noticed by lookouts. The message was relayed back to the Durbar and the army led by Sham Singh Attariwala with 6,000 troopers overtook the fleeing party. There was an exchange of fire and eventually, Hira Singh and his party were all killed. One part of the Dogra hegemony had now come to an end and the Queen Mother, Jindan Kaur, had the army to contend with. This led to the new government of the Panjab which was composed of Jindan Kaur and her brother Jawahir Singh.[5] Lal Singh and Tej Singh provided military counsel which was restricted to certain people.

The power of the army and the increase in pay, described in the tables in Chapter 5, are most profound. They show how the promises to prop up the army were empty promises and this ultimately led to a new power answerable only to themselves. The financial resources of the state were depleted and the treasury was running dry. The figures for the *Fauj-i-Ain* in all branches rose from Rs35,242 in 1839–40 to Rs51,452 in 1843–44. The salary receipts rose from Rs4,211,292 to Rs8,730,108 with similar increases in the Irregular Army.[6]

Essentially, since the death of Ranjit Singh in 1839, the state was spending twice the amount of money on the army. The Durbar was now in an untenable state. They were no longer receiving the revenues which they had received before, despite attempts being made to raise the revenue. This included the *Jagirdars* not paying their due stipends.

---

5   Jawahir Singh also fell afoul of the army and he was killed, much to the dismay and indignation of Jindan Kaur. She was helpless against them.

6   Kohli, *Sunset of the Sikh Empire*, p.85.

Dismantling the Sikh State from the Outside

Whilst the above would suggest that this was all internal politics playing out, the part of the EIC is also not beyond suspicion and there are many anecdotes to suggest that the British were also looking to ensure that they came out winners in any power plays. As a result, we need to consider the correspondence and despatches to see what the motive was to take over the Panjab. The letters written by Lord Ellenborough to Queen Victoria and the Duke of Wellington are not just revelatory but actually support the idea of the British preparing for war, turning conjecture into actual fact. Reports from the time suggest that the time for taking over the Panjab was ripe in October 1843, after the intrigues at Lahore:

> …it is impossible not to perceive that the ultimate tendency of the late events at Lahore is, without any effort on our part, to bring the plains first, and at a some-what, later period the hills, under our direct protection or control.[7]

In November 1843, Lord Ellenborough stated that the areas below the Sutlej were now being strengthened for any impending Sikh attack:

> On our side we have one European and two native regiments of infantry at each of the points of Ferozepore and Loodianah, besides cavalry and artillery, and there will be a strong force at Umballah [Ambala], besides a European regi-ment at Kassowley. Mud works are in process of erection round the magazine at Ferozepore. The old fort of Loodianah will be strengthened.'[8]

They were uncertain whether the Sikh army would make an attack but by April 1844, Lord Ellenborough's thoughts were 'we cannot but feel that the termination of the present state of things in the Punjab is essential to the security of the British power in India; but he will wait, cautiously preparing our strength for a contest he would will-ingly defer, but which he considers inevitable.'[9]

The British had also made a mistake in allowing Attar Singh Sandhanwalia to leave Thanesar and cause further issues in the Panjab. Hira Singh's forces had crossed the Sutlej to intercept him and were fearful that the British were causing a rift in Lahore. This caused apprehension on the part of the Sikhs that the British were going to attack the Panjab. Another incident, not well-known, centred on Suchet Singh who had been killed in the intrigues of Panjab. He had considerable amounts of money and treasury below the Sutlej. The Lahore Durbar deemed this as their property and so

---

7   Lord Colchester, *History Of The Indian Administration Of Lord Ellenborough in his Correspondence with the Duke of Wellington* (London: Richard Bentley and Son, 1874), p.98.
8   Colchester, *History Of The Indian Administration*, p.406.
9   Colchester, *History Of The Indian Administration*, p.124.

petitioned the EIC for this. They were non-committal and this led to further distrust between the British and the Sikhs.

Interestingly, there were also reports of mutineers and deserters in the British camp. The EIC were worried about this and fearing an attack, Ellenborough wrote to the Duke of Wellington in April 1844: 'I earnestly hope nothing may compel us to cross the Sutlej, and that we may have no attack to repel till November 1845. I shall then be prepared for anything. In the meantime we do all we can in a quiet way to strengthen ourselves.'[10] This statement was repeated in May 1844 when Dhian Singh was plunging Panjab into chaos: 'Everything is going on there as we could desire, if we looked forward to the ultimate possession of the Punjab.'[11] The date is very interesting, as if it was almost planned for the First Sikh War to start in December 1845. Almost a year and a half would be required for planning a war against the Sikhs. Hugh Gough, who won both Sikh wars for the British, would later be condemned for his military tactics in view of the high casualties the British received.

Ellenborough doubted that Hugh Gough should be in charge of military operations and felt his abilities lay in leading the initial attack and in essence a Divisional Commander.[12] Henry Hardinge would replace Ellenborough as Governor-General in December 1844 and would now be in charge of seeing the war through in that capacity. Whilst initially hesitant about the war, Hira Singh's death was the catalyst. Another catalyst was the appointing of Major George Broadfoot (1807–45), the British Resident at Ludhiana, who unlike his predecessor was following a line of incitement and provocation. During this time, the British were accused of breaking the 'Treaty of Friendship' in four instances.[13] His access to information on Sikh positions seemed to have reached him directly and not through proper channels; 'Broadfoot, though somewhat more remote from the frontier than some of his Assistants, got important and trustworthy news before it reached them.'[14] Together with Captain Nicholson,

---

10   Colchester, *History Of The Indian Administration*, p.435.
11   Colchester, *History Of The Indian Administration*, p.437.
12   'I ought not to conceal from you that the anxiety I feel not to be called too suddenly into the field is much increased by a want of confidence in Sir Hugh Gough, who, with all his personal courage and many excellent qualities, certainly does not appear to possess the grasp of mind or the prudence which is essential to the successful conduct of great military operations. He would do admirably, I have no doubt, at the head of an advanced guard. … We are altogether very ill-provided with officers for the higher commands. The whole army requires a great deal of teaching, and I am satisfied the eighteen months I ask are not more than enough to make it what it ought to be.' Colchester, *History Of The Indian Administration*, p.435.
13   According to Broadfoot's biographer, 'The cases cited were: that Hakim Bai and his Sowars had been treated with indignity; that Lai Singh, Adalati, had not been allowed to cross the Sutlej; that the Lahore Ahlkars had been disrespectfully used; and that Suchet Singh's gold had not been handed over to the Darbar.' Major W. Broadfoot, *The Career of Major George Broadfoot, C. B. … In Afghanistan and the Punjab*, (London: John Murray,1888), p.375.
14   Broadfoot, *The Career of Major George Broadfoot*, p.379.

they were in contact with Lal Singh and Tej Singh. According to Captain Humbly, 'It cannot be denied, that the Sikhs had considerable cause for provocation.'[15] He continues that '...so great was the influence which Captain Nicolson exercised over some of their chiefs, that he prevailed upon Lall Singh to divide his forces; and it was only a division of Sikhs which fought at Moodkee on the 18th December.'[16] This is the reason why the Sikh commanders in history have been seen as being treacherous and disloyal to the Sikh Durbar. Many Sikhs disbelieve they lost the war against the British but rather were sold down the river with plans of their attack being given away. The prime reason for doing this was to break the Sikh army and to be part of any new world order after the war. Gulab Singh Dogra is also cited as colluding with the British to dismantle the Sikh state in order to gain favour with them if the Sikhs lost the war.[17] He intimated that 'the Lahore Government meant to make war against the British, wished to cast in his lot with the latter, as his existence depended on their success.'[18]

The Battle of Mudki

The battle of Mudki was fought on 18 December 1845.[19] It pitted Raja Lal Singh and Tej Singh against Lieutenant General Hugh Gough and Governor-General Henry Hardinge. On 9 December 1845, several units of the Sikh army had moved towards Ferozepur where the British cantonment was, the other being at Ludhiana. The locations of the EIC were not heavily guarded and the Sikh army could have easily attacked these areas with minor losses. They knew the British army was still at Ambala and would take a few days to reach the Sutlej. Lal Singh had split the Sikh forces, a plan which he had discussed with the British, across four areas of the Panjab: Ferozepur, Ferozeshah, Mudki and Phillour.[20] Under the orders of Tej Singh, Commander-in-Chief of the Sikh army, Kanh Singh Mann, Shumsher Singh,

---

15   W.W.W Humbly, *Journal of a Cavalry Officer: Including the Memorable Sikh Campaign of 1845–46* (London: Longman, Brown, Green, and Longmans, 1854), p.37 Also cites several reasons similar to W. Broadfoot.

16   Humbly, *Journal of a Cavalry Officer*, pp.40–41.

17   Letter from Frederick Currie to Major Broadfoot, 25 November 1845: 'Goolab Singh's game, to induce the Ranee [Jindan Kaur] and Sirdars to urge the army to this demonstration, with a view to bringing a solemn re- monstrance at least from us; this remonstrance and our impending anger to be used by the troops as a plea for putting those obnoxious to Goolab Singh to death, and thus smoothing his way to power,' Broadfoot, *The Career of Major George Broadfoot*, p.370.

18   Broadfoot, *The Career of Major George Broadfoot, p.*373.

19   Alternative variations of the area include Mudkee/Moodkee. Fought on the south bank of the Sutlej River in the Panjab.

20   Amarpal Singh, *The First Anglo–Sikh War* (Stroud: Gloucestershire: Amberley Publishing, 2010), p.42.

Chutter Singh, Mewa Singh and Rattan Singh Mann were to remain at Ferozepore. On 13 December, Tej Singh and the *Fauj-i-Khas* had crossed the Sutlej into their own territories and surrounded Ferozepur. The location where they crossed was at the fords deemed as Sikh demarcated areas. This was a defensive position. There was no declaration of war by the Sikhs. Governor-General Hardinge issued a proclamation declaring war on the Sikhs and an erroneous one at that. The Sikh army's strategy was to neutralise the limited threat posed by Major-General Littler (1783–1856), and his small force of the 27th Native Infantry who fortified the garrison, and then set about protecting the area. However, Tej Singh had ample opportunity to destroy the Ferozepur cantonment, but he chose not to order any attack, which gave the British a huge advantage later at Ferozeshah. When Littler and his forces came out to rout the Sikhs, Lal Singh retreated, much to the chagrin of the Sikh army. Further lack of ambition was exhibited by Tej Singh when he asked Ranjodh Singh Majithia who was stationed at Phillaur, Ludhiana, to remain static. These forces could have been pivotal to the fight at Mudki. No engagements took place and this was the starting of what Sikhs saw as their betrayal by the Sikh commanders. Lal Singh was entrenched at Ferozeshah awaiting the main British army.

The stage was now being set for the actual battle at Mudki which pitted a number of Sikh generals and commanders against the main British and Bengal army, under its commander in chief, Hugh Gough, which had begun marching rapidly from its garrisons at Ambala and Meerut. The British forces were known as the 'Army of the Sutlej' hence the campaign named after these battles. On 16 December, Gough had reached Bussean and a rendezvous took place with Governor-General Hardinge who was at Ludhiana. The Wadni garrison of the Sikhs came under fire from the British and this became the first skirmish in the war. Lal Singh sent part of his detachment to face Gough at Mudki. Advance parties from both parties arrived at Mudki with the main British force arriving around 4:00 p.m. Shah Mohammed notes:

> There is a village by the name of Mudki
> Where a moat filled with water separated the armies.
> The freshly-recruited Akali horsemen
> Had just planted their flags in the battlefield,
> When the Feringhee guns started booming.[21]

It was during this initial encounter that the Nihangs captured a British officer. Ganda Singh Nihang, the officer in charge of the Nihangs, confident that his horse could go anywhere on earth and could cover any distance, arrived in the neighbourhood of

---

21   Shah Mohammed gives an interesting and glowing account of the First Sikh War. He is critical of both the Sikhs and the British. He was considered to be related to Sultan Mohammed of the artillery division. *Jangnamah*, p.189.

Mudki. There he captured an Englishman and some servants, who had arrived there in the train of the Governor-General, and sent them to the Sikh camp.[22]

The Englishman in question was Captain Biddulph of the 3rd Irregular cavalry who was captured in the early skirmish by Ganda Singh's Akalis. He was taken to Lal Singh's tent at Ferozeshah where he was treated humanely. He would later supply key information on Sikh positions.[23] Ganda Singh Nihang received word that the Governor-General's forces had arrived nearby; this information was relayed to Lal Singh.

These forces, tired after the march from Ambala, were in need of food, drink and rest. Lal Singh essentially kept a defensive position. The kettle drums of the Khalsa had started; Bahadur Singh's brigade was on the right, *Fauj-i-Khas* in the middle, Mehtab Singh on the left, *Ghorchurahs* (cavalry) and regular units were pitched on both sides, with Sikh snipers in the trees.[24] Their artillery was polished and ready for action.[25] There was a jungle between the two armies. The numbers of both forces were around 13,000. The Sikhs had around 10,000 cavalry and around 3,000 infantry plus 22 guns.[26] The British had Europeans as one-third of the army. In terms of artillery, they also had more guns; maybe two to one. Hugh Gough was on the right flank, together with Henry Hardinge. Behind them were the units under Lieutenant-General Harry Smith (1787–1860) who were positioned on the right flank. Major-General Gilbert (1785–1853) was in the centre whilst General John McCaskill commanded another division positioned on the left.

Major Broadfoot, the political officer, approached the British camp and shouted, 'The Sikhs are upon us.' The campaign started with gun bombardment on both sides, with Brigadier Brooks who limbered up his '12 field battery 9-pounders' and '30 horse artillery 6-pounders.' There was no sign of leadership on the part of the Sikhs commanders; Lal Singh was nowhere to be seen, with some reports saying he was hiding under a bush. Bahadur Singh's brigade was the first to face the British forces with guns and matchlocks.[27] After some time, Gough ordered a cavalry charge led by the 3rd Light Dragoons – who took the heaviest losses – charged at the *Ghorchurahs*. They managed to capture a Sikh battle standard. Their action in battle labelled them

22   Vidya Sagar Suri, *Some Original Sources Of Punjab History* (Lahore: Punjab University Historical Society, 1956), p.71. This text *Waqai-i-Jang-i-Sikhan* contains eyewitness testimony by Sikhs on the battlefield at Mudki and Ferozeshah. It was compiled by Ajudhia Prashad of the *Fauj-i-Khas*.
23   Kohli, *Sunset of the Sikh Empire*, p.109.
24   Singh, *The First Anglo-Sikh War*, p.57
25   'Mahmud Ali marched out from his Majha country, Taking awesome artillery pieces out of the city. The brigade of Sultan Mahmud also came out, With invincible Imam Shahi guns in tow. Elahi Baksh brought out his guns after polishing them, And showing them worshipful burning incense sticks. O Shah Mohammed! In such a way did the guns shine, As if these were the flashes of lightning, out to dispel darkness.' *Jangnamah*, p.173.
26   Hugh Cook, *The Sikh Wars*, (London: Leo Cooper Ltd, 1975), p.44.
27   Suri, *Some Original Sources*, p.72.

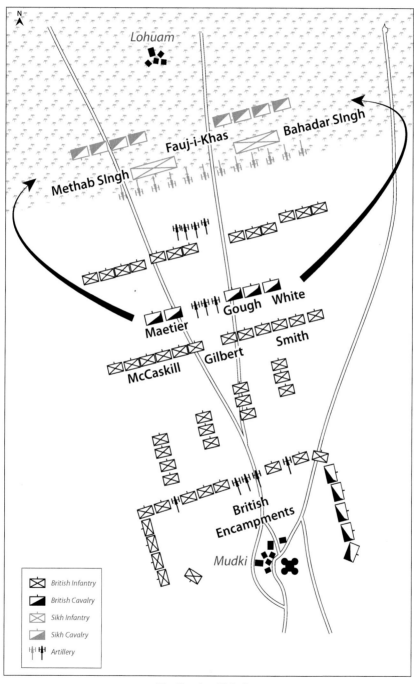

The Battle of Mudki.

The Battle of Moodkee on 18 December 1845. (By Henry Martens, 1846)

the '*Moodkee Wallahs*' whilst the Sikhs had a different label, '*Shaitan ke Bacchi*' – children of Satan.[28] The *Ghorchurahs* were dealt with by an attack from the Native Cavalry Lancers and the Dragoons which led to a Sikh withdrawal.

The British Infantry was now poised to attack but the air was full of thick dust leading to a confused state for them. This allowed Sikh snipers to start firing on the British cavalry, aided by the jungle the Sikh line of defence maintained itself, leading to a British withdrawal. The Khalsa attack was sustained by the Muslim gunners and Sikh infantry. This all led to hand-to-hand combat between both forces, but the Sikhs sustained heavy losses due to this direct action. The Akalis were noted for their usual bravado with one offering to take on a whole British regiment. The British became detached from their own regiments and confusion was paramount, the thickness of the jungle providing a distraction. In the melee, Hugh Gough took over and directed the charge at the Sikh guns. Most of the Muslim gunners and infantry fell in this charge who, to their credit, did not leave their positions. The assault was disastrous for the British with General Robert Sale, Joseph McCaskill, Brigadier Bolton and two aides of the Governor-General being amongst the 215 or so killed and 655 wounded. The 31st Regiment of Foot sustained heavy losses with both of their officers carrying

---

28   Cook, *The Sikh Wars*, p.47. The war cry for the 3rd Light Dragoons would be 'remember Mudki' in future conflicts.

the colours killed. The Sikhs certainly suffered more losses but no records were kept. This untidy encounter came to an end. The Sikhs made their way to Lohaum and then Ferozeshah. Yet the confusion continued with Lieutenant-Colonel Bunbury drifting into the Sikh positions after the battle had ended. The British captured 17 guns, yet interestingly they were not damaged by British fire.[29] This was all due to the British missing the Sikh artillery hidden behind the dust and in the jungle. So, in essence, a small force of the total Sikh army was deployed in this encounter and Gough's insistence on fighting as soon as he arrived at Mudki left the British with major casualties. Henry Hardinge, with his experience in the field, offered his services as second in command under Gough, which he accepted. The British may have expected an easier confrontation, as they were so often used to seeing native armies crumbling from the ferocity of the EIC forces. The Sikhs were also reflecting and questioning the motives of Lal Singh and Tej Singh. However, both armies were still ready for another confrontation.

The Battle of Ferozeshah

The Battle of Ferozeshah was fought between 21 and 22 December 1845.[30] There was no change in the generals that fought in the battle: Hugh Gough and Henry Hardinge were pitted against Raja Lal Singh and Tej Singh. The day after the Battle of Mudki, the dead on both sides were buried or cremated where possible. However, many bodies were left to rot. The British went to secure the Mudki Fort where they were met by Sikh snipers. Lal Singh conveyed the Sikh position to the British through emissary Shams-ud-Din, and this reached Major Broadfoot; the information was essentially favouring an attack to the north.[31] Gough preferred a direct attack from the south and for it to be undertaken imminently. Hardinge, in view of the fighting spirit of the Sikhs and receiving intelligence at Mudki, overruled Gough and ordered that the attack be deferred till Littler's force from Ferozepur joined the main army. The undermining of Gough's authority had begun. This suggests that Gough was not privy to any secret correspondence being received by Hardinge.

On the other hand, Tej Singh with a force of ten thousand under him, remained idle in the neighbourhood of the battlefield, absurdly pretending that he was guarding Ferozepur, although Littler's force of 5,000 had left clearly in broad daylight.[32] Lal Singh was being admonished by his own artillery for not moving quickly enough and for failing at Mudki. It has often been asked that if Lal Singh was treacherous why did none of the Sikhs do anything about it?. Interestingly, Diwan Ajudhia Prashad notes

29   Cook, *The Sikh Wars*, p.50.
30   Pronounced or originally called Pheru-shah. The pronunciation has changed over time.
31   Singh, *The First Anglo-Sikh War*, p.69.
32   Kohli, *Sunset of the Sikh Empire*, p.112.

that Lal Singh was subjected to abuse and others were looking to plunder his camp: 'They spoke roughly to Raja Lal Singh and the officers and **accused them of aiding the British**. [author emphasis]'[33] A mutiny had now begun; they were going to attack Lal Singh's camp when the battle was afoot.

The Sikhs were estimated as having between 25,000 and 30,000 troops.[34] However, not all of them were deployed in the battle. Only 17,000 engaged, with others stationed at a standstill at Ludhiana. The *Fauj-i Khas* was commanded by Diwan Ajudhia Prashad and the artillery was headed by General Ilahi Bakhsh, together with Methab Singh and Bahadur Singh's brigade. The Sikhs had essentially formed a triangle. The British figures were recorded as 18,000 with one-third of these Europeans and two-thirds being native units. They were aided by the arrival of Littler's troops, but the battle had been now delayed.[35] The fighting began at 3:30 p.m. when Hugh Gough led the right, together with General Gilbert's division, Hardinge in the centre and Littler on the left-wing of the assailing force. Such was the quick volleys of Sikh fire that within ten minutes, two hundred British soldiers were either killed or crippled and Littler, with a fear of his division being destroyed, retired with his force to Misreewallah.[36] The power of the Sikh guns was superior to the British; made of heavy metal they were firing at the rate of three to one.[37] The British were making no dent with their artillery and were depleting their reserves of their ammunition.[38] It is also worth describing the fight between the Akalis and the 29th and 80th regiments during the capture of the Sikh colours:

> Suddenly a number of Sikhs dressed in chain mail, Akalis who had been lying 'doggo' wrapped in their razhias, appeared in their midst, while numbers of dismounted Ghorchurras came forward from the camp...Against the 80th the Sikhs were led by a man with a large black flag, around which the fiercest fighting occurred. Two of the Company commanders were killed at this time but the black flag was captured by Colour Sergeant Kirkland.[39]

---

33   Suri, *Some Original Sources,* p.72.
34   Kohli has estimated this number based on his analysis of the KDR. See KDR Vol. 1, pp.87–90.
35   Gough wanted to take the initiative without waiting for reinforcements of Littler's division. He was overruled by Hardinge enforcing his view on the battle.
36   Singh, *The First Anglo-Sikh War,* p.79.
37   'Not one single Sikh Gun bore signs of being hit by British fire after the battle was over. They included 24-, 32- and 36- pounders, pretty serious opposition for the British 6-pounders.' Cook, *The Sikh Wars,* p.57.
38   Colonel James Robertson of the HM 31st Foot described the dire situation of their guns. 'We had not a gun left, or if there were, the ammunition was all expended; but most of them were smashed; and dead horses and broken limbers were lying about, having been completely outmatched by the heavier artillery of the Sikhs.' Peter James Robertson, *Personal Adventures and Anecdotes of an Old Officer* (London: Edward Arnold, 1906), p.75.
39   Kirkland of the HM 29th Foot. Cook, *The Sikh Wars,* p.60.

The description of the black flag being captured by a certain Captain Kirkland has been subject to scrutiny and found to be without merit.[40] As darkness fell, Harry Smith's division launched a renewed attack that overran several Sikh batteries and penetrated into the midst of the Sikh camp, around the village of Ferozeshah itself. Major Broadfoot noticed Avitabile's infantry moving forward and launched an attack; however, he was killed in the encounter. This was a quick end to the instigator of the Sikh war. Fierce hand-to-hand fighting continued until midnight. The casualties were considerable on both sides; a Sikh magazine exploded and British losses increased.[41] Gilbert and Wallace showed some success but still lost 270 men in the exploit. The Sikh horsemen were driven back by a British cavalry regiment, the 3rd Light Dragoons, at which time the British then withdrew. This is outlined in the following: 'Neither Gough nor Hardinge knew what had happened to Harry Smith's Division nor where Littler was. In fact Smith thought that they had won the day when Sikh forces began to converge on his position. Under these circumstances, Gough ordered the troops to retire 300 yards from the entrenchment and bivouac for the night.'[42] The Sikh camp did not understand the predicament of the British, for if they had known, then they might have been able to undertake the complete destruction of Gough's 'Army of the Indus.' In fact, there was dissension among the Sikhs who were still reeling from the tactics of their leaders.[43]

The British now found themselves in a grave position without food or water throughout the night. Cunningham, who was present in the battle, gives a graphic description of the battle scene: 'Darkness, and the obstinacy of the contest, threw the English into confusion; men of all regiments and arms were mixed together: generals were doubtful of the fact or of the extent of their own success and colonels knew not what had become of the regiments they commanded or of the army of which they formed a part.'[44] The future of British India remained in the balance. Robert Cust, who was also present in the battle states, 'December 22nd. News came from the Governor-General that our attack of yesterday had failed, that affairs were desperate, that all State papers were to be destroyed, and that if the morning attack failed, all would be over; this was kept secret by Mr. Currie and we were concerting measures to make an unconditional surrender to save the wounded, the part of the news that grieved me the most.'[45] General Sir Hope Grant stated that, 'Sir Henry Hardinge thought it was all up and gave his sword, a present from the Duke of Wellington and which once belonged to Napoleon and his Star of the Bath to his son, with directions to proceed to Ferozepur

---

40   I have discussed this in my book *British and the Sikhs*. The debate centres on the alleged eyewitness testimony of an officer who was not present at the battle.
41   Singh, *The First Anglo-Sikh War*, p.79. Suri, *Some Original Sources*, p.75.
42   Cook, *The Sikh Wars*, p.60.
43   Suri, *Some Original Sources*, p.75.
44   Cunningham, *History of the Sikhs*, p.266.
45   Robert Needham Crust, *Linguistic and Oriental Essays. Written from the year 1840 to 1901*, Sixth Series (London: Luzac & Co., 1901), p.48.

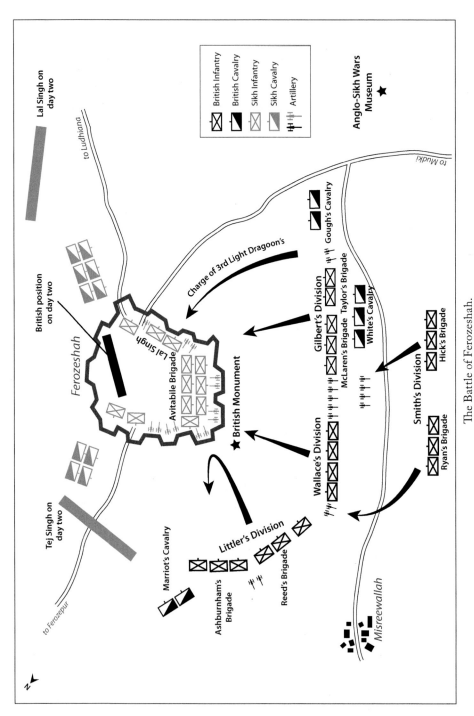

The Battle of Ferozeshah.

remarking that if the day were lost, he must fall.'[46] With the cold setting in, fires were lit, allowing the Sikhs to fire at their positions.[47] Suggestions were made for a full retreat but the ramifications for British prestige would have been huge. Gough sensed the low morale in the camp.[48] There was no option but for the British to continue, they couldn't just retreat leaving the wounded and abandoning their guns.

On the 22 December, the second day of fighting, the Sikhs had the advantage of having full rations of food and ample ammunition. However, frustration was building against Lal Singh who had deliberately failed to attack the British lines, which left his *Ghorchurahs* ineffective in the battle. The Akali Nihangs attacked his camp and he precipitately fled in the night, leaving his subordinates without orders and without an objective.

This was a critical moment as British artillery had been exhausted on the first day of the battle. Harry Smith and his troops were near Sikh positions trying desperately to meet up with the main army. He learnt that General Littler's army was nearby and they met up. At the same time, confusing orders were given by Captain Lumley to Smith and Littler advising them to move to Ferozepur. These were not obeyed, and a disaster was averted. Surprisingly, Lumley was left in his position, and as the two sides were lining up for battle on the 22nd this officer ordered all the cavalry and artillery to leave the field and march to Ferozepur. This time there was no Smith to exercise his judgement and the young staff officers order was obeyed. This was all unknown to Gough at the time.[49] Sensing a Sikh win, Lal Singh withdrew a large part of the army with him and left the remaining Sikhs in a precarious position.[50] Tej Singh was also restricting his forces for the next day of battle.

On the right of the British line, Gough committed Brigadier White's cavalry brigade; 3rd The King's Own Light Dragoons, 4th Bengal Light Cavalry (Lancers) and the 9th Bengal Irregular Cavalry, to attack on the corner of the fortifications. Hardinge and his units were on the left. However, the British and Bengal army units rallied and drove the Sikhs from the rest of their fortifications. The brigades of Mehtab Singh and Bahadur Singh opened fire, but the British wheeled to the right and left and bombarded the Sikhs. Considerably reduced by their casualties at Mudki, the 3rd charged through a battery and the infantry positioned behind it, before breaking into the Sikh camp and engaging in ferocious hand-to-hand combat with crowds of swordsmen and matchlock men. Much of the Sikh army had now fled. After four days, Tej Singh, who had remained stationary near Ferozepore, finally arrived near

---

46   Prince Waldemar (1817–1849) of Prussia who was in the British camp as an observer was instructed to take the sword to Mudki. He later wrote a book with many illustrations of the Sutlej campaign.
47   Singh, *The First Anglo-Sikh War*, p.85.
48   Singh, *The First Anglo-Sikh War*, p.86.
49   Cook, *The Sikh Wars*, pp.65-66.
50   Singh, *The First Anglo-Sikh War*, p.89. 'The darkness of that night was as the life of the vanquished. Raja Lal Singh was wounded and a fugitive.' Suri, *Some Original Sources*, p.75.

Battle of Ferozeshah, day 2. (Colour engravings by Harris, after Martens 'from a sketch by Major G.F. White, HM 31st Regt.', published April 5, 1849)

Ferozeshah.[51] The British were caught unaware of his intentions and proceeded to regroup their forces northwest of the village. Some shots were fired by the troops, which were returned by the British. The Sikh flanks had a large body of cavalry; the infantry formed a square; the artillery opened fire and inflicted some casualties.[52] Unknown to the Sikhs, the British were out of ammunition and again this seemed like a desperate situation. With this exchange lasting no more than two hours, Tej Singh ordered a retreat, to the bewilderment of his Sikh forces and the British alike. With the commanders of the Sikh army retreating within a space of two days, the dual role of their leaders and the treachery of their cause were openly seen on all sides. The British losses totalled 2,415 with 694 killed and 1721 wounded; Sikh losses were estimated at 3,000.[53] Much of the Sikh artillery which had caused many of the British casualties was now captured. The treachery of the Sikh commanders was noted:

> Many, however, are of opinion, that the sudden attack of Tej Singh, with his 30,000 troops was a mere feint. It was well known that he was in correspondence with Captain Nicolson; and it is even affirmed, that he had privately furnished an officer with a plan of the intended operations of the Sikh army. It was his object to ingratiate himself with both parties. His position as leader of the army demanded that he should make the attack; while at the same time he foresaw that the British would ultimately triumph in the Punjaub and that it would be for his interest to make friends of them.[54]

Broadfoot and Nicholson, who collaborated with the Sikhs, both died in this battle.[55]

Descriptions of Ferozeshah

Hugh Gough records the verdict of Ferozeshah in these terms: 'Never did a native army having so relatively slight an advantage in numbers fight a battle with the British in which the issue was so doubtful as at Ferozeshah; and if the victory was decisive, opinion remains divided as to what the result might have been if the Sikh troops had found commanders with sufficient capacity to give their qualities full opportunity.'[56]

---

51 Diwan Ajudhia Prashad gives the impression that Kanh Singh Man, Shamsher Singh, Chatter Singh, Mewa Singh, and their artillery, together with the brigade of Rattan Singh Man and the rest of the troops only found at about the Ferozeshah battle after hearing of cannon fire. This further leads to the fact that Tej Singh was purposely keeping his forces aloof from the battle. Suri, *Some Original Sources*, p.76.
52 Cook, *The Sikh Wars*, p.67.
53 Singh, *The First Anglo-Sikh War*, p.101.
54 Humbly, *Journal of a Cavalry Officer*, pp.40–41.
55 Broadfoot was also buried at Ferozepur Cemetery.
56 Sir G. Gough and Arthur Donald, *The Sikhs and the Sikh Wars: The Rise, Conquest, and Annexation of the Punjab State* (London: A.D. Innes & Company, 1897), p.42.

Cunningham describes the artillery in these terms: '...the guns of the Sikhs were served with rapidity and precision, and the foot soldiers stood between and behind their batteries, firm in their order and active with their muskets.'[57] The resistance met by the English on this occasion was wholly unexpected, and Ferozeshah proved for the first time that Indian and the British soldiers of the English armies met an equal antagonist with their own weapons — even down to the ranks and the fire of artillery. Sita Ram Kohli notes, 'Thus the value of discipline and the European methods of fighting introduced among his men by the sagacious Ranjit had borne their fruit, and if the Sikhs lost the day at Ferozeshah, it was mainly for want of competent and honest commanders.'[58] Colonel James Robertson stated, 'I always believed, and I still do, that the Sikh General had received an enormous bribe to retire.'[59] It was common knowledge that the Sikhs had been sold down the river. After the battle, the Sikh army crossed the Sutlej at Sobraon, while Gough led his army on to Ferozepore. If the Sikhs had initially attacked Ferozepore, the best option to strike first, the British would have had nowhere to go except to fall back. Now, only when reinforcements and additional ammunition arrived in the new year would Gough resume his offensive and attack the main Sikh army in Sobraon. However, there was Buddowal and Aliwal to contend with first.

Buddowal

A temporary cessation of hostilities followed the battle of Ferozeshah. The English were not in a position to assume the offensive and they waited for heavy guns and reinforcements to arrive from Delhi. They would be reinforced with 10,000 troops composed of HM 10th (North Lincolnshire) Regiment of Foot, 9th and 16th Lancers and 3rd Native Light Infantry. Lal Singh and Tej Singh allowed them the much-needed respite in as much as they kept the Sikhs from recrossing the Sutlej. No additional troops appeared to be forthcoming from Lahore. To add to this, no other Cis-Sutlej states came to aid the Sikh Empire and for that matter no other group in India. These battles were the true battle for independence as the Sikh Empire was the only one still standing in the EIC controlled regions.

To induce desertions, Henry Hardinge issued a proclamation inviting all natives of Hindustan to quit the service of the Sikh state on pain of forfeiting their property and to claim protection from the British government. He also boosted the morale of his own forces by ensuring that 1,000 mince pies were distributed to the British troops on Christmas Day 1845. However, he was dismissive of Gough's tactics and he wrote to Prime Minister Robert Peel suggesting that he be replaced.[60]

---

57   Cunningham, *History of the Sikhs*, p.266.
58   *Khalsa Darbar Records*, Vol. 1, p.6
59   Robertson, *Personal Adventures and Anecdotes*, p.76.
60   Generally this is noted in the second Sikh war but it appears both Governor-Generals Hardinge and Dalhousie were at odds with Gough's tactics. Cook, *The Sikh Wars*, p.72.

Ranjodh Singh Majithia. (Watercolour by a Company artist, Punjab, 1865.
Courtesy of the Council of the National Army Museum, London.)

Ranjodh Singh Majithia, a 25-year-old of the Majithia clan, commanded a large army of 10,000 infantry, 2,000 regular cavalry and sixty guns.[61] He had been patiently waiting at Phillaur, ten miles from Ludhiana. He crossed the Sutlej in force and was joined by Ajit Singh with his irregulars from the British protectorate state of Ladwa. This chief of the strong Karorasinghia Misl had a disdain of the British unlike other leaders of the Cis-Sutlej states which provided little support to the Sikh Empire during these wars.[62] The theatre of war now moved 56 miles east towards Ludhiana. This, like Ferozepur, should have been an easy location for the Sikhs to capture and in fact, the residents were expecting this.

61   Son of Desa Singh Majithia, and half-brother to the described Lehna Singh Majithia.
62   Ajit Singh was the son of the Gurdit Singh, who held large estates in the area of Karnal. A chief ally of the Karorasinghia Misl head, Baghel Singh. The Misl had fought against the British at the time of General Lake's war with the Marathas. Ajit Singh had received the title of Raja from Lord Auckland due to the construction of a bridge over the River Sarasvati.

On 5 January 1846, Ajit Singh burnt a portion of the British cantonment. The Sikh army moved to Buddowal where the *Jagirs* and estates of Ajit Singh were located, presumably to receive adequate shelter and support. The Buddowal Fort was now fortified with Ranjodh Singh's cannons. Taking a defensive position, his main cavalry was positioned behind a wooded area with other parts digging trenches in the sandy area. On 21 January, Harry Smith was sent to relieve Ludhiana and to meet Colonel Godby. Gough ordered him to capture the forts at Dharamkot and Fatehgarh. Smith marched eastwards from Ferozepur, keeping a few miles away from the Sutlej and away from Ranjodh Singh's movements.[63] However, Ranjodh Singh's intelligence was better and could see Smith's troops. The British were composed of 4,000 men and 42 guns and so were highly outnumbered.[64] Smith also had a number of casualties from Mudki and Ferozeshah as well as a number of untried men from the 'young' 53rd regiment.[65] Smith's column, realising their predicament, tried to make a detour at Buddowal. The Sikhs appeared on Smith's left on a wide track whilst Smith was moving in thick sand. The Sikhs moved forward with their guns and opened fire, the British horse artillery replying. The Sikh cavalry now looked to attack the rear of Smith's column; their infantry was also sent. Smith was in no position to attack and had to take a defensive position.

The Khalsa attacked the EIC army at the rear with great vigour and were met with resistance by the 53rd, the 16th Lancers and some Native forces. The Sikhs captured the baggage train and stores.[66] Harry Smith states, '...the enemy, with a dexterity and quickness not to be exceeded, formed a line of seven battalions directly across my rear, with guns in the intervals of battalions, for the purpose of attacking my column with his line. This was a very able and well-executed move, which rendered my position critical and demanded nerve and decision to evade the coming storm.'[67] The result was 69 killed, 68 wounded and 77 missing, presumably captured by the Sikhs, with no Sikh losses reported.[68] It was indeed a reprieve for the British. The inexperience of Ranjodh Singh was noted whilst another reason was that Lal Singh had advised him not to engage.[69] Smith recognised his fragile situation at the time, writing, 'He [Ranjodh Singh] should have attacked me with the vigour his French tutors would [have displayed, and] destroyed me, for his force compared to mine was overwhelming; then turned about upon the troops at Loodiana, beaten them, and sacked and burnt the city—when the gaze I speak of in India would have been one general blaze of revolt!'[70]

63   Afterwards governor of Cape Colony.
64   Singh, T*he First Anglo-Sikh War*, p.111.
65   Cook, *The Sikh Wars*, p.76.
66   This included the loss of the regimental silver of the 16th Lancers.
67   G. C. Moore Smith, *The Autobiography of Lieutenant-General Sir Harry Smith Baronet of Aliwal on the Sutlej G.C.B, Vol. 2* (London: John Murray, 1902), p.173.
68   Singh, *The First Anglo-Sikh War*, p.118.
69   However there seems to be no evidence of this.
70   Moore, *The Autobiography of Lieutenant-General Sir Harry Smith*, pp.186–187. Smith also erroneously assumed the whole Khalsa army was trained by the Europeans. Also see *Jangnamah*, p.219.

Ajit Singh of Ladwa. (James Skinner, *Tazkirat al-umara*, Add.MS 27254, British Library)

The Buddowal Fort. (Watercolour by Prince Waldemar)

A few days later on 24 January, the Fort of Buddowal was captured by the British and the inhabitants of the villages who had sided with the Sikhs met with an unfortunate end: 'British soldiers and camp followers now fanned out that evening, burning and looting the nearby villages and killing locals suspected of helping the Sikhs.'[71] This event is remembered by locals of the area to this day and was hardly reported in British chronicles at the time. Of all the battles during the Sutlej Campaign, this should be singled out for the indiscriminate killing of Sikhs by the British. After the Battle of Aliwal, the fort of Ajit Singh was blown up.[72]

Aliwal

The Buddowal attack was a reprieve for Smith, who was now ordered to march to Jagraon on the more southerly road, where he was to take command of HM 53rd Foot. He reached there on 21 January and the sons of Fateh Singh Ahluwalia allowed him to occupy the fort. He then marched to Ludhiana, where he would find Colonel Godby, who had not followed his orders fully. Smith was critical of Godby; he was sent several messages asking to support him at Buddowal which never materialised.[73] He had with him four native regiments, including two battalions of Gurkhas (later the 1st and 2nd Gurkha Rifles), and four guns. He was also aided by a cavalry unit of Brigadier Cureton, amongst others. The British strength was 10,000 to 12,000 composed of 3,000 cavalry and around 7,000 infantry with 32 guns. Ranjodh Singh Majithia was joined by Jodha Ram's (Avitabile's) Brigade, *Ghorchurah* Khas Derah and Fateh Singh's/ Mubarak Khan Artillery Brigade. Again Smith describes the situation: 'For the purpose of protecting the passage of a very considerable reinforcement of twelve guns and 4,000 of the regular, or "Aieen" troops, called Avitabile's battalion, entrenching himself strongly in a semi-circle, his flanks resting on a river, his position covered with from forty to fifty guns generally of large calibre, howitzers, and mortars.'[74] The Sikh strength was now between 14,000 to 18000 men, including the 4,000 *Fauj-i-Ain*, irregulars and local villagers.[75]

The British were approaching from the village of Porein and from there they could see the Sikh army from the rooftops of the houses, in essence being able to see the Sikh army positions at the villages at Aliwal and Bhundri.[76] The Sikh guns started

---

71   Singh, *The First Anglo-Sikh War*, p.124. Smith also had his scouts executed who he felt had led him intentionally towards Buddowal.

72   On my visit to Buddowal there were little or any signs of the old fort. The locals showed me where it was possibly located. They also informed that there once existed a tunnel from Ajit Singh's Buddowal Fort to one of his Havelis.

73   Moore, *The Autobiography of Lieutenant-General Sir Harry Smith*, p.175.

74   Moore, *The Autobiography of Lieutenant-General Sir Harry Smith*, p.179.

75   Singh, *The First Anglo-Sikh War*, p.129.

76   On my visit to Aliwal in 2018, I went to the rooftop of a house to see the locations of Porein and Bhundri to gain a better understanding of the battle locations.

firing with the British responding in the same vein. Brigadiers Godby and Hicks on the right flanks charged at the Aliwal outpost which was manned by Dogra irregulars. There was little opposition which led to immediate success for the British. Ranjodh Singh sent his cavalry to support from his position, but this was met with a strong attack by Brigadier Cureton's cavalry. The left side was now very weak with parts of the Khalsa army retreating across the Sutlej. The British took control of the village of Aliwal. The centre and right would be where the main battle would take place. The Sikh guns fired in Smith's direction, narrowly missing him and hitting his telescope. The British used their strategy of lying down then getting up and advancing several times and were able to move up to the Sikh line. Major Lawrenson and Brigadier Stedman charged into the Sikh line which collapsed. The *Ghorchurahs* came in contact with the 3rd Light cavalry and 16th Lancers. This now led to a retreat of the Sikh forces towards Bhundri some distance away. Ranjodh Singh had left the battle yet the Sikh forces made an orderly retreat. The *Fauj-i-Ain* and the Avitabile units now made a last stand. The Sikhs began to form the military squares to repel the cavalry attack, with which this battle is synonymous. The Avitabile Regiment formed their square, which was more of a triangular formation. This classic manoeuvre was based on the French system; composed of two or three lines of infantry, it bristled with bayonets and was trained to deliver horrific volleys to take out attacking horsemen. The 16th Lancers and the 3rd Light Cavalry under Captain Bere and Captain Fyler charged the Sikhs. The square opened up and the British were now behind the Sikh line; the square formed again and the second charge took place, but this had no impact. The third charge was undertaken and was now successful and broke the Sikh formation. The Sikh line needed to be supported by cannon fire for this manoeuvre to be completely effective, which did not materialise. This led to the Avitabile regiment retreating.[77]

However they kept fighting as they moved towards the Sutlej. Captain Daniel Henry Mackinnon wrote:

> Those troops, the pupils of Avitabile, did credit that day to themselves and their master; and, however we may abhor their treachery and thirst of blood, displayed in the revolutionary annals of the Punjaub since the death of the old Lion of Lahore, we must at least bear witness to their resolute courage and soldierlike bearing.[78]

---

77 Cook, *The Sikh Wars*, p.81.
78 Daniel Henry Mackinnon, *Military service and adventures in the Far East: including sketches of the campaigns against the Afghans in 1839, and the Sikhs in 1845–6. By a cavalry officer, in two Volumes,* (London: Charles Ollier, 1847), p.197. Shah Mohammed states 'The brunt was borne by the Avitabile forces Which fought a furious action for quite a few hours.' *Jangnamah,* p.223.

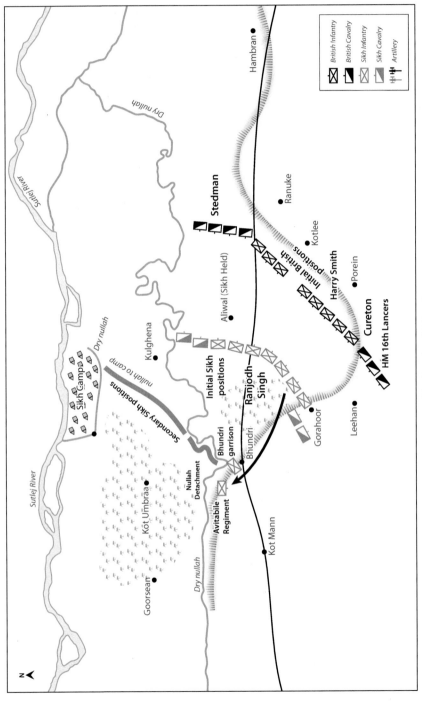

The Battle of Aliwal.

The Sikh infantry was also based at the *Bhuda Nullah* or riverbed and was attacked by the 30th Native Infantry which led to a general retreat by the Sikhs. The Sikh gunners at Bhundri were also dispossessed of their cannons. As they were crossing the Sutlej and entering into an open area they became easy prey for the British cannons. The disadvantage of having their backs to the river became apparent. The battle was won by the British. The Sikh losses were considered to be in the hundreds whilst the British losses were 151 killed, 422 wounded and 25 missing.[79] Essentially Ranjodh Singh's army was still intact despite the loss of baggage and loss of guns and supplies. He was to later blame the Ahluwalia troops of not supporting his efforts. The British went to tend to their wounded and bury the dead; the battlefield was over a five-mile radius. Harry Smith seems to have received a mixed reaction to this contest, and it has been subject to scrutiny, particularly from Lord Dalhousie who later was scathing of his tactics.[80] The Village of Aliwal commemorates the battle every year.[81]

Rani Jindan Kaur

A deputation of the army was sent to the regent Rani Jindan requesting additional supplies including food and rations. Colonel Gardener describes the scene at the court:

> I could detect that the Rani was shifting her petticoat; I could see that she stepped out of it, and then rolling it up rapidly into a ball, flung it over the screen at the heads of the angry envoys, crying out, "Wear that, you cowards! I'll go in trousers and fight myself!" The effect was electric. After a moment's pause, during which the deputation seemed stunned, a unanimous shout arose, "Dhulip Singh Maharaja, we will go and die for his kingdom and the Khalsaji!" and breaking up tumultuously and highly excited, this dangerous deputation dispersed, and rejoined the army. The courage and intuition displayed by this extraordinary woman under such critical circumstances filled us all with as much amazement as admiration.[82]

The qualities of Rani Jindan Kaur was noted by many, with Colchester writing, 'The mother of the boy Dhuleep Singh seems to be a woman of determined courage, and she is the only person apparently at Lahore who has courage.'[83] The situation was

---

79   Singh, *The First Anglo-Sikh War*, p.138.
80   J.G. Baird (ed), *Private Letters of the Marquess of Dalhousie*, (Edinburgh and London: William Blackwood and Sons, 1910), pp.195-196. Letter dated 4 April 1852.
81   A memorial has been raised in Aliwal as recently as 2015. Due to the success of the Sikh Museum Initiative 'Anglo Sikh Wars: Battles, Treaties and Relics' exhibition, I was awarded a plaque by Pargat Singh the *Sarpanch* or (head of the village).
82   Pearse, *Soldier and Traveller*, pp.272–273
83   Colchester, *History Of The Indian Administration*, p.406.

changing and she despatched ten horsemen with an urgent message to the veteran General Sham Singh Attariwala to help in the next encounter. He in turn rounded up the support of additional irregular troops headed by Akali Hanuman Singh and his Akali Nihangs. It is not known why Sham Singh did not participate earlier; one reason may be that he was disgusted with the appointments of Lal Singh and Tej Singh.[84] His non-involvement in the earlier campaigns should be a note of concern.

Sobraon

By the close of the first week of February 1846, one part of the Sikh army had constructed formidable entrenchments about two and a half miles long on the left bank of the Sutlej near Sobraon. The other part of the Sikh army, again like the previous battles, were kept away and were at the north bank of the river. The Sikhs were expecting additional support from Gulab Singh Dogra which never came. They were also suffering from depleted artillery due to it being captured in the previous battles. Despite these odds and the loss at Aliwal, the Sikhs were still in high spirits or *Chardi Kala*. The Sikh batteries were placed about six feet high protected by deep trenches. These defensive works were connected with the right bank with a bridge of boats. Some 20,000 to 25,000 soldiers and seventy guns were placed behind these entrenchments. Sham Singh was commanding the left flank, the middle was with Mehtab Singh Majithia, Kahn Singh Mann and Gulab Singh Povindia, with the Avitabile troops in the centre-left.[85] The weakest point in the Sikh line was its right flank where the loose sand made it impossible to build high parapets or place heavy guns there; it was to be protected by the *Ghorchurahs* and light camel guns which only fired balls one or two pounds in weight. Stationed here were Attar Singh Kalianwala and the Frenchman Francois Henri Mouton (1804–76). The latter and the Spanish Engineer Colonel Domingo Hurbons constructed the entrenchments.[86] Moreover, the command of this wing was reserved conveniently by Lal Singh for himself. His objective was still to destroy the Sikh army.[87] It was notable to the Sikh soldiers that the leadership of Tej Singh and Lal Singh was non-existent. William Edwards, writing about the treachery states, 'While there [Ferozepore], emissaries from Rajah

84   'But on the 25th of December, just after the news of Lal Singh's defeat at Ferozeshah had reached Lahore, the Maharani [Jindan Kaur] heard that Sham Singh was at Atari, and sent there ten horsemen, who were to be quartered on the sardar till he joined the army. Sham Singh sent, again and again, to the Maharani, denouncing the war and the policy that was destroying the country, but in vain; and at last, when told he was a coward and afraid to die, he determined to join the camp.' Griffin, *Chiefs and Families*, Vol. 1, p.476.

85   Singh, *The First Anglo-Sikh War*, pp.189–190.

86   C. Grey, (ed. H.L.O. Garrett), *European Adventurers Of Northern India 1785-1849* (Lahore: Printed by the Superintendent, Government Printing, Punjab, 1929), pp.338-340.

87   Singh, *The First Anglo-Sikh War*, p.161.

Lall Singh arrived, and gave us valuable information respecting the enemy's position. From the intelligence thus received, it was determined to attack the entrenchment on its extreme right, where Lall Singh reported the defences to be low and weak.[88]

The British had similar numbers to the Sikhs in the region of 20,000 and 108 guns of various calibre. Robert Dick's division was ordered to commence the attack on the right flank with Walter Gilbert's division in immediate support on the right. Harry Smith's division was to be close to Gilbert's right to support him. Dick's division advanced according to plan and found the defences on the right flank weak and easily surmountable. The 10th Queen's Regiment broke through totally unopposed, but when the entire division had penetrated some way, it was suddenly fallen upon by the Sikhs and driven back. Robert Dick was himself mortally wounded. Now both Gilbert's and Dick's divisions engaged in what may be described as a deadly hand-to-hand encounter with the Sikh infantry.

For some time, the issue of the Battle of Sobraon was hanging in the balance as the conflict raged fiercely. The guns on both sides had been firing for several hours but leading to massively depleted ammunition on the British side. The field was resplendent with embattled warriors and as Sir Herbert Edwards says, 'The artillery galloped up and delivered their fire within 300 yards of the enemy's batteries and infantry charged home with the bayonet and carried the works without firing a single shot.'[89] Gilbert now concentrated on the Sikh centre. Mounting on one another's shoulders, the attackers gained a footing on the entrenchments and as they increased in number they rushed at the Sikh guns and captured them. Soon the news spread down the line that enemy troops had won their way through to Sikh positions. The tide of battle now turned against the gallant defenders and to make its turn irrevocable, the treacherous commanders Tej Singh and Lal Singh, instead of leading their fresh men to bolster up the defences, fled across the bridge of boats sinking the central boat after crossing. According to Major Carmichael Smyth, 'Tej Singh ordered up eight or ten guns and had them pointed at the bridge as if ready to beat it to pieces or to oppose the passage of the defeated army.'[90] Robert Smith states, 'The Sikh troops, basely betrayed by their leaders who had come so it was said, and not without some appearance of truth, **to a secret understanding with us**, [author emphasis] fought like heroes.'[91] General Sham Singh, brought into to make a final stand with the British, did not waver. He was not expecting to come back to his native area of Attari; he had settled his accounts amongst other important matters. He took an oath on the Guru Granth Sahib and seeing his army facing defeat, he

88   William Edwards, *Reminiscences of a Bengal civilian* (London: Smith, Elder and Co.,1866), p.99.

89   Karnail Singh, *Winston Churchill's Account of Anglo Sikh Wars and Its In-side Tale* (Amritsar: S.G.P.C, 1968), p.32.

90   Smyth, *A History of the Reigning Family of Lahore*, pp.183–84.

91   R. Bosworth Smith, *Life of Lord Lawrence*, Vol.1 (London: Smith, Elder, & Co.,1885), pp.63–64

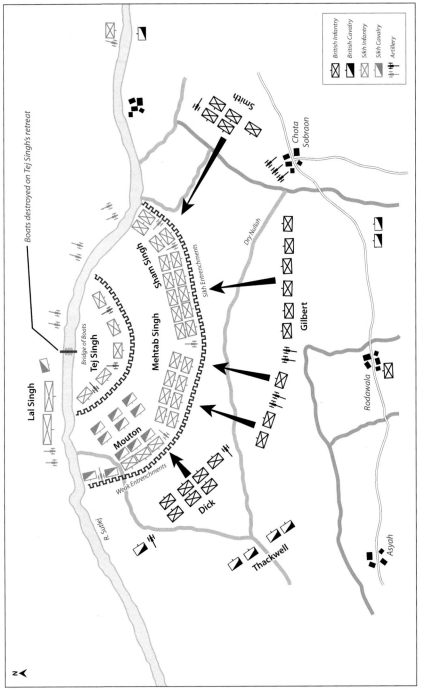

The Battle of Sobraon.

took the final fatal plunge. He moved forward against the 50th Foot, brandishing his sword and calling on the Khalsa to follow him. During the battle, he fell from his horse, his body pierced with several cannon balls. Cunningham describes the scene: 'The dangers which threatened the Sikh people pressed upon their mind and they saw no escape from foreign subjection. The grey headed chief, Sham Singh of Attari, made known his resolution to die in the first conflict with the enemies of his race and so to offer himself as a sacrifice of propitiation to the spirit of Gobind Singh ji and to the genius of his mystic Commonwealth.'[92] Shah Mohammed states, 'Sham Singh, the honourable sardar of Attari, was resplendent in the battlefield despite his years.'[93] All commentators are in agreement that the spirited Sham Singh was a credit to the Sikh nation and to soldiery in general.

> One old chief, whose name should be recorded — Sham Sing — 'among the faithless faithful only found,' clothed in white garments, and devoting himself to death, like Decius of old, called on those around him to strike for God and the Guru, and, dealing death everywhere around him, rushed manfully upon his own.[94]

As proof of this, his dead body, according to the British Commander-in-Chief, 'was sought for in the captured camp by his followers', who were permitted to search for their dead leader. His body was discovered where the dead lay thickest. His servants placed the body on a raft and swam with it across the river. The self-sacrifice of sardar Sham Singh, the hero of Sobraon, had an inspiring effect. Henry Hardinge stated, 'Few escaped; none, it may be said, surrendered. The Sikhs met their fate with the resignation which distinguishes their race.'[95]

The final retreat across the Sutlej saw many deaths of the Khalsa; with boats already broken, and under the relentless fire of grape and canister shots and at the hands of British bayonets. Shah Mohammed sums up the battle:

> Where the French-trained soldiers and Charyari cavalry was.
> They advanced in an arc-like formation.
> But it was indeed a very difficult battle for the Khalsa.
> For, Teja Singh had destroyed the bridge from behind
> So that the army could not even retreat.
> O Shah Mohammed! They could only die and earn martyrdom,
> Unmindful of what happened to their lives.[96]

92 Cunningham, *History of the Sikhs*, p.281.
93 *Jangnamah*, p.233.
94 Smith, *Life of Lord Lawrence*, pp.63–64
95 Charles Stewart Hardinge, *Rulers of India: Viscount Hardinge* (Oxford: Clarendon Press, 1891), p.119.
96 *Jangnamah*, p.235.

Retreat at the destroyed bridge of boats at Sobraon. (Archibald Forbes, Major Arthur Griffiths, and others, *Illustrated Battles of the Nineteenth Century*. (London: Cassell & Co., 1895))

Robert Peel (1788-1850), the British Prime Minister quoted Gough's letter whilst giving a vote of thanks to the British victory in the Sutlej Campaign in the Houses of Parliament, which stated: '...were it not from a deep conviction that my country's good required the sacrifice, I could have wept to witness the fearful slaughter of so devoted a body of men.'[97] Akali Hanuman Singh, who also fought in the battle, lost many of the Akali forces in the hand-to-hand combat that took place. However, whilst information is sparse, Hanuman Singh left the battlefield where he was hunted down at Patiala and eventually killed at Sohana (Chandigarh). Other notable losses included Gulab Singh Gupta, Hira Singh Topee, Kishan Singh (son of Jamadar Singh Khushal Singh), Mubarak Ali and Shah Nawaz (son of Fateh Din of Kasur); all died in this battle which essentially finished off the majority of the older guard of Maharajah Ranjit's Singh army. British losses amounted to

97   Robert. S. Rait, *The Life and Campaigns of Hugh, First Viscount Gough, Field-Marshal*, Vol. 2 (Westminster: Archibald Constable & Co Ltd, 1903), pp.108–109. This was on 2 April 1846; in the same speech, Harry Smith, Hugh Gough and Henry Hardinge were singled out for the victories. Pensions and honours were conferred on them.

320 killed, and 2,083 wounded. Sikh losses were not known though an estimate of 8,000 has been noted.[98]

Governor-General Henry Hardinge entered the Sikh capital of Lahore on 20 February 1846. On 9 March he imposed terms upon the young Maharajah Duleep Singh, then aged seven and a half years, referred to as a 'treaty of peace.' This Treaty of Lahore was followed by additional articles supplementary to it on 11 March 1846. By the terms of the treaty, Maharajah Duleep Singh had engaged to reduce the Sikh army to 25 battalions of regular infantry, 12,000 cavalry, and surrender all the guns which were pointed against the British army.[99] The complicated connotations of a young child signing a treaty about which he had little understanding are still contested and the whole act is seen as troublesome. Duleep Singh would question the legality of the treaty in his later years. Gulab Singh also secured the territory of Kashmir and Jammu by paying an indemnity. His reluctance to help the Lahore Durbar and also his negotiations from the time of Governor-General Ellenborough to Governor-General Hardinge paid dividends. This, however, was not the end of the matter and trouble would once again start brewing in the Panjab.

98   This is based on Hugh Gough's assessment.
99   The strength of the regular army was brought down to 35,547 men, distributed over 28 battalions of infantry, 4 regiments of cavalry and 17 derahs of artillery. *Khalsa Darbar Records*, Vol. 1, p.94.

11

Second Anglo-Sikh War

The insinuation by the EIC was that the Treaties enacted were to benefit the Lahore Durbar but by December 1846, it was looking like a more permanent plan was in motion. The idea that British troops were being stationed in Panjab until Maharajah Duleep Singh reached the age of 16 was more of a smokescreen. Through the Treaty of Bhyroval enacted on 26 December 1846, Henry Lawrence was appointed resident with 'full authority to direct and control all matters in every department of the State.' A new eight-member Council of Regency was created, composed of leading Chiefs and sardars: Tej Singh, Sher Singh Attariwala, Diwan Dina Nath, Faqir Nur-ud-Din, Ranjodh Singh Majithia, Bhai Nidhan Singh, Atar Singh Kalianwala and Shamsher Singh Sandhanwalia. They were assured that their *Jagirs* would be intact. This was important, as a week earlier Lal Singh was banished from the Panjab.[1] This effectively gave the British control of the government. The regency ceased to exist as a sovereign political body. It was more an instrument for serving British interests and rubber-stamping any decisions or policies.

Maharani Jindan Kaur, as a result, was removed as a regent and awarded a pension of Rs150,000. The idea was to reduce her power and effectively separate her from her son, Duleep Singh. Hardinge, in December 1846, noted that for the Treaty to be effective, Jindan Kaur's 'deprivation of power is an indispensable condition.' This caused resentment within the Sikh Empire and would be a cause for which the Khalsa would rally, calling for freedom in the Panjab. In January 1847, Henry Hardinge would be replaced by the Earl of Dalhousie, James Andrew Broun-Ramsay, and the Lawrence brothers would govern the Panjab unabated. In February 1847, Prema, a Brahman who had been a soldier in Gulab Singh`s service, came to Lahore and set up a secret campaign against the British and started associating himself with officers and officials of the Sikh army. This became known as the Prema plot; the idea was to restore the power of Maharani Jind Kaur as the Regent of the minor Maharajah

---

1 This was an untidy end for Lal Singh who had been seen as treacherous. Indeed, this was not lost on the British and they eventually got rid of him from the Panjab.

Duleep Singh and terminate British control by assassinating Henry Lawrence and Tej Singh. The plotters lost heart and did not undertake the attack.[2] Information, however, had reached the Panjab Government and the plotters were arrested and sentenced or deported out of the state. Jindan Kaur was implicated but there was no definite proof she was involved. However, a pretext had been set and next, an unjustified act led to the removal of the Maharani from Lahore. On 7 August 1847, Maharajah Duleep Singh refused to confer an honour to the treacherous Tej Singh.[3] This was seen as an act instigated by Jindan Kaur who had told her son to take this course of action. Lord Dalhousie, the Governor-General, had already been briefed on the Queen Regent and he would take Hardinge's policy to its conclusion. She was removed from the Panjab and sent to the fort at Sheikhupura, 25 miles away from Lahore.[4] Her allowance was reduced from Rs150,000 to Rs48,000 annually.

There was growing dissatisfaction within the Sikh Empire but this did not lead to any premeditated war on the EIC. In fact, it was due to events at Multan far removed from Lahore which lit the fuse. This was a protracted affair between the Hindu ruler Diwan Mulraj and the Sikh Durbar and then the EIC. This was from 19 April 1848 to 22 January 1849, when the last defenders surrendered.

After the end of the First Sikh War, Multan was still considered an independent territory.[5] However, the newly appointed Commissioner in the Panjab, Frederick Currie, requested from Multan the duties and taxes previously paid to the Lahore Durbar which was now in arrears. The amount was also raised from Rs20 lacs to Rs30 lacs (1 lac is 100,000 rupees). Mulraj decided to resign and sardar Khan Singh Mann was appointed as his successor. He was accompanied by a British Political Agent, Patrick Vans Agnew and another officer, Lieutenant Anderson (Bombay Army) and an escort of Gurkha troops from Lahore. On 19 April 1848, after the keys were being handed over at the main citadel, the two officers began to ride out and were attacked. Both officers were wounded, and together with Khan Singh they made their way to the mosque outside the city. Anderson despatched letters, with one going to Frederick Currie in Lahore, while a second took a copy via a different route, across the Indus River. With the main escort leaving their sides, individuals from Multan killed both of them. It was not known if Diwan Mulraj was involved but this now set the scene for the beginnings of the so-called second Anglo-Sikh War. Mulraj presented Vans Agnew's head to Khan Singh and told him to take it back to Currie. It was now a question of whether this was a local rebellion or a full-scale war against the British.

---

2   Atar Singh Kalianwala, Sher Singh Attariwala, Ranjodh Singh and Mian Jawahar Singh (nephew of Gulab Singh) were said to be involved or supported it.

3   Ganda Singh, 'Some New Light on the Treaty of Bharowal (December 16, 1846)', *Proceedings Indian Historical Records Commission*, Vol.17, 1940, pp.265–266.

4   The Sheikhupura Fort during the Sikh Empire was the *Jagir* of Mai Nakkain until 1838. So effectively the history of the two wives of Ranjit Singh is intertwined within this fort.

5   Multan was incorporated into the Sikh Empire of Ranjit Singh in 1818 and was predominantly a Muslim area.

The exile of Maharani Jindan Kaur was being considered and again she was impli-cated in the rebellion at Multan without any proof. It was taken as a given, by the British that she had a hand in this. On 15 May she was taken from Sheikhupura and put under house arrest. This would become another factor and rallying cry for a local rebellion to turn into a full-scale war. Lieutenant Herbert Edwardes, the British Political Agent in Bannu, had intercepted the second copy of Vans Agnew's letter to Currie and immediately began to concentrate troops. He wrote to the Lahore authori-ties insisting that this revolt could be suppressed quickly. It appears that the newly appointed Governor-General Dalhousie together with Hugh Gough did not want to commit their forces during the hot weather and monsoon season. There was also the usual time needed to prepare and send for forces stationed elsewhere. However, it appears that this would also be a pretext for the annexation of the Panjab. Edwardes would write to Major Hodson, the political assistant of the Resident at Lahore: 'You express a hope we shall seize the opportunity to annex the Punjab. In this I cannot agree with you, for I think, for all that has happened, it would be unjust and inexpedient.'[6]

The Battle of Kineyri

Mulraj was now in charge of the rebellion and was reinforced by several other regi-ments of the Sikh Khalsa army of the Sikh Empire, which rebelled or deserted. He also took other measures to strengthen his defences, digging up guns that had previ-ously been buried and enlisting more troops. Edwardes began to lead an army against Multan. On 18 June, Pashtun irregulars from the Nawab of Bahawalpur crossed the Chenab River on ferry boats. They were fired on by Mulraj's artillery and forced to take cover for several hours. Mulraj's infantry and cavalry, with a strength of 8,000 to 10,000 strong, began to advance and inflicted the initial casualties. Edwardes was reinforced at the last minute by two regiments of the Lahore Durbar under Colonel Henry Charles Van Cortlandt (1814–88).[7] His artillery caused heavy losses among the Multani troops and Edwardes's Pashtuns counter-attacked. Mulraj's forces retreated to Multan, having suffered 500 casualties and losing several guns. Edwardes' men lost 58 with 89 wounded.

Edwardes now pushed towards Surajkhund and by 30 June he was joined by a Durbar Column under Imma-ud-din with his Muslim-only troops. Edwardes now had 18,000 troops and around 30 guns.[8] There was an intention not to commit Sikh

6   Major Hodson was second in command under Lieutenant-General Harry Lumsden of
     the Corps of Guides which was raised in 1846 combining British and Indian (mainly
     Pathans) listed officers. There were also some Sikh officers. See final chapter.
7   An Anglo-Indian soldier of fortune who joined the Sikh army under Maharajah Ranjit
     Singh.
8   Cook, *The Sikh Wars*, p.122.

troops to the affray in case they rebelled during the attacks on Multan. It is not clear where this directive came from but this started to play into the minds of the Sikh troops. General William Whish of the Bengal Artillery was despatched to begin the siege of Multan.[9] However, they still required more troops as their numbers were too small to encircle the city. Multan had a reputation of strength and even Ranjit Singh had difficulty securing it in 1818 as described earlier. Whish would be joined by Captain Lumsden and his corps of guides. Currie also decided to reinforce them with a substantial detachment of the Khalsa under Sher Singh Attariwala. He had with him some regular infantry of *Purbias*, with 500 irregular cavalry, 3,000 Sikh cavalry and two mortars.[10] There had been a long-standing suggestion that Sher Singh was a willing partner to rebel against the British but this was not borne out by the facts. He was loyal to the EIC until some months later. However, his father Chattar Singh Attariwala, the Governor of Hazara, was preparing to revolt in the north of the Panjab. Despite warnings, Currie nevertheless ordered a detachment from Chattar Singh's army under his second in command, Jundial Singh, to reinforce Sher Singh. This allowed Jundial Singh and other officers to influence Sher Singh and spread disaffection among his regiments.

There was, however, another problem for the British; the Sikh leader by the name of Maharaj Singh was also in contact with Diwan Mulraj and could muster support against the EIC.[11] Due to him being a religious leader, he was referred to as 'Guru.' He was implicated in the Prema Plot and had his movements restricted to Naurangabad. His estates were confiscated. This course of action led him to also raise the banner of freedom for the Sikhs. On 1 July, Mulraj proceeded towards Sadoosam and the next battle took place at Suraj Khand. There was continued gunfire from both sides for several hours. In the course of the battle, Mulraj's elephant *Howdah* (seat) was shot at, which sent him in a panic. He ordered a retreat and there was confusion within his lines. He then left the battlefield and went back to the Multan Fort; the retreat was disorderly and led to further losses.[12] This led to disaffection in the Multan camp and led to soldiers deserting him. Chattar Singh made his move against the British at Haripur on 6 August and tried to seize the guns there, but his subordinate Colonel Canora refused unless he received orders from Abbott.[13] He was killed in the melee that ensued. Colonel Nicholson secured the Attock Fort, hence preventing any other

9   His specialty was commanding a rocket troop which saw action in the siege of Bhurtpore. Later promoted to Lieutenant-General and made a K.C.B.
10   Cook, *The Sikh Wars*, p.126.
11   He was born as Nihal Singh and was head of a community with many soldiers. He was respected by the Lahore Durbar. He was successor to the pious Bir Singh who died in 1844.
12   Amarpal Singh, *The Second Anglo-Sikh War* (Gloucester: Amberley Publishing, 2016), p.160.
13   John Francis Canora (1799–1848) was an Irishman who joined the Sikh Durbar in 1831 and was employed in the artillery division.

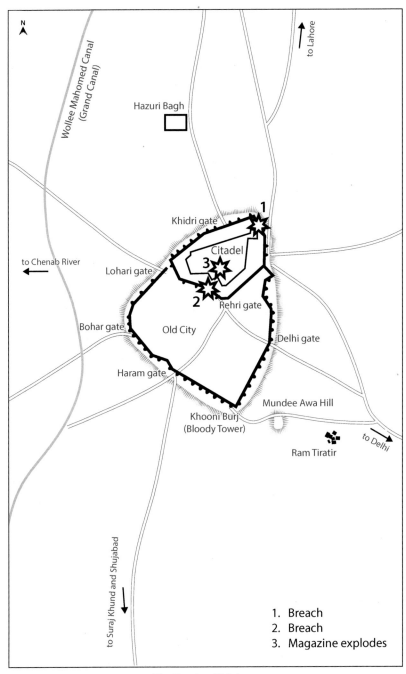

The Battle of Multan.

disaffected Khalsa troops from having any connection with Chattar Singh.[14] This move was not known by the Lahore Durbar and so they could not be considered as conspiring in this action. In fact, the opposite was taking place; Lahore troops had reached Multan on the 18 and 19 August followed by elements of the Ferozepore Brigade on the 25th. Various types of artillery were sent, including 32 siege and heavy guns, six were 24-pounders, another six were 18-pounders together with 12 mortars amongst them.

Initially, Whish's and Edwardes' camps were six miles apart with Multan troops in the middle; these were cleared by Lumsden's Guides which involved taking *Zamburaks* and spiking the guns. Sher Singh helped in this connection by using his Muslim troops, but Sikhs in his forces were now reluctant to fight. Indeed, the fight was with Multani troops consisting of Akali Nihangs and Rohillas. A trench was now being dug at Ramtirat, from where the attack on Multan would take place. This would allow an approach to both the Delhi Gate and Khonee Burj (Bloody Tower), a bastion on the south of the city. Several skirmishes now started with Diwan Mulraj's forces being bombarded by guns. Indeed, if Lahore Durbar troops were going to take the city, it would be with cannonade, and the assault started on 12 September when they captured the outpost of Jumoondar Ke Kiree, 800 yards from the Khonee Burj. They continued going from compound to compound until they were met with heavy fire. The EIC troops were now recalled, not without confusion amongst the ranks and with friendly fire taking place. This advancement of 800 yards led to 550 Multan troops dead, and over 50 dead on the EIC side and 203 wounded. Sher Singh was advised to remove himself after this offensive and take a back seat. As a result, on 14 September, Singh after being influenced by Sikh troops and family loyalty, openly left the battle-field. This now made the EIC forces too weak to maintain the siege, and they were forced to retreat. There was a fear that Sher Singh would attack Lahore and EIC forces from behind. Many of Edwardes' and Bahawalpur's troops dispersed to their homes whilst two sardars abandoned Sher Singh.[15] It was now time for Sher Singh to meet Diwan Mulraj; however, forged letters written by the British were intercepted by Multani troops which suggested that he was in league with the British.[16] This led to distrust. After some discussions they met at a neutral point of a mosque outside the city, it was agreed that Sher Singh would move north into the mainly Sikh-populated areas of the Panjab.[17] One thing that was agreed upon was that they would work to

---

14 The fort covered the crossing of the River Indus on the route from Peshawar to Lahore so effectively cutting off any Sikh attack at Lahore.
15 Uttar Singh and Shumsher Singh and some others went to Edwardes' side and advised that they had not been treacherous.
16 Cook, *The Sikh Wars*, p.134. The letter by Edwardes to Sher Singh was intentionally allowed to fall in the hands of Multanis inferring this.
17 This issue was never resolved, Mulraj still fearing that Sher Singh was with the British. If an amicable agreement had been reached, this would have led to a different course of events.

rid the British in the name of Maharani Jindan Kaur who had been disrespected and humiliated for no reason.

Sher Singh declared his manifesto to rid the Panjab of the British and extorted the Panjabis of all creeds and races to join him in his crusade. Letters were sent in all directions for the people to rise up:

> By the direction of the Holy Gooroo, Rajah Sher Sing and others, with their valiant troops, have joined the trusty and faithful Dewan Moolraj, on the part of Maharajuh Duleep Sing, with a view to eradicate and expel the tyrannous and crafty Feringhees.[18]

Placards for revolt were also found outside the Harimandir Sahib in Amritsar. Diwan Mulraj also sent his proclamation asking the populace to rise up and 'come out openly in the field to fight so that both sides, having been freed from the misery of this world, go to heaven, because there is no other [better] occasion than this.'[19] This would now effectively start two theatres of war. Sher Singh wanted to take the fight to Lahore. However, he collected some troops from Multan as well as sending emissaries to Edwardes' men to encourage them to defect and take part in their struggle. This did not have the desired effect but Mulraj received more recruits. On 9 October, Sher Singh marched along the River Chenab not far from where General Whish was stationed. It is a matter of wonder that Sher Singh did not attack Whish but there was more at stake and 'Multan had become a sideshow.' However, it can also be questioned why General Whish either allowed or was ignorant of Sher Singh moving freely past him. Word was now reaching Lahore of the activities in Multan and the British authorities took steps to guard Lahore, with the 53rd Regiment taking control of the Treasury and the guarding of the Koh-i-Noor diamond. The other treasury at Gobindgarh Fort in Amritsar was also secured by Lahore troops.[20] Effectively, Sikh or Lahore Durbar troops were being replaced by the EIC and other regiments which had confirmed loyalty to the British. Hugh Gouch had sent instructions to Dalhousie that he had assembled the forces required for action in the Panjab.

Gough was not clear whether he was suppressing a rebellion on behalf of the Durbar or whether the Durbar was the enemy. The Governor-General's speech at a banquet was, however, clear enough and this was for all and out war: 'Unwarned by precedents, uninfluenced by example, the Sikh Nation has called for War and on my word, sirs will have it with a vengeance.'[21] However, this information was not sent to the Lahore Durbar which further gave impetus for the annexation of the Panjab, without any fault of Maharajah Duleep Singh.

---

18   Major Herbert Edwardes, *A Year on the Punjab Frontier, in 1848–49*, Vol. 2 (London: Richard Bentley, 1851), pp.623–624

19   To see 'Diwan Mulraj's Proclamation to the Khalsa', see my *British and the Sikhs*, p.149

20   Hodson, *Twelve years of a Soldier's life*, pp.125–126. Cook, *The Sikh Wars*, p.139.

21   Cook, *The Sikh Wars*, p.141.

Interestingly, the protagonist of the First Sikh War, Gulab Singh of Kashmir, was also being watched. The EIC was unsure whether he would switch sides; however, this was not to materialise. Gulab Singh was happy to watch things play out and stay aloof in his usual way. Gough's 'Army of the Punjab' consisted of one cavalry and three infantry divisions headed by Brigadier Cureton, Walter Gilbert and Joseph Thackwell. Sher Singh's intention was to take over Lahore but he would be thwarted. He stationed some of his forces at Gujranwala. Cureton was despatched to block the passageway to Lahore. Also, some of the Muslim regions were aware of the rebellion and were not willing to help the sardar. Sher Singh moved with his forces to the River Chenab where he was joined by 6,000 troops from Bannu and thirty guns.[22] Some small skirmishes took place with the *Ghorchurahs* but there was still little contact between the warring parties.

Battle of Ramnuggar

On 9 November, Hugh Gough crossed the Sutlej and by the 21st, his 'Army of the Panjab' was eight miles from Sher Singh's army. Gough had suffered some mishaps with robbers attacking his baggage trains. The village of Ramnuggar was two miles from the Chenab. The Khalsa army occupied strong positions on both banks of the river and on an island mid-stream, hoping that the EIC would come through the broken ground around the bank of the river, where their artillery would be more effective. On 22 November at dawn, the British force assembled opposite the fords. The 3rd Light Dragoons and 8th Light cavalry drove some Sikhs back across the river from positions on the east bank but concealed Sikh batteries opened fire. The British cavalry was submerged in the soft ground. Gough's horse artillery was struggling and being outgunned and forced to retire, a 6-pounder gun and a couple of limbers sank in the ground. Retrieval of the gun was not possible with Sikh artillery firing on the EIC positions.[23]

3,000 Sikh horsemen composed of the *Ghorchurahs* crossed the fords to take advantage of the right position. The cavalry, composed of the 14th Light Dragoons and the 5th Bengal Light Cavalry, was sent to attack them. Sikh horsemen retreated but halted and using the *Dhai Phat* method turned around, hitting the 5th Light Cavalry and causing casualties. Colonel William Havelock of the 14th Light Dragoons saw another body of Sikh horseman along the river and he decided to lead another charge. This ill-thought-out plan was disastrous; his troops were cut down and they fell into the river bed. The horses were unable to move out of the deep sand. Havelock was killed and 50 of his regiment suffered casualties. Brigadier Cureton, witnessing the disaster that was falling on the troops, galloped up and tried to order a retreat. He

---

22   Cook, *The Sikh Wars*, p.144.
23   Cook, *The Sikh Wars*, p.146.

was then killed by musket fire. There was no further action as Gough was unwilling to commit any more troops.

The battle saw many hand-to-hand encounters with the Sikhs showing their sword-wielding skills against the bayonet charges of the British. 'The weakness of the British Sword against the Sikh Tulwar' was witnessed within the battle. A note reported in *The Illustrated London News* stated, 'No nation could exceed them in the rapidity of their fire…No men could act more bravely than the Sikhs. They faced us the moment we came on them, firing all the time…their individual acts of bravery were the admiration of all.'[24] Indeed, the army of Sher Singh was boosted by the courageous Nihangs, and the Chakkar was used by them with much success:

> In the magnificent army that Shere Singh led against the British all the Hindoo weapons, both ancient and modern, were represented. There were large bodies of troops carrying firearms, and drilled in the European manner, as well as squadrons of horsemen in complete suits of armour, with plumed helmets on their heads, and bearing lances. Besides these there were many thousands of irregular soldiers, both horse and foot; and amongst the latter some who carried several chakras arranged on their high-peaked caps. Their practice was to hurl their sharp quoits at the advancing foe, and then to rush on them with their swords. Nothing could exceed the bravery of the Sikhs; and it was only after numerous battles, in which the British troops suffered severely, that they were subdued.[25]

The Sikhs then withdrew to the north. Official British casualties were 26 killed or missing, 59 wounded; Sikh casualties were not known.

Gough's intention was to cross the Chenab and defeat the Sikhs before being reinforced. However, the location of the crossing was proving difficult due to Sikh defences at Ghuriki, Runiki and Ali Sher Ke Chuck. The next entry point lay 22 miles from Ramnuggar. It was decided to push towards Wazirabad under John Nicholson. The Sikhs did not notice the detachment of the EIC forces. The British crossed at Wazirabad after securing a number of boats and General Thackwell was sent to start the next offensive. The idea was to attack the fords and for Thackwell to attack behind the Sikhs. Advancing to Sadulpore on 3 December, Thackwell did not realise that Sher Singh's forces of 10,000 men were nearing. Indeed, it was a surprise for the Sikhs to see the British advancing from this vantage point. The British infantry retired, with the Sikhs not following up. The Sikh cavalry were met by the British horse artillery; however, this was just a light interaction, with cannons now firing on both sides. This lasted three hours with no conclusion. The fords had now been crossed by the EIC

24   Report dated 25 November 1848, in *The Illustrated London News*. The Bengal Light Cavalry did not use their regulation swords and 'preferred to use their pistols…to this extent, they were inferior to the irregular cavalry, who were themselves armed with tulwars and who used them with complete confidence.' Cook, *The Sikh Wars*, p.147.

25   This was noted in the Victorian Magazine, *Chatterbox* (1892), pp.41–42

Chakkar wielded by an Akali during the Second Sikh War. (*Chatterbox*, 1892)

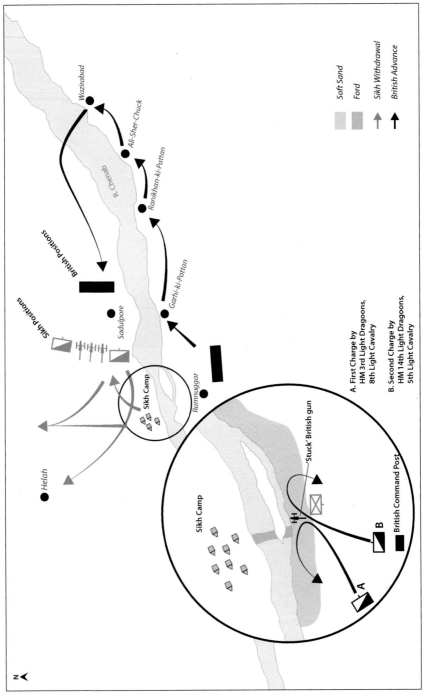

The Battle of Ramnuggar.

which was a rather late reaction. The ill-thought-out manoeuvres of Thackwell could have proved a Sikh win and later there were questions as to who ordered the attack at Sadulpore.[26] When dawn broke, the Sikhs had moved to Jhelum without Gough realising. Sher Singh was one step ahead of the British, the idea being to draw the British forces higher up to the North West Frontier regions and to secure more reinforcements from Chattar Singh and the Afghans, whilst Gouch waited for Multan to fall and to expand his force.

The Second Siege of Multan

Late in November, Whish was reinforced by a substantial force of the Bombay Army. His combined force amounted to 32,000 men and 150 pieces of artillery, many of which were heavy guns or mortars. Steamships brought supplies along the Indus River to within a short distance of the city. There was also the call-up of Colonel Dundas's 60th Rifles which led to further delays of EIC action at Multan; he arrived on 21 December. Mulraj now had at his disposal 12,000 troops, with 54 guns and 12 mortars.[27] On 27 December, Whish ordered four columns of troops to attack Mulraj's forces outside the city from every vantage point. His force had moved up to 500 yards from the city walls, eventually allowing him to set up breaching batteries 80 yards from the walls. At the same time, they being subjected to fire from the Multani forces. On 30 December, the main magazine in the citadel exploded. This explosion has been considered one of the largest in the nineteenth century and sent shockwaves across the area.[28] Debris and smoke rose 1,000 feet in the air and an eerie silence fell at Multan. The explosion resulted in the death of 800 people inside the fort including the family members of Diwan Mulraj.

Mulraj was still defiant and sent a message to General Whish, stating that he still had enough powder to last a year.[29] In fact, the fort walls were still intact despite the explosion. He attempted to mount a sortie against the EIC on 31 December but this was driven back. More guns were now brought to the siege to keep up the attack on

26   Conflicting evidence centred on Pennycuick, Campbell, Thackwell and Gough not clearly communicating orders after crossing at Wazirabad.
27   Some sources state there were 80 guns mounted in the citadel.
28   There were between over 800,000 lbs of gunpowder stored in the magazine. Singh, *The Second Anglo-Sikh War*, p.216.
29   A mortar shell fired from the Multan Fort can be seen at the National Army Museum, London. The mortar is inscribed with the words 'THIS BRASS SHELL (Weighing 87lbs)/ was fired from the ramperts [sic] of/ MOOLTAN IN THE PUNJAUB [sic]/ by the Seikhs into the British Camp during the siege/ and capture of the City on 2nd January 1849./ It was secured and brought to England as a Trophy/ BY THE LATE MAJOR GENERAL I. B. BELLASIS./ who with his cousin COLONEL E. MAUDE/ was present throughout the Siege/ H.I.B. 1904.' See colour pages.

the fort walls.[30] On 2 January 1849, Whish ordered a general assault leading to two breaches, one at Delhi gate and the other at Khonee Burj. The attackers successfully scaled the breaches, and the battle became a bloody house-to-house fight in the city. They made their way to Lahore Gate on the western side after capturing two Sikh colours. It was now getting dark and confusion reigned. Whish for some unknown reason rounded up the civilians and placed them in the main square. Looting now took place before order was restored in the morning.

By midday, the fall of the city was nearly complete with only the already-scarred citadel remaining. Yet Diwan Mulraj held out for another fortnight against heavy bombardment. On 12 January, the Sikh forces made a sortie against the British sap-heads but they were beaten back. By 21 January, three mines had exploded under its walls, causing heavy losses and destroying large sections of its walls. Some of the garrison slipped away, sensing that all was lost. Mulraj had offered to surrender if his life was spared, but Whish insisted on an unconditional surrender. On 22 January, Mulraj gave himself up, with 550 of his men. This ended one of the most expensive campaigns for the EIC in terms of ammunition, second only to Bhurtpore (Bharatpur).[31] Mulraj was arrested, sent to Lahore and placed on trial for the murders of Vans Agnew and Anderson. He was found guilty of being an accessory to the officer's death despite there being relatively little evidence to support this. He was given the death penalty but this was later commuted to life imprisonment. In January 1850, he was taken to Calcutta where he fell seriously ill. He died on 11 August 1851 near Buxar on his way to Banaras. His personal property was also confiscated, leading to suggestions of a major injustice for his family.[32] Multan was one of the wealthiest parts of the Sikh Empire and had now fallen to the British.

Battle of Chillianwallah

General Whish, after leaving the Multan garrison, would support the main operation against Sher Singh. Despite the events at Multan, Sher Singh was aware that his

---

30   This included eleven 8-inch mortars, ten 10-inch mortars, four 5 ½ inch mortars, six 18-pounders, two 8-inch howitzers, two 10-inch howitzers and ten 24-pounders. Cook, *The Sikh Wars*, p.159.

31   Cook, *The Sikh Wars*, p.161. The siege of Bhurtpore took place between 1825–1826 between Field Marshall Combermere and Balwant Singh of the Marathas. The 17.75-ton Bhurtpore gun, captured during the siege, stood outside the Royal Artillery Barracks in Woolwich, London.

32   The *Talwar* of Diwan Mulraj was taken by Captain Whish and bequeathed by his descendants to the Royal Artillery in Woolwich in 1965. An inscription inside the handguard reads 'Akaal Sahai Mulraja 1893' which translates to 1836. It is contained in a green scabbard. A descendant of Mulraj, Jarat Chopra has petitioned for the sword to be given back to his family without success. He has been supported by a descendant of General Whish.

father, Chattar Singh, would be joined by Afghan reinforcements. The fort at Attock had fallen after Herbert Edwardes had surrendered, so this now only a matter of time. The Afghan contingent was that of Amir Dost Mohammed Khan, once an enemy of the Sikhs. Hugh Gough was also not waiting for the end of the siege; he was aware that Sikh agents were trying to undermine the loyalty of Indian native troops and that this could be met with success. As a result, he advanced to Chillianwallah, which was a Sikh outpost.[33] This, however, was driven out. Gough was based at Russol, some distance away, but he could see the positions along Luckanwalla. No patrols had been sent and when the Sikhs saw the presence of the EIC they suddenly started firing, which caught Gough and his cavalry by surprise. Again, Sher Singh had got the better of Gough although the plan might have been to ensure that all his forces were at Chillianwallah. Ram Singh and his Bannu troops consisted of one regiment of cavalry, four regiments of infantry and seventeen guns, positioned on their right flank. Lall Singh and Ata Singh had two regiments of cavalry and ten regiments of infantry and 17 guns in the centre.[34] Their left or main line was headed by Sher Singh together with his *Ghorchurahs* consisting of regiments of cavalry, five regiments of infantry, five guns and irregular horse.[35] Other irregulars were held up at the village of Moong. The Sikh strength has been disputed but British sources state that it numbered a top figure of 30,000 with 62 guns.[36] The Sikhs were arranged in a shape of a *Talwar*. Once again thick forest separated the two forces and the Sikhs' left flank was a steep climb upwards. Sher Singh had indeed picked the correct spot but like Aliwal, they had their backs to the river.

Gough's army was composed of two infantry divisions with a total of 66 guns, Bengal Artillery and Bengal Horse Artillery. On the left was deployed Colin Campbell, with another division under Walter Gilbert. Gough's cavalry was headed by Joseph Thackwell and covered each flank; the right under Brigadier Pope and the left under Brigadier White. The centre was composed of two heavy artillery batteries with eight 18-pounder guns and four 8-inch howitzers. Brigadier Penney held a reserve unit of Bengal Native troops. Gough had around 12,000 men and was thought to be outnumbered but his troops may be considered more experienced. The battle commenced at 3:00 p.m. and the jungle separating the forces was going to be an issue for the EIC. The firing started on both sides, with Campbell's division pushing into the Sikh infantry line. The HM 24th Regiment was given orders to go forth with the

33   Interestingly the area was synonymous with the battle undertaken 2,000 years earlier between Alexander the Great and Porus the King of Panjab.
34   The Lall Singh mentioned here should not be confused with the treacherous Lal Singh of the First Sikh War. His forces were also composed of 6 veteran Khalsa units.
35   Several guns sent by Chattar Singh had now reached Sher Singh. Singh, *The Second Anglo-Sikh War*, p.332. Narain Singh a commander under Diwan Mulraj also made his way to the Khalsa camp with 3000–4000 troops. He evaded interception by EIC troops sent to block his path.
36   Amarpal Singh notes it as 50 guns.

Raja Sher Singh, his bodyguard, and Sikh troops. (*The Illustrated London News*, 1849)

bayonet as opposed to opening fire. Pennycuick's brigade also teamed up with the 24th. The EIC reached the Sikh lines and took some of their guns. The Khalsa army now took the offensive and recaptured some of the trenches and soon the 24th was in retreat. Pennycuick, his son, and Colonel Brookes the commanding officer, fell as soon as they had reached the Sikh position. All the members of the EIC colour party were killed; the 25th and 45th Bengal Native Infantry lost all but one of their colours, the 24th losing one colour with another being recaptured.[37] The *Ghorchurahs* pursued the EIC forces for a short distance. The remaining 24th regrouped under Captain Blachford.[38]

The Sikh cavalry came face to face with HM 61st foot and was driven away whilst the Sikh Infantry headed by Atar Singh was repulsed by the 36th Bengal Native Infantry. The 24th Bengal Native Infantry took their fight to the Sikh line and captured 13 guns and then joined up with Gilbert's division.[39] Brigadier Mountain came under fire from Sikh snipers hidden in the trees and the colours of the 29th were shot out. The Khalsa army was seen throwing away their muskets and fighting with their *Talwars* but they were attacked by the 29th. The Sikh gunners

37   The Queen's colour was also lost or captured by the Sikhs.
38   The sword worn by Captain Blachford 24th Regiment of Foot at the Battle of Chillianwallah can be seen at Regimental Museum of The Royal Welsh Brecon. It was exhibited at the Sikh Museum Initiative 'Anglo Sikh Wars: Battles, Treaties and Relics' Exhibition in 2017 at Newarke Houses Museum, Leicester.
39   Cook, *The Sikh Wars*, p.173.

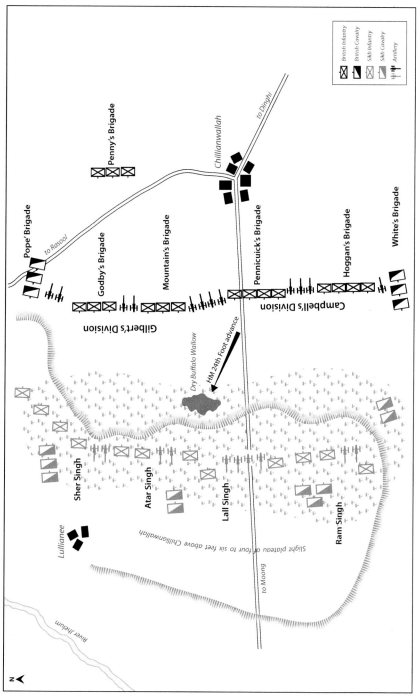

The Battle of Chillianwallah.

also received praise for trying to capture their opponents' bayonet with their hands; however, 12 guns were lost to the 29th. The *Ghorchurahs* fought on the left flank with Captain White's cavalry. Captain Unett and his 3rd King's Own Light Dragoons went through the jungle, cutting their way through the Sikh lines, but every member of their squadron was wounded.[40] On the right flank, Sikh cavalry met with Pope's brigade and supporting units; during the melee, they repulsed the EIC forces. Brigadier Pope's forces, however, drifted into the path of Gilbert's forces, causing a nuisance. Pope himself was severely injured by a Sikh who slashed his face with a sabre. As he was leaving the battlefield, some of the British saw this as an order to retreat, including the 14th Light Dragoons.[41] The *Ghorchurahs* burst through the British hospital where injured soldiers and animals were located. This caused further panic. Their battery was left unprotected and as a result, they captured two guns. Eventually, British guns drove them back. Penny's reserve brigade was sent to face the Sikhs; however, they lost their way in the jungle and met up with Godby's unit. At one point in the battle, the Sikhs came within near distance of Gough but did not see him. As much as the thick jungle provided cover for the Sikhs, it also masked what was happening on the other side, where the British were.

Darkness was now approaching. Sher Singh and his forces were now withdrawing along the banks of the Jhelum. Gough was also weighing his options and whether he should withdraw to Chillianwallah. Both sides recovered their dead, with Sikhs returning two privates of the 9th Lancers as well as allowing a Lieutenant Bowie out on parole.[42] Even though there were excesses on both sides, this was a notable gesture. The British losses amounted to 2,331 of all ranks with the previously mentioned 24th suffering the most together with HM 3rd King's Own Light Dragoons. Sikh losses were estimated to be 4,000. The Sikhs considered this a success if not a bloody nose for the British; this is despite the prominent gunner, General Ilahi Bakhsh, defecting.[43] The battle had created a bad impression of the British not just in India but in England as well. A replacement was sought for Hugh Gough, who was blamed for the loss of personnel, guns and their colours. This was to come in the form of General Charles James Napier (1782–1853); however, even before he was appointed the battle of Gujarat had been fought and the war was effectively over.[44]

A number of matchlock guns were found at the scene of the battle, one of which can be seen in the colour pages.

---

40   I was able to inspect some of the remaining relics of Captain Unett at the Queen's Royal Hussars Museum, Warwick together with some other Sikh relics.
41   Recriminations continued for years between individual soldiers as to who was to blame for the order to retreat. Singh, *The Second Anglo-Sikh War*, pp.346–350. Cook, *The Sikh Wars*, p.176–177.
42   Cook, *The Sikh Wars*, p.179.
43   This included his sons and the artillery commander Amir Khan; a split in the army between the Sikhs and Muslims might have contributed towards this act.
44   Napier was a veteran of the Napoleonic wars and was governor of Sind, defeating the regime there in 1843. He had gone back to England in 1847.

Battle of Gujarat

Gough's idea to follow up the next day was hampered by three days of incessant rain which kept the two armies apart. The British strategy was to wait for Multan to fall, and receive additional troops and guns under General Whish, whilst the Sikhs under Sher Singh would rendezvous with his father, Chattar Singh. Sher Singh was trying to tempt Gough to attack him; realising the predicament, however, Gough was not prepared to undertake a full-scale attack. A number of skirmishes took place between 30 January and the first week of February. Sher Singh now moved off in a south-easterly direction towards Gujarat. The route to attack Lahore was still on the cards but was not taken by the Sikhs. The British reconnaissance was very poor throughout this campaign. Sher Singh left Rasool on 4 February but he moved out without Gough realising.[45] In fact, he did not even know which direction he had taken. A skirmish also took place between Lumsden's guides and around 6,000 Sikhs from Ramnuggar. The location had not been garrisoned, so they tried crossing at Wazirabad, which had now been blocked off by the British.

On 15 February, Gough moved towards Lassorie, an area between Chillianwallah and Sadulpore. Now General Whish's troops, tired but upbeat from their success at Multan, had fully joined up with Gough's main army which was the intended objective. By 20 February he was three miles from the Sikh position at Gujarat. The Sikhs had entrenched themselves once again in a crescent style position between two *Nullahs*. They set up at Bara Kalra and Chota Kalra. The position was held by infantry interspersed with artillery; backup cavalry was at the rear of Chota Kalra. Many of the Afghan forces of Dost Mohammed were under Akram Khan on the right. Gough's army composition had some changes in terms of the brigades which now had different commanders. General Gilbert was stationed in the middle, with Penny's division on his right and Mountain's division on the left. Under Captain Whish on the right were the Lockwood and Hersey divisions. On the left were the divisions of Dundas, McLoed and Carnegie. Gough's position was now advantageous with additionally artillery support consisting of eighteen guns positioned on his left next to the dry *Nullah*. It was now 21 February and the clear skies allowed Gujarat to be seen in full view all the way to the Himalayas. The Sikhs commenced the action at 9:00 a.m., disclosing their positions immediately and the British guns were sent to respond. In the initial action, the British would face the most casualties due to some attacks by their infantry; however, after the heavy pounding of around two hours they seemed to get the better of the Sikhs. The British frontline now advanced with the Sikh cavalry looking towards crossing the *Nullah*, but their advancement was blocked. A party of 30 Afghan horsemen made it through to Hugh Gough's position but were checked by the 5th Bengal Light Cavalry.[46]

45   Cook, *The Sikh Wars*, p.183.
46   Cook, *The Sikh Wars*, p.188.

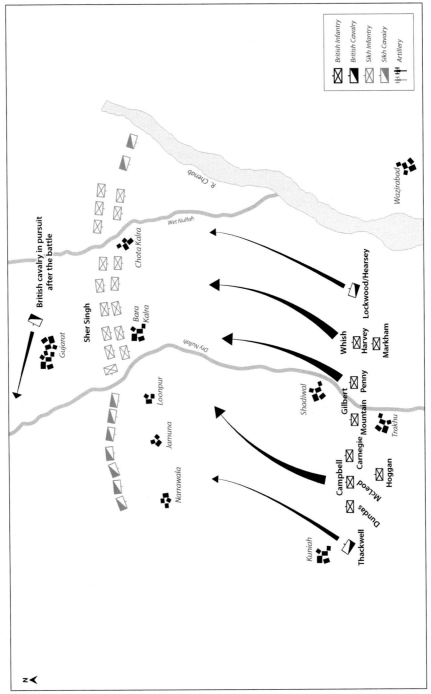

The Battle of Gujarat.

The fighting at the village of Gujarat intensified, with the 10th Regiment and the 8th Bengal Native Infantry driving out the Sikhs. The Khalsa regrouped at Bara Kalra but they were blocked. There was now desperate hand-to-hand fighting at the small fortified villages of Burra Kalra and Chota Kalra. The attack by Penny's brigade led to many Sikhs battling to the last man and losing three battle standards in the process. The Sikh guns continued to fire, inflicting 140 casualties on the 31st Bengal Native Infantry. The Sikh attack now focused on the dry *Nullah* but it was neutralised by Gilbert and Campbell's gunners. The Sikh cavalry on the right was more offensive in this campaign and got through to Campbell's infantry. The Sikhs, with a battery of six guns, were attacked by 60th Rifles, leading to the guns being spiked by the 3rd Light Dragoons. The cavalry of Afghan troops was met by Scinde's horse and 9th Lancers and this led to a Sikh retreat with four Sikh colours lost and interestingly a British cannon previously captured by the Sikhs at Chillianwallah.[47]

Approaching 12:30 p.m., the Sikh line was now in retreat, the cannonade being too much from them. Sher Singh had now left the battle. The infantry was seen leaving in an orderly fashion but the British cavalry had caught up with many of them and this led to many Sikh losses. The pursuit led by General Thackwell and Hearsay's regulars covered up to 15 miles, showing the British determination to finish the Sikhs once and for all. Much of the Sikh forces were unable to be caught, leading to the chase being called off. The EIC had initially taken over India by using their artillery strength at the Battle of Plassey (1757) and the last battle of strategic importance at Gujarat was completed by effectively using the same branch of the army. This showed that for a complete battle, it required not just the mechanics but the strategy behind it.[48] In history, the battle of Gujarat is referred to as the 'Battle of Guns' for this reason. The Sikhs had the training and the military know-how to engage their own superior guns but this was in short supply at this engagement. The British losses were 96 killed and 750 wounded, with the artillery suffering the most. Sikh losses were estimated at 2,000 killed and 53 to 56 guns being captured. Gough, despite his criticism, was triumphant against Sher Singh. On 22 February, Gilbert accompanied Brigadiers Mountain and Dundas and set out against Sher Singh. It was thought some of the army was in the region of Bhimbar so Campbell's division was despatched in that direction. The remnants of the Sikh army crossed the River Jhelum on the 24 February, and Sher Singh had now sent George Lawrence (as an envoy) asking for terms.[49] This was essentially the full reinstatement of Maharajah Duleep Singh and for the British to leave Lahore.[50] He also released some prisoners in his care. But Dalhousie would only accept unconditional surrender. Sher Singh, now short of supplies, advanced

47   Cook, *The Sikh Wars*, pp.189–190.
48   Brig. R.C. Butalia, *The Evolution of the Artillery in India: From the Battle of Plassey 1757 to the Revolt of 1857* (New Delhi: Allied Publishers, 1998), p.318.
49   Cook, *The Sikh Wars*, p.191.
50   Kohli, *Sunset of the Sikh Empire*, p.181.

Battle of Gujarat. (W. S. Simmons, 1849)

to Rawalpindi but was met with hostilities from the Muslim villagers. Gulab Singh again showed his true colours by helping Major Abbott block Sher Singh's retreat and by supplying boats to the British to cross the Jhelum.[51]

On 14 March the Attariwala sardars, Sher Singh and Chattar Singh, finally surrendered to the East India Company. The British however wanted a formal ceremony with the Sikhs laying down their swords to Gilbert. The mighty Khalsa had been now vanquished. The following description gives a vivid account of the surrender:

> 'With noble self-restraint' – to use the words of Edwin Arnold – 'thirty-five chiefs laid down their swords at Gilbert's feet, while the Sikh soldiers, advancing, one by one, to the file of the English drawn across the road, flung down tulwar, matchlock, and shield upon the growing heap of arms, salaamed to them as to the "spirit of the steel," and passed through the open line, no longer soldiers.' But it must have been a more touching sight still, when – as it has been described to me by eye-witnesses – each horseman among them had to part, for the last time, from the animal which he regarded as part of himself – from the gallant charger which had borne him in safety in many an irresistible charge over many a battle-field. This was too much even for Sikh endurance. He caressed and patted his faithful companion on every part of his body, and then turned resolutely away. But his resolution failed him. He turned back, again and again, to give one caress more, and then, as he tore himself away for the very last time, brushed a teardrop from his eye, and exclaimed, in words which give the key to so much of the history of the relations of the Sikhs to us, their manly resistance, and their not less manly submission to the inevitable, 'Runjeet Sing is dead to-day!'[52]

The defeat was immortalised by the British issuing medals to soldiers depicting the Sikhs surrendering their weapons to Sir Walter Gilbert.[53] Interestingly, only one other individual who received a special medal for his fight against the Sikhs was Herbert Edwardes.[54] (See colour pages). Indeed, Sher Singh was made to watch the proceedings and in his mind, the war was justified to stop the transgressions made by the

---

51   Kohli, *Sunset of the Sikh Empire*, p.183.
52   Smith, *Life of Lord Lawrence*, Vol. 1, pp.240. The Panjabi rendering of the final line is 'Aj Ranjit Singh mar Gaya.' Referencing the foundation and stability of the Sikh Empire was all due to Ranjit Singh.
53   These were known as the 'Punjab Medal.'
54   This special medal was conferred on him by the Court of Directors. The medal depicts on the obverse Queen Victoria with the words 'the fountain of all honour', and on the reverse, the Edwardes family arms surmounting the inscription, 'To Lieutenant Herbert Benjamin Edwardes, Brevet-Major and C.B., for his services in the Punjab, 1848'. The inscription is flanked by the figures of Valour and Victory, and beneath the inscription, the figure of the infant Hercules (emblematic of Edwardes youth) strangles the serpent. It is indeed a very rare medal.

British on Rani Jindan Kaur. At Multan, this was still a localised war and one in which he did not participate until September 1848. For the British, it was a Sikh Empire versus East India Company campaign, in which the Lahore Durbar played little part and did not participate or send any forces to fight against the British. In fact, it was a war with many disaffected groups which also included the Afghans, who by 16 February were still being pursued by Gilbert. The small Afghan contingent destroyed the pontoon bridge at Attock behind them. Dost Mohammed later concluded peace negotiations with the East India Company, acknowledging their possession of the Peshawar region.

The Second Sikh War was now over and the British undertook to annexe the Panjab. The policy was always intended by Governor-General Dalhousie; he wanted to place blame on the Lahore Darbar, with Maharajah Duleep Singh still a minor. Ultimately he wanted to replace the Sikh Raj – the last bastion which remained independent of the EIC. The Council of Regency was worked on by Currie and Dalhousie to the extreme where the Maharajah was to be banished from Panjab and to be given a pension, but it was more of a threat than a negotiation. This was the logic of the strong over the weak. On 29 March at the Durbar with the Regency and the EIC, Duleep Singh was passed a paper by Tej Singh who affixed his signature 'by tracing the initials of his name in English letters.' A declaration was made that the sovereignty of Panjab was now assumed by the British and the annexation of the Panjab was now complete. The British colours were now hoisted on the Lahore Citadel. The Sikhs once had it all, but this all gave way during the First Sikh War and the successive battles.

Conclusion

In regards to the First Sikh War, according to the historian Hari Ram Gupta, 'Such a shameless and treasonable transaction is a thing of rare occurrence in the history of a free people in the world.'[55] This was freedom taken from the lands of the Sikhs after years of subjection; it brought individual prejudices to the fore. After the great and astonishing achievement of Ranjit Singh, the Panjab had become a state of lawlessness. Yet they had had an army equipped using both Indian and European modes of warfare. This is before we can even start to consider the British intention of weakening the Panjab from the outside, yet the Khalsa state did it to themselves. This was a British victory against a people afflicted with internal treachery and treason which ultimately led to the end of the great Sikh Durbar. The Second Sikh War was not even supported by a majority of the populace. In both conflicts, the question of 'where did all the good people go' must be asked and even then, would they have been able to direct efforts to a positive conclusion? Despite all of this, the Sikh soldiers performed admirably and these conflicts would live on in the

---

55   Gupta, *Punjab on the Eve*, p.17.

psyche of both the Sikhs and the British. The ramifications of the annexation of the Panjab would continue into the nineteenth century during the partition of India and Pakistan where the Sikh homeland was cut in two, and then again in the early 1980s when calls for a Sikh homeland known as Khalistan were rejected and instead the Indian Army attacked the Sikh separatists at Amritsar. In between all of this, a new world order would arise where the vanquished would form a major part of the British Indian Army.

12

Sikh Conquests in the 'British Indian Army'

At the close of the First Sikh War in 1846, it was decided to conciliate the men of the defeated Khalsa Army and enlist them into the EIC's service. This prospect of turning a foe into a willing partner was going to be interesting. The annexation of the Panjab provided the impetus for this. Yet the major recruitment was also undertaken during the so-called Indian Mutiny or Rebellion (the Sepoy uprising of 1857 and erroneously called the first Indian War of Independence). The British turned to various enlisting schemes guided by the martial races concept which gave precedence to recruiting races and groups based on certain traits. Sikh village after village was visited by EIC officers, as well as enlisted Sikh officers, promoting the virtues of the British Indian Army and the benefits it would give them. It is important at the outset to explain that the employment with the British was initially part of the East India Company, and then part of specific Presidency Arms and post 1895 the Indian Army. For simplicity, the in term British Indian Army has been used although this was not a formal title given to the Indian Army.

Early Regiment Formation

In 1846 a frontier brigade was created, consisting of a Corps of Guides, four regiments of Sikh Local Infantry, five regiments of Punjab Infantry, five regiments of Punjab Cavalry and one Light Battery of Artillery.

The idea was to police the North West Frontier as well as to become a pivotal part of policing parts of the Panjab. The Second Sikh War had disrupted this plan but it was recommenced in 1849, with the addition of three light batteries of artillery from the disbanded Sikh Horse Artillery. This set the scene for all recruitment of Sikhs into the British Indian Army.

Two of the first regiments raised in 1846 included the Regiment of Ferozepore and the 15th Ludhiana Sikhs. These units were composed of soldiers who fought against the Sikh Empire. The idea was to initially raise a Sikh irregular battalion, for service with the Bengal Army of the EIC. The 1st Sikh infantry was raised just after the First Anglo-Sikh War, a fact that many may not be aware of. Hence it begs the question, as to how this was this undertaken? It would be presumed that the regiment would be from Patiala or the Cis-Sutlej states but this could not be further from the truth. To defend the newly annexed districts, a fresh raising of troops was required, and, for this purpose, a brigade termed 'The Frontier Brigade' was created, consisting of one company of artillery and four regiments of Native Infantry, of which the 1st Sikhs was the first regiment.[1] Captain Hodgson, the Commandant, reported to Henry Lawrence at Lahore, on 29 November 1846, and received orders to proceed immediately to the station of Hoshiarpur and to commence raising his regiment.[2] On 10 December 1846, he issued his first regimental order, announcing the arrival of his second in command, Captain Troup, and on the same day, he enlisted his first 17 men.[3] The regiment was intended to be completely Sikh but was abandoned. The reason is unknown, but the names of Panjabi Mahomedans and Hindustanis also appear among his enlistments. The recruitment policy of a completely Sikh unit would be checked or balanced due to fears of a possible insurrection or mutiny. This was a continuing theme throughout the late nineteenth century. They were armed with muskets using common flint which were considered to be of inferior quality. On 3 February 1847 Captain Hodgson reported having got 400 men; on 1st March, 700; and on 15 April, the unit was complete. A constitution was created defining their regulations, their orders and pension and pay status. (See Appendix).

This established four regiments of Sikh Local Infantry and the term Frontier Brigade was discontinued: '...our Infantry regiments, which formed a portion of the brigade, are to be designated the 1st, 2nd (or Hill Corps), 3rd and 4th Regiments of Sikh Local Infantry.'[4] Many duties of the unit consisted chiefly of guarding over the jail, treasury, and other civil posts, and these duties required 183 men. They would not be employed across the Jamuna or in any major campaigns at this stage, hence the term local was pivotal. To the Frontier Brigade was later added the Corps of Guides (mentioned earlier) which had also been raised in 1846 at Peshawar by Lieutenant Harry Burnett Lumsden, by order of Sir Henry Lawrence, and which was largely inspirational for the creation of the two brigades. The Guides were long considered an ultimate 'crack' unit of the later-constituted Punjab Infantry Force (PIF). Lumsden had also pioneered the use of khaki in their uniform.

With the advent of the Second Sikh War in 1848, Ram Singh of Chattar Singh's army had stationed himself at Bassa, 60 miles from Hoshiarpur. The first action

---

1   Anonymous, *History of the 1st Sikh Infantry 1846–1886*, Vol. 1 (Calcutta: Printed by Thacker, Spink and Co.,1903), p.1. From here on, *History of the 1st Sikh Infantry*.
2   *History of the 1st Sikh Infantry*, p.2.
3   This was then boosted with Regular Infantry regiments of the line and some police. That of the 1st Regiment consisted of ten men from each of the following regiments: 6th Native Infantry, 12th Native Infantry, 43rd Native Infantry, 47th Native Infantry, and 68th Native Infantry, and one hundred men from the Umballah (Ambala) police — in all 150 men.
4   *History of the 1st Sikh Infantry*, pp.6–7.

of the 1st Sikhs was against him and his troops. Reaching there sometime after 18 September, Ram Singh was dislodged and the 1st Sikhs were praised for their actions. In November, Jodh Singh who was again part of Chattar Singh's army had captured the surrounding areas around Dinannagar. Again the party was dislodged. Umed Singh had captured the areas of Amb and Akrot, and Major Hodgson's men once more dislodged the Sikhs. All these small but important interventions led Lord Dalhousie, in a letter dated 8 December 1848, to praise the regiment:

> Lord Dalhousie is much gratified also by the conduct of the Sikh Regiment and of all those employed on this occasion, and he desires that his approbation of the conduct of the troops, both officers and men, may be communicated to them.' Similarly, Major Hodgson was confident about the unit: 'The Commanding Officer is assured that the Regiment will on every occasion strive to prove itself worthy of this good opinion by the same zealous, faithful, and soldier-like discharge of duty both in quarters and in the field against the enemy.[5]

Ram Singh, who had given the unit trouble earlier, had in 1849 stationed himself around Pathankot on the left bank of River Ravi. Brigadier-General Wheeler, together with Major Hodgson, were detached to counter this move. On 16 January, Ram Singh's positions were attacked but the Sikh lines stayed intact, and Lieutenant Peel was hit in the chest and later died. The 1st Sikh infantry force charged with their swords. Several soldiers, including Jemadar Ram Krishan Singh for the British forces, lost their lives in their defence.

In 1846, Colonel Brasyer (1812–97), who had fought in the First Sikh War and so had a good understanding of the Sikhs, was sent to tour the villages south of the Sutlej River or the Malwa region.[6] He visited many villages, where he persistently spoke to the Sikhs in their own language and collected all able men who were willing to serve as soldiers in the company's service. In less than two months he had collected four hundred men, many of whom had recently been fighting against the British. He brought them all to Ferozepore, where he handed them over to Captain Watt and Captain Tebbs, who had been appointed to raise the Regiment of Ferozepore which was later to be known as the 14th King George's Own Ferozepore Sikhs. This began to be known as the 14th Ferozepore Sikhs or just 14th Sikhs. Brasyer writes, 'Thus I had the honour of being myself the first to form the nucleus of that invaluable Seikh element of the Bengal Army, that has since served the British Government with so, much credit in every campaign since 1857.'[7] In December 1846, the Commander-in-Chief, Gough, reviewed the regiment in Ambala and presented them with their first

5   *History of the 1st Sikh Infantry*, p.15.
6   Jeremiah Brasyer of the Bengal Army. He had also fought in the First Afghan War.
7   <https://www.allaboutsikhs.com/biographies/british/brasyer-cb-colonel-j/> (accessed 12 October 2021).

Lieutenant-Colonel Jeremiah Brasyer of the 14th Sikhs Regiment of Ferozepore, 1858–1859. (By Felice Beato. Courtesy of Getty's Open Content Program)

colours. At the same time, the Regiment of Ludhiana (or the Loodiana Regiment) was also formed which went on to have many successful operations and battles which are recounted later in the chapter.

Further formalisation of Sikh Regiments took place in 1851, with The Punjab Irregular Force (PIF) later known as the Punjab Frontier Force, which was created to protect the North West Frontier. This was created from the previously mentioned Sikh Local Infantry Regiments. In time this gave rise to their name 'Piffer' which was adopted by the officers and men of the regiments of the PIF and is still used to this day by their successor regiments. The 4th Punjab Infantry was raised at Lahore in 1849 by Captain George Gladwin Denniss II (1821–62) of 1st European Bengal Fusiliers. He skilfully recruited soldiers who participated in the Second Sikh War: 60 followers of Diwan Mulraj, who had delivered themselves up as prisoners to the British Government on the capture of Multan, 200 men of sardar Dhara Singh's regiment and more significantly 300 men of Sher Singh's regiment. The selection process seemed to work: 'It was in this Force that the Pathan, Jatsikh and Dogra was first taught to serve in the ranks of the British Army; and it was in these Regiments that the Afreedees and other Afghan tribes were gradually reduced to obedience, and are now as well behaved as any of our Native Soldiery.'[8]

Recruitment Tactics

The EIC wanted to enlist Sikh soldiers but at the same time test their loyalty. Every campaign or law enforcement would lead to greater confidence by the British for Sikh recruitment. They also had to tap into the inner workings of the Sikhs and this was undertaken by ensuring that the religious element was kept intact rather than being completely absorbed or dismantled. This led to a number of innovations across the next half-century. The early promotion of Sikh belief in their scriptures was paramount and would be adopted in recruitment. Captain Thomas Wilde (4th Punjab Infantry), writing in 1850, refers to the oaths sworn by Sikh soldiers on commencement of their recruitment:

> I...inhabitant of...son of...swear by the Gooroo Grunth Sahibjee [holy scripture of Sikhism] and if I tell a falsehood may the Gooroo Grunth Sahib cause misfortune to descend upon me, that I will never forsake or abandon my Colours, that I will march wherever I am directed whether within or beyond the Company's Territories, that I will implicitly obey all the orders of my Commanders, and in everything behave myself as becomes a good Soldier and faithful servant of the

8   Appendix 2. Anon., *Regimental History of the 4th Battalion:13th Frontier Force Rifles (Wilde's)* (East Sussex: The Naval & Military Press Ltd., 2005).

Company, and failing in any part of my duty as such I will submit to the penalties ascribed in the Articles of War, which have been read to me.[9]

This prescription of using the scriptures to ensure loyalty would work wonders for the enlistment into the British Indian Army. Indeed, the idea of the Guru Granth Sahib being kept with a unit or battalion would become a norm.[10] This was in keeping with the traditions of the Khalsa, where the *Giani* or reciter of scriptures would be part of a battalion.

Many of the battles in the forthcoming pages have been overlooked in the face of the mutiny and the battle of Saragarhi. After the annexation of the Panjab, the Sikh soldier adjusted not just their loyalty but also the way they accepted the British Indian Army model. The Sikh soldier operated across many battlefields across the world, from the continued campaigns against the Afghans, in parts of Africa, and closer to home in Burma. As part of the allied forces in the World Wars, they were seen in action in France, Italy, and the Middle East. These were not just fringe campaigns and the Sikhs became the backbone of the British Indian Army. The honours received initially included the Indian Order Of Merit (IOM) and later the Sikhs became recipients of the Victoria Cross (VC). In 1911 King George V extended the Victoria Cross to the officers and men of the Indian Army. This was the highest honour of valour for the British and the British Empire (later the Commonwealth countries). The campaigns in which the Sikhs operated extended to many spheres of the world. The continuation of the policing of the North West Frontier would become a norm for the Sikhs, leading to epic encounters with various tribes who held their own against the British and other adversaries. Other areas were the campaigns in Africa which are seldom discussed and for which the Sikhs were singled out for their bravery and courage.

Early Campaigns and the Indian Rebellion

In 1853, the Sikhs were in action against the Afridis.[11] The campaign resulted in two Sikhs receiving the IOM.[12] In 1857, the 2nd Punjab Infantry and the Corps of Guides took action against the Bozdar tribes, also in the NWF. The Sikhs had previously been in action against them during the days of the Sikh Empire. 1857 was also pivotal as a huge uprising in India was beginning to take shape at the Meerut and this would spread to other areas. The conflict centred on the introduction of the new Enfield

9   Appendix 3. Anon., *Regimental History of the 4th Battalion*.
10   For a portrait showing the swearing-in of soldiers in the presence of the Guru Granth Sahib, see *Illustrated London News*, 17 January 1891, in my *British and the Sikhs*.
11   The Afridis are a Pathan tribe from the Khyber and Darra Adam Khel districts of the Khyber Pakhtunkhwa.
12   The information for the recipients of the IOM has been taken from Narindar Singh Dhesi, *Sikh Soldier – Gallantry Awards*, Vol. 2 (East Sussex: Naval & Military Press, 2010).

rifle. To load it, the soldiers had to bite off the ends of lubricated cartridges. Thoughts were spread among the soldiers that the grease used to lubricate the cartridges was a mixture of pig and cow fat. This oral contact was considered blasphemous to both Muslims and Hindus. This led to dissatisfaction among Indian army soldiers, mainly that this was encroaching on their beliefs and undermining traditional society. This began what is termed the Indian Rebellion or Indian Mutiny.

Starting in March 1857, a Hindu soldier named Mangal Pandey of the 34th Bengal Native Infantry attacked British officers at the military garrison in Barrackpore. He was arrested and then executed by the British in early April. In the same month, Indian soldiers at Meerut refused the Enfield cartridges, and as punishment they were fettered and put in jail with long prison terms. This punishment incensed their comrades, who rose up on 10 May, shot their British officers, and marched to Delhi, where there were no European troops. The local garrison joined the Meerut men, and by the evening the aged Mughal emperor Bahadur Shah II (1775–1862) had been nominally restored to power by a tumultuous soldiery.[13] The seizure of Delhi provided a focus and set the pattern for the whole mutiny, which then spread throughout northern India. However, this uprising needs to be qualified on many grounds; firstly, it was supported by the Mughal emperor and his sons, Maratha, Nana Sahib and Lakshmibai, the Queen of Jhansi (1828–58). They all had personal motives against the British which was not necessarily related to the cartridges. No other important Indian princes joined the mutineers. There had also been many sustained attacks on the Sikhs, citing them as the only community which aided the British in the Mutiny, but this is not true either.

The Bengal Presidency army recruited heavily from among high-caste Hindus and comparatively elite Muslims. The Muslims formed a larger percentage of the 18 irregular cavalry units within the Bengal Army, whilst Hindus were mainly to be found in the regular infantry and cavalry regiments. The soldiers were therefore affected to a large degree by the concerns of the landholding and traditional members of Indian society. The EIC tolerated and even encouraged caste privileges and customs within the Bengal Army, which recruited its regular soldiers almost exclusively amongst the landowning Rajputs and Brahmins of the Bihar and Awadh regions. These soldiers were known as *Purbias*. This recruitment had its disadvantages; as in this case, it could lead to one type of community easily rebelling. Many of these soldiers had also fought against the Sikhs in the Anglo-Sikh Wars and so there was no love lost between them. It was only eight years after the Sikh Wars and there was still bitterness regarding this. The treacherous Tej Singh and Lal Singh were both *Purbias* who had moved up the ranks in the Sikh Empire. Sikh persecution from the Mughals in the eighteenth century was also something that brought about negative connotations.

---

13   Bahadur Shah Zafar, the twentieth and last Mughal Emperor of India. He was only a figurehead and held no real power. The British exiled him to Rangoon (Burma) after convicting him on several charges.

If anything, the Anglo-Sikh Wars were the most opportune time to revolt against the British but Bengal soldiers helped the British to defeat Sikhs – this was a real battle for independence that no parties across Hindustan supported. Furthermore, the support of a Mughal Emperor was not something that was going to happen. This was partly due to the Anglo–Sikh Wars and partly the long memory of Sikh persecution by the Mughals. Nationalistic tendencies were still in their infancy. Singh writes,

> Apart from the Panjab, the Hindus, the Muslims[…]kept aloof from the mutineers, but the people of Bengal, Madras, Maharashtra, Gujarat, Sindh, Rajasthan, Jammu and Kashmir and the North-Western Frontier Province also did not join them. Some of them actually opposed them. Not only this. Out of the three Presidency Armies – Bengal, Madras and Bombay – it was only a part of the Bengal Army that had mutinied. The other parts fought on the side of the British Government to suppress it. The Madras and Bombay armies remained quiet and loyal. Evidently, the Poorbia soldiers had failed to win the sympathies of their own class of people in the south and south-west as in the west and north-west.[14]

Maratha's ruler Sindhia of Gwalior, Holkar of Indore and Gaikwad of Baroda actively helped the British even though Nana Sahib, the adopted son of Peshwa Balaji Baji Rao II, had plunged into the rebellion.

This point in time became a focal point of Sikh recruitment into the EIC. Firstly, support came from the Sikh allies of the Cis-Sutlej states who had sided with the British from 1809. This included Patiala under Narendra Singh who was based at Ambala and who provided loans to the British. It also included the state of Kapurthala under Randhir Singh, who was stationed in Jullundur. The Raja of Nabha, Bharpur Singh, sent his force to Ludhiana. The Raja of Faridkot, Wazir Singh, sent his forces under the jurisdiction of Ferozepur and would cut off any mutineers crossing the Sutlej. The Raja of Jind, Sarup Singh, left for Karnal with the British so to create a boundary between Thanesar and Delhi. Essentially they would patrol around the Grand Trunk Road. Raja Sobha Singh and his son Lehna Singh of Kalsia guarded the ferries at the River Jamuna and his troops were also sent to Oudh. Other *Jagirdars* sent their private contingents to the Ambala division and Sher Singh of Amritsar sent his men which would form Hodson's Horse.[15] The Cis-Sutlej states also sent carts, camels, and grain to support the effort. Two new pioneer regiments were formed. The 15th (Pioneer) Regiment of Punjab Infantry, later to become the 23rd Sikh Pioneers, were raised at Lahore in 1857, together with the 24th (Pioneer) Regiment of Punjab

---

14 Ganda Singh, *The Indian Mutiny Of 1857 And The Sikhs* (Delhi: Gurdwara Parbandhak Committee, 1969), pp.37-38.
15 Shamsul Islam, *Rebel Sikhs in 1857* (New Delhi: Vani Prakashan), pp.17–30. The author also labours the point that there were many Sikhs in support of the rebellion.

Infantry at Madhopur. The regiments were raised principally from the Mazhbi Sikh community of the Panjab, who had been recruited into pioneer and engineer units since 1850.[16]

There were several theatres of war beginning at Delhi on 11 May 1857; aided by a mob from the bazaar, the rebels killed Europeans and Indian Christians. On 7 June 1857, a hastily raised force of 4,000 men succeeded in occupying a ridge overlooking Delhi, but was too weak to retake the city. Between July and August 1857, faced by over 30,000 mutineers, the British came under increasing pressure. The army began to suffer losses through cholera. In the searing heat, the British held off repeated rebel efforts to take the ridge. On 14 August 1857, reinforcements arrived from the Panjab, including a siege train of 32 guns and 2,000 men under Brigadier-General John Nicholson. He executed without trial hundreds of mutineers and innocent civilians.[17] By September the British had 9,000 men before Delhi. A third were British, the rest Sikhs, Panjabi Muslims, and Gurkhas. Their assault began when artillery breached the walls and blew up the Kashmir Gate. Between 14 and 21 September 1857, there was continuous fighting. It took a week of vicious street fighting before Delhi was taken. It was then ransacked in an orgy of looting and killing. But Delhi's recapture proved the decisive factor in the suppression of the revolt.

Another area of concern was Allahabad. Colonel Brasyer dismissed members of the 6th Native Infantry who appeared to be mutinous. He was attacked by his troops when he asked them to surrender. However, he was supported by the Sikhs, although at this time he was not sure of their loyalties. They helped dislodge the disaffected elements. Brasyer organised the defence of the fort, which he held against the rebels with his four hundred Ferozepore Sikhs. Allahabad was the key to the north-west and, once secured, it formed an advance base of operations. Brasyer also asked the Sikhs to dispense with any company attire and to fight as they saw best, so they 'discarded their caps and heavy coats and wore red turbans and Sikh blouses throughout the Mutiny.' This led to success on 17 June and the rebels were defeated.

In June 1857, soldiers rebelled at Cawnpore (Kanpur). They were led by Nana Sahib, a local ruler who had suffered from the British seizure of his estate. They laid siege to Major-General Sir Hugh Wheeler's garrison. The situation at Cawnpore was worsening which led to Sikhs being deployed under General Havelock. On 16 July, the force advanced to within a few miles of the town before meeting any resistance. The 78th Highlanders were in the lead and rolled up the enemy's left flank with a brilliant charge. The 64th and 84th Foot and Brasyer's Sikhs then passed through and carried the enemy's position. They captured the guns on the right and the enemy retreated. Leaving the guns behind, protected by Brasyer's Sikhs, the British infantry

16   Mazhbi refers to individuals considered to be of low caste; whilst the Sikh faith had tried to eradicate Casteism, it has continued to prevail. This is together with recruits from the Ramdasia community, these groups contributed significantly to the Sikh Pioneers Regiments (later the Sikh Light Infantry).

17   Pramod K. Nayar, *The Penguin 1857 Reader* (New Delhi: Penguin Books India), pp.15–16.

regiments followed up their success and inflicted further losses on the enemy, who eventually lost heart and fled in disorder. They entered Cawnpore on 17 July but they were too late to stop the brutal murder of the women and children by the mutineers. Further skirmishes took place around the area which ended in a British Indian Army success.[18] When trials were held, those convicted of mutiny were blown from cannons and hanged for public display. It was a cruel punishment with a religious dimension but something that was considered official punishment at the time.[19] The people of northern India called the long period of reprisals as 'the Devil's Wind.'

The relief of Lucknow (Oude) was now the main cause of concern. Henry Lawrence, the Chief Commissioner of Oudh, fortified his Lucknow Residency, and stockpiled supplies, ready for a siege. On 21 September, two brigades about three thousand strong set out for Lucknow under General Havelock. He was accompanied by reinforcements under James Outram. They managed to secure the fort after heavy fighting but they could not leave as they were being targeted by additional mutineer forces. The Residency was besieged as closely as ever, and Outram who was now in command had to stand on the defensive and await relief in his turn. They held out for a further two months until the 17 of November, when a relieving force under General Colin Campbell, the newly appointed Commander-in-Chief in India, arrived at Lucknow. There would be continued attacks and in December 1857, the Ferozepore Sikhs were instrumental in defeating a large number of the enemy. The protracted affair continued into 1858 and in March, the enemy was holding three lines of defences north of the city covering the Kaiserbagh, their citadel. They captured the Bara Imambara Magazine with colours planted after their success.[20] The Sikhs and the 90th Light Infantry, led by Captains Brasyer and Havelock (the son of Major General Sir Henry Havelock) rushed forward and fought their way into an enclosure adjoining the Kaiserbagh under terrible fire. On 16 March Brasyer's Sikhs formed part of General Outram's force which captured the Residency and the iron bridge. The rebels had been completely defeated in these battles and Lucknow was back in British hands.[21] After the capture of Lucknow, the Ferozepore Regiment joined the Oudh Field Force and took part in several encounters while rounding up parties of rebels and pacifying the countryside

18   'Soldiers, your labours, your privations, your sufferings and your valour will not be forgotten by a grateful country.' The statue in Trafalgar Square, London quotes these lines and on the reverse, The Regiment of Brasyer's Ferozepore Sikhs is included amongst the units listed as the Defenders of Lucknow.

19   It was also something that would have been adopted from the Mughals. See Stuart Flinders, *Cult of a Dark Hero: Nicholson of Delhi* (London: Bloomsbury Publishing 2018).

20   Bara Imambara was built by Asaf-ud-Daula, Nawab of Awadh, in 1784.

21   The regiment was allowed to bear on its colours the inscription 'Lucknow, Defence and Capture,' while as a special mark of distinction for its outstanding conduct the issued orders that the men of the Regiment of Ferozepore were permitted to wear red *safas* (turbans), Governor-General like those in which they had fought, instead of native infantry caps – a privilege of which the regiment still avails itself on ceremonial parades.

From the time of the mutineers' seizure of Delhi, the British operations to suppress the mutiny were divided into three parts. First came the desperate struggles at Delhi, Kanpur, and Lucknow during the summer; then the operations around Lucknow in the winter of 1857–58, directed by Colin Campbell; and finally the campaigns of Hugh Rose in early 1858. The tensions ended on July 8, 1859. The mutiny of 1857 failed because it had no noble sentiment behind it, no plan to guide it, and no sincere leader to see it through.[22] The rebellion also had repercussions on the EIC which was abolished, and the government of India was now transferred to the British Crown. A secretary of state for India was appointed and the Crown's viceroy became head of the government. The Sikh chiefs of the Cis-Sutlej states were thanked and rewarded for their services and given prestigious titles over the following years.[23]

China Campaigns

These centred on the British involvement in the trade of opium from India to China. There was a growth in this trade from 1820 onwards. This led to a backlash from the Chinese resulting in the so-called Opium Wars, the first being between 1839–1842. The Second Opium War was between the Qing Dynasty and an allied force of the British and the French. Relations had increasingly become strained, with the boarding of the British ship named the Arrow and the death of a French missionary being the early catalysts. The Russians and the Americans also had a stake in negotiations for improving their trade deals, hence they were part of the movement which included legalisation of the opium trade, expansion of the transport of cheap labourers opening all of China to British merchants and opium traffickers, and exempting imports from internal transit duties. Lieutenant Hope Grant had with him four infantry brigades; the Sikh support involved the 15th Ludhiana Sikhs, 23rd Sikh Pioneers, 20th Punjab Regiment and 27th Punjab Infantry. The recently raised cavalry units during the Indian Rebellion of 1857 also brought in troops of Probyn's Horse and Fane's Horse. In total, the BIA had 11,000 troops together with 6,000 French troops. On 1 August, landing at Odin Bay, they went straight into action. At Sinho, the engagement with the Tartar Cavalry took place with soldiers of Probyn's Horse armed with lances.[24] The allied forces entered Peking (Beijing) on 6 October when Emperor Xianfeng fled the capital. This resulted in the sacking of the Old Summer Palace and the occupation of the Forbidden City palace complex in Peking. The Treaty was confirmed by the Convention of Peking in 1860.[25]

22 Singh, *The Indian Mutiny Of 1857*, p.23.
23 Narendra Singh and Sarup Singh were given additional land rights and later were awarded the title of K.C.S.I. Bharpur Singh and Randhir Singh were given additional land rights. Wazir Singh, Sobha Singh and Lehna Singh also received favours from the British.
24 Tartar horseman employed from the Mongols.
25 Whilst the Treaty of Nanking had been signed in 1842, this treaty resulted in opening up trade ports and increasing diplomatic representations of the British in Hong Kong. The

Sikh forces composed of Probyn's Horse landing at Odin Bay. (*The Illustrated London News*, October 1860)

In 1864 the disputed areas around Bhutan became a focal point of activity. The area was annexed 1864, but a year there was a number of Bhutanese raids into Indian territory. The British Indian Army met these incursions head-on. Initially they suffered a setback at Dewanigiri, but a later detachment under Brigadier General Sir Harry Tombs saw the Bhutanese being defeated.[26] Sikh Officers from the 14th Bengal Cavalry and 19th Punjabis regiments received the IOM. In 1866–67 the Sikhs were in action against Sulliman Khel tribespeople from across the NWF. In 1871 a campaign termed the Lushai raids took place into Manipur, Tripura, and Sylhet. The tea planter by the name of Mr Winchester was killed and his daughter taken captive. This became a rescue and a punitive mission from November 1871 to February 1872. 4,000 Indian troops were involved and the child was rescued. The condition of peace was one of the bargaining chips for surrender. One IOM was given to a Sikh, Naik Bughet Singh. In 1877, the Jowaki Afridis were disenchanted after being told that their payments for securing the Kohat Pass were to be reduced. This led to them attacking Peshawar and the Kohat Pass. The tribe was considered to be a powerful Pathan group in the NWF. Under the command of Colonel Federic David Morcotta, of the Bengal Staff Corps, the 3rd Sikh Infantry burnt thirty villages and inflicted considerable damage. They made massive gains in pushing the Afridis out of Jammu.[27] However, the Jowaki were not defeated and skirmishes continued into 1878. No terms could be accepted by the tribesmen when they met with Generals Keyes and Pollack. Not soon after this, they were completely defeated. One Sikh was awarded the IOM, Havildar Dharum Singh (14th Ferozepore Sikhs).

Africa

One of the first campaigns which involved the Sikhs travelling by sea was the Abyssinia Expedition of 1868, in present-day Ethiopia. Additionally, forty-four trained elephants were brough from India to carry the heavy guns over four hundred miles of mountainous terrain. Emperor Tewodros II (c.1818–68), a Coptic Christian ruler, known as Theodore to the British, was holding European hostages including many craftsman, artisans, missionaries, and the British Consul and his staff. The Abyssinian Campaign was led by Lieutenant-General Robert Napier (1810–90). The decisive victory took place on 10 April 1868 at Arogee (Arogi), after which the hostages were released. Three days later the fortress of Magdala was stormed by the British, and Emperor Tewodros committed suicide.[28]

biggest winners however were the Russians and the French. See Philip J. Haythornthwaite, *The Colonial Wars Sourcebook* (London: Caxton Editions, 2000), p.238.

26   Haythornthwaite, *The Colonial Wars Sourcebook*, pp.110-111.

27   James Grant, *Recent British Battles on Land and Sea* (London, Paris and New York: Cassell & Company, Ltd, 1884), pp.9–10

28   Field Marshal Robert Cornelis Napier received the title of 1st Baron Napier of Magdala after this campaign.

23rd Punjab Pioneers attack with the bayonet at Magdala, Abyssinian Campaign, April 1868. (Archibald Forbes, Major Arthur Griffiths, and others, *Illustrated Battles of the Nineteenth Century* Vol. II, (London: Cassell & Co., 1895))

Sikh involvement centred primarily on the 23rd Sikh Pioneers who provided vital support and time for the 4th Foot to push back the enemy at the battle of Arogee. Had the Pioneers not held the left, then the 4th would not have unable to attack and this would have led to fighting on several fronts. Four IOMs were issued to Sikhs after this campaign. For their exceptional fighting during the campaign, the regiments involved, including the 23rd Sikh Pioneers, were awarded the battle honour of Abyssinia which is carried to this day by the Sikh Light Infantry Regiment.

Another campaign in Africa was the Second Suakin expedition of 1885 which centred on the British involvement in Sudan. Britain's interest was the protection of trade and travel routes along the Red Sea and the Suez Canal. Sudan was under the Egyptian regime, but they faced hostilities under Mohammed Ahmed or Mahdi, 'the highly guided one' to his followers. The original campaign saw the sacking of Khartoum, the killing of General Gordon and the massacre of thousands of civilians at the hands of Mahdist warriors in January 1885. The failure of the relief effort of General Wolseley's Nile Expedition prompted further measures.[29] In March, General Gerald Graham led the combined force of 13,000 British and Indian troops against the Mahdist forces led by Osman Digna (c.1840–1926). The Sikh soldiers from the 15th Ludhiana Sikhs and the 9th Bengal Cavalry took action against the insurgents at the Battle of Tofrek. The 15th Ludhiana Sikhs saved many of the unarmed work party of the Berkshire Regiment which was being attacked by the Arabs of the Hadendoa tribe. It was noted that 'two soldiers of the Berkshires were saved from certain death by the magnificent daring of Subedar Gurdit Singh of 15th Ludhiana Sikhs, who placing himself between the pursuers and their prey, killed three Arabs in succession by rapid sword cuts.'[30] Four Sikhs of the Bengal Cavalry were awarded the IOM for their gallantry.

The Malta Expeditionary Force

Whilst the African campaigns showed the ability of Sikhs to fight in different terrains, the first Sikhs to be part of a BIA in Europe was in Malta. The intent was for the soldiers to be deployed to support Turkey (the Ottoman Empire) against any aggression from Russia. This followed the Turkish defeat by the Russians in 1877 and the loss of Balkan territories to them. HRH Field Marshal the Duke of Cambridge, Commander in Chief of the British Army, inspected the force on the Floriana Parade in Malta on 17 June 1878. The expeditionary force was sent to undertake the transfer of power and territory of Cyprus from Turkey to the British.[31] The Hodson Horse

---

29   Field Marshall Garnet Joseph Wolseley, 1st Viscount Wolseley (1833-1913).
30   Taken from the *Frontier and Overseas Expedition*, quoted in Dhesi, *Sikh Soldier*, vol.5, p.108.
31   Steven Purewal, *Duty, Honour & Izzat: From Golden Fields to Crimson – Punjab's Brothers in Arms in Flanders* (Canada: Renegade Arts Entertainment, 2019), p.74.

Indian Troops ordered for Service in Europe, the 31st Bengal Native Infantry.
(*The Illustrated London News*, 4 May 1878)

Cavalry units at that time known as 10th Bengal (Duke of Cambridge's Own) Lancers and 9th Bengal Cavalry were pivotal in this work, providing escorts and security to officers and ensuring a peaceful transfer. The advance party was made up of Indian units of the Madras Sappers and Miners, who arrived at Larnaca on July 16. The combined British and Indian force was then placed under the command of Wolseley. A case of poisoning prevented the Sikhs from the 9th Bengal Cavalry from actually going to Cyprus. A few died and the rest were disabled. Yet this would be a forerunner of European deployments of Indian and Sikh units in the future.[32]

Second Afghan War, 1878 to 1880

With the possible threat posed by the Russian regime, the prevailing view by political officer's was a permanent diplomatic mission to Kabul. The Afghan ruler Sher Ali Khan (c.1825–79) was the son of the aforementioned Dost Mohammed Khan. He refused to accommodate any mission from the Russians and then from the British. In September 1878 an expedition took place to counteract any Russian influence and try and compel him to meet and come to terms with the British. The mission was turned away. This led to the battle of Ali Masjid taking place where once previously the British and the Sikhs had taken the fort in 1839. The Sikhs received numerous IOMs of which the soldiers of the 14th Ferozepore Sikhs, 5th Punjab Cavalry, 2nd Sikh Infantry and many other regiments were shown their appreciation. The descriptions of the acts of the Sikhs were indicative of their bravery. Examples include Jowahir Singh dashing through 15 of the enemy, killing two of them with his bare hands. Subedar Major Gurbax Singh and Ala Singh (2nd Sikh Infantry) attacked numerous Ghazis through rifle fire and were wounded. The number involved was endless. The campaign ended on 26 May 1879 after the Treaty of Gandamak. The Guides Infantry were singled out for their capture of Kabul.

The Defence of the Kabul Residency

The British Residency was situated at Bala Hisar in Kabul. It was on 3 September 1879 that Afghan soldiers attacked the Residency. British and Indian troops of the Queen's Own Corps of Guides were met with over 1,000 Afghan troops together with the general populace joining in. All British officers were killed in the attack including the British Resident, Sir Louis Cavagnari (1841–79) and his escort.[33] They

32 'Russian interest in the Med, and the Indian army in Malta', Times of Malta, 5 September 2015 (https://timesofmalta.com/articles/view/russian-interest-in-the-med-and-the-indian-army-in-malta.583460 accessed April 2022).

33 Pierre Louis Napoleon Cavagnari was an Italian-British soldier whose family was in service with the Bonaparte family. He was appointed Assistant Commissioner of Panjab in

faced artillery fire whilst the guides fought with bayonets coming out of the Residency on a periodical basis. The Residency was burning during the twelve hours of fighting. The Afghans' offer of surrender was refused and the few remaining Guides under Jamadar Jewand Singh and many Sikhs fought to the death, charging the enemy as part of their last stand. This small resistance also led to 600 Afghan deaths. A memorial was erected at the Residency commemorating the action of the Sikhs, consisting of Guides Cavalry and Infantry:

> The annals of no army and no regiment can show a brighter record of devoted bravery than has been achieved by this small band of Guides [Sikh], by their deeds they have conferred undying honours not only on the regiment to which they belong but on the whole British Army. [34]

However, there was still no end in sight, with several other battles taking place at Charasia (1879) and the British defeat at Maiwand in July 1880. The latter battle involved attacking Emir Ayub Khan's (1857–1914)'s forces before he captured Ghazni. However, the BIA were heavily outnumbered with around 2,500 compared with the 20,000 Afghan forces. They still managed to inflict between 2000-3000 casualties. This led to a retreat to Kandahar. There was a loss of 1,000 men, but Sikhs from the 3rd Sind Horse were awarded the IOM. After a siege, which was lifted by reinforcements led by the future Field Marshal Lord Roberts, the latter fought a decisive battle leading to the defeat of Emir Khan's forces at Kandahar in August 1880.[35] This led to the installation of Abdur Rahman (d.1901) as the next Afghan King and the end of the second Anglo-Afghan War.

Martial Races Theory and Identity

It would be wise to digress from the chronological narration of Sikhs in the BIA and consider a concept that sought further recruitment of Sikhs. Field Marshal Frederick Sleigh Roberts (1832–1914), Commander-in-Chief of the Indian Army from 1885–93, was a principal proponent of the martial race theory. This theory implied that the Sikhs should be employed and their military prowess should be encouraged but within the confines of a distinct identity. The martial races were a designation created by army officials of British India, whereby they classified each ethnic group into two

---

1861.

34 Dhesi, *Sikh Soldier*, Vol 2, p.322. There is another memorial to the guides at Mardan in the NWF established in 1892. This place is also famous for the rock edict attributed to Buddhist King Ashoka. A plaque commemorating the bravery of the guides is also at the National Army Museum, Acc.No:1998-10-48. It was previously at the Frontier Forces' Chapel/Sanctum, St Luke's Church, Kensington and Chelsea, London.

35 Ayub Khan is considered a national hero in Afghanistan due to the battle at Maiwand.

categories, martial and non-martial. A martial race was typically thought to be brave and well-built for fighting, while the non-martial races were those whom the British believed to be unfit for battle. This theme, however, was extended to groups who were against the British in the Indian Rebellion.[36] The martial races included but were not limited to: the Sikhs, Gurkhas, Rajputs, Dogras, Marathas, and Jats.

Alongside this was the tension between retaining Sikh symbology and traits which made the Sikhs the bravest of the brave, but within a fixed identity of the British Indian Army. Interestingly, many of the Sikh insignia and even phrases were borrowed from the traditional Khalsa vanguard, the Akali Nihangs, as well as war slogans which were employed from the martial scripture, the Dasam Granth.[37] However, as noted earlier, the majority of soldiers undertaking oaths did so in the presence of the Guru Granth Sahib; the presence of both scriptures has been noted but was not as frequent.[38] Whilst the Nihangs were seen as thorns in the side of the British, much of their symbology was adopted in many cases by Sikh personnel and regiments. In comparison to the British Army recruits, many Sikhs were more militarised than the British wanted them to be so maybe this was one idea to make this identity fixed. The prescription of the '5 Ks' (*Kesh, Kangha, Kara, Kachera*, and *Kirpan*) was enforced and promoted, leading to later commentators that the British created the 5 Ks for the Sikhs. The Akali Nihangs, whose defiance against the British which we have discussed, were opposed to British interventions, were armed to the teeth. So to suggest that Sikhs could limit their weaponry would not be something to which they would adhere to. This would affect the Sikhs when the British initiated the Arms Act; whether they would try and curtail the weapons that anybody could carry. Towards this end, the colonial government, under Lord Lytton as Viceroy (1874–80), brought into existence the Indian Arms Act, 1878, an act which exempted Europeans and ensured that no Indian could possess a weapon of any description unless the British masters considered him a 'loyal subject of the British Empire.' Secondly, this Act restricted the number of guns that were licenced out. Disarmament was the key in all of this. This dual policy is interesting to note, because Sikhs who enlisted as part of the British Army could carry weapons within reason. The Akalis, who were the most militarised, were to be sanctioned. The idea that the British banned *Shastarvidia* or

---

36　High-caste Hindus were described as treacherous, faithless etc. Whilst Muslim sepoys were against the British, Panjabi Muslims were welcomed into the army. Heather Streets, *Martial Races: The Military, Race and Masculinity in British Imperial Culture*, 1857–1914 (Manchester: Manchester University Press, 2005).

37　Based on my lecture 'Sikh Army identity in World War 1', *Concurrences in Postcolonial research– perspectives, methodologies, engagements* at Linnaeus University, Kalmar, Sweden, 20–23 August 2015.

38　The use of the Guru Granth Sahib in other ceremonial rituals would also be evident. Major A.E. Barstow, *A Handbook for the Indian Army: Sikhs* (Calcutta: Govt of India, Central Publications Dept, 1928). p.21.

any other martial act was not a direct policy decision but moreover was to deal with lawless Indian subjects and to ensure there was no repeat of the Indian Rebellion.

Whilst generally the attire was prescribed by the British military, there was still some retention of Sikh clothing. This did, however, differ from regiment to regiment. Each regiment had its own brooches so the 1st Sikhs would wear regalia bearing the words '1st Sikh', a new innovation as previous Sikhs did not carry any emblem bearing letters and words, however, the symbol adorned on the turban was something different. A comparison should be made with the Akali Nihangs who traditionally wore the turban with quoits and small words inscribed on them. The symbol of the *Ad Chand* (half-moon) is a case in point. This metal is composed of a crescent moon symbol with a sword or *Khanda* pointing upwards; alternatively it can be described as two curved swords with the third pointing upwards. It was this symbol which in various guises was adopted by British regiments. Interestingly, this symbol was only seen amongst the Nihang Singhs as opposed to the traditional or mainstream Sikhs. The *Chakkar*, which was used by the Khalsa, was retained in some cases and again worn on turbans. This would continue into the twentieth century. Regiments included the Rattray Sikhs and the 15th Sikhs; 14th Sikhs adopted the tradition of either the *Ad Chand* or the *Chakkar* amongst the various regiments. Eventually, the use of the *Ad Chand* in derivative ways would morph into the present day *Khanda* symbol of the Sikhs. It is not known when this took place but it could be as late as post-1900.

There has also been an assertion that miniature Guru Granth Sahibs would be given to Sikh soldiers in later campaigns. It does beg the question as to why would a small manuscript be required together with a microscopic device to read them? The daily liturgy or the *Nitnem* would be small enough to be carried within the baggage of the Sikhs. Traditionally, Sikhs kept small liturgies known as *Safari* recensions which would be carried in the *Tarkas* or quivers in battle. There is little or no records confirming the reason for creating miniature manuscripts for army personnel. However, some miniatures do exist and they may have been produced for symbolical reasons as opposed to the traditional reading of the compositions. The number created appear to be limited.[39]

1890–1900s

Somaliland

A British protectorate area was being threatened by the Mullah from the Sahilya Order who embarked on a *jihad* against the British.[40] In response, the Zaila Field

39   Thanks to Dr Kristina Myrvold, Sweden for sharing this information with me. Also see 'Sikh devotees pay respects to 100-year-old Guru Granth Sahib' <http://www.sikhnet. com/news/sikh-devotees-pay-respects-100-year-old-guru-granth-sahib> (accessed 10/08/2021). The article suggests 13 were created for the First World War.
40   The area termed Somaliland continued to be a British protectorate up until 1960.

Force was deployed. On 13 January 1890, the 17th Regiment Bombay Infantry travelled via Aden and landed at Zaila. The initial strike resulted in the capture of prisoners and livestock. Subedar Jamail Singh of the 17th was awarded an IOM for his repulse of the enemy at Hussain on 29 January.

Burma

The Anglo-Manipur war (Burma) took place after a coup in 1891 which resulted in the death of the British Chief Minister and several of his staff. The city of Imphal was captured and the Kingdom of Manipur was annexed which was effectively the last kingdom to be taken by British India. Subedar Amar Singh was awarded IOM for his gallantry at Mona where he overcame Manipur resistance.[41]

Gulistan

The Orakzai tribes were again in action against the British on the NWF on 20 April 1891.[42] The Orakzai lost 200 men with one killed and four wounded on the British India side. A few months later in December at Nilt Fort in Hunza, Sapper Hazara Singh (Bengal Sappers and Miners) blew open the gates of the fort whilst taking heavy fire from the towers gateway. Whilst he received the IOM, his colleague Captain Aylmer received the VC, showing the disparity in awards at that time.[43]

Central Africa

Trouble was again brewing in Central Africa and interestingly the next incursion centred on taking action against Arab and African slave traders. The notion of slavery has taken many forms across the world and many groups have been singled out for this crime against humanity. The British were seen as one of those groups but during the early part of the nineteenth century, the slave trade was banned in the British Empire.[44] An attempt at removing slavery from their colonies was also evident at this time.[45]

Some of the best Sikh soldiers from the BIA were used to form the Central African Rifles in 1891, the first regular army to operate in East and Central Africa. The campaigns lasted for four years. The Sikhs were in action fighting against the slaver Makanjira at Lake Nysa in November 1891.[46] His town and defences were destroyed.

---

41   Dhesi, *Sikh Soldier*, Vol 2, p.23.
42   Orkazi are a Pashtun tribe from the area of Kuram district of Kohat of the North West Frontier.
43   Dhesi, *Sikh Soldier*, Vol 2, p.23.
44   The Slavery Abolition Act of 1833 was an act of the UK Parliament that abolished slavery in most British colonies.
45   Between 1808 and 1860 it is estimated they intercepted over 1,600 slave ships and freed over 150,000 African slaves.
46   Better known as Lake Malawi, located between Malawi, Mozambique and Tanzania. Named Lake Nyssa by explorer and Christian Missionary David Livingstone (1813–1873) who sought to end the slave trade in East Africa.

The Sikhs were also in action against the slavers at Kisungle on Lake Nysa. The Sikhs were on board the African Lakes Steamer named the Domira which was loaded with a 7-pounder gun. They came under fire and, according to Johnston:

> After setting fire to a portion of the town with other shells, I effected a landing with a small number of Sikhs, whilst Captain Maguire kept the enemy at bay by bombarding the town from the steamer. We managed to land with only one or two casualties, and the Sikhs carried off two of Makanjira's cannon and set fire to one of his daus [Arab sailing vessel].[47]

The enemy came back in large numbers, but the BIA managed to overcome their attackers and made a retreat back to the ship. Not soon after, the slaver Kawinga of the Yao tribe was also attacking villagers in the Chikala hills. He managed to thwart the attack by the BIA led by Captain Maguire. However, he had no option but to sue for peace. Yet the fighting continued, and gallant action was noted when Captain Maguire landed on ground to destroy the other *Daus* vessels belonging to Makanjira. The boat had run aground and the wind blew the Domira amongst the rocks. Captain Maguire ordered a retreat to the Domira, but he was killed in the melee. The Sikhs were repulsing the enemy with the bayonet but made for the steamer which was now coming under attack. This fighting lasted for three days but in the end, the populace made peace terms; however, not without the BIA being attacked one last time. The Domira left under heavy attacks. Harry Johnston, who was tasked with setting up the British Central Africa Protectorate, referred to the Sikhs in glowing terms:[48]

> Soon afterwards they had, in fact, to be sent back to India, though there were men amongst them who had strikingly distinguished themselves. It must be remembered, however, that they were all cavalry men, and not used to fighting on foot, or on board a ship, and all things considered behaved as well as might be expected. The Sikhs, however, throughout all this crisis, never showed their sterling worth more effectually.[49]

These battles proved that Sikhs were capable of adapting to different terrains far removed from their native villages or regular areas of combat.

---

47 Harry Hamilton Johnston, *British Central Africa: An attempt to give some account of a portion of the territories under British influence north of the Zambesi* (London: Methuen & Co.,1897), p.102.

48 Henry Hamilton Johnston GCMG KCB (1858–1927) explorer, administrator and author of many books on Africa.

49 Johnston, *British Central Africa*, p.105.

Burma

The Kachins of Burma during the years 1892–3 were accustomed to police operations.[50] However, they raided the town of Myitkyina, attacking the police post there. A force of 1200 troops was sent to quell the uprising. This resulted in many BIA casualties but the Kachins were defeated at Palap soon afterwards. Many IOMs were given to Sikhs for their bravery at Palp. In 1886, a Burma Military Patrol was sanctioned to oversee the withdrawal of BIA regular forces. This Battalion consisted of 3,937 Sikhs and also took law and order duties.

1893–1894

In 1893, Indian soldiers were sent to Central Africa replacing the ones which fought earlier in Central Africa. They had come under the command of Lieutenant W.H.Manning. Additional gunboats had been completed. Makanjira continued his war by inciting other regional leaders to rebel. The Rifu peninsula was where the slaver was held up and he received support from a large Arab slave-trading caravan. However, local natives, and the Sikhs made their way to the main town and after 5 hours of fighting Makanjira's forces escaped leaving just the villagers. Fort McGuire, which had been named after the fallen captain was built with Sikh support.[51] In 1894 Makanjira after attacking the fort was finally defeated by soldiers of the 45th Rattray Sikhs. In the same year, Sikhs of the 15th Ludhiana Sikhs and the 23rd Sikh Pioneers were once again in action at Fort Johnston which helped end the slave trade.[52]

In January 1894, trouble was brewing with the Waziris of Waziristan on the NWF. The tribes were defeated. A year later in Chitral (NWF) the local chief was killed and the war of succession led to the British being driven out. This led to a 16,000 strong expedition attacking the rebels. The Malakand Pass was the centre of the battle which saw 2,000 Swati Tribes being defeated by the charge of 50 sabres of the Guides Cavalry of which Sikhs played a major role.

However, Chitral Fort in the Hindu Kush mountains was besieged. Defended only by 88 men of the 14th Ferozepore Sikhs, they held out for 46 days. Captain Townsend praised the Sikhs for their reluctance to lay down their arms. They were relieved by forces of the 32nd Sikh Pioneers from Gilgit under Colonel Kelly who forced the Chitralis to withdraw. They had covered 220 miles of ground. The importance of the Sikh pioneers' march was never fully recognised, with most of the publicity and fame for the relief being lavished on the more well-known British Regiments.[53] The Gordon Highlanders received major praise for the campaign. However, six Sikhs received the IOM together with an additional reward bonus of six months of pay. At the action at Koragh, in Chitral, only 18 Sikhs survived the entrapment there. They cut their

---

50   The Kachin state is the northernmost state of Myanmar now bordered by China and India.
51   Johnston, *British Central Africa*, p.126.
52   Haythornthwaite, *The Colonial Wars Sourcebook*, p.162.
53   Dhesi, *Sikh Soldier*, Vol 4., p.92.

way through the enemy to save their lives. Meanwhile, the Sikhs within the Bengal Sappers and 6th Punjab Infantry were recipients of the IOM at the related action at Reshun, Chitral.

1895

The final battle against the slave traders was with the Sultan of Nkode (modern-day Malawi) named Mlozi bin Kazbadema in 1895. The Sultan had attacked several villages, killed the men and abducted women and children. The small but important contingent of Sikhs and natives were named the 'ever-victorious army.'[54] The Sikhs were described as fighting like demons. They scaled the city walls and Mlozi was found hiding in a secret bunker. He was tried and hanged. This ended the ruthless streak of the slave trade within the region.[55]

Also in 1895, BIA was attacked by the tribes of the Maliks of the Maizar region of the NWF. Whilst out to settle tribe differences, British officers were set upon and many were wounded. Sikhs were awarded the IOM from the 6th and 8th Mountain Batteries, and the officers from the 1st Regiment Sikh Infantry (posthumous awards).

Malakand 1897

In 1893, a border was negotiated between British India and Afghanistan, the idea being conceived under administrator Mortimer Durand and Abdur Rahman Khan, Emir of Afghanistan.[56] This demarcation, known as the Durand Line, would limit each power's level of influence and improve diplomatic relations. However, over the many decades, the border would be disputed and many incursions and battles would continue to take place to the present day. The garrison at Malakand was attacked by Pashtun tribesman whose lands were bisected by the Durand Line. Between July and August 1897, the garrison was besieged with many of the men outside the fort. The poorly defended small forts around the area would come under attack. The BIA was commanded by Brigadier-General William Meiklejohn (1845–1909). This led to British officers being attacked with Sikhs defending the camps. The uprising and *jihad* were inspired by the Muslim cleric Saidullah who had been given the title of 'Mad Mullah.' Between 26 and 30 July, the garrison was subjected to day and night attacks. The 45th Rattray Sikhs despatched the enemy advancing on the garrison. On 30 July, a bayonet charge scattered the tribesman which saw them fleeing to the hills. The Malakand Field Force was sent as the relief force. The 45th under Lieutenant Macrae, as well as the Sikhs from the 24th Punjabis and 35th Sikhs, Guides Cavalry and

---

54   Johnston, *British Central Africa*, p.136.
55   Between 1891 and 1894, 861 slaves were released by officials of the Protectorate, and 170 between 1894 and 1896. Johnston, *British Central Africa*, p.149.
56   Henry Mortimer Durand, GCMG, KCSI (1850–1924) was a British Anglo-Indian diplomat and member of the Indian Civil Service, who also served as a Foreign Secretary of India from 1884-94.

Infantry, were noted for their actions.[57] Winston Churchill (4th Hussars), later Prime Minister of the United Kingdom, acted as a war reporter for *The Times* newspaper who described the bravery of the Sikhs. He records that Colonel McCrae was stabbed in the neck and rallied the Sikhs:

> But he called upon the men to maintain the good name of 'Rattray's Sikhs,' and to hold their position till death or till the regiment came up. And the soldiers replied by loudly shouting the Sikh war cry [*Jaikara*] and defying the enemy to advance.[58]

The encounter at Chakdara Fort some ten miles away was commanded by Lieutenant H.B. Rattray, (son of Colonel Thomas Rattray). The enemy, numbering 14,000, besieged the fort which comprised of six British officers and 240 BIA personnel. The battle, lasting for two hours, saw the attacks being beaten off using the Maxim and Martini-Henry rifles. Sikh signallers of the 45th were noted for using the heliograph to signal to Malakand, whilst coming under heavy fire.[59] They managed to send the words 'Help us.' They were saved by the cavalry; the main force of the 11th Bengal Lancers arrived, leading to the Swatis fleeing. This battle stood apart from others in the NWF but has been overshadowed by local campaigns in the area.

Samana: The Battle of Saragarhi

These battles centred on the Afridi incursion of the Kyber and Samana ranges. The Samana is a ridge of hills running east-west, south of Khanki valley, marking the southern edge of the Tirah region. It is about 12 miles long and its highest point is 6,000 feet. The Khyber Pass is some 30 miles to the north. It had been captured by the British in 1891 and two main forts built on it, Fort Lockhart in the middle and Fort Gulistan on the western end. The two forts were three miles apart and in between was a smaller fort called Saragarhi which was used as a signalling post. Another outpost, called Sangar, was on the highest peak to the east.

Samana was garrisoned by five companies of the 36th Sikhs. The commanding officer was acting Lieutenant-Colonel John Haughton.[60] Major Charles Des Voeux commanded the Fort Cavagnari at Gulistan. The Battle of Saragarhi formed part of the Tirath Campaign on 12 September 1897 between Sikh soldiers of the BIA and Pashtun Orakzai tribesmen. This single battle is world-renowned due to the last stand taken by the Sikhs. The British Indian contingent comprised of 22 Sikh soldiers of the

57   21 men of the 35th Sikhs had died from heatstroke after marching all day.
58   Winston, L. Spencer Churchill, *The Story of the Malakand Field Force: An Episode of Frontier War* (London: Thomas Nelson & Sons, Ltd., 1916), p.72.
59   Heliograph – a system that uses mirrors to reflect sunlight and create flashes of light, in essence a system of Morse code.
60   Whilst born in India, John Haughton came to the United Kingdom and was educated at Uppingham School, Leicestershire, where there is a plaque commemorating his service.

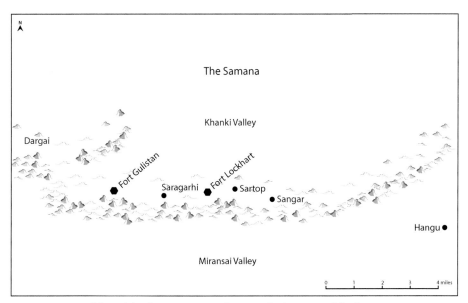

Map of the Samana region showing the location of the forts.

36th Sikhs (now the 4th Battalion of the Sikh Regiment), who were stationed at the army post, and were attacked by around 10,000 tribesmen.[61] They were offered passage out but the soldiers inside the outpost, led by Havildar Ishar Singh, chose to fight to the death rather than surrender. Gurmukh Singh signalled events to Fort Lockhart by heliograph as they occurred. At last, asking for permission to stop signalling, he took up his rifle to join combat. He fell fighting single-handed. The outpost was set ablaze resulting in all 21 Sikhs perishing in the attack. This single event has magnified into the mighty stand of the Sikhs and is commemorated around the world.[62] For their actions, the defenders of Saragarhi were awarded the IOM. Their battalion, 36th Sikhs, also received Battle Honours. To commemorate the men, the British built two Saragarhi Gurdwaras: one in Amritsar, nearby the Harmandir Sahib, and another in Firozpur Cantonment, in the district that most of the men hailed from.

After Saragarhi, the enemy proceeded towards Fort Gulistan commanded by Major Des Voeux which held 175 men of the 36th Sikhs.[63] The garrison was besieged from 12 to 14 September. The fort walls came under attack from the Pathans. Havildar Kala Singh took a party and attacked the enemy at the southern side of the fort. Meanwhile, Havildar Sundar Singh using ropes scaled-down the fort and supported

---

61   This figure has been contested.
62   Saragarhi Day is commemorated around the world and in the UK a yearly event takes place. On 12 September 2021 at Wolverhampton, UK, a monument to Saragarhi was unveiled.
63   The Major's wife was pregnant and gave birth during this attack.

the Sikhs who were seen to be under attack by another group of Pathans. Three battle standards of the enemy were captured as part of their sorties. Injured Sikh soldiers were brought back into the fort. Forty-four men were killed or wounded. They held the fort with great vigour. When it reached night-time, BIA forces started firing their guns from the Miranzai valley. The battle continued into the next day and on 14 September the enemy was continually being bombarded from Miranzai. This was coupled with a relief force under General Biggs with the 2nd Punjab moving towards Saragarhi and Lockhart. The Pathans now started retreating. General Bingham also reached Lockhart, meeting up with Colonel Haughton they made their way to Gulistan. The Sikhs fired upon the enemy on seeing the relief forces, and the Pathans lifted the siege. On reaching the fort, Bingham and Haughton met no opposition and the fort was secured.[64] The gallant stand at Fort Gulistan was recognised with the awarding of the Samana honour to the 36th and numerous IOMs conferred on them.

Tirah Campaign, September 1897 to April 1898

The Pathans gained nothing by attacking the outposts and in response, the Army of India amassed the largest force in expedition history to combat the continued threat: this was General Lockhart with his Punjab Army Corps and over 34,000 BIA troops and additional 20,000 followers. The frontier post at Kohat was selected as the base of operations.

In October 1897 a combination of the Dorsetshire's, Gordon Highlanders, Gurkhas, and 3rd Sikhs were in action at the Dargai Heights. There was an initial success but the outpost was abandoned due to a lack of supplies. By 20 October, the operation was a success after the Gordon Highlanders and the Sikhs rushed across the heights, which they had apparently taken 40 minutes to ascend.

The Tirah Campaign employed by far the largest force in Frontier expeditions. There was fierce fighting at the Khyber pass, Tesri, Kando, Maidan and the Arhanga Pass. The defeated Afridis had no option but to surrender and pay heavy fines for the trouble they had caused. Sikhs of the 2nd Mountain Battery, 3rd Sikhs, 14th Ferozepore Sikhs, and 15th Ludhiana Sikhs were amongst those awarded the IOM.

The Sikh Soldier Beyond 1900

At the beginning of 1900, the Sikhs were employed to quell an 'anti-foreigner' uprising in China. The Boxer Rebellion was an attempt to throw the foreign powers out of the country.[65] They were particularly resentful of foreign missionaries. The Chinese Government was unable to quell the disturbances and in the end unofficially

---

64   Gurinderpal Singh Josan, *A Saga of Valour The Epic Battle of Saragarhi* (Patiala: Sarbat Da Bhala Charitable Trust, 2017).
65   Also known as the Boxer Uprising or the Yihetuan Movement.

supported them. This led to the foreign legation Quarter in Peking being besieged for three months and coming under attack. An International relief force of eight countries was organised. Their trading interests within the country were a major concern for them.[66] Indian troops arrived at Yang Tsun from the 24th Punjab Infantry. The 14th Regiment of Americans worked in tandem with them to capture strategic trenches. As part of the multi-national force 3,000 Sikh soldiers contributed to the capture of Peking and the 'Siege of the International Legations' was lifted. The Boxer protocol of 1901 ended the uprising this also saw the execution of high-ranking officials linked to the outbreak and other officials who were found guilty of the slaughter of foreigners in China.[67] In all 30,000 Chinese Christians were killed by the Boxers.[68] The government paid a heavy price monetarily with an indemnity considered to be around 67 million pounds which severely weakened the Qing Dynasty.

Policy
Lord Horatio Herbert Kitchener (1850–1916), Commander-in-Chief of the Indian Army from 1902–09, now carried Field Marshal Roberts' policy of martial races selection to its conclusion. This would later result in separate kitchens created for the different martial races, based on religious dietary requirements.[69] This was most notable in the World Wars. An interesting depiction in *The Graphic* of 1906 suggests that each regiment of Sikhs was allowed duly enlisted boy recruits, who drew a monthly pay of three rupees and eight annas. At the age of sixteen, they would be transferred to the ranks. Indeed, further research is required to make conclusions from this assertion.

The World Wars

There were continued campaigns across the world and there was no decrease in the numbers employed in the British Indian Army; in fact, employment increased notably during the World Wars. The previous century had set up the Sikhs as a loyal set of troops for the British. A new medal for bravery was also introduced called the Indian Distinguished Service Medal, to ensure loyalty and pride in their work. This would now continue unabated with the onset of the First World War which lasted from 28 July 1914 to 11 November 1918. It is important to note that the Panjab and Sikh support for the wars provided a vital and much-needed boost to the war effort.

---

66 Apart from the BIA, there was the American, Austro-Hungarian, French, German, Italian, Japanese and Russian forces.
67 Haythornthwaite, *The Colonial Wars Sourcebook*, pp.246-147.
68 Some of the rebels were beheaded in public.
69 This included having separate kitchens for Muslims, Hindus, and Sikhs. Muslim kitchens would have meat prepared according to the Halal or Islamic traditions, whilst Hindus abstained from eating beef.

The importance of Indian troops including the Sikh contribution has been ignored, forgotten and erased in popular media. This has prompted many Sikh organisations to counter this narrative, which in turn has been receptive, encouraged and supported by the public at large.[70] Sikh statues have been erected across the UK and regular exhibitions and engagement take place between the armed forces and the Sikhs.

There has been some uncertainty regarding exactly how many Sikhs fought during the World Wars but we can try and shed some light on the numbers. Although accounting for just two per cent of the population of British India at the time, the Sikhs are understood to have made up more than twenty per cent of the British Indian Army at the outbreak of the First World War.[71] Barstow states, at the outbreak of the war:

> The soldierly qualities of the Sikhs have been fittingly recognised in the extent to which they have been employed in the Indian Army, in which on the outbreak of the war they numbered 33,000 out of 174,000, or somewhat less than 1/5th of the total strength.

Whilst less than twenty per cent at that time, other figures estimate by the end of the war around 130,000 Sikhs saw active service. They fought on most of the war's major fronts, from the Somme to Gallipoli (Turkey), fighting with distinction. Many of them were in action at Ypres and stopped the German advance there in the autumn of 1914, soon after the war broke out, while the British were still recruiting and training their own forces. As well as this, they fought against the Ottoman Empire in the Mesopotamian theatre of war. Indian Army troops also served in Aden, Egypt, Palestine, Persia, Italy, Salonica, Russia, East and West Africa, on the Gallipoli peninsula and China. The Sikh warriors were given the name of 'Black Lions of the East.'[72] It has been originally estimated, 'In the last two World Wars 83,005 turban-wearing Sikh soldiers were killed and 109,045 were wounded. They all died or were wounded for the freedom of Britain and the world, and during shell fire, with no other protection but the turban, the symbol of their faith.'[73] These figures are considered to be on the higher end. There is a suggestion that all turban-wearing soldiers

---

70   Several movies have been criticised for not recognising the contribution of Indian soldiers. The actor Laurence Fox caused resentment when he referred to 'the oddness in the casting of a Sikh soldier' in the film 1917. He later apologised. See 'Laurence Fox apologises to Sikhs for 'clumsy' 1917 comments', on the BBC News site, <https://www.bbc.co.uk/news/entertainment-arts-51233734> (accessed 21 November 2021). Also note my rebuttal 'Sikh scholar vs Laurence Fox: Sikhs did fight in the World Wars' broadcast on BBC Radio Leicester 23 February 2020.

71   Barstow, *A Handbook for the Indian Army: Sikhs*, p.21.

72   Apparently the Arabs gave them this title during the fighting at Mesopotamia. Francis Yeats-Brown, *Martial India* (London: Eyre and Spottiswood, 1945), p.31

73   General Sir Frank Messervy in the foreword of Colonel F.T. Birdwood, *The Sikh Regiment in the Second World War* (East Sussex: Naval and Military Press, 2014).

are equated with this number. The actual figure is not known at this time and after extensive scrutiny of the records can the true figure be revealed.

Conclusion

The Sikhs were forged from the concept of Saint Soldier to uphold the duties of righteousness and freedom. The Sikhs led by their Gurus were persecuted, culminating in Guru Hargobind creating the initial army and his grandson, Guru Gobind Singh consecrating the Khalsa. After persecution from the Afghans and the Mughals during the eighteenth century, the Sikh Misls carved out territories and started shaping themselves towards statehood and governance. This was not just limited to menfolk, and many women proved their mettle during this period. The success was based on irregular attackers of cavalry or a guerrilla mode of warfare. This would lead to Maharajah Ranjit Singh maintaining a Sikh Empire which shaped a world-class army. Adding infantry and artillery to his cavalry, it now came to be regarded as the mainstay of military strength, conquering many Afghan strongholds like Peshawar in the process. This was an amalgamation of Sikh innovations with the incorporation of European methods which worked wonders. After his demise, the Sikhs held on for some years but anarchy within the court and the unruly behaviour of the army meant it now met its end by the aggressive nature of the East India Company. The successive Anglo-Sikh Wars of 1845–1846 and 1848–1849 would once again show the Sikhs at their most formidable. Praised by their enemies for their bravery but without any strong leaders, this Empire would now be at its end. Indeed, the treachery singled out during these campaigns would put a major dent into any nationalistic ambition. With the Panjab annexed in 1849, the British would look to the vanquished and seek them out for recruitment in many campaigns across the world. From the North West Frontier to Africa, the Sikhs would be visible and acting in the interest of the colonial powers. This would lead to the conferring of the Order of Merit to many soldiers. This would be a forerunner to the equally global operations during the World Wars, where once again they would prove themselves, adding Europe to the countries in which they fought. In the process, they would also be recipients of the Victoria Cross. So in essence, the Sikh Soldier would be seen in different terrains and fighting with different enemies but they would always uphold their dignity and their values from the day they were incorporated. The Sikh Soldier is recognised by their signature turbans, ones which made them stand out from their counterparts and which made them truly sons and daughters of Guru Gobind Singh.

Appendix I

Treaty of Friendship between the East India Company and the Sirdars Ranjit Singh and Fateh Sing, 1806

Sirdar Runjeet Sing and Sirdar Futteh Sing have consented to the following Articles of Agreement concluded by Lieutenant-Colonel John Malcolm, under the special authority of the Right Honorable Lord Lake, himself duly authorized by the Honorable Sir George Hilaro Barlow, Baronet, Governor-General, and Sirdar Futteh Sing, as principal on the part of himself and plenipotentiary on the part of Runjeet Sing.

Article 1. Sirdar Runjeet Sing and Sirdar Futteh Sing Aloowalia hereby agree that they will cause Jeswunt Rao Holkar to remove with his army to the distance of 30 coss from Amritsar immediately, and will never hereafter hold any further connection with him, or aid or assist him with troops, or in any other manner whatever, and they further agree that they will not in any way molest such of Jeswunt Rao Holkar's followers or troops as are desirous of returning to their homes in the Deccan, but, on the contrary, will render them every assistance in their power for carrying such intention into execution.

Article 2. The British Government hereby agrees that in case a pacification should not be effected between that Government and Jeswunt Rao Holkar, the British Army shall move from its present encampment on the banks of the River Beas as soon as Jeswunt Rao Holkar aforesaid shall have marched with his army to the distance of 30 coss from Amritsar; and that in any Treaty which may hereafter be concluded between the British Government and Jeswunt Rao Holkar, it shall be stipulated that, immediately after the conclusion of the said Treaty, Holkar shall evacuate the territories of the Sikhs and march towards his own, and that he shall in no way whatever injure or destroy such parts of the Sikh country as may lie in his route. The British Government further agrees that as long as the said Chieftains Runjeet Sing and Futteh Sing abstain from holding any friendly connection with the enemies of that Government, or from committing any act of hostility on their own parts against the said Government, the British Armies shall never enter the territories of the said Chieftains, nor will the British Government form any plans for the seizure or sequestration of their possessions or property.

Dated 1st January, 1806, corresponding with 10th Shawal, 1220 H.E.
Seal of Runjeet Sing / Seal of Futteh Sing

Appendix II

Letter to Maharajah Ranjit Singh from Generals Ventura and Allard

---

TO HIS MAJESTY THE KING.

Sire,— The favours showered on us by your majesty since our arrival in this capital are innumerable, and correspond to the high opinion we had formed of his [your] benevolence, Fame, which had borne the name of the King of Lahor as far even as our abode, said nothing in comparison of what we worthy of a sovereign who aspires to immortality. Sire, when we first had the honour of being presented to your majesty, we disclosed to him [you] the motive of our journey: the reply he [you] vouchsafed sets us at ease, but leaves us uncertain as to the future. We, therefore, had the honour of addressing your majesty a few days ago, to know whether our arrival in this state is agreeable to him [you], and whether we can render him [you] any service by our knowledge in the art of war, acquired as superior officers, under the immediate command of the Great Napoleon Bonaparte, Sovereign of France. Your majesty has not yet relieved us from this suspense, and we are still without his [your] commands. We have, therefore, reiterated our request in the French language, according to the advice of Nurudin Sahib, who leads us to believe that an individual employed about your august person understands our tongue. In this uncertainty, we beseech your majesty to condescend to forward us his [your] instructions which we shall follow with the utmost punctuality.

We have the honour to be, with the deepest respect.
Sire, your majesty's most humble,
Most obedient, and most devoted servants,

C. Venture Allard. Lahore, 1 April 1822.

Major H. M. L. Lawrence, *Adventures Of An Officer In The Punjab* (Vol. 1) (New Delhi: Punjab National Press, pp.15–16.

Appendix III

Letter from Lord Ellenborough to Maharajah Ranjit Singh

A COPY OF A LETTER FROM HIS MAJESTY'S MINISTER FOR THE AFFAIRS OF INDIA TO MAHARAJA RUNJEET SING, DELIVERED TO HIS HIGHNESS AT LAHORE, ON THE 20 OF JULY, 1831.

To His Highness Maharaja Runjeet Sing, Chief of the Seik Nation and Lord of Cashmere.

Maharaja,

The King, my most gracious master, has commanded me to express to your Highness his Majesty's acknowledgements of your Highnesses' attention in transmitting to his Majesty, by the esteemed and excellent Lord, Earl, Amherst, the splendid manufacture of your Highnesses' subjects of Cashmere.

The King, knowing that your Highness is in possession of the most beautiful horses of the most celebrated breeds of Asia, has thought that it might be agreeable to your Highness to possess some horses of the most remarkable breed of Europe; and, in the wish to gratify your Highness in this matter, has commanded me to select for your Highness some horses of the gigantic breed which is peculiar to England. These horses, selected with care requiring much time, I now send to your Highness and as their great weight makes it inexpedient that they should undergo the fatigue of a long march in a hot climate, I have directed that they shall be conveyed to your Highness by the Indus, and such river of the Punjab as may be most easy of navigation.

The King has given me his most special com-mands to intimate to your Highness the sincere satisfaction with which his Majesty has witnessed the good understanding which has for so many years subsisted, and which may God ever preserve, between the British Government and your Highness.

His Majesty relies with confidence on the continuance of a state of peace, so beneficial to the subjects of both powers; and his Majesty earnestly desires that your Highness may live long in health and honour, extending the blessings of beneficent government to the nations under your Highness's rule.

By the King's command.

(Signed) Ellenborough.

Appendix IV

Letter describing Akali Phula Singh's attack on Lieutenant White, 1810

From A. Seton, Resident at Delhi to C, Lushington Acting Secretary to the Government in the Political Department, Fort William, 11th May 1810.

On the 7th instant I had the honor to acquaint you that Phola Sing, the Ukaulee [Akali] or Sikh priest who was the ringleader of the gang of banditti who attacked Lieutenant White's party, had fled from Dumdumah [Damdama] to Umritser [Amritsar]. I at the same time submitted my reasons for not having made an application to Runjeet Sing for his surrender.

In continuation of the subject, I now have the honor to acquaint you, for the information of Government, that Runjeet Sing, on hearing that Phola Sing had taken refuge in the temple at Umritser, and being apprehensive that his being allowed to remain there would give offence to the British Government, desired Futteh Sing of Allooa [Ahluwalia] to remove him from thence, but at the same time to give him 100 rupees for his support. On receiving a message to this effect from Futteh Sing, Phola Sing sent a harsh and indignant reply, declaring that Umritser had been the place of residence of Gooroo Baba Nanak; that he, Phola Sing, was one of that Gooroo's priests and would not leave the place, adding that, in the event of an attempt being made to expel him by force, he and forty or fifty Ukaulees who were devoted to him would resist to the last, being determined rather to perish than to yield- It now remains to be seen whether Runjeet Sing will support his first order against this desperate murderer.

Appendix V

Account of the Khalsa Army by Baron Hugel

I requested leave to inspect them (the *Ghorchurahs*) and never beheld a finer nor a more remarkably striking body of men. Each one was dressed differently, and yet so much in the same fashion that they all looked in perfect keeping. The handsome Raja Sushet [Suchet] Singh was in a similar costume, and reminded me of the time when the fate of empires hung on the point of a lance, and when the individual whose bold heart beat fearlessly under his steel breastplate, was the sole founder of his own fortunes. The strange troop before me was most peculiarly Indian. The uniform consisted of a velvet coat or gaberdine, over which most of them wore a shirt of mail. Others had this shirt made to form a part of the tunic. A belt round the waist, richly embroidered in gold, supported the powder-horn, covered with cloth of gold, as well as the Persian katar and the pistols which many of them carried in addition to those weapons. Some wore a steel helmet, inlaid with gold, and surmounted with the kalga [kalgi] or black heron's plume; others wore a cap of steel, worked like the cuirass in rings: this cap lies firmly on the turban, and covers the whole head, having openings for the eyes. The left arm is often covered from the hand to the elbow with a steel cuff inlaid with gold. The round Sikh shield hangs at the back, fastened with straps across the chest, a quiver at the right side and a bow slung at the back being carried as part of the equipment; a bag made in the belt holds the balls, and a tall bayonet, frequently ornamented with gold, held in the right hand when the man is on foot, and carried over the shoulder when in the saddle, completes the dress. One would suppose that the arms that each man carried would be enough to weigh him down, but this is not the case, and though the Sikhs are anything but strongly-built men, they seemed to bear them with the greatest ease; the black curly beard which hangs as low as the chest giving them an appearance of power which they do not in reality possess. It is a strange sight to a European to see their slippers embroidered in gold covering their naked feet. Some few among them wear high jack boots.

Hugel's *Travels In Kashmir And The Punjab*, p.331.

Appendix VI

Manifesto Issued by Sher Singh against the British

Seal of Sher Sing

It is well known to all the inhabitants of the Punjab, to the whole of the Sikhs, and those who have been cherished by the Khalsajee, and, in fact, to the world at large, with what oppression, tyranny, and undue violence, the Feringhees have treated the widow [Jindan Kaur] of the great Maharajuh Runjeet Sing, now in bliss, and what cruelty they have shown towards the people of the country.

In the first place, they have broken the treaty by imprisoning and sending away to Hindoostan, the Maharanee, the mother of her people. Secondly, the race of Sikhs, the children of the Maharajuh (Runjeet Sing), have suffered so much from their tyranny that our very religion has been taken away from us. Thirdly, the kingdom has lost its former repute. By the direction of the Holy Gooroo, Rajah Sher Sing and others, with their valiant troops, have joined the trusty and faithful Dewan Moolraj, on the part of Maharajuh Duleep Sing, with a view to eradicate and expel the tyrannous and crafty Feringhees. The Khalsajee must now act with all their heart and soul All who are servants of the Khalsajee, of the Holy Gooroo, and the Maharajuh, are enjoined to gird up their loins and proceed to Mooltan without delay. Let them murder all Feringhees, wherever they may find them, and cut off the daks. In return for this service they will certainly be recompensed by the favour of the Holy Gooroo, by increase of rank, and by distribution of rewards. Fourthly, let all cling closely to their religion. Whoever acts accordingly will obtain grace in this world and hereafter, and be who acts otherwise is excluded from the pale of the Sikh faith.

Seal of Sooka Singh / Seal of Soorutt Singh
Seal of Urjun Sing / Seal of Baluk Sing
Seal of Jeer Singh / Seal of Rutun Sing
Seat of Futteh Sing / Seal of Sahib Sing
Seal of Lal Sing

Edwardes, Herbert, *A Year on the Punjab Frontier,* in 1848–49, pp.623–624

Appendix VII

Constitution of the 1st Sikh Infantry

1. The term "Frontier Brigade" is to be discontinued, and the four Infantry regiments, which formed a portion of the brigade, are to be designated the 1st, 2nd (or Hill Corps), 3rd and 4th Regiments of Sikh Local Infantry.
2. They will not, save on emergency, be employed beyond the Jumna to the eastward, nor beyond the Bias or the Satlaj below its junction with the Bias to the westward.
3. The regiments are to be considered local corps, and the rules relating to such corps will be held applicable to them, except on such points as are differently laid down herein.
4. Gives the establishment with rates of pay of all ranks, and differs from that already given only in doing away with color havildars and reducing the lascars from ten to five.
7. Each regiment will be allowed half the number of Sepoys' pals allotted to a Native Infantry regiment of the line, A tent will be supplied for each Staff Sergeant.
9. Extra batta will not be allowed on account of regiments or detachments marching within the bounds specified in the 2nd paragraph, but should a regiment or detachment be ordered beyond those boundaries, extra batta will be granted from the date of passing the specified limits to the date of returning within them.
14. Men of these regiments will be entitled to pension on the same scale and under the same conditions as those of other local corps, viz., to the pension of their rank (provided they shall have completed three years in such rank) when worn out after having completed 20 years' service.
17. Wound pension will be granted under the Regulation for local corps.
23. A Queen's Color and also a Regimental Color are allowed for each regiment to be of the same dimension and pattern in every respect, as those allowed for corps of the line.
24. The revision of establishment as above directed will have effect from 1st November 1847.

History of the 1st Sikh Infantry, pp.6–7.

Glossary

Adi Granth/Ad Granth: See *Guru Granth Sahib*

Akal Takht: Literally the timeless throne; seat of temporal authority of the Guru. Also known as the *Akal Bunga*, meaning the tower or palace of Akal. Located in the complex of the Harimandir Sahib or Golden Temple at Amritsar. It is the highest seat of Sikh temporal authority; this was declared by Guru Hargobind Sahib in 1609. Traditionally only the Buddha Dal Jathedar was the historical leader of the Akal Takht, for example, Akali Phula Singh.

Akali: Worshiper of Akal. A warrior Sikh, clad in blue and high turbans, with steel weapons. The term was copied from this traditional order and used by political parties, such as the *Akali Dal*. The term is synonymous with the word *Nihang*.

Akali Nihang: The traditional Singh warrior guardians of orthodox Sikhism. Under the British, this order suffered heavily. A high-ranking Nihang Singh who has a plume on top of a high conical turban.

Amrit: Immortal. Also the nectar of immortality used in the initiation ceremony of the Sikhs and Khalsa.

Ardas: A prayer or invocation at the end of every Sikh ceremony. This is from the first stanza of the Dasam Granth composition *Chandi di Var* – The ballad of Chandi.

Baba: A term used for an elderly father or grandfather. It is a term of affection and respect used for holy figures and saints, for example, Baba Baghel Singh.

Bhai: An address, to mean brother or friend. Also given for piety and learning, for example, Bhai Mani Singh.

Brahmin: The members of the Indian high caste. They are normally priests. In Sikhism, a *Brahmin* is irrespective of caste but a person who knows *Braham*. This is in line with ancient Indian texts such as *Bhagavad Gita*.

Chakkar/Chakram: A quoit a favoured weapon of the Sikhs. Also worn as regalia on a turban and on the body by the Akali Nihangs.

Chakravarti: Always on the move. A reference to the Akali Nihangs who would move from place to place. Reminiscent of the Misls from the eighteenth century.

Buddha Dal: The moving throne (*Takht*) of the Akali Nihangs. Deriving its name from Baba Buddha, the martial instructor of the sixth preceptor, Guru Hargobind. Various Akali Nihangs Dals are all subordinate to the Buddha Dal. The leader of the Buddha Dal was traditionally seen as the head of the entire Sikh nation and commander of the Sikh army, as well as being the custodian or Jathedar of the Akal Takht.

Bunga: The word *bunga* is derived from a Persian word that means abode, a rest-house or a place of dwelling

Darshan: The vision or experience of being in the presence of God. To have an audience. The appearance of an eminent person. To have the audience of the Guru.

Dasam Granth : The scripture written by the tenth Guru, compositions of which instil warrior spirit into the Sikhs. A text of various themes, mostly focussing on fighting a righteous war. It is respected by the non-martial Sikh orders of Udasis, Nirmala and Seva Panthis. It is worshipped as equal to Guru Granth Sahib by the Akali Nihangs and the school of learning the Damdami Taksal. It is enthroned at two of the thrones of Sikh polity and was also enthroned at the Akal Takht and numerous Gurdwaras across the Indian subcontinent prior to 1920.

Degh-Tegh-Fateh: A popular slogan used by the Khalsa in the eighteenth and nineteenth century. Initially used by Guru Gobind Singh followed by Banda Singh Bahadur.

Dhai Phat: Literally, two-and-a-half strikes. A military manoeuvre where you strike and retreat twice, and then finally attack wholeheartedly.

Dhal: Shield.

Durbar: The court of a ruler.

Farman: A royal or governmental decree.

Fauj-i-Khas: Special royal corps in the Sikh Empire. Trained in the French system of drill and other military matters.

Ferengi: A western person. A reference to the western generals in Ranjit Singh's army.

Ghazis: Title given to Muslim warriors or soldiers.

Ghallughara: Holocaust. A reference to the two holocausts in the eighteenth century known as the *Vadhha/Choota Ghallughara*, or big/smaller holocausts.

Ghorchurahs: Literally, horse-riders, cavalrymen who formed the bulk of the irregular divisions in the *Fauj-i-Khas*.

Guru: The Divine Master, Enlightener or Teacher.

Gurdwara: Literally, Guru's door, a Sikh place of worship; in which the Sikh scriptures are venerated.

Gurmukhi: Literally, from the Guru's mouth; the script in which the poetry of the Gurus is written. It has become the script in which Panjabi is written by Sikhs in India.

Guru Granth Sahib: The first scripture of spirituality compiled by Guru Arjan Dev in 1603–04. The sacred scriptures of the Sikhs are known as Granth. The Granth is the paramount Sikh scripture that enshrines the spirit of peace (*Shanti ras*). Also referred to as *Sri Guru Granth Sahib* and *Guru Granth Sahib*. To differentiate one from later scriptures, this recension was known as the first Granth, that is, Adi Granth. When the Granth received Guruship in the form of the *Damdami* recension, it was then termed *Sri Guru Granth Sahib*, literally translated as the first Granth, in relationship to the Dasam Granth being the second.

Harimandir Sahib: The Temple of God. The most sacred Sikh shrine at Amritsar, referred to as the Golden Temple under the British.

Hukamnama: An edict originally sent by the Gurus. In modern days a reference to the taking of a verse from a randomly selected left-hand side page from the Guru Granth Sahib each morning. This is then published by the Gurdwara.

Jathedar: The leader or commander of a Takht; or the leader of a military army.

Kalgi: Plume.

Kaur: Literally, princess, a name used by female initiates of the Khalsa, as an equal to Singh (lion) for men.

Khila'at: A grant to recognised distinguished service or occasionally demonstrating friendship. Composed of clothing and jewellery.

Kirpan: A reference to the sword of the Sikhs. This is one of the '5Ks' or prescribed symbols worn by a Sikh initiated into the Khalsa.

Khalsa: A religious/chivalrous order established by Guru Gobind Singh in 1699. Literally, the pure, the ones from one source, the sovereign.

Khande ki pahul: Mystical 'knighthood' and 'initiation of the double-edged sword.' The ceremony where five compositions are read (from the Guru Granth Sahib and the Dasam Granth) and a cauldron of water and sugar is stirred with a sword. The initiation ceremony which new spiritual aspirants/warriors undergo to enter the Khalsa fraternity.

Kurehats: Conduct from which an initiated Sikh should refrain, including the use of tobacco, consumption of alcohol and so on.

Koftgari: A type of gold/silver decorative inlaying on metal objects

Langar: The Gurdwara kitchen from which sacred food is served to all, regardless of caste or creed; the sacred food from such a kitchen.

Mughal: Dynasty of Muslim rulers of India. During the time of the Sikh Gurus, the rise of the Sikh Misls up to the time of the EIC domination in India.

Nazrana: Gift or tribute, payment after losing territory or after a battle.

Nitnem: The liturgy of Sikh prayers that are recited daily.

Panchayats: Generally elected council holding large powers, both executive and judicial. Based on the idea of deriving authority from the *Panj Pyare* (five beloved).

Panth: This keyword refers to the Sikh community or congregation; the path, way or system of religious belief.

Rahit: The code of chivalry or conduct of the Khalsa.

Rahitnama: A Gurmukhi record of the *rahit*. There were several *Rahitnamas* written by the Guru's followers. These early codes of conduct were used to form the modern Sikh Rahit *Maryada*.

Raja: A chief of a certain area or battalion within India. Sometimes short for Maharajah.

SGPC: Shiromani Gurdwara Parbandhak Committee. The Sikh organisation which controls the main Gurdwaras in Panjab. It was formed in the early twentieth century during the British Raj.

Sahib: Master/lord; term of respect.

Sardar/sirdar: Originally a term to denote a title of nobility to describe princes, nobles and aristocrats. More synonymous with the Sikhs and generally someone who wears a turban. Leaders of the Sikh Misls, equivalent to the senior British generals.

Sant sipahi: Literally, saint-soldier. A reference to the Khalsa, which is an amalgamation of the saintly and soldierly aspects.

Sawa Lakh: The Khalsa concept of one Sikh being equal to 125,000 on the battlefield.

Shastarvidia: The science of weapons. Seen as a martial art of the Sikhs. Seldom practised by the Sikhs in the modern age, but some Akali Nihangs still preserve this old tradition.

Samadhi: A tombstone/memorial. Recognition of a fallen Sikh.

Takht Hazur Sahib: Situated at Nanden, Maharashtra, India, where Guru Gobind Singh ascended to heaven. It was here that the Guru Granth Sahib was declared to be the Guru of the Sikhs.

Takht Keshgarh Sahib: Situated at Anandpur Sahib, Panjab, where Guru Gobind Singh gave birth to the fraternity of the pure or Khalsa.

Takht Patna Sahib: Situated in Patna, Bihar, India, the birthplace of the Guru Gobind Singh.

Takht: Throne; one of the five centres of temporal power within the religion. The five *Takhts* are situated at Amritsar, Anandpur Sahib, Damdama Sahib (Bhatinda district), Patna Sahib (Bihar) and Hazur Sahib, Nanded (Maharashtra). Traditionally there were four physical *Takhts*: Akal Takht Sahib, Patna Sahib, Keshgarh Sahib, Hazur Sahib and the Buddha Dal (Khalsa), traditionally seen as the fifth.

Talwar: A curved sword from the Indian Subcontinent.

Taruna Dal: In 1734, Nawab Kapur Singh split the Khalsa into the Buddha Dal (superior and comprising older, wiser and battle-hardened warriors) and the Taruna Dal (comprising younger warriors).

Toshkhana: Persian. Treasury. Reference to the Treasury of the Sikhs in Lahore built up by Maharajah Ranjit Singh.

Vakil: Representative/agent of the court.

Var: Ballad. One of the most famous compositions is the *Vars* attributed to Bhai Gurdas, scribe to Guru Arjan Dev. These are in the poetic form of an ode. In the Guru Granth Sahib, these are poetical compositions consisting of stanzas (*pauris*) with preceding *saloks*. Var is used in the Sikh scriptures.

Bibliography

Ahluwalia, M.L., *Bhai Maharaj Singh* (Patiala: Punjab University)

Aijazuddin, Fakir S., *The Resourceful Fakirs: Three Muslim Brothers at the Sikh Court of Lahore* (New Delhi: Three River Publishers, 2014)

Anon., *Inscriptions on the Seikh Guns Captured by the Army of the Sutledge 1845–46 Volume of 64 hand-coloured engravings by and after C. Gomeze* (Calcutta: 1846)

Anon., *Papers Relating to the Punjab, 1847–1849* (London: Printed by Harrison and Son, 1849)

Anon., *History of the 1st Sikh Infantry*, 1846-1886, Vol. 1 (Calcutta: Printed by Thacker, Spink and Co., 1903. Originally published in 1887.)

Anon., *Regimental History of the 4th Battalion: 13th Frontier Force Rifles (Wilde's)* (East Sussex: The Naval & Military Press Ltd., 2005)

Arnold, Edwin, *The Marquis of Dalhousie's administration of British India, Volume the First* (London: Saunders, Otley and Co., 1862)

Arshi, P.S., *The Golden Temple: History Art And Architecture* (New Delhi: Harman Publishing House, 1989)

Atkinson, James, *The Expedition into Afghanistan; notes and sketches descriptive of the country, contained in a personal narrative during the campaign of 1839 and 1840. Up to the surrender of Dost Mahomed Khan* (London: W.H. Allen & co., 1842)

Atwal, Priya, *Royals and Rebels: The Rise and Fall of the Sikh Empire*, (London: C Hurst & Co. Publishers Ltd, 2020)

Bance, Peter, *Sovereign, Squire and Rebel: Maharajah Duleep Singh and the Heirs of a Lost Kingdom* (London: Coronet House, 2009)

Lieut. William Barr, *Journal of a March from Delhi to Peshawur, and from thence to Cabul, with the mission of Lieut.-Colonel Sir c. M. Wade, kt. C.b. Including travels in the Punjab, a visit to the city of Lahore, and a narrative of operations in the Khyber Pass, undertaken in 1839* (London, James Madden & Co., 1844)

Barstow, Major A.E., *A Handbook for the Indian Army: Sikhs* (Calcutta: Govt of India, Central Publications Dept, 1928)

Bayly, C.A., *Empire and Information: Intelligence Gathering and Social Communication in India, 1780–1870*, Cambridge Studies in Indian History and Society, No. 1. (Cambridge: Cambridge University Press, 1996)

Bhargava, Krishna Dyal (ed.), *Browne Correspondence* (Delhi: Pub. for the National Archives of India by the Manager of Publications, Government of India, 1960)

Birdwood, Colonel F.T., *The Sikh Regiment in the Second World War* (East Sussex: Naval and Military Press, 2014)

Bonarjee, P.D., *A Handbook of the Fighting Races of India* (Calcutta: Thacker, Spink and Co, 1899)

Buckle, Capt. E. Ed. J.W. Kaye, *Memoir of the Services of the Bengal Artillery, from the formation of the corps to the present time, with some account of its internal organization* (London W.H. Allen, 1852)

Burnes, Alexander, *Travels into Bokhara; being the account of a journey from India to Cabool, Tartary and Persia, 3 Vols.* (London: John Murray, 1834)

Brice, Christopher, *Brave As a Lion: The Life and Times of Field Marshal Hugh Gough, 1st Viscount Gough* (Solihull: Helion & Company, 2017)

Broadfoot, Major W., *The Career of Major George Broadfoot, C. B. … In Afghanistan and the Punjab,* (London: John Murray, Albemarle Street, 1888)

Brown, Kerry (ed.), *Sikh Art and Literature* (London: Routledge, 1999)

Browne, Major J., *India Tracts: Containing a Description of the Jungle Terry Districts, Their Revenues, Trade, and Government: with a Plan for the Improvement of Them. Also an History of the Origin and Progress of the Sicks* (London: Logographic Press, 1788)

Butalia, Brig. R.C., *The Evolution of the Artillery in India: From the Battle of Plassey 1757 to the Revolt of 1857* (New Delhi: Allied Publishers, 1998)

Caldwell, Rev. J., 'Journal of a Missionary tour amongst Towns and villages in the neighbourhood of Lodhiana', *The Missionary Chronicle*, Volume 11 (New York: Mission House, 1843)

Campbell, George, *Memoirs of my Indian Career* (London: Macmillan and Co, 1893)

Chopra, Gulshan Lall, *The Punjab as a Sovereign State (1799–1839)* (Lahore: Uttar Chand Kapur & Sons, 1928)

Churchill, Winston, L. Spencer, *The Story of the Malakand Field Force: An Episode of Frontier War* (London: Thomas Nelson & Sons, Ltd., 1916)

Clarke, Caspar Purdon (Intro. Robert Elgood), *Arms and Armour at Sandringham: The Indian Collection Presented by the Princes, Chiefs And Nobles Of India…In 1875–1876* (Cambridge: Ken Trotman Publishing, 2008; reprint of the original from 1898)

Clarke, Caspar Purdon (Intro. Robert Elgood), *Indian Art in Marlborough House: A Catalogue of Indian Arms and Objects of Art presented by the Princes and Nobles of India to H.R.H. the Prince on the Occasion of His Visit to India in 1875–1876* (Cambridge: Ken Trotman Publishing, 2008; reprint of the original from 1910)

Cook, Hugh, *The Sikh Wars* (London: Leo Cooper Ltd., 1975)

Crust, Robert Needham, *A Sketch of the Modern Languages of the East Indies* (London: Trubner & Co., Ludgate Hill, 1878)

Crust, Robert Needham, *Linguistic and Oriental Essays. Written from the year 1840 to 1901, Sixth Series* (London: Luzac & Co., 1901),

Cunningham, J.D. and Garret, H.L.O. (eds), *A History of the Sikhs* (Delhi: S. Chand and Co., 1955)

Dalhousie, E. Login, *Lord Login's Recollections: Court Life and Camp Life 1820–1904* (London: Smith, Elder & Co., 1916)

Daly, Major H., *Memoirs of General Sir Henry Dermot Daly G.C.B., C.I.E., Sometime Commander of Central India Horse, Political Assistant for Western Malwa, etc., etc.* (London: John Murray, Albemarle Street, 1905)

Dennie, William H., *Personal Narrative of the Campaigns in Afghanistan, Sinde, Beloochistan* (Dublin: William Curry, Jun. and Company, 1843)

Dunbar, Janet (ed.), *Tigers, Durbars And Kings: Fanny Eden's Indian Journals* (London: John Murray, 1988)

Dhesi, Narindar Singh, *Sikh Soldier – Gallantry Awards*, Vol. 2 (East Sussex: Naval & Military Press, 2010)

East India Company, *An Authentic Copy of the Correspondence in India: Between the Country Powers and the Honourable the East India Company's Servants: Containing Amongst Many Others the Letters of Governor Hastings, J. Macpherson, Esq., J. Stables, Esq. … &c., Together with the Minutes of the Supreme Council at Calcutta: the Whole Forming a Collection of the Most Interesting India-papers, which Were Laid Before Parliament in the Session of 1786, Volume 4* (London: Printed for J. Debrett, 1787)

Eden, Emily, *Portraits of the Princes & Peoples of India by the Honorable Miss Eden, Drawn on the Stone by L. Dickinson* (London: J. Dickinson & Son, 1844)

Eden, Emily, *Up the Country: Letters Written to Her sister from the Upper Provinces of India* (London: Richard Bentley, 1867)

Edwards, William, *Reminiscences of a Bengal Civilian* (London: Smith, Elder And Co., 1866)

Edwards, Major Herbert Benjamin, *A Year on the Punjab Frontier, in 1848–49* (London: Richard Bentley, 2 Vols, 1851)

Falcon, Capt. R.W., *Handbook on Sikhs for the use of Regimental Officers* (Allahabad: Pioneer Press, 1896)

Henry Edward Fane, *Five years in India; comprising a narrative of travels in the presidency of Bengal, a visit to the court of Runjeet Sing, a residence in the Himalayah mountains, an account of the late expedition to Cabul and Affghanistan, voyage down the Indus, and Journey overland to England Vol. 1* (London: Henry Colburn, Great Marlborough Street, 1842)

Faroodi, Main Bashir Ahmed, *British Relations With The Cis-Sutlej States(1809–1823)* (Delhi: Punjab National Press, 1942)

Flinders, Stuart, *Cult of a Dark Hero: Nicholson of Delhi* (London: Bloomsbury Publishing 2018)

Forster, George, *A Journey from Bengal to England: Through the Northern part of India, Kashmire, Afghanistan, and Persia, and into Russia by the Caspian Sea 2 Volumes* (London: Printed for R. Faulder, 1798).

Francklin, William, *The History of the Reign of Shah-Aulum, the present emperor of Hindostaun: Containing the transactions of the court of Delhi, and the neighbouring states, during a period of thirty-six years: interspersed with geographical and topographical observations on several of the principal cities of Hindostaun* (London: Cooper and Graham, 1798)

Francklin, William, *Military Memoirs of Mr. George Thomas; Who, by Extraordinary Talents and Enterprise* (London: Reprinted for John Stockdale, Piccadilly, 1805)

Fraser, James Baillie, *Military Memoir of Lieut-Col. James Skinner, C.B.: For Many Years a Distinguished Officer, Vol. II* (London: Smith, Elder and Co., 1851)

Fox, Richard G., *Lions of the Punjab: Culture in the Making, 1st Edition* (Berkeley: University of California Press, 1985)

Garrett, H.L.O. (trans. and ed.), *The Punjab A Hundred Years Ago: As Described by V. Jacquemont (1831) & A. Soltykoff (1842)* (Delhi: Nirmal Publishers, 1986)

Gill, D.S., 'Relics of Guru Gobind Singh ji', *Sikh Review*, Issue 548, 47 (August 1999).

Gopal, Madan, *Dyal Singh Majithia* (New Delhi: Publication Division, Ministry of Information and Broadcasting, Govt. of India, 1994)

Gott, Richard, *Britain's Empire: Resistance, Repression and Revolt* (London: Verso Books, 2011)

Gough, Sir Charles and Innes, Arthur Donald, *The Sikhs and the Sikh Wars: The Rise, Conquest, and Annexation of the Punjab State* (London: A.D. Innes & Company, 1897)

Grant, James, *Recent British Battles on Land and Sea* (London, Paris and New York: Cassell & Company, Ltd, 1884)

Grierson, G.A., *The Modern Vernacular Literature of Hindustan* (Calcutta: Asiatic Society, 1889)

Griffin, Lepel, *The Rajas of the Punjab Being the History of the Principal States in the Punjab and their Political Relations with the British Government, 2nd Ed* (London: Trubner & Co., 1873)

Griffin, Sir L.H., *Ranjit Singh and the Sikh Barrier Between Our Growing Empire and Central Asia* (Oxford: Clarendon Press, 1905)

Griffiths, Charles John, *A Narrative of The Siege of Delhi with an Account of The Mutiny at Ferozepore in 1857* (London: John Murray, 1910)

Gupta, Hari Ram, *History of the Sikhs*, 5 Vols (New Delhi: Munishiram Manoharlal Publishers Pvt. Ltd, 2014).

Hasrat, Bikrama Jit, *Anglo Sikh Relations 1799–1849. A reappraisal of the Rise and Fall of the Sikhs* (Hoshiarpur: V. V. Research Institute Book Agency, 1968)

Havelock, Henry, Captain, *Narrative of the War in Afghanistan in 1838–39*, Vol. II (London: Henry Colburn, 1840)

Heath, Ian, *The Sikh Army 1799–1849* (Oxford: Osprey, 2005)

Hugel, Baron Charles, *Travels In Kashmir And The Panjab Containing a Particular Account of the Government and Character of the Sikhs* (London: John Petheram, 1845)

Humbly, W.W.W, *Journal of a Cavalry Officer: Including the Memorable Sikh Campaign of 1845–46* (London: Longman, Brown, Green, and Longmans, 1854)

Islam Shamsul, *Rebel Sikhs in 1857* (New Delhi: Vani Prakashan, 2012. Original edition 2008.)

Kaur, Balvinder, *Sukerchakia Misl Uptil 1799* (Unpublished MA Dissertation, Punjabi University Patiala, 1982)

Imperial Record Department, *Calendar of Persian Correspondence: Volume 2 (1767–9)* (Calcutta: Superintendent Government Printing, 1914)

Johar, Surinder Singh, *Sikh Warrior: Hari Singh Nalwa* (Delhi: National Book Shop, 2012)

Johnston Harry Hamilton, *British Central Africa: An attempt to give some account of a portion of the territories under British influence north of the Zambesi* (London: Methuen & Co.,1897)

Josan, Gurinderpal Singh, *A Saga of Valour The Epic Battle of Saragarhi* (Patiala: Sarbat Da Bhala Charitable Trust, 2017)

Kaur, Madanjit, *The Golden Temple Past and Present* (Amritsar: Guru Nanak Dev University Press,1983)

Khera, Paramdip Kaur, *Catalogue of Sikh Coins in the British Museum* (London: The British Museum, 2011)

Kipling, Rudyard, *Kim* (New York: Doubleday Page and Company, 1912)

Kohli, Sita Ram, *Catalogue of Khalsa Darbar Records*: *Volume 1* (Lahore: Printed by the Superintendent, Government Printing, 1919)

Kohli, Sita Ram, *Catalogue of Khalsa Darbar Records*: *Volume 2* (Lahore: Printed by the Superintendent, Government Printing, 1927)

Kohli, Sita Ram, *Sunset of the Sikh Empire* (New Delhi: Orient Blackswan Private Limited, 2012)

Lafont, Jean-Marie, *Fauj-i-Khas: Maharajah Ranjit Singh and his French officers* (Amritsar: Guru Nanak Dev University, 2002)

Lafont, Jean-Marie, *La Présence Française dans le Royaume Sikh du Penjab 1822–1849*, Ecole Française d'Extrême-Orient, Vol.168, Paris, 1992

Lafont, Jean-Marie, *Maharajah Ranjit Singh Lord of the Five Rivers* (New Delhi: Oxford University Press, 2002. Third Impression 2013)

Lal, Mohan, *Life of the Amir Dost Mohammed Khan of Kabul with his political proceedings towards the English, Russian and Persian Governments including the victory and disasters of the British army in Afghanistan* (London: Longman, Brown, Green and Longmans, 1846)

Lawrence, Major, H. M. L., *Adventures Of An Officer In The Punjab (Vol. 1)* (New Delhi: Punjab National Press, 1970. Originally published in 1883)

Leitner, G.W., *History of indigenous Education in Punjab Since Annexation and in 1882* (Calcutta: Printed by the Superintendent of Government Printing, India, 1883)

Login, Lady, *Sir John Login and Duleep Singh by Lady Login with an introduction by Colonel G.B. Malleson, c.s.i.* (London, W.H. Allen & Co., 1890)

Lowrie, Rev. John. C., *Travels in North India: Containing notices of the Hindus; journals of a voyage on the Ganges and a tour to Lahor; notes on the Himalaya mountains and the hill tribes, including a sketch of missionary undertakings* (Philadelphia: Presbyterian Board of Publication, 1842)

Macauliffe, Max Arthur, *The Sikh Religion: Its Gurus, Sacred Writings and Authors*, 6 *Vols* (Oxford: Clarendon Press, 1909)

Mackenzie, C., *Life in the Mission, the Camp, and the Zenana, or, Six Years in India, Vol. 1* (London: Richard Bentley, 1853)

Mackinnon, Daniel Henry, *Military service and adventures in the Far East: including sketches of the campaigns against the Afghans in 1839, and the Sikhs in 1845–6. By a cavalry officer, in two Volumes* (London: Charles Ollier, 1847)

Malcolm, Lt.-Col. John, *The Sketch of the Sikhs: A Singular Nation Who Inhabit the Provinces of the Punjab Situated Between the Rivers Jamnu and Indus* (London: John Murray, 1812)

Mann, Gurinder Singh, and Singh, Kamalroop, *Sri Dasam Granth: Questions and Answers* (London: Archimedes Press, 2011)

Mann, Gurinder Singh, and Singh, Kamalroop, *Akali Phula Singh and his Turban*, (Unpublished manuscript)

Martin, Robert Montgomery, *The History, Antiquities, Topography, and Statistics of Eastern India: comprising the districts of Behar, Shahabad, Bhagulpoor, Goruckpoor, Dinajepoor, Puraniya, Rungpoor, & Assam, in relation to their geology, mineralogy, botany, agriculture, commerce, manufactures, fine arts, population, religion, education, statistics, etc* (London: W.H. Allen and Co., 1838)

Maunsell, Colonel E.B., 'An Historic Durbar', *Journal of the United Service Institution of India*, Vol. LXII, Jan.–Oct. 1932, (Lahore: Printed by E.A. Smedley at the Civil and Military Gazette Press, 1932)

Meghani, Kajal, *Splendours of the Subcontinent: A Prince's Tour of India 1875–76* (London: Royal Collection Trust, 2017)

Nalwa, Vanit, *Hari Singh Nalwa Champion of the Khalsaji*, 1791-1837 (New Delhi: Manohar, 2009)

Nayar, Pramod K., *The Penguin 1857 Reader* (New Delhi: Penguin Books India)

Nijhawan, P.K., *The First Punjab War Shah Mohammed's Jangnamah* (Amritsar: Singh Brothers, 2001)

Nijahawan, Michael, *Dhadi Darbar: Religion, Violence, and the Performance of Sikh History* (New Delhi: Oxford University Press, 2006).

Osbourne, W.G., *The Court and Camp of Runjeet Singh* (London: Henry Colburn Publishers, 1840)

Owen, Edward Farley, *European Travellers in India: During the Fifteenth, Sixteenth and Seventeenth Centuries, the Evidence Afforded by Them with Respect to Indian Social Institutions, & the Nature & Influence of Indian Government* (Delhi: Asian Educational Services, 1991; originally published in 1909)

Pal, M.K., *Historical Gurdwaras of Delhi* (Delhi: Niyogi Books, 2013)

Pall, S.J.S., *The Beloved Forces of the Guru* (Amritsar: B. Chattar Singh, Jiwan Singh, 2007)

Pearse, Major Hugh, *Soldier and Traveller; memoirs of Alexander Gardner, Colonel of Artillery in the service of Maharaja Ranjit Singh* (London: William Blackwood and Sons, 1898)

Powell, B.H. Baden, *Handbook Of The Manufactures And Arts Of The Punjab, Vol.2* (Lahore: Punjab Printing Company, 1872)

Prinsep, Henry Thoby, *Origin of the Sikh Power in the Punjab and political life of Maharaja Ranjit Singh; with an account of the Religion, Laws, and Customs of Sikhs* (Calcutta: G.H. Huttmann, Military Orphan Press, 1834)

Purewal, Steven, *Duty, Honour & Izzat: From Golden Fields to Crimson – Punjab's Brothers in Arms in Flanders* (Canada: Renegade Arts Entertainment, 2019)

Rait, Robert, S., *The Life and Campaigns of Hugh, First Viscount Gough, Field-Marshal*, 2 Vols. (Westminster: Archibald Constable & Co Ltd, 1903).

Ramgharia, Sundar Singh, *Guide to the Darbar Sahib or Golden Temple of Amritsar* (Lahore: Mufid-i-Am Press, 1903)

Randhawa, T.S., *The Sikhs: Images of a Heritage* (New Delhi: Prakash Book Depot, 2007)

Records Of The Ludhiana Agency (Lahore: Punjab Government Press, 1911)

Rennell, James, *Memoir of a map of Hindoostan; or The Mogul Empire: with an introduction, illustrative of the geography and present division of that country: and a map of the countries situated between the head of the Indus, and the Caspian Sea* (London: Printed by M. Brown for the author, 1788)

Richardson, Thom (ed.), *East Meets West: Diplomatic Gifts of Arms and Armour between Europe and Asia* (2013)

Robertson, James Peter, *Personal Adventures and Anecdotes of an Old Officer* (London: Edward Arnold, 1906)

Roebuck, Thomas, *The Annals of the College of Fort William* (Calcutta: Printed by Philip Pereira at the Hindoostanee Press, 1819)

Roy, Kaushik, 'Race and Recruitment in the Indian Army: 1880–1918', *Modern Asian Studies*, Volume 47, Issue 4 (July 2013)

Sandhra, Sharanjit Kaur, 'The Nihangs Within the Great Sikh Court of 19th Century India' (unpublished MA thesis, The University of the Fraser Valley, 2005)

Sandhu, Gurmukh Singh, *Maharaja Duleep Singh, The King in Exile* (Chandigarh: Institute of Sikh Studies, 2006)

Sandhu, Jaspreet Kaur, *Sikh Ethos: Eighteenth Century Perspective* (Delhi: Vision & Venture, 2000)

Scott, George Batley, *Religion and Short History of The Sikhs–1469 to 1930* (London: The Mitre Press, 1930)

Seth, Mesrovb Jacob, *Armenians in India, from the Earliest Times to the Present Day* (New Delhi: Asian Educational Services, 2005)

Shackle, C., *Catalogue of The Panjabi and Sindhi Manuscripts in the India Office Library* (London: India Office Library and Records, 1977)

Sidhu, Amarpal Singh, *The First Anglo–Sikh War* (Stroud, Gloucestershire: Amberley Publishing, 2010)

Sidhu, Amarpal Singh, *The Second Anglo–Sikh War* (Stroud, Gloucestershire: Amberley Publishing, 2016)

Simpson, William, *India Ancient and Modern: a series of illustrations of the country and the people of India and adjacent territories; executed in chromo-lithography from drawings by William Simpson; with descriptive literature by John William Kaye* (London: Day and Son, 1867)

Singh, Attar, *Sakhee Book: or, the Description of Gooroo Gobind Singh's Religion and Doctrines* (Allahabad: The Indian Public Opinion Press, 1876)

Singh, Attar (trans.), *The Travels of Guru Tegh Bahadar and Guru Gobind Singh* (Lahore: Indian Public Press, 1876)

Singh, Bhagat, *A History of the Sikh Misals* (Patiala: Punjabi University, 1993)

Singh, Colonel Iqbal, *The Quest for the Past – Retracing the History of the Seventeenth-Century Sikh Warrior* (US: XLIBRIS, 2017)

Singh, Darshan (ed.), *Western Image of the Sikh Religion – A Sourcebook* (New Delhi: NBO, 1999)

Singh, Duleep, *A Reprint of two sale catalogues of jewels & other confiscated property belonging to his Highness the Maharajah Duleep Singh (1837–1893): which were put up to auction and sold at Lahore, in the years 1850 and 1851 by the government of India. With introductory remarks* (privately printed, 1885)

Singh, Ganda (ed.), *Maharajah Duleep Singh Correspondence* (Patiala: Punjabi University, 1977)

Singh, Ganda, *The Indian Mutiny Of 1857 And The Sikhs* (Delhi: Gurdwara Parbandhak Committee, 1969)

Singh, Ganda, *A Select Bibliography of the Sikhs and Sikhism* (Amritsar: SGPC, 1965)

Singh, Ganda (ed.), *Early European Accounts of the Sikhs* (Calcutta: Indian Studies, Past and Present, 1962; reprint)

Singh, Ganda, *The Panjab In 1839–40 Selections from the Punjab Akhbars, Punjab Intelligence, etc preserved in the National Archives of India* (Amritsar: Sikh History Society, 1952)

Singh, Harbans, *Guru Nanak and the Origins of the Sikh Faith* (Bombay: Asia Publishing House, 1969)

Singh, Harbans (ed.), *The Encyclopaedia of Sikhism, 4 Vols* (Patiala: Punjabi University, 1992)

Singh, Karnail, *Winston Churchill's Account of Anglo Sikh Wars and Its In-side Tale* (Amritsar: S.G.P.C, 1968; Enlarged 1984)

Singh, Kamalroop and Mann, Gurinder Singh, *The Granth of Guru Gobind Singh: Essays, Lectures and Translations* (New Delhi: OUP, 2015)

Singh, Khushwant, *Ranjit Singh Maharaja of the Punjab* (London: George Allen and Unwin Ltd, 1962)

Singh, Kulwant (trans.), *Sri Gur Sobha Sainapati* (Chandigarh: Institute of Sikh Studies, 2014)

Singh, Nahar and Singh, Kirpal (eds), *Rebels Against the British Rule (Guru Ram Singh and the Kuka Sikhs)* (New Delhi: Atlantic Publishers and Distributors, 1995)

Singh, Sikandar (Bhayee) and Singh, Roopinder, *Sikh Heritage: Ethos & Relics* (New Delhi: Rupa & Co., 2012)

Smith, R. Bosworth, *The Life of Lord Lawrence, 1849–1852* (London: Smith Elder & Co., 1883)

Smith, G. C. Moore, *The Autobiography of Lieutenant-General Sir Harry Smith Baronet of Aliwal on the Sutlej G.C.B, 2 vols.* (London: John Murray, 1902)

Smyth, G. Carmichael, *A History of the Reigning Family of Lahore, with some account of the Jummoo Rajahs, the Seik soldiers and their Sirdars; with notes on Malcolm, Prinsep, Lawrence, Steinbach, McGregor, and the Calcutta Review* (Calcutta: W. Thacker and Co., 1847)

Sotheby's, *Sotheby's Colstoun Auction Catalogue; May 21–22*; 1990

Steinbach, H., *The Punjaub; Being a Brief Account of the Country of the Sikhs, its Extent, History, Commerce, Productions, Government, Manufactures, Laws, Religion, etc.* (London: Smith, Elder, & Co., 1845)

Streets, Heather, *Martial Races: The Military, Race and Masculinity in British Imperial Culture, 1857–1914* (Manchester: Manchester University Press, 2005)

Stronge, Susan (ed.), *The Arts of the Sikh Kingdoms* (London: V&A Publications, 1999)

Suri, Lala Sohan Lal, (trans, V.S. Suri), *An Outstanding Original Source Of Panjab History Umdat-Ut-Tawarikh, Four Vols.* (Delhi: S. Chand & Co., 1961)

Suri, Vidya Sagar, *Some Original Source Of Punjab History* (Lahore: Punjab University Historical Society, 1956)

Tanner, Brigadier J.K., 'Immortal Fame – The 80th (Staffordshire Volunteers) at Ferozeshah', *Soldiers of the Queen – Journal of the Victorian Military Society*, Issue 130, September 2007

The Sessional Papers of the House of Lords, Session 1849, (12 & 13 victoria), Vol. Xv (London: Harrison and Sons, 1849)

Haythornthwaite, J. Philip, *The Colonial Wars Sourcebook* (London: Caxton Editions, 2000)

The Sikh Review, Volume 31, Issues 355–60 (Calcutta: Sikh Cultural Centre, 1983)

The Indian News and Chronicle of Eastern Affaire (London: 24 April 1848)

Verma, Devinder Kumar, *Foreigners at the Court of Maharaja Ranjit Singh* (Patiala: Arun Publications, 2006)

Wilson, C.R., *The Early Annals of the English in Bengal, Volume II, Part II* (Calcutta: The Asiatic Society, 1911)

Wilson, H.H., *The Journal of the Royal Asiatic Society of Great Britain and Ireland, Vol. 13* (1852)

Wolff, Joseph, *Researches and Missionary Labours among the Jews, Mohammedans, and other sects by the Rev. Joseph Wolff During his travels between the years 1831 and 1834* (Philadelphia: Orrin Rogers, 1837)

Yeats-Brown, Francis, *Martial India* (London: Eyre and Spottiswood, 1945)

Special Papers and Manuscripts

British Library: Add MS. 27254, Add Or. 5259, Add Or. 1403, Add Or. 1248, Add Or. 1385

Websites

The Encyclopaedia of Sikhism: www.advancedcentrepunjabi.org/eos/
www.sikhmuseum.org.uk
www.anglosikhwars.com
www.sikhscholar.co.uk
www.anglosikhmueum.com
www.Bl.org.uk
https://britishmuseum.org/
www.vam.ac.uk
www.worldcat.org
www.rct.uk
www.archive.org

Index

The period 1815-1914 is sometimes called the long century of peace. It was in reality very far from that. It was a century of civil wars, popular uprisings, and struggles for Independence. An era of colonial expansion, wars of Empire, and colonial campaigning, much of which was unconventional in nature. It was also an age of major conventional wars, in Europe that would see the Crimea campaign and the wars of German unification. Such conflicts, along with the American Civil War, foreshadowed the total war of the 20th century.

It was also a period of great technological advancement, which in time impacted the military and warfare in general. Steam power, electricity, the telegraph, the radio, the railway, all became tools of war. The century was one of dramatic change. Tactics altered, sometimes slowly, to meet the challenges of the new technology. The dramatic change in the technology of war in this period is reflected in the new title of this series: From Musket to Maxim.

The new title better reflects the fact that the series covers all nations and all con ict of the period between 1815-1914. Already the series has commissioned books that deal with matters outside the British experience. This is something that the series will endeavour to do more of in the future. At the same time there still remains an important place for the study of the British military during this period. It is one of fascination, with campaigns that capture the imagination, in which Britain although the world's predominant power, continues to field a relatively small army.

The aim of the series is to throw the spotlight on the conflicts of that century, which can often get overlooked, sandwiched as they are between two major conflicts, the French/Revolutionary/Napoleonic Wars and the First World War. The series will produced a variety of books and styles. Some will look simply at campaigns or battles. Others will concentrate on particular aspects of a war or campaign. There will also be books that look at wider concepts of warfare during this era. It is the intention that this series will present a platform for historians to present their work on an important but often overlooked century of warfare.

For more information go to:
https://www.helion.co.uk/series/from-musket-to-maxim-1815-1914.php

Submissions

The publishers would be pleased to receive submissions for this series. Please contact series editor Dr Christopher Brice via email (christopherbrice@helion.co.uk), or in writing to Helion & Company Limited, Unit 8, Amherst Business Centre, Budbrooke Road, Warwick, Warwickshire, CV345WE.

Books in the series:

1. *The Battle of Majuba Hill: The Transvaal Campaign 1880-1881* John Laband
   (ISBN 978-1-911512-38-7)

2. *For Queen and Company: Vignettes of the Irish Soldier in the Indian Mutiny*
   David Truesdale
   (ISBN 978-1-911512-79-0)

3. *The Furthest Garrison: Imperial Regiments in New Zealand 1840-1870* Adam Davis
   (ISBN 978-1-911628-29-3)

4. *Victory over Disease: Resolving The Medical Crisis In The Crimean War, 1854-1856*
   Michael Hinton (ISBN 978-1-911628-31-6)

5. *Journey Through the Wilderness: Garnet Wolseley's Canadian Red River Expedition of 1870*
   Paul McNicholls (ISBN 978-1-911628-30-9)

6. *Kitchener: The Man Not the Myth* Anne Samson (ISBN 978-1-912866-45-8)

7. *The British and the Sikhs: Discovery, Warfare and Friendship (c.1700–1900)* Gurinder
   Singh Mann (ISBN 978-1-911628-24-8)

8. *Bazaine 1870: Scapegoat for a Nation* Quintin Barry (ISBN 978-1-913336-08-0)

9. *Redcoats in the Classroom: The British Army's School for Soldiers and Their Children During
   the 19th Century* Howard R. Clarke (ISBN 978-1-912866-47-2)

10. *The Rescue They Called A Raid: The Jameson Raid 1895-96* David Snape
    (ISBN 978-1-913118-77-8)

11. *Hungary 1848: The Winter Campaign* Johann Nobili (ISBN 978-1-913118-78-5)

12. *The War of Two Brothers: The Portuguese Civil War 1828-1834* Sérgio Veludo Coelho
    (ISBN 978-1-914059-26-1)

14. *Forgotten Victorian Generals* Christopher Brice (editor) (ISBN 978-1-910777-20-6)

15. *The German War of 1866: The Bohemian and Moravian Campaign* Theodor Fontane
    (ISBN 978-1-914059-29-2)

16. *Dust of Glory: The First Anglo-Afghan War 1839-1842, its Causes and Course*
    (ISBN 978-1-914059-33-9)

17. *Saarbruck to Sedan: The Franco-German War 1870-71. Uniforms, Organisation and Weapons
    of the Armies of the Imperial Phase of the War* (ISBN 978-1-914059-88-9)

18. *The Battle of Lissa 1866: How the Industrial Revolution Changed the Face of Naval Warfare*
    (ISBN 978-1-914059-92-6)

19. *The Zulu Kingdom and the Boer Invasion of 1837–1840* John Laband
    (ISBN 978-1-914059-89-6)

20. *The Fire of Venture Was in His Veins Major Allan Wilson and the Shangani Patrol 1893*
    David Snape (ISBN 978-1-914059-90-2)

21. *From the Atacama to the Andes Battles of the War of the Pacic 1879–1883* Alan Curtis
    (ISBN 978-1-914059-90-2)

22 *The Rise of the Sikh Soldier: The Sikh Warrior through the ages, c.1700-1900* Gurinder Singh
    Mann (ISBN 978-1-915070-52-4)